U.S. Private-Sector Privacy

Law and Practice for Information Privacy Professionals

Peter Swire, CIPP/US
DeBrae Kennedy-Mayo, CIPP/US

An IAPP Publication

Copy editor and Proofreader: Julia Homer
Indexer: Jeanne R. Busemeyer, Hyde Park Publishing Services

ISBN: 978-0-9983223-6-0

Library of Congress Number: 2017959816

Contents

About the IAPP .... *vii*

Preface .... *ix*

Acknowledgments .... *xi*

Introduction .... *xiii*

Chapter 1: Introduction to Privacy

1.1 Defining Privacy 1

1.2 Classes of Privacy 2

1.3 The Historical and Social Origins of Privacy 2

1.4 Fair Information Practices 4

1.5 Information Privacy, Data Protection and the Advent of Information Technology 13

1.6 Personal and Nonpersonal Information 13

1.7 Sources of Personal Information 16

1.8 Processing Personal Information 17

1.9 Sources of Privacy Protection 18

1.10 World Models of Data Protection 19

1.11 Conclusion 23

Chapter 2: U.S. Legal Framework

2.1 Branches of the Government 27

2.2. Sources of Law in the United States 28

2.3. Key Definitions 32

2.4. Regulatory Authorities 34

2.5. Self-regulation 35

2.6. Understanding Laws 35

2.7. Conclusion 37

Chapter 3: Federal and State Regulators and Enforcement of Privacy Law

3.1 Types of Litigation and Enforcement ... 39
3.2 Federal Privacy Enforcement and Policy Outside of the FTC and the FCC ... 40
3.3 FTC Jurisdiction ... 42
3.4 FTC Enforcement Process and Consent Decrees ... 44
3.5 Privacy Policies and Notices and Early FTC Enforcement Actions ... 45
3.6 Enforcement Actions and Deceptive Trade Practices ... 47
3.7 Enforcement Actions and Unfair Trade Practices ... 48
3.8 Future of Federal Enforcement ... 52
3.9 State Enforcement ... 57
3.10 Self-Regulation and Enforcement ... 58
3.11 Cross-border Enforcement Issues ... 60
3.12 Conclusion ... 61

Chapter 4: Principles of Information Management

4.1 The Role of the Privacy Professional ... 67
4.2 Risks of Using PI Improperly ... 68
4.3 Developing an Information Management Program ... 69
4.4 Data Sharing and Transfer ... 72
4.5. Privacy Policies and Disclosure ... 75
4.6 Managing User Preferences and Access Requests ... 78
4.7 Contract and Vendor Management ... 82
4.8 Global Perspective ... 84
4.9 Conclusion ... 86

Chapter 5: Online Privacy

Using Personal Information on Websites and Other Internet Technologies

5.1 Overview of Web Technologies ... 91
5.2 Privacy Considerations for Online Information ... 96
5.3. Online Privacy Notices and Methods for Communication ... 107
5.4. Collection and Use of Electronic Data ... 111
5.5. Digital Advertising ... 116
5.6. Conclusion ... 126

Chapter 6: Information Security and Data Breach Notification Laws

6.1 Information Security 136

6.2 Information Security Laws 136

6.3 Types of Data Breach Incidents 139

6.4. Fundamentals of Incident Management for Data Breaches 140

6.5 Lack of Federal Data Breach Law 142

6.6 State Breach Notification Laws 142

6.7 State Data Destruction Laws 151

6.8 Conclusion 152

Chapter 7: Medical Privacy

7.1 Confidentiality of Substance Use Disorder Patient Records Rule 164

7.2 The Health Insurance Portability and Accountability Act of 1996 166

7.3. The Health Information Technology for Economic and Clinical Health Act 173

7.4. Genetic Information Nondiscrimination Act of 2008 175

7.5 The 21st Century Cures Act of 2016 177

7.6 Conclusion 178

Chapter 8: Financial Privacy

8.1 The Fair Credit Reporting Act 187

8.2 The Fair and Accurate Credit Transactions Act 196

8.3 Gramm-Leach-Bliley Act 199

8.4 Dodd-Frank Wall Street Reform and Consumer Protection Act 205

8.5 Required Disclosure Under Anti-Money-Laundering Laws 206

8.6 Online Banking and Mobile Banking 210

8.7 Conclusion 211

Chapter 9: Education Records and Technology

9.1 An Overview of the Family Educational Rights and Privacy Act 217

9.2 FERPA and the Protection of Pupil Rights Amendment 222

9.3 Interaction Between FERPA and the HIPAA Privacy Rule 224

9.4 Education Technology 224

9.5 Conclusion 225

Chapter 10: Telecommunications and Marketing

10.1 Regulations Governing Telemarketing 231
10.2 Fax Marketing........ 243
10.3 Controlling the Assault of Nonsolicited Pornography and Marketing Act of 2003 244
10.4 The Telecommunications Act of 1996 248
10.5 The Cable Communications Policy Act of 1984........ 250
10.6 The Video Privacy Protection Act of 1988........ 251
10.7 Digital Advertising 252
10.8 Conclusion 255

Chapter 11: Workplace Privacy

11.1 Legal Overview 263
11.2 Privacy Issues Before, During and After Employment 268
11.3 Conclusion 292

Chapter 12: Privacy Issues in Civil Litigation and Government Investigations

12.1 Disclosures Required, Permitted or Forbidden by Law........ 302
12.3 Law Enforcement and the Role of Privacy Professionals 313
12.4. National Security and the Role of Privacy Professionals........ 323
12.5 Conclusion 330

Chapter 13: Emerging Issues

Big Data and the Internet of Things

13.1 Historic Context........ 344
13.2. Big Data 346
13.3 Internet of Things........ 352
13.4 Conclusion 359

About the Authors 367

Index........ 369

About the IAPP

The International Association of Privacy Professionals (IAPP) is the largest and most comprehensive global information privacy community and resource, helping practitioners develop and advance their careers and organizations manage and protect their data.

The IAPP is a not-for-profit association founded in 2000 with a mission to define, support and improve the privacy profession globally. We are committed to providing a forum for privacy professionals to share best practices, track trends, advance privacy management issues, standardize the designations for privacy professionals and provide education and guidance on opportunities in the field of information privacy.

The IAPP is responsible for developing and launching the only globally recognized credentialing programs in information privacy: the Certified Information Privacy Professional (CIPP®), the Certified Information Privacy Manager (CIPM®) and the Certified Information Privacy Technologist (CIPT®). The CIPP, CIPM and CIPT are the leading privacy certifications for thousands of professionals around the world who serve the data protection, information auditing, information security, legal compliance and/or risk management needs of their organizations.

In addition, the IAPP offers a full suite of educational and professional development services and holds annual conferences that are recognized internationally as the leading forums for the discussion and debate of issues related to privacy policy and practice.

Preface

As I write this during the 2017 Thanksgiving holiday, I believe privacy professionals have much to be thankful for. The field of privacy and data protection has doubled and redoubled in size since my first privacy publication over 20 years ago, "Markets, Self-Regulation, and Legal Enforcement in the Protection of Personal Information." This growth is rooted in the nature of the Information Age. Privacy involves the governance of personal information, and many of our most pressing social, technical, legal and business issues implicate precisely that governance of information.

Privacy professionals thus work daily on today's key issues. Technology drives constant change, as entire new sectors and privacy topics emerge within a short time. This third edition of the textbook adds a new chapter on the subject: "Emerging Technologies—Big Data and the Internet of Things." When the second edition went to press in 2012, the terms *Big Data* and *Internet of Things* were hardly known, but now these sectors are expected to generate more than a trillion dollars annually within the coming years. As they generate new innovation and economic growth, they also will pose challenging questions about how to maintain privacy and personal dignity. Privacy professionals will play a central role in answering these and many other questions.

When Sol Bermann and I wrote the first edition of this book, published in 2007, it was the first official International Association of Privacy Professionals textbook and was created to prepare for the first Certified Information Privacy Professional examination. Kenesa Ahmad and I revamped and updated the text for the second edition, which was published in 2012. For the third edition, DeBrae Kennedy-Mayo and I have again rewritten and updated the material. Sol, Kenesa and DeBrae worked tirelessly to make sure every piece of text and endnote was correct. I have had the great fortune to work with all of them, seeking to create a book that gives you, a new person in the field, a readable and understandable introduction to our profession. For this edition, Jesse Woo and Justin Hemmings also provided valuable assistance to DeBrae and me.

At the IAPP, Nicole Russell was our lead contact for this edition. Under the direction of Trevor Hughes, the IAPP, which was founded in 2001, has grown into a vibrant, global organization with more than 35,000 members. Omer Tene has played a growing role in recent years in developing the content and thought leadership from the IAPP, assisted by the great professionals who provide the Daily Dashboard that so many of us read, as well as the many other publications.

On a personal level, my special thanks to my wife Annie Antón, for her wisdom and partnership in privacy and more importantly in life.

I believe that we, as privacy professionals, have a profound ethical responsibility to handle personal information in responsible ways. I hope this book fosters the knowledge and awareness to help make that a reality.

Peter Swire, CIPP/US
Atlanta, Georgia, USA
November 2017

I want to express my appreciation to Peter Swire for the opportunity to coauthor this book with him. In addition, I want to thank Annie Antón for reminding all of us that the conversation about privacy should include both lawyers and technologists. On a personal note, thank you to my wonderful husband Garrett for his support and for his unique perspective. I want to express my appreciation to my mother-in-law Gladys for her wisdom regarding an older generation's perspective on these issues. Finally, thank you to my sons Austin and Brayden, who provide me with insights into privacy and technology from the viewpoint of a younger generation.

DeBrae Kennedy-Mayo, CIPP/US
Atlanta, Georgia, USA
November 2017

Acknowledgments

The IAPP is pleased to present the second edition of *U.S. Private-Sector Privacy: Law and Practice for Information Privacy Professionals* in support of the Certified Information Privacy Professional/United States (CIPP/US®) program.

We would like to express our gratitude to the many professionals who contributed their time and expertise to the development of this important resource.

We are fortunate for the ongoing guidance of, and support from, our Training Advisory Board. Thank you, members past and present, for generously sharing your knowledge and experiences. These members are highly respected privacy and data protection professionals from around the world and include:

Sol Bermann, CIPP/US
Andy Bloom, CIPP/E, CIPP/US, CIPM, CIPT, FIP
Orrie Dinstein, CIPP/US
Renee Fehr, CIPP/US, CIPM
Mark Francis, CIPP/US, CIPT, FIP
D. Reed Freeman, CIPP/US
Nick Graham, CIPP/E
Sachin Kothari, CIPP/US
Susan Lyon-Hintze, CIPP/US
Siobhan MacDermott
Judy Macior, CIPP/C, CIPP/G, CIPP/US, CIPT, FIP
Hyder Masum, CIPP/C, CIPP/E, CIPP/US, CIPM
Sabine O'Keeffe, CIPP/C
Aurélie Pols
K Royal, CIPP/E, CIPP/US, CIPM, FIP
Todd Ruback, CIPP/E, CIPP/US, CIPT
Stephanie Salih, CIPP/G
James Shreve, CIPP/US, CIPT, FIP
Robert Streeter, CIPP/E, CIPP/US
Jessica Tay, CIPP/E, CIPM
Charlotte Tschider, CIPP/E, CIPP/US

Carlos Vela-Treviño, CIPM
Mr. Robert Yonaitis, CIPM, CIPT
Ernst-Oliver Wilhelm, CIPP/E, CIPM, CIPT, FIP

We are ever-so-grateful that Peter Swire, with DeBrae Kennedy-Mayo, agreed to write this revision of *U.S. Private-Sector Privacy.* The first edition, written by Peter and Sol Berman and published in 2007 as *Information Privacy: The Official Reference for the Certified Information Privacy Professional,* was the IAPP's very first certification textbook. Peter wrote the revision of *Information Privacy* with Kenesa Ahmad. This book was published in 2012 as *U.S. Private-Sector Privacy.* This third edition of the CIPP/US textbook, and second edition of *U.S. Private-Sector Privacy,* is the result of tireless research and writing by Peter and DeBrae. Our heartfelt thanks to you both.

Thank you to Judy Macior, CIPP/C, CIPP/G, CIPP/US, CIPT, FIP; Mark Francis, CIPP/US, CIPT, FIP; Ernst-Oliver Wilhelm, CIPP/E, CIPM, CIPT, FIP; Lothar Determann; Damion Jurrens; K Royal, CIPP/E, CIPP/US, CIPM, FIP; Todd Ruback, CIPP/E, CIPP/US, CIPT; and Charlotte Tschider, CIPP/E, CIPP/US for reviewing and providing feedback on the draft manuscript. We appreciate your guidance and support. To Justin Hemmings and Dan Felz, thanks for your thoughtful comments and input during the editing process. Jesse Woo, thank you for your assistance updating endnotes. Many thanks to Julia Homer, for her meticulous work in both copyediting and proofreading the text, and to Jeanne Busemeyer, who created the book index.

We are grateful to the many professionals who contributed to the publication of this book. We think you will find this textbook to be a valuable resource in preparing for your certification as well as a practical reference in your daily professional lives.

Marla Berry, CIPT
Training Director
International Association of Privacy Professionals

Introduction

Has there ever been a time when privacy was front and center like it is today? New technologies—from artificial intelligence and the Internet of Things to Big Data and the cloud—are reshaping the market at a dizzying pace. Data breaches of epic magnitude hit the news every week. International developments affecting global multinationals and consumers are seemingly commonplace. All of this makes privacy a front-page news item, a central public policy issue and, importantly, a thriving profession. To be a privacy professional means being steeped in an ever-growing and constantly shifting body of knowledge ranging from protecting children's data online to administering healthcare to governing machine-to-machine communications in smart cars, systems and homes. It means understanding not only the law but also the technology and business of data in organizations.

Since this book was last published, in 2012, much has changed on the privacy landscape. The Federal Trade Commission (FTC) has reinvigorated its privacy and data security enforcement efforts, bringing actions against Yelp, Snap, Uber, Ashley Madison, VIZIO and more. On two occasions, defendants challenged the agency's enforcement jurisdiction in court; each time, the FTC was vindicated in litigation—against Wyndham Hotels and LabMD. Privacy enforcement has spread beyond Washington, D.C., to encompass the states, with attorneys general leading the way and private litigants following suit with class action filings.

In June 2013, Edward Snowden shook the privacy world with leaks of highly classified information concerning the nature and scope of government surveillance of private-sector communications data in the United States and beyond. The revelations sent shudders through the intelligence community, resulting in international incidents (such as repeal of the EU-U.S. Safe Harbor Framework), legislative reforms and a public awakening to the value of privacy in a connected world. Two years later, privacy once more occupied top news headlines, as Apple challenged the Federal Bureau of Investigation's authority to order the unlocking of a terrorist's phone.

Few if any experts can match the depth and breadth of Peter Swire's expertise on privacy issues ranging from encryption policy and surveillance oversight to de-identification, online behavioral advertising, cookies and apps. The Nancy J. and Lawrence P. Huang Professor in the Scheller College of Business at the Georgia Institute of Technology,

Swire, who is also a senior fellow at the Future of Privacy Forum, was the first person to hold the position of chief counselor for privacy in the Office of Management and Budget under President Bill Clinton. In this role, he helped shape the Health Insurance Portability and Accountability Act Privacy Rule. In November 2012, he was named co-chair of the Tracking Protection Working Group of the World Wide Web Consortium, leading the group's effort to set forth a Do Not Track standard. In August 2013, pursuant to the Snowden revelations, President Barack Obama appointed Swire as one of five members of the Director of National Intelligence Review Group on Intelligence and Communications Technologies.

In this updated edition of *U.S. Private-Sector Privacy: Law and Practice for Information Privacy Professionals,* Professor Swire provides the definitive resource for privacy law and regulation in the United States. The book covers everything from general information privacy principles to data breach notification statutes, as well as sector-specific privacy laws in healthcare, finance, education, marketing and more. It is an indispensable guide to the richness and texture of U.S. privacy law.

Omer Tene
VP of Research and Education
International Association of Privacy Professionals

CHAPTER 1

Introduction to Privacy

This chapter provides an introduction to the subject of protection of information about individuals. In the United States and other countries, laws in this area are known as **privacy law**, or sometimes **data privacy** or **information privacy law**. In the European Union (EU) and other countries, laws in this area are known as **data protection law**. The discussion introduces the relevant vocabulary and describes the common principles and approaches used throughout the world for information privacy and data protection. This chapter continues by providing an understanding of the legal and policy structures for privacy and data protection around the world. It then outlines key models of privacy protection: the comprehensive, sectoral, self-regulatory or co-regulatory, and technology models.

1.1 Defining Privacy

In 1890, Samuel Warren and Louis Brandeis published "The Right to Privacy" in the *Harvard Law Review*, setting forth the essential definition of privacy as "the right to be let alone."[1] Both fundamental and concise, this definition underscored the personal and social dimensions of the concept that would linger long after publication of this landmark essay. Similar to this U.S. experience, most other countries have historical reasons that individuals, organizations, and government bodies have proposed their own privacy definitions. International organizations have also addressed the issue of privacy.

Privacy has been defined as the desire of people to freely choose the circumstances and the degree to which individuals will expose their attitudes and behavior to others.[2] It has been connected to the human personality and used as a means to protect an individual's independence, dignity and integrity.[3] Establishing an understanding of how privacy is defined and categorized—as well as how it has emerged as a social concern—is critical to understanding data protection and privacy law as they have been established today in the United States, Europe and elsewhere around the world.

1.2 Classes of Privacy

As discussed above, privacy can be defined in many ways. When examining data protection and privacy laws and practices, it can be helpful to focus on four categories or classes of privacy.[4]

1. **Information privacy** is concerned with establishing rules that govern the collection and handling of personal information. Examples include financial information, medical information, government records and records of a person's activities on the Internet.
2. **Bodily privacy** is focused on a person's physical being and any invasion thereof. Such an invasion can take the form of genetic testing, drug testing or body cavity searches. It also encompasses issues such as birth control, abortion and adoption.
3. **Territorial privacy** is concerned with placing limits on the ability to intrude into another individual's environment. "Environment" is not limited to the home; it may be defined as the workplace or public space. Invasion into an individual's territorial privacy typically takes the form of monitoring such as video surveillance, ID checks, and use of similar technology and procedures.
4. **Communications privacy** encompasses protection of the means of correspondence, including postal mail, telephone conversations, email, and other forms of communicative behavior and apparatus.

While some of these categories may interrelate, this book will focus primarily on the legal, technological and practical components of information privacy.

1.3 The Historical and Social Origins of Privacy

The concept of information privacy as a social concept is rooted in some of the oldest texts and cultures.[5] Privacy is referenced numerous times in the laws of classical Greece and in the Bible. The concept of the freedom from being watched has historically been recognized by Jewish law.[6] Privacy is similarly recognized in the Qur'an and in the sayings of Mohammed, where there is discussion of the privacy of prayer as well as in the avoidance of spying or talking ill of someone behind his or her back.[7]

The legal protection of privacy rights has a similarly far-reaching history. In England, the Justices of the Peace Act, enacted in 1361, included provisions calling for the arrest of "peeping Toms" and eavesdroppers.[8]

In 1765, British Lord Camden protected the privacy of the home, striking down a warrant to enter the home and seize papers from it. He wrote, "We can safely say there is no law in this country to justify the defendants in what they have done; if there was, it would destroy all the comforts of society, for papers are often the dearest property any man can have."[9] Parliamentarian William Pitt shared this view, declaring that "[t]he poorest man may in his cottage bid defiance to all the force of the Crown. It may be frail: its roof may shake; the wind may blow through it; the storms may enter; the rain may enter—but the King of England cannot enter; all his forces dare not cross the threshold of the ruined tenement."[10]

This British tradition of privacy protection was built into the U.S. Constitution, ratified in 1789. Although the word *privacy* does not appear in the Constitution, a number of provisions relate to privacy, including: the Third Amendment, banning quartering of soldiers in a person's home; the Fourth Amendment, generally requiring a search warrant before the police can enter a home or business; the Fifth Amendment, prohibiting persons from being compelled to testify against themselves; and, later, the Fourteenth Amendment, with its requirement of due process under the law, including for intrusions into a person's bodily autonomy.

By contrast, the California Constitution contains an explicit guarantee of the right to privacy, which the people of California added to the California Constitution by a ballot measure in November 1972. Article 1, Section 1 of the California Constitution states:

> *All people are by nature free and independent and have inalienable rights. Among these are enjoying and defending life and liberty, acquiring, possessing, and protecting property, and pursuing and obtaining safety, happiness, and privacy.*[11]

In many parts of the world, modern privacy has arisen within the context of human rights. In December 1948, the General Assembly of the United Nations adopted and proclaimed the Universal Declaration of Human Rights.[12] This declaration formally announced that "[n]o one shall be subjected to arbitrary interference with his privacy, family, home or correspondence."[13] In 1950, the Council of Europe set forth the European Convention for the Protection of Human Rights and Fundamental Freedoms.[14] Article 8 of that Convention, which has been the subject of extensive litigation, provides that "[e]veryone has the right to respect for his private and family life, his home and his correspondence," with this right conditioned where necessary to protect national security and other goals, as necessary to preserve a democratic society.[15]

1.4 Fair Information Practices

Since the 1970s, fair information practices (FIPs), sometimes called fair information privacy practices or principles (FIPPs), have been a significant means for organizing the multiple individual rights and organizational responsibilities that exist with respect to personal information. The precise definitions of FIPs have varied over time and by geographic location; nonetheless, strong similarities exist for the major themes. In practice, there are various exceptions to the clear statements provided here and the degree to which the FIPs are legally binding.

Important codifications of FIPs include:

- The 1973 U.S. Department of Health, Education and Welfare Fair Information Practice Principles
- The 1980 Organisation for Economic Co-operation and Development Guidelines Governing the Protection of Privacy and Transborder Flows of Personal Data ("OECD Guidelines")
- The 1981 Council of Europe Convention for the Protection of Individuals with Regard to the Automatic Processing of Personal Data ("Convention 108")
- The Asia-Pacific Economic Cooperation (APEC), which in 2004 agreed to a Privacy Framework
- The 2009 Madrid Resolution—International Standards on the Protection of Personal Data and Privacy

1.4.1 Overview of Fair Information Practices

FIPs are guidelines for handling, storing and managing data with privacy, security and fairness in an information society that is rapidly evolving.[16] These principles can be conceived in four categories: rights of individuals, controls on the information, information lifecycle, and management.

1.4.1.1 Rights of Individuals

With regard to the rights of individuals, organizations should address notice, choice and consent, as well as data subject access.

- **Notice**. Organizations should provide notice about their privacy policies and procedures, and should identify the purpose for which personal information is collected, used, retained and disclosed.

- **Choice and consent.** Organizations should describe the choices available to individuals and should get implicit or explicit consent with respect to the collection, use, retention and disclosure of personal information. Consent is often considered especially important for disclosures of personal information to other data controllers.
- **Data subject access.** Organizations should provide individuals with access to their personal information for review and update.

1.4.1.2 Controls on the Information

Regarding controls on the information, organizations should focus on information security and information quality.

- **Information security.** Organizations should use reasonable administrative, technical and physical safeguards to protect personal information against unauthorized access, use, disclosure, modification and destruction.
- **Information quality.** Organizations should maintain accurate, complete and relevant personal information for the purposes identified in the notice.

1.4.1.3 Information Lifecycle

Organizations should address the lifecycle of information, including collection, use and retention, and disclosure.

- **Collection.** Organizations should collect personal information only for the purposes identified in the notice.
- **Use and retention.** Organizations should limit the use of personal information to the purposes identified in the notice and for which the individual has provided implicit or explicit consent. Organizations should also retain personal information for only as long as necessary to fulfill the stated purpose.
- **Disclosure.** Organizations should disclose personal information to third parties only for the purposes identified in the notice and with the implicit or explicit consent of the individual.

1.4.1.4 Management

Regarding management, organizations should ensure that they address both management and administration as well as monitoring and enforcement.

- **Management and administration**. Organizations should define, document, communicate and assign accountability for their privacy policies and procedures.
- **Monitoring and enforcement**. Organizations should monitor compliance with their privacy policies and procedures and have procedures to address privacy-related complaints and disputes.

1.4.2 U.S. Health, Education and Welfare FIPs (1973)

The FIPs used widely today date back to a 1973 report by the U.S. Department of Health, Education and Welfare Advisory Committee on Automated Systems.[17]

The original Code of Fair Information Practices provided:

- There must be no personal data record-keeping systems whose very existence is secret
- There must be a way for a person to find out what information about the person is in a record and how it is used
- There must be a way for a person to prevent information about the person that was obtained for one purpose from being used or made available for other purposes without the individual's consent
- There must be a way for a person to correct or amend a record of identifiable information about the person
- Any organization creating, maintaining, using or disseminating records of identifiable personal data must assure the reliability of the data for its intended use and must take precautions to prevent misuse of the data

1.4.3 OECD Guidelines (1980)

In 1980, the OECD, an international organization that originally included the United States and European countries but has since expanded, published a set of privacy principles entitled "Guidelines Governing the Protection of Privacy and Transborder Flows of Personal Data."[18] The OECD Guidelines, updated in 2013, are perhaps the most widely recognized framework for FIPs and have been endorsed by the U.S. Federal Trade Commission (FTC) and many other government organizations.[19]

The Guidelines provide the following privacy framework:

> ***Collection Limitation Principle.*** *There should be limits to the collection of personal data and any such data should be obtained by lawful and fair means and, where appropriate, with the knowledge or consent of the data subject.*
>
> ***Data Quality Principle.*** *Personal data should be relevant to the purposes for which they are to be used, and, to the extent necessary for those purposes, should be accurate, complete and kept up-to-date.*
>
> ***Purpose Specification Principle.*** *The purposes for which personal data are collected should be specified not later than at the time of data collection and the subsequent use limited to the fulfillment of those purposes or such others as are not incompatible with those purposes and as are specified on each occasion of change of purpose.*
>
> ***Use Limitation Principle.*** *Personal data should not be disclosed, made available or otherwise used for purposes other than those specified in accordance with [the* Purpose Specification Principle*] except: (a) with the consent of the data subject or (b) by the authority of law.*
>
> ***Security Safeguards Principle.*** *Personal data should be protected by reasonable security safeguards against such risks as loss or unauthorized access, destruction, use, modification or disclosure of data.*
>
> ***Openness Principle.*** *There should be a general policy of openness about developments, practices and policies with respect to personal data. Means should be readily available of establishing the existence and nature of personal data, and the main purposes of their use, as well as the identity and usual residence of the data controller.*
>
> ***Individual Participation Principle.*** *An individual should have the right: (a) to obtain from a data controller, or otherwise, confirmation of whether or not the data controller has data relating to him; (b) to have communicated to him, data relating to him, within a reasonable time, at a charge, if any, that is not excessive, in a reasonable manner, and in a form that is readily intelligible to him; (c) to be given reasons if a request made under subparagraphs (a) and (b) is denied, and to be able to challenge such denial; and (d) to challenge data relating to him and, if the challenge is successful to have the data erased, rectified, completed or amended.*
>
> ***Accountability Principle.*** *A data controller should be accountable for complying with measures which give effect to the principles stated above.*

1.4.4 Council of Europe Convention (1981)

In 1981, the Council of Europe passed the Convention for the Protection of Individuals with Regard to the Automatic Processing of Personal Data ("Convention 108"). This convention required member states of the Council of Europe that signed the treaty to incorporate certain data protection provisions into their domestic law.[20]

Convention 108 provided for the following:

- **Quality of data.** Data of a personal nature that is automatically processed should be obtained and stored only for specified and legitimate purposes. Data should be stored in a form that permits identification of the data subject no longer than needed for the required purpose.
- **Special categories of data.** Unless domestic law provides appropriate safeguards, personal data revealing the following categories cannot be automatically processed: racial origin, political opinions, religious beliefs, health, sex life or criminal convictions.
- **Data security.** Appropriate security measures should be taken for files containing personal data. These measures must be adapted for the particular function of the file as well as for risks involved.
- **Transborder data flows.** When transferring data from one party of the Convention to another party, privacy concerns shall not prohibit the transborder flow of data. Exceptions to this provision include special regulations concerning certain categories of personal data.[21]

The Convention was broadly similar to the OECD Guidelines, and its principles were important contributors to national data protection laws in Europe in the 1980s and 1990s.[22]

1.4.5 APEC Privacy Framework (2004)

APEC is a multinational organization with 21 Pacific coast members in Asia and the Americas. Unlike the EU, the APEC organization operates under nonbinding agreement. It was established in 1989 to enhance economic growth for the region.

In February 2003, the APEC Privacy Subgroup was established under the auspices of the Electronic Commerce Steering Group in order to develop a framework for privacy practices. This framework was designed to provide support to APEC-member economic legislation that would both protect individual interests and ensure the continued economic development of all APEC member economies. The APEC Privacy Framework was approved by the APEC ministers in November 2004.[23]

It contains nine information privacy principles that generally mirror the OECD Guidelines, but in some areas are more explicit about exceptions. The APEC privacy principles spelled out in the framework are:

1. ***Preventing Harm***. *Recognizing the interests of the individual to legitimate expectations of privacy, personal information protection should be designed to prevent the misuse of such information. Further, acknowledging the risk that harm may result from such misuse of personal information, specific obligations should take account of such risk and remedial measures should be proportionate to the likelihood and severity of the harm threatened by the collection, use and transfer of personal information.*

2. **Notice**. *Personal information controllers should provide clear and easily accessible statements about their practices and policies with respect to personal information that should include:*

    a. *the fact that personal information is being collected;*

    b. *the purposes for which personal information is collected;*

    c. *the types of persons or organizations to whom personal information might be disclosed;*

    d. *the identity and location of the personal information controller, including information on how to contact it about its practices and handling of personal information;*

    e. *the choices and means the personal information controller offers individuals for limiting the use and disclosure of personal information, and for accessing and correcting it.*

    All reasonably practicable steps shall be taken to ensure that such information is provided either before or at the time of collection of personal information. Otherwise, such information should be provided as soon after as is practicable. It may not be appropriate for personal information controllers to provide notice regarding the collection and use of publicly available information.

3. ***Collection Limitation.*** *The collection of personal information should be limited to information that is relevant to the purposes of collection and any such information should be obtained by lawful and fair means, and, where appropriate, with notice to, or consent of, the individual concerned.*
4. ***Uses of Personal Information.*** *Personal information collected should be used only to fulfill the purposes of collection and other compatible purposes except:*
    a. *with the consent of the individual whose personal information is collected;*
    b. *when necessary to provide a service or product requested by the individual; or,*
    c. *by the authority of law and other legal instruments, proclamations and pronouncements of legal effect.*
5. ***Choice.*** *Where appropriate, individuals should be provided with clear, prominent, easily understandable, accessible and affordable mechanisms to exercise choice in relation to the collection, use and disclosure of their personal information. It may not be appropriate for personal information controllers to provide these mechanisms when collecting publicly available information.*
6. ***Integrity of Personal Information.*** *Personal information should be accurate, complete and kept up-to-date to the extent necessary for the purposes of use.*
7. ***Security Safeguards.*** *Personal information controllers should protect personal information that they hold with appropriate safeguards against risks, such as loss or unauthorized access to personal information, or unauthorized destruction, use, modification or disclosure of information or other misuses. Such safeguards should be proportional to the likelihood and severity of the harm threatened, the sensitivity of the information and the context in which it is held, and should be subject to periodic review and reassessment.*
8. ***Access and Correction.*** *Individuals should be able to:*
    a. *obtain from the personal information controller confirmation of whether or not the personal information controller holds personal information about them*
    b. *have communicated to them, after having provided sufficient proof of their identity, personal information about them*
        i. *within a reasonable time;*
        ii. *at a charge, if any, that is not excessive;*

iii. in a reasonable manner;

iv. in a form that is generally understandable; and,

c. challenge the accuracy of information relating to them and, if possible and as appropriate, have the information rectified, completed, amended or deleted.

d. such access and opportunity for correction should be provided except where:

i. the burden or expense of doing so would be unreasonable or disproportionate to the risks to the individual's privacy in the case in question;

ii. the information should not be disclosed due to legal or security reasons or to protect confidential commercial information; or

iii. the information privacy of persons other than the individual would be violated

If a request under (a) or (b) or a challenge under (c) is denied, the individual should be provided with reasons why and be able to challenge such denial.

9. ***Accountability.*** *A personal information controller should be accountable for complying with measures that give effect to the principles stated above. When personal information is to be transferred to another person or organization, whether domestically or internationally, the personal information controller should obtain the consent of the individual or exercise due diligence and take reasonable steps to ensure that the recipient person or organization will protect the information consistently with these principles.*

1.4.6 Madrid Resolution (2009)

In 2009, the Madrid Resolution was approved by the independent data protection and privacy commissioners (not the governments themselves) at the annual International Conference of Data Protection and Privacy Commissioners, held in Madrid, Spain.[24] There were dual purposes for the Madrid Resolution: to define a set of principles and rights guaranteeing (1) the effective and internationally uniform protection of privacy with regard to the processing of personal data and (2) the facilitation of the international flows of personal data needed in a globalized world.

The resolution has several basic principles:

- **Principle of lawfulness and fairness.** Personal data must be fairly processed, respecting the applicable national legislation as well as the rights and freedoms of individuals. Any processing that gives rise to unlawful or arbitrary discrimination against the data subject shall be deemed unfair.
- **Purpose specification principle.** Processing of personal data should be limited to the fulfillment of the specific, explicit and legitimate purposes of the responsible person; processing that is noncompatible with the purposes for which personal data was collected requires the unambiguous consent of the data subject.
- **Proportionality principle.** Processing of personal data should be limited to such processing as is adequate, relevant and not excessive in relation to the purposes. Reasonable efforts should be made to limit processing to the minimum necessary.
- **Data quality.** The responsible person should at all times ensure that personal data is accurate, sufficient and kept up to date in such a way as to fulfill the purposes for which it is processed. The period of retention of the personal data shall be limited to the minimum necessary. Personal data no longer necessary to fulfill the purposes that legitimized its processing must be deleted or rendered anonymous.
- **Openness principle.** The responsible person shall provide to the data subjects, as a minimum, information about the responsible person's identity, the intended purpose of processing, the recipients to whom their personal data will be disclosed, and how data subjects may exercise their rights. When data is collected directly from the data subject, this information must be provided at the time of collection, unless it has already been provided. When data is not collected directly from the data subject, the responsible person must inform him or her about the source of personal data. This information must be provided in an intelligible form, using clear and plain language, in particular for any processing addressed specifically to minors.
- **Accountability.** The responsible person shall take all the necessary measures to observe the principles and obligations set out in the resolution and in the applicable national legislation and have the necessary internal mechanisms in place for demonstrating such observance both to data subjects and to the supervisory authorities in the exercise of their powers.

1.5 Information Privacy, Data Protection and the Advent of Information Technology

Modern ideas about privacy have been decisively shaped by the rapid development of information technology (IT). Mainframe computers emerged by the 1960s to handle the data processing and storage needs of business, government, educational and other institutions. As hardware and software evolved, there were clear and large benefits to individuals and society, ranging from increased economic growth to easier communications for individuals. The unprecedented accumulation of personal data, and the resulting potential for increased surveillance, also triggered an acute interest in privacy practices and the privacy rights of individuals. A vivid image of the risk came from George Orwell's 1949 book *1984*, in which the government kept citizens under surveillance at all times, warning them with the slogan "Big Brother is watching you."[25] To prevent the creation of "Big Brother," by the late 1960s, nearly two decades after Orwell wrote his masterpiece, there were increasing demands for formal rules to govern the collection and handling of personal information.

In response to this sort of concern, in 1970 the German state of Hesse enacted the first known modern data protection law. This German law was motivated in part by the growing potential of IT systems as well as a desire to prevent a reoccurrence of the personal information abuses that took place under Hitler's Third Reich before and during World War II. Such concerns were not confined to Germany, and over the next decade, several European countries enacted national privacy laws of differing objectives and scope. The United States passed its first national privacy law in 1970, the Fair Credit Reporting Act, which focused solely on information about consumer credit.

1.6 Personal and Nonpersonal Information

Because information privacy is concerned with establishing rules that govern the collection and handling of personal information, an understanding of what constitutes personal information is key. A central issue to determine is the extent to which information can be linked to a particular person. This can be contrasted with aggregate or statistical information, which generally does not raise privacy compliance issues.

1.6.1 Personal Information

In the United States, the terms *personal information* and *personally identifiable information* (PII) are generally used to define the information that is covered by privacy laws. These definitions include information that makes it possible to identify an individual. Examples include names, Social Security numbers or passport numbers. The terms also include information about an "identified" or "identifiable" individual. For instance, street address, telephone number, and email address are generally considered sufficiently related to a particular person to count as identifiable information within the scope of privacy protections. The definitions generally apply to both electronic and paper records. **Sensitive personal information** is an important subset of personal information. The definition of what is considered sensitive varies depending on jurisdiction and particular regulations. In the United States, Social Security numbers and financial information are commonly treated as sensitive information, as are driver's license numbers and health information. In general, sensitive information requires additional privacy and security limitations to safeguard its collection, use and disclosure.

1.6.2 Nonpersonal Information

If the data elements used to identify the individual are removed, the remaining data becomes nonpersonal information, and privacy and data protection laws generally do not apply. Similar terms used include *de-identified* or *anonymized* information. This type of information is frequently used for research, statistical or aggregate purposes. "Pseudonymized" data exists where information about individuals is retained under pseudonyms, such as a unique numerical code for each person, that renders data temporarily nonpersonal. Pseudonymized data can be reversed, re-identifying the individuals. This reversibility can be important in certain situations, for instance, in a drug trial where the medicine is discovered to have adverse side effects.[26]

1.6.3 The Line Between Personal and Nonpersonal Information

The difference between personal and nonpersonal information depends on what is identifiable. The line between these two categories is not always clear, and regulators and courts in different jurisdictions may disagree on what counts as personal information.

Other Information Assets of an Organization

As part of their normal activities, organizations also may collect and generate information that by its nature would not be considered personal information, but is nevertheless a key part of the information assets of the organization. Examples of such information include:

- *Financial data*
- *Operational data*
- *Intellectual property*
- *Information about the organization's products and services*

Though not personal information, such information needs to be protected and secured to ensure its confidentiality.

As an example of how different regimes have defined the line between personal and nonpersonal information, consider the Internet protocol (IP) address, the numbers that identify the location of computers in communications over the Internet. The EU considers IP addresses "personal data," taking the view that IP addresses are identifiable.[27] A court in Ireland, however, determined that IP addresses did not constitute personal information.[28] In the United States, federal agencies operating under the Privacy Act do not consider IP addresses to be covered by the statute.[29] The FTC, an independent agency in the United States, has stated, however, that in connection with breaches of healthcare information, IP addresses are personal information.[30] For the privacy professional, it is important to check the line between personal and nonpersonal information for the appropriate regulatory regime.

Assessing an Organization's Personal Information Responsibilities

The line between personal and nonpersonal information illustrates a critical first step in assessing an organization's personal information responsibilities—is the organization covered by a law or other obligation?

With globalization, information privacy professionals may need to determine when the laws of a particular jurisdiction apply. In addition, some laws apply only to particular sectors or types of information. The Health Insurance Portability and Accountability Act in the United States, for instance, applies only to certain organizations ("covered entities") and certain information. ("personal health information").

Changes in technology can also shift the line between personal and nonpersonal information. For instance, historically, IP addresses were usually "dynamic"—individuals would generally get a new IP address assigned by their Internet service provider each time they logged on to the Internet. Over time, more individuals have had "static" IP addresses, which stay the same for each computer device, linking the device more closely to an identifiable person. The increasingly used version of the Internet protocol (IPv6) employs a new numbering scheme that, by default, uses information about the computer to generate an IPv6 address, making it even easier to link devices (including smartphones) and their users.

1.7 Sources of Personal Information

Sometimes the same information about an individual is treated differently based on the source of the information. To illustrate this point, consider three sources of personal information: public records, publicly available information and nonpublic information.

1. **Public records** consist of information collected and maintained by a government entity and available to the public. These government entities include the national, state or provincial, and local governments. Public records laws vary considerably across jurisdictions.

   For instance, real estate records in some jurisdictions contain detailed information about ownership, assessed value, amount paid for the parcel, taxes imposed on the parcel, and improvements. Making this information public has certain advantages, such as enabling a person who owns real estate to determine if the taxes assessed are fair relative to other parcels in the area. Other jurisdictions, by contrast, do not release such information, considering it to be private.

2. **Publicly available information** is information that is generally available to a wide range of persons. Some traditional examples are names and addresses in telephone books and information published in newspapers or other public media. Today, search engines are a major source of publicly available information.

3. **Nonpublic information** is not generally available or easily accessed due to law or custom. Examples of this type of data are medical records, financial information and adoption records. A company's customer or employee database usually contains nonpublic information.

Organizations should be alert to the possibility that the same information may be public record, publicly available and nonpublic. For example, a name and address may be a matter of public record on a real estate deed, publicly available in the telephone book, and included in nonpublic databases, such as in a healthcare patient file. To understand how to handle the name and address, one must understand the source that provided it—restrictions may apply to use of the name and address in the patient file, but not to public records or publicly available information.

1.8 Processing Personal Information

As introduced above, almost anything that someone may do with personal information might constitute processing under privacy and data protection laws. The term *processing* refers to the collection, recording, organization, storage, updating or modification, retrieval, consultation and use of personal information. It also includes the disclosure by transmission, dissemination or making available in any other form, linking, alignment or combination, blocking, erasure, or destruction of personal information. The following common terms, first widely used in the EU, apply to data processing:

- **Data subject** is the individual about whom information is being processed, such as the patient at a medical facility, the employee of a company or the customer of a retail store.
- **Data controller** is an organization that has the authority to decide how and why personal information is to be processed. This entity is the focus of most obligations under privacy and data protection laws—it controls the use of personal information by determining the purposes for its use and the manner in which the information will be processed.[31] The data controller may be an individual or an organization that is legally treated as an individual, such as a corporation or partnership.
- **Data processor** is an individual or organization, often a third-party outsourcing service, that processes data on behalf of the data controller. Under the Health Insurance Portability and Accountability Act (HIPAA) medical privacy rule, these data processors are called "business associates." A data controller might not have the employees or expertise in-house to do some types of activity, or might find it more efficient to get assistance from other organizations. For instance, a data controller may hire another organization to do accounting and back-office operations. The first data processor, in turn, might hire other organizations to act as data processors on its behalf, for example, if a company providing back-office operations hired a subcontractor to manage its website. Each organization in the chain—from data controller, to data processor, to any subsequent data processor acting on behalf of the first data processor—is expected to act in a trusted way, doing operations that are consistent with the direction of the data controller. The data processors are not authorized to do additional data processing outside of the scope of what is permitted for the data controller itself.

1.9 Sources of Privacy Protection

There is no single approach to protecting privacy and security. Rather, privacy protection is derived from several sources: market forces, technology, legal controls and self-regulation.

- **Markets**. The market can be a useful way of approaching privacy protection. When consumers raise concerns about their privacy, companies respond. Businesses that are brand sensitive are especially likely to adopt strict privacy practices to build up their reputations as trustworthy organizations. In turn, this can create market competition, spurring other companies to also implement privacy practices into their operations.
- **Technology**. Technology also can provide robust privacy protection. The rapid advancement of technology such as encryption provides people with new and advanced means of protecting themselves. Even if privacy protection from law or market forces is weak, information privacy and security best practices can remain strong.
- **Law**. Law is the traditional approach to privacy regulation. However, simply enacting more laws does not necessarily result in better privacy and security. Laws may not be well drafted and may be poorly enforced. Laws should be understood as one very important source of privacy protections, but in practice, actual protection also depends on markets, technology and self-regulation.
- **Self-regulation and co-regulation**. Self-regulation (and the closely related concept of co-regulation) is a complement to law that comes from the government. The term self-regulation can refer to any or all of three components: legislation, enforcement and adjudication. Legislation refers to the question of who defines privacy rules. For self-regulation, this typically occurs through the privacy policy of a company or other entity, or by an industry association. Enforcement refers to the question of who should initiate enforcement action. Actions may be brought by data protection authorities, other government agencies, industry code enforcement, or in some cases the affected individuals. Finally, adjudication refers to the question of who should decide whether an organization has violated a privacy rule. The decision maker can be an industry association, a government agency or a judicial officer. Thus, the term self-regulation covers a broad range of institutional arrangements. For a clear understanding of data privacy responsibilities, privacy professionals

should consider who defines the requirements, which organization brings enforcement action, and who actually makes the judicial decisions.

1.10 World Models of Data Protection

As of the writing of this book, well over 100 countries have privacy or data protection regimes, and more than half of them first enacted such laws after the year 2000.[32] In varying degrees, the different data protection models around the world all draw upon law, markets, technology and self-regulation as sources for privacy protection. Comprehensive data protection laws are those in which the government has defined requirements throughout the economy. On the other hand, sectoral laws, such as those in the United States, exist in selected market segments, often in response to a particular need or problem. The scope of data protection laws, as described above, varies depending on how much the specific country relies on government laws versus industry codes and standards. The various data protection models used globally also differ in enforcement and adjudication. However, each regime falls along a continuum, with clearly defined legislative, enforcement and adjudication mechanisms established by the government at one end, and no stated, defined baseline at the other. In practice, no regime is so comprehensive that all laws are written, enforced and adjudicated by the government. Even in the United States, however, which is often used as an example of a less regulatory-oriented regime, the government has written numerous privacy laws.

Some of the most common data protection models in use today are comprehensive and sectoral frameworks, co-regulatory or self-regulatory models, and the technology-based model. Following are the basic approaches, along with major arguments for and against each approach.

1.10.1 Comprehensive Model

Comprehensive data protection laws govern the collection, use and dissemination of personal information in the public and private sectors.[33] Generally speaking, a country that has enacted such laws hosts an official or agency responsible for overseeing enforcement.[34] This official or agency, often referred to as a data protection authority (DPA) in Europe, ensures compliance with the law and investigates alleged breaches of the law's provisions. In many countries, the official also bears responsibility for educating the public on data protection matters and acts as an international liaison for data protection issues. Enforcement and funding are two critical issues in a comprehensive data protection scheme. Data protection officials are granted varying degrees of enforcement power from country to country. Further, countries choose to allocate varying levels of resources to the enforcement of data protection laws, leaving some countries inadequately funded to meet the laws' stated goals.

Over time, countries have adopted comprehensive privacy and data protection laws for a combination of at least three reasons:[35]

1. **Remedy past injustices.** A number of countries, particularly those previously subject to authoritarian regimes, have enacted comprehensive laws as a means to remedy past privacy violations. For instance, Germany is widely regarded as having one of the strictest privacy regimes. At least part of the reason is likely a reaction to its history during the Nazi regime and under the heavy surveillance by the Stasi (Ministry of State Security) in East Germany before the two parts of Germany were reunified in 1990.
2. **Ensure consistency with European privacy laws.** As discussed below, the Data Protection Directive in the EU limits transfer of personal data to countries that lack "adequate" privacy protections. Some countries passed privacy laws as part of the process of joining the EU. Other countries have enacted privacy laws at least in part to prevent any disruption in trade with EU countries.
3. **Promote electronic commerce.** Countries have developed privacy laws to provide assurance to potentially uneasy consumers engaged in electronic commerce.

Critics of the comprehensive approach express concern that the costs of the regulations can outweigh the benefits. One-size-fits-all rules may not address risk well. If the rules are strict enough to ensure protection for especially sensitive data, such as medical data or information that can lead to identity theft, that same level of strictness may not be justified for less sensitive data. Along with the strictness of controls, comprehensive approaches can involve costly paperwork, documentation, audit and similar requirements even for settings where the risks are low.

A different critique of comprehensive regimes is that they may provide insufficient opportunity for innovation in data processing. With the continued evolution of IT, individuals have access today to many products and services that were unimaginable a decade or two ago, from smartphones to social networks and the full range of services that have developed since the Internet emerged in the 1990s. To the extent that comprehensive laws may discourage the emergence of new services involving personal information or require prior approval from regulators, the pace and diversity of technological innovation may slow.

1.10.2 Sectoral Model (United States)

This framework protects personal information by enacting laws that address a particular industry sector.[36] For example, in the United States, different laws delineate conduct and specify the requisite level of data protection for video rental records, consumer financial transactions, credit records, law enforcement and medical records. In a comprehensive model, laws addressing specific market segments may be enacted to provide more specific protection for data particular to that segment, such as the healthcare sector.

Supporters of the sectoral approach emphasize that different parts of the economy face different privacy and security challenges; it is appropriate, for instance, to have stricter regulation for medical records than for ordinary commerce. Supporters also underscore the cost savings and lack of regulatory burden for organizations outside of the regulated sectors.

Critics of the sectoral approach express concern about the lack of a single data protection authority to oversee personal information issues. They also point out the problems of gaps and overlaps in coverage. Gaps can occur when legislation lags technological change, and unregulated segments may suddenly face privacy threats with no legislative guidance. Whereas laws under the comprehensive approach apply to new technologies, there are no similar governmental rules under the sectoral approach until the legislature or other responsible body acts. As a recent example, drones are becoming more common in the United States, but there have not been any national privacy rules governing surveillance by drones. Moreover, there can be political obstacles to creating new legislation if industry or other stakeholders oppose such laws. An example of a gap being filled is the Health Information Technology for Economic and Clinical Health (HITECH) Act of 2009, which introduced a breach notification requirement for vendors of personal health records vendors. These were not "covered entities" under HIPAA. The new law addressed a gap, where entities not traditionally involved in healthcare offered services involving the collection and use of large volumes of healthcare information.

Similarly, overlaps can exist in a sectoral approach. For instance, HIPAA-covered entities such as medical healthcare providers are subject to enforcement either by the U.S. Department of Health and Human Services under HIPAA or by the FTC under its general authority to take action against unfair and deceptive practices. As the boundaries between industries change over time, previously separate industries can converge, potentially leading to different legal treatment of functionally similar activities.

1.10.3 The Co-Regulatory and Self-Regulatory Models

Co-regulation and self-regulation are quite similar, with co-regulation generally referring to laws such as those in Australia, which are closer to the comprehensive model, and self-regulation generally referring to approaches such as those in the United States, where there are no general laws applying to personal information.[37] Under both approaches, a mix of government and nongovernment institutions protects personal information.

The **co-regulatory model** emphasizes industry development of enforceable codes or standards for privacy and data protection against the backdrop of legal requirements by the government. Co-regulation can exist under both comprehensive and sectoral models. One U.S. example is the Children's Online Privacy Protection Act in the United States (COPPA), which allows compliance with codes to be sufficient for compliance with the statute once the codes have been approved by the FTC.

The **self-regulatory model** emphasizes creation of codes of practice for the protection of personal information by a company, industry or independent body. In contrast to the co-regulatory model, there may be no generally applicable data protection law that creates a legal framework for the self-regulatory code.[38] A prominent example that affects the wide range of businesses that process credit card data is the Payment Card Industry Data Security Standard (PCI-DSS), which enhances cardholder data security and facilitates the broad adoption of consistent data security measures globally.

Seal programs are another form of self-regulation. A seal program requires its participants to abide by codes of information practices and submit to some variation of monitoring to ensure compliance.[39] Companies that abide by the terms of the seal program are then allowed to display the program's privacy seal on their website. Seal programs recognized by the FTC for the COPPA are Aristotle International Inc., Children's Advertising Review Unit (CARU), Entertainment Software Rating Board (ESRB), iKeepSafe, kidSAFE, PRIVO, and TrustArc (formerly TRUSTe).[40]

Supporters of a self-regulatory approach tend to emphasize the expertise of the industry to inform its own personal information practices, and thus use the most efficient ways to ensure privacy and security.[41] Self-regulatory codes may also be more flexible and quick to adjust to new technology without the need for prior governmental approval.

Critics of the self-regulatory approach often express concerns about adequacy and enforcement. Industry-developed codes can provide limited data protection, and may not adequately incorporate the perspectives and interests of consumers and other stakeholders who are not part of the industry. The strength of enforcement can also vary.

In some cases, where an organization has signed up for a code, any violation is treated just like a violation of a statute. In others, however, penalties can be weak, and there may be no effective enforcement authority.

An alternative to the protections that arise from an organization's administrative compliance with laws or self-regulatory codes that is worth considering is a technology-based model. Individuals and organizations in some settings can use technical measures that reduce the relative importance of administrative measures for overall privacy protection. For example, global web email providers such as Google and Microsoft have increased their use of encryption between the sender and recipient. Chapters 4 and 5 further discuss the interrelated roles of technical, administrative and physical safeguards for personal information.

1.11 Conclusion

This chapter introduced key terminology about privacy and data protection laws and policies. It traced the history of these topics and the continued growth of legal requirements to accompany the evolution of information technology since the 1960s. As legal requirements have increased, the number of data protection and privacy professionals has grown rapidly, and their role has expanded in many organizations. Similar but not identical forms of fair information practices have been the basis of privacy and data protection laws in numerous countries around the globe. This chapter introduces the reader to the legal and policy structures for privacy and data protection around the world. The key models of privacy protection have been examined: the comprehensive, sectoral, self-regulatory or co-regulatory, and technology models.

Endnotes

1 Samuel Warren and Louis Brandeis, "The Right to Privacy," *Harvard Law Review* 4 (1890): 193, http://groups.csail.mit.edu/mac/classes/6.805/articles/privacy/Privacy_brand_warr2.html (accessed November 2017). There are numerous sources of legal privacy, including tort privacy (Warren and Brandeis' original conception), Fourth Amendment privacy, First Amendment privacy, fundamental-decision privacy and state constitutional privacy. Ken Gormley, "One Hundred Years of Privacy," *Wisconsin Law Review* 1335 (1992), https://cyber.law.harvard.edu/privacy/Gormley--100%20Years%20of%20Privacy--%20EXCERPTS.htm (accessed November 2017).

2 Alan F. Westin, *Privacy and Freedom* (New York: Atheneum, 1967).

3 Edward J. Bloustein, "Privacy as an Aspect of Human Dignity: An Answer to Dean Prosser," *39 New York University Law Review* 962, 971 (1964): 962 at 971.

4 David Banisar and Simon Davies, "Global Trends in Privacy Protection: An International Survey of Privacy, Data Protection, and Surveillance Laws and Developments," *John Marshall Journal of*

Computer & Information Law 18 (Fall 1999), http://papers.ssrn.com/sol3/papers.cfm?abstract_id=2138799 (accessed November 2017).

5 *Colloquium on Privacy & Security,* transcript, Gary M. Schober, moderator, *Buffalo Law Review* 50 (2002): 703, 726; *Privacy and Human Rights: An International Survey of Privacy Laws and Developments,* Electronic Privacy Information Center (EPIC) & Privacy International (2002).

6 *Privacy and Human Rights,* 5; *see EPIC-Privacy and Human Rights Report* (2006), www.worldlii.org/int/journals/EPICPrivHR/2006/PHR2006-The.html (accessed November 2017).

7 an-Noor 24:27–28 (Yusufali); al-Hujraat 49:11–12 (Yusufali).

8 Justice of the Peace Act 1361, Legislative.gov.uk, www.legislation.gov.uk/aep/Edw3/34/1 (accessed November 2017).

9 Entick v. Carrington [1765] EWHC KB J98, www.bailii.org/ew/cases/EWHC/KB/1765/J98.html (accessed November 2017).

10 William Pitt, Speech on the Excise Bill, House of Commons (March 1763).

11 Cal. Const. art. I, § 1. *See,* Lothar Determann, California Privacy Law - Practical Guide and Commentary Chapter 2-2 (2016).

12 Universal Declaration of Human Rights, United Nations, www.un.org/en/universal-declaration-human-rights/ (accessed November 2017).

13 *Id.* at Article 8.

14 Convention for the Protection of Human Rights and Fundamental Freedoms, Council of Europe (April 11, 1950), www.coe.int/en/web/conventions/full-list/-/conventions/treaty/005 (accessed November 2017).

15 *Id.* at Article 8.

16 Pam Dixon, "A Brief Introduction to Fair Information Practices," World Privacy Forum, https://www.worldprivacyforum.org/2008/01/report-a-brief-introduction-to-fair-information-practices/ (accessed November 2017). To view the code itself, *see* Code for Fair Information Practices, EPIC, https://www.epic.org/privacy/consumer/code_fair_info.html (accessed November 2017).

17 "Records, Computers, and the Rights of Citizens: Report of the Secretary's Advisory Committee on Automated Personal Data Systems, Records, Computers, and the Rights of Citizens," U.S. Department of Health, Education and Welfare, vii (July 1973), https://www.justice.gov/opcl/docs/rec-com-rights.pdf (accessed November 2017).

18 *Guidelines Governing the Protection of Privacy and Transborder Data Flows of Personal Data,* Sept. 23, 1980, OECD. An important distinction between the OECD and the COE is the involvement and support of the U.S. government. For more information, *see* www.oecd.org/internet/ieconomy/oecdguidelinesontheprotectionofprivacyandtransborderflowsofpersonaldata.htm (accessed November 2017).

19 The OECD Privacy Framework, www.oecd.org/internet/ieconomy/privacy-guidelines.htm (accessed November 2017); Jordan M. Blanke, "'Safe Harbor' and the European Union's Directive on Data Protection," *Albany Law Journal of Science & Technology* (2000).

20 Convention for the Protection of Individuals with Regard to the Automatic Processing of Personal Data, January 8, 1981, Council of Europe, https:// www.coe.int/en/web/conventions/full-list/-/conventions/treaty/108 (accessed November 2017); *see* Council of Europe Privacy Convention, EPIC, https://epic.org/privacy/intl/coeconvention/ (accessed November 2017).

21 *See* Explanatory Report to the Convention for the Protection of Individuals with Regard to Automatic Processing of Personal Data, European Treaty Series – 108, Council of Europe (January 28, 1981), https://rm.coe.int/16800ca434 (accessed November 2017).

22 Banisar and Davies, "Global Trends," 11. *See* also Jeffrey B. Ritter, Benjamin S. Hayes and Henry L. Judy, "Emerging Trends in International Privacy Law," *Emory International Law Review* (Spring 2001).

23 APEC Privacy Framework, https://www.apec.org/Publications/2017/08/APEC-Privacy-Framework-(2015) (accessed November 2017).

24 Madrid Resolution–International Standards on the Protection of Personal Data and Privacy, https://www.gov.im/lib/docs/odps/madridresolutionnov09.pdf (accessed November 2017).

25 https://images-na.ssl-images-amazon.com/images/I/51AZNmwwgxL._SY550_.jpg (accessed November 2017).

26 *See* Phil Lee, "Anonimisation is Great, but Don't Undervalue Pseudonymisation," *Privacy, Security and Information Law*, fieldfisher, April 26, 2014, http://privacylawblog.fieldfisher.com/2014/anonymisation-is-great-but-dont-undervalue-pseudonymisation/ (accessed November 2017).

27 *See*, for example, Case C-461/10, ECLI:EU:C:2012:219 – Bonnier Audio, European Court of Justice, http://curia.europa.eu/juris/document/document.jsf;jsessionid=9ea7d2dc30d553a7d7593643447981718ccc0151a006.e34KaxiLc3qMb40Rch0SaxuSchv0?text=&docid=121743&pageIndex=0&doclang=EN&mode=lst&dir=&occ=first&part=1&cid=589823 (accessed November 2017).

28 EMI Records (Ireland) Limited, Sony Music Entertainment Ireland Limited, Universal Music Ireland Limited, Warner Music Ireland Limited and WEA International Incorporated v. UPC Communications Ireland Limited, Case No. 2009 No. 5472 P, www.trefor.net/wp-content/uploads/2010/10/EMI-v-UPC-copyright-inadequacy-of-legislation.doc (accessed November 2017). Additional analysis of this line of cases can be found at www.lexology.com/library/detail.aspx?g=31626ec8-5dbe-4819-86c5-cd403593f05d (accessed November 2017).

29 OMB Memorandum 07-16, "Safeguarding Against and Responding to the Breach of Personally Identifiable Information," Office of Management and Budget (2007), https://obamawhitehouse.archives.gov/sites/default/files/omb/memoranda/fy2007/m07-16.pdf (accessed November 2017).

30 Federal Register, FTC 16 CFR Part 318 Health Breach Notification Rule (2009); https://www.ftc.gov/sites/default/files/documents/federal_register_notices/health-breach-notification-rule-16-cfr-part-318/090825healthbreachrule.pdf (accessed November 2017).

31 Data Protection Directive at Article 2(d).

32 http://unctad.org/en/PublicationsLibrary/dtlstict2016d1_en.pdf (accessed November 2017); "Graham Greenleaf's Global Table of Data Privacy Laws," http://papers.ssrn.com/sol3/papers.cfm?abstract_id=2000034 (accessed November 2017). For a searchable database, see https://www.dlapiperdataprotection.com/#handbook/world-map-section/c1_RU (accessed November 2017).

33 Banisar and Davies, "Global Trends." 18.

34 *Id.* at 14.

35 *Id.* at 11.

36 *Id.* at 14.

37 Australian Privacy Principles, Office of the Australian Information Commissioner, Australian Government, https://www.oaic.gov.au/privacy-law/privacy-act/australian-privacy-principles (accessed November 2017); *see* Australia, Data Protection Laws of the World, DLA Piper

(March 17, 2017), https://www.dlapiperdataprotection.com/index.html?t=law&c=AU (accessed November 2017).

38 Banisar and Davies, "Global Trends." 13-14.

39 "COPPA Safe Harbor program," FTC, https://www.ftc.gov/safe-harbor-program (accessed November 2017).

40 "FTC gives nod to 7th Safe Harbor program under COPPA," Law360, www.law360.com/articles/564715/ftc-gives-nod-to-7th-safe-harbor-program-under-coppa (accessed November 2017).

41 For a discussion of the pros and cons of self-regulation, *see* Peter Swire, "Markets, Self-Regulation, and Government Enforcement in the Protection of Personal Information," U.S. Department of Commerce, Privacy and Self-Regulation in the Information Age (1997), http://papers.ssrn.com/sol3/papers.cfm?abstract_id=11472 (accessed November 2017).

CHAPTER 2

U.S. Legal Framework

This chapter introduces basic concepts and terms used by privacy professionals in the United States. Much of the material in this chapter will be familiar to lawyers. Privacy compliance in most organizations today, however, involves substantial participation by nonlawyers, including people whose primary background ranges from marketing, information technology and human resources to public relations and other areas. For all readers, the goal of this chapter is to provide a helpful introduction to the terminology used by privacy professionals.

2.1 Branches of the Government

The U.S. Constitution establishes the framework of the legal system, creating three branches of government. The three branches—legislative, executive and judicial—are designed to provide a separation of powers with a system of checks and balances among the branches. These three branches are also found at the state (and often the local) levels. The legislative branch is made up of elected representatives who write and pass laws. The executive branch's duties are to enforce and administer the law. The judicial branch interprets the meaning of a law and how it is applied, and may examine such issues as a law's constitutionality and the intent behind its creation.

Table 2-1: Three Branches of U.S. Government

	Legislative Branch	Executive Branch	Judicial Branch
Purpose	Makes laws	Enforces laws	Interprets laws
Who	Congress (House and Senate)	President, vice president, cabinet, federal agencies (such as FTC)	Federal courts
Checks and Balances	Congress confirms presidential appointees, can override vetoes	President appoints federal judges, can veto laws passed by Congress	Determines whether the laws are constitutional

The U.S. Congress, consisting of the Senate and the House of Representatives, is the legislative branch. Aside from passing laws, Congress can override presidential vetoes; the Senate confirms presidential appointees. When enacting legislation, Congress may also delegate the power to promulgate regulations to federal agencies. For example, Congress has enacted several laws that give the U.S. Federal Trade Commission (FTC) the authority to issue regulations to implement the laws.

The executive branch consists of the president, the vice president, the president's cabinet and federal agencies that report to the president. The agencies implement the laws through rule making and enforce the laws through civil and criminal procedures. In addition, the president has veto power over laws passed by Congress and the power to appoint federal judges.

The judicial branch encompasses the federal court system. The lowest courts in the federal system are the district courts, which serve as federal trial courts. Cases decided by a district court can be appealed to a federal appellate court, also referred to as a circuit court. The federal circuit courts are not trial courts but serve as the appeals courts for federal cases. The appeals courts are divided into 12 regional circuits and each district court is assigned to a circuit; appeals from a district court are considered by the appeals court for that circuit. In addition, there are special courts such as the U.S. Court of Federal Claims and the U.S. Tax Court.

At the top of the federal court system is the U.S. Supreme Court, which hears appeals from the circuit courts and decides questions of federal law, including interpreting the U.S. Constitution. In certain circumstances, the Supreme Court may also hear appeals from the highest state courts. In rare instances, the Supreme Court also has the ability to function as a trial court.

As mentioned above, when given the authority by Congress, federal agencies may promulgate and enforce rules pursuant to law. In this sense, agencies may wield power that is characteristic of all three branches of government. This means that agencies may operate under statutes that give them legislative power to issue rules, executive power to investigate and enforce violations of rules and statutes, and the judicial power to settle particular disputes.

2.2 Sources of Law in the United States

The numerous sources of law in the United States include federal and state constitutions, legislation, case law (such as that concerning contracts and torts) and regulations issued by agencies.

2.2.1 Constitutions

The supreme law in the United States is the U.S. Constitution, drafted originally by the Constitutional Convention in 1787. The Constitution does not contain the word *privacy*. Some parts of the Constitution directly affect privacy, such as the Fourth Amendment limits on government searches. The Supreme Court has also recognized an individual's right to privacy over personal issues, such as contraception and abortion, by discussing a "penumbra" of unenumerated constitutional rights arising from numerous constitutional provisions as well as the more general protections of due process of law.[1]

State constitutions are also sources of law and may create stronger rights than are provided in the U.S. Constitution. For example, the California state constitution expressly recognizes a right to privacy.

2.2.2 Legislation

Both the federal Congress and the state legislatures have enacted a variety of privacy and security laws. These regulate many different matters, including certain applications of information (such as use of information for marketing or preemployment screening), certain industries (such as financial institutions or healthcare providers), certain data elements (such as Social Security numbers or driver's license information) or specific harms (such as identity theft or children's online privacy).

In the United States, law-making power is shared between the national and state governments. The U.S. Constitution states that the Constitution, and laws passed pursuant to it, is "the supreme law of the land." Where federal law does not prevent it, the states have power to make law. Under the Tenth Amendment to the Constitution, "[t]he powers not delegated to the United States by the Constitution, nor prohibited by it to the States, are reserved to the States respectively, or to the people." In understanding the effect of federal and state laws, it's important to consider whether a federal law "preempts," or overrides, any state laws on the subject. In many instances, such as for the Health Insurance Portability and Accountability Act (HIPAA) medical privacy rule, states may pass privacy or other laws with stricter requirements than federal law. In other instances, such as the limits on commercial emails in the Controlling the Assault of Non-Solicited Pornography and Marketing (CAN-SPAM) Act, federal law preempts state law, and the states are not permitted to pass stricter provisions.

Aside from this governmental ability to make and enforce laws and regulations, the U.S. legal system relies on legal precedent based on court decisions, the doctrines implicit in those decisions, and their customs and uses. Two key areas of the common law are contracts and torts, discussed in Sections 2.2.6 and 2.2.7.

2.2.3 Regulations and Rules

Some laws require regulatory agencies such as the FTC or the Federal Communications Commission (FCC) to issue regulations and rules. These place specific compliance expectations on the marketplace. For example, in 2003 the U.S. Congress passed the CAN-SPAM Act, which requires the senders of commercial email messages to offer an "opt-out" option to recipients of these messages. CAN-SPAM provides the FTC and the FCC with the authority to issue regulations that set forth exactly how the opt-out mechanism must be offered and managed.

2.2.4 Case Law

Case law refers to the final decisions made by judges in court cases. When similar issues arise in the future, judges look to past decisions as precedents and decide the new case in a manner that is consistent with past decisions. The following of precedent is known as *stare decisis* (a Latin term meaning "to let the decision stand"). As time passes, precedents often change to reflect technological and societal changes in values and laws.

Common law refers to legal principles that have developed over time in judicial decisions (case law), often drawing on social customs and expectations. Common law contrasts with law created by statute. For privacy, the common law has long upheld special privilege rules such as doctor-patient or attorney-client confidentiality, even in the absence of statutes protecting that confidentiality.

2.2.5 Consent Decree

A consent decree is a judgment entered by consent of the parties whereby the defendant agrees to stop alleged illegal activity, typically without admitting guilt or wrongdoing.[2] This legal document is approved by a judge and formalizes an agreement reached between a federal or state agency and an adverse party. The consent decree describes the actions the defendant will take, and the decree itself may be subject to a public comment period. Once approved, the consent decree has the effect of a court decision.

In the privacy enforcement sphere, for example, the FTC has entered into numerous consent decrees with companies as a result of alleged violations of privacy laws, such as the Children's Online Privacy Protection Act (COPPA).[3] These consent decrees generally require violators to pay money to the government and agree not to violate the relevant law in the future.

Aside from promulgating rules and enforcing them, agencies provide guidance in the form of formal opinions. Agency opinions do not necessarily carry the weight of law, but do give specific guidance to interested parties trying to interpret agency rules and regulations.[4] Agencies often provide even more informal guidance through published reports, content on their websites, congressional testimony, and speeches at conferences or industry gatherings. These channels are not so much explicit requirements as they are valuable insight into the agency's mindset, view of the law, and priorities in enforcement.

2.2.6 Contract Law

A contract is a legally binding agreement enforceable in a court of law. The contract may include provisions on issues such as data usage, data security, breach notification, jurisdiction and damages. For example, a company often has a contract with its service providers, requiring the latter to implement privacy and security protections when processing personal data provided by the first company.

However, not every agreement is a legally binding contract. There are certain fundamental requirements for forming a binding contract:[5]

- An **offer** is the proposed language to enter into a bargain. An offer must be communicated to another person and it remains open until it is accepted, rejected, retracted or has expired. Some terms of an offer, such as price, quantity and description, must be specific and definite. Note: A counteroffer ends the original offer.
- **Acceptance** is the assent or agreement by the person to whom the offer was made that the offer is accepted. This acceptance must comply with the terms of the offer and must be communicated to the person who proposed the deal.
- **Consideration** is the bargained-for exchange. It is the legal benefit received by one person and the legal detriment imposed on the other person. Consideration usually takes the form of money, property or services. Note: An agreement without consideration is not a contract.

It is important to understand that contracts that would otherwise be valid may be unenforceable due to reasons such as conflict with public policy, or misrepresentation.[6]

A privacy notice may be a contract if a consumer provides data to a company based on the company's promise to use the data in accordance with the terms of the notice.

2.2.7 Tort Law

Torts are civil wrongs recognized by law as the grounds for lawsuits. These wrongs result in an injury or harm that constitutes the basis for a claim by the injured party. Primary goals of tort law are to provide relief for damages incurred and deter others from committing the same wrongs.

There are three general tort categories:

1. **Intentional torts.** These are wrongs that the defendant knew or should have known would occur through his or her actions or inactions; for example, intentionally hitting a person or stealing personal information.
2. **Negligent torts.** These occur when the defendant's actions were unreasonably unsafe; for example, causing a car accident by not obeying traffic rules or not having appropriate security controls.
3. **Strict liability torts.** These are wrongs that do not depend on the degree of carelessness by the defendant, but are established when a particular action causes damage.[7] Product liability torts fall into this category since they concern potential liability for making and selling defective products, without the need for the plaintiff to show negligence by the defendant.

Historically, the concept of a personal privacy tort has been a part of U.S. jurisprudence since the late 1890s.[8] Privacy torts continue today for actions such as intruding on seclusion, public revelation of private facts, interfering with a person's right to publicity, and casting a person in a false light. These traditional privacy torts, however, are often subject to the defense that the speaker is exercising free speech rights under the First Amendment. In addition, courts in recent years have considered a range of other privacy-related torts, such as allegations that a company was negligent for failing to provide adequate safeguards for personal information, and thus caused harm due to disclosure of the data. The lack of adequate safeguards thus may expose a company to damages under tort law. Privacy torts remain an unsettled area of law, and courts across the United States have not taken a uniform approach in applying tort principles to privacy-related cases.

2.3 Key Definitions

Here are a few legal terms and definitions that are important for understanding the framework of U.S. privacy law:

- **Person.** Any entity with legal rights, including an individual (a "natural person") or a corporation (a "legal person").
- **Jurisdiction.** The authority of a court to hear a particular case. A court must have jurisdiction over both the type of dispute ("subject matter jurisdiction") and the parties ("personal jurisdiction"). Government agencies have jurisdictional limits also.

- **General versus specific authority.** A governmental body can have two types of authority. "General authority" is blanket authority to regulate a field of activity. "Specific authority" is targeted at singular activities that are outlined by legislation. Many agencies have both types of authority. For example, the FTC has general authority over "unfair and deceptive trade practices" and specific authority to enforce COPPA.
- **Preemption.** A superior government's ability to have its laws supersede those of an inferior government. For example, the U.S. federal government has mandated that state governments cannot regulate email marketing. The federal CAN-SPAM Act preempts state laws that might impose greater obligations on senders of commercial electronic messages.
- **Private right of action.** The ability of an individual harmed by a violation of a law to file a lawsuit against the violator.

It is also useful to review the concepts of notice, choice and access in the context of U.S. privacy law.

2.3.1 Notice

Notice is a description of an organization's information management practices. Notices have two purposes: (1) consumer education and (2) corporate accountability. The typical notice tells the individual what information is collected, how the information is used and disclosed, how to exercise any choices about uses or disclosures, and whether the individual can access or update the information. However, it is important to note that many U.S. privacy laws have additional notice requirements. With the states enacting breach notification laws that have varying requirements for notice, the federal government is now considering a preemptive law to standardize breach-related notification. In addition, for most industries, the promises made in a company's privacy notice are legally enforceable by the FTC and the states.

Privacy notices may also be called privacy statements or even privacy policies, although the term *privacy policy* is often used to refer to the internal standards used within the organization, whereas *notice* refers to an external communication issued to consumers, customers or users. Additionally, protocols, standards and instructions are used by companies to direct their employees to comply with data privacy laws.[9]

2.3.2 Choice

Choice is the ability to specify whether personal information will be collected and/or how it will be used or disclosed. Choice can be express or implied.

The term *opt in* means an affirmative indication of choice based on an express act of the person giving the consent. For example, a person opts in if he or she says yes when asked, "May we share your information?" Failure to answer would result in the information not being shared.

The term *opt out* means a choice can be implied by the failure of the person to object to the use or disclosure. For example, if a company states "unless you tell us not to, we may share your information," the person has the ability to opt out of the sharing by saying no. Failure to answer would result in the information being shared.

Choice is not always appropriate, but if it is offered, it should be meaningful—that is, it should be based on a real understanding of the implication of the decision.

2.3.3 Access

Access is the ability to view personal information held by an organization. This may be supplemented by allowing updates or corrections to the information. U.S. laws often provide for access and correction when the information is used for substantive decision making, such as for credit reports.

2.4 Regulatory Authorities

At the federal level, a number of agencies engage in regulatory activities concerning privacy in the private sector. The FTC has general authority to enforce against unfair and deceptive trade practices, notably including the power to bring "deception" enforcement actions where a company has broken a privacy promise.[10] In certain areas, such as marketing communications and children's privacy, the FTC has specific regulatory authority.

Other federal agencies have regulatory authority over particular sectors. These include the federal banking regulatory agencies (such as the Consumer Financial Protection Bureau, Federal Reserve, and Office of the Comptroller of the Currency), the FCC, the U.S. Department of Transportation, and the U.S. Department of Health and Human Services, through its Office of Civil Rights. The U.S. Department of Commerce does not have regulatory authority for privacy, but often plays a leading role in privacy policy for the executive branch.

At the state level, state attorneys general bring a variety of privacy-related enforcement actions, often pursuant to state laws prohibiting unfair and deceptive practices.[11] Each state attorney general serves as the chief legal advisor to the state government and as the state's chief law enforcement officer. Many states have successfully pursued such actions, including Washington and Minnesota.[12]

2.5 Self-Regulation

As discussed in Chapter 3, self-regulatory regimes play a significant role in governing privacy practices in various industries. Examples include the Network Advertising Initiative,[13] the Direct Marketing Association[14] and the Children's Advertising Review Unit.[15] Some trade associations also issue rules or codes of conduct for members. In some regulatory settings, government-created rules expect companies to sign up for self-regulatory oversight.

2.6 Understanding Laws

To understand any law, statute or regulation, it is important to ask six key questions:

1. Who is covered by this law?
2. What types of information (and what uses of information) are covered?
3. What exactly is required or prohibited?
4. Who enforces the law?
5. What happens if I don't comply?
6. Why does this law exist?

The first two questions relate to the scope of the law. Even if an organization or person is not subject to the law, it may still be useful to understand it. For example, the law may suggest good practices that an organization or individual would want to emulate. It may provide an indication of legal trends. It may also provide a proven way to achieve a particular result, such as protecting individuals in a given situation.

Assuming one is subject to the law, question three explains how to comply with it. Questions four and five help the individual or corporation assess the risks associated with noncompliance or less than perfect compliance. In most cases, companies do what it takes to be materially compliant with applicable laws. There may, however, be a situation where the costs of compliance outweigh the risks of noncompliance for a particular period of time. For example, if a system that is not appropriately compliant with a new law is going to be replaced in a few months, a company may decide that the risks of noncompliance outweigh the costs and risks of trying to accelerate the system transition.

The final question helps foster understanding of the motivation behind the law. Most companies try to comply with both the letter and the spirit of the law. Knowing why the law was written helps them understand the spirit of the legislation and can also help improve other processes and thus achieve desired results. It may also help companies anticipate regulatory trends.

As an example, consider the security breach notification law in California (California SB 1386), which was the first such law enacted and covers the largest population.[16]

- **Who is covered?** This law regulates entities that do business in California and that own or license computerized data, including personal information. It applies to natural persons, legal persons and government agencies.

  Those that do business only in Montana or New York are not subject to this law (although they may wish to be careful about what counts as "doing business"). Even if they conduct business in California, they are not subject to this law if they don't have computerized data.

- **What is covered?** This law regulates the computerized personal information of California residents. "Personal information" is an individual's name in combination with any one or more of the following: (1) Social Security number; (2) California identification card number; (3) driver's license number; or (4) financial account, credit, or debit card number in combination with security code, access code or password information required to permit access to an individual's financial account, when either the name or the data elements are not encrypted.

  Databases that contain only names and addresses or only encrypted information are not subject to this law.[17]

- **What is required or prohibited?** This law requires all persons to disclose any breach of system security to any resident of California whose unencrypted personal information was or is reasonably believed to have been acquired by an unauthorized person. A breach of the security of the system means unauthorized acquisition of computerized data that compromises the security, confidentiality or integrity of personal information maintained by the person. The disclosure must be made in as expedient a manner as possible.

  There is an exception for the good faith acquisition of personal information by an employee or agent of the business, provided the personal information is not used or subject to further unauthorized disclosure. One may also delay providing notice, if law enforcement requests such a delay.

- **Who enforces the law?** The California attorney general enforces the law, and there is a private right of action.

- **What is the consequence for noncompliance?** The California attorney general or any citizen can file a civil lawsuit against a noncompliant party seeking damages and forcing compliance.
- **Why does this law exist?** SB 1386 was enacted because security breaches of computerized databases are feared to cause identity theft—and individuals should be notified about these breaches so they can take steps to protect themselves. Anyone with a security breach that puts people at real risk of identity theft should consider notifying them even if they are not subject to this law.

2.7 Conclusion

This chapter has introduced legal concepts and terminology about basic topics, including the structure of the U.S. government and legal system. Privacy compliance requires knowing the applicable legal rules as well as fulfilling each organization's policies and goals. The next chapter examines the structure of enforcement actions for alleged privacy violations in the United States.

Endnotes

1 Many of the cases relevant to this discussion have their foundation in protecting private sexual conduct. Cases include Griswold v. Connecticut (1965), voiding a state statute preventing the use of contraceptives; Roe v. Wade (1973), overturning state law that barred abortion; and Lawrence v. Texas (2003), striking down antisodomy laws. *See* "The Right to Privacy," Section 3.4, Criminal Law, Open Textbooks at University of Minnesota Libraries, http://open.lib.umn.edu/criminallaw/chapter/3-4-the-right-to-privacy/ (accessed November 2017).

2 *Black's Law Dictionary*, 9th ed., 2009, s.v. "consent decree." http://thelawdictionary.org/consent-decree/ (accessed November 2017).

3 "Ohio Art Consent Decree," April 2004, https://www.ftc.gov/enforcement/cases-proceedings/022-3028/ohio-art-company (accessed May, 2016); "FTC Protecting Children's Privacy Online," FTC, April 22, 2002, https://www.ftc.gov/news-events/press-releases/2002/04/ftc-protecting-childrens-privacy-online (accessed November 2017).

4 "Advisory Opinions," FTC, https://www.ftc.gov/policy/advisory-opinions (accessed May 2016).

5 "Contracts: The Basics," nolo.com, www.nolo.com/legal-encyclopedia/contracts-basics-33367.html (accessed November 2017).

6 *See* "What Makes a Contract Valid," *Forbes*, November. 20, 2006, https://www.forbes.com/2006/11/20/smallbusiness-statelaw-gifts-ent-law-cx_nl_1120contracts.html (accessed November 2017); "Unenforceable Contracts: What to Watch Out For," Nolo.com, https://www.nolo.com/legal-encyclopedia/unenforceable-contracts-tips-33079.html (accessed November 2017).

7 "Tort," Cornell University Law School, Legal Information Institute, https://www.law.cornell.edu/wex/Tort (accessed November 2017).

8 "The Privacy Torts," Privacilla, www.privacilla.org/business/privacytorts.html (accessed November 2017).

9 For more guidance on the function and drafting considerations regarding privacy notices, policies, protocols and other documentation, *see* Lothar Determann, *Determann's Field Guide to Data Privacy Law,* Chapter 3 (2nd Ed. 2015).

10 15 U.S.C. § 45 (2011), "[U]nfair or deceptive acts or practices in or affecting commerce, are hereby declared unlawful. . . . The [FTC] is hereby empowered and directed to prevent persons, partnerships, or corporations, except [certain institutions] . . . from using unfair methods of competition in or affecting commerce and unfair or deceptive acts or practices in or affecting commerce." For a listing of recent enforcement actions, *see* https://www.ftc.gov/enforcement/cases-proceedings (accessed November 2017).

11 For general information on actions by state attorneys general, view Danielle Citron, "Privacy Enforcement Pioneers: The Role of State Attorneys General in the Development of Privacy Law," *Notre Dame Law Review* (2016). http://papers.ssrn.com/sol3/papers.cfm?abstract_id=2733297 (accessed November 2017).

12 "Washington e-Commerce Company May Owe You Money," Office of the Attorney General, State of Washington, http://atg.wa.gov/news/news-releases/washington-e-commerce-company-may-owe-you-money (accessed November 2017); ConsumerAffairs.com, "Minnesota Settles Consumer Fraud Suit with MemberWorks," https://www.consumeraffairs.com/news/index/2000/04/ (accessed November 2017). For an in-depth discussion of state actions, view Danielle Citron, "The Privacy Policymaking of State Attorney Generals," http://papers.ssrn.com/sol3/papers.cfm?abstract_id=2733297 (accessed November 2017).

13 The NAI Code and Enforcement Program: An Overview, NAI Code and Enforcement, Network Advertising Initiative (NAI), https://www.networkadvertising.org/code-enforcement (accessed November 2017).

14 Self-Regulation, Data & Marketing Association, https://thedma.org/accountability/self-regulation/ (accessed November 2017).

15 ARSC Snapshot, Advertising Self-Regulatory Council, www.asrcreviews.org/about-us/ (accessed November 2017).

16 California Legislative Information, Customer Records, https://leginfo.legislature.ca.gov/faces/codes_displaySection.xhtml?lawCode=CIV§ionNum=1798.82 (accessed May 2016). For a summary of the current statute, view "California amends its breach notification statute," *Data Privacy Monitor* (accessed November 2017), www.dataprivacymonitor.com/data-breach-notification-laws/california-amends-its-breach-notification-statute/ (accessed November 2017).

17 As of January 1, 2016, the definition of personal information has been expanded to include data collected from automated license plate recognition systems. https://leginfo.legislature.ca.gov/faces/billNavClient.xhtml?bill_id=201520160SB34 (accessed November 2017).

CHAPTER 3

Federal and State Regulators and Enforcement of Privacy Law

This chapter discusses the enforcement of privacy law by U.S. federal and state regulators. Enforcement through civil and criminal litigation in the courts is covered, as well as agency enforcement actions, self-regulation and other forms of accountability.

This chapter focuses particular attention on the Federal Trade Commission (FTC). The FTC is an independent agency governed by a chairperson and four other commissioners. Their decisions are not under the U.S. president's control. With certain exceptions, the FTC has authority to enforce against "unfair and deceptive trade practices." Along with this general authority, the FTC has specific statutory responsibility for issues such as children's privacy online and commercial email marketing. Among federal agencies, the FTC has played a prominent role in the development of U.S. privacy standards, including public workshops on privacy issues and reports on privacy policy and enforcement. In recent years, the Federal Communications Commission (FCC) has played a more prominent enforcement role as well.

This leading role for the FTC exists in a context where numerous other federal agencies are involved in privacy enforcement, as well as more general privacy oversight and policy development. This chapter outlines the roles for these agencies, many of which are discussed in more detail in later chapters. It then examines FTC enforcement in more detail before turning to privacy enforcement in the states, concluding with discussion of enforcement in self-regulatory systems and across borders.

3.1 Types of Litigation and Enforcement

For nonlawyers, it is useful to define the main categories of legal action: civil litigation, criminal litigation and administrative enforcement.

Civil litigation occurs in the courts, when one person (the plaintiff) sues another person (the defendant) to redress a wrong. The plaintiff often seeks a monetary judgment from the defendant. The plaintiff may also seek an injunction, which is a court order mandating the defendant to stop engaging in certain behaviors. Important categories of civil litigation include contracts and torts. For instance, a plaintiff might sue for a breach of a contract that promised confidential treatment of personal information. In a tort action, a plaintiff might sue for an invasion of privacy—for example, where the defendant surreptitiously took pictures in a changing room and broadcast the pictures to the public. Some privacy laws create "private rights of action," enabling an individual plaintiff to sue based on violations of the statute. The Fair Credit Reporting Act (FCRA), for instance, has a private right of action, allowing individuals to sue a company if their consumer reports have been used inappropriately.

Criminal litigation involves lawsuits brought by the government for violations of criminal laws. This contrasts with civil litigation, which generally involves an effort by a private party to correct specific harms. Criminal prosecution can lead to imprisonment and criminal fines. In the federal government, criminal laws are prosecuted by the Department of Justice (DOJ). States typically place criminal prosecutorial power in the hands of the state attorney general and local officials such as district attorneys.

Administrative enforcement actions are carried out pursuant to the statutes that create and empower an agency, such as the FTC and the FCC. In the federal government, the basic rules for agency enforcement actions occur under the Administrative Procedure Act (APA).[1] The APA sets forth basic rules for adjudication within an agency, where court-like hearings may take place before an administrative law judge (ALJ). Federal agency adjudications can generally be appealed to federal court. In addition, a federal agency may sue a party in federal court, with the agency as the plaintiff in a civil action. How the FTC and the FCC typically conduct privacy enforcement actions, notably by the use of consent decrees, is discussed in more detail in Section 3.4 below.

3.2 Federal Privacy Enforcement and Policy Outside of the FTC and the FCC

Depending on the statutes or regulations violated, agencies other than the FTC and the FCC may be responsible for privacy enforcement. For example, the following agencies are discussed in the chapters noted:

- **Medical privacy**—the Office of Civil Rights in the Department of Health and Human Services (HHS), for the Health Insurance Portability and Accountability Act (HIPAA), Chapter 7
- **Financial privacy**—the Consumer Financial Protection Bureau (CFPB) for financial consumer protection issues generally; federal financial regulators such as the Federal Reserve and the Office of Comptroller of the Currency,

for institutions under their jurisdiction under the Gramm-Leach-Bliley Act (GLBA), Chapter 8

- **Education privacy**—Department of Education for the Family Educational Rights and Privacy Act, Chapter 9
- **Telemarketing and marketing privacy**—the FCC Commission (together with the FTC), under the Telephone Consumer Protection Act and other statutes, Chapter 10
- **Workplace privacy**—agencies including the Equal Employment Opportunity Commission, for the Americans with Disabilities Act and other antidiscrimination statutes, Chapter 11

In addition, other federal agencies are involved in privacy oversight, enforcement and policy. Privacy professionals should thus be alert to the possibility that federal agencies other than the FTC will be relevant to their organizations' activities.

- The U.S. Department of State has been increasingly active over time on privacy, especially by negotiating internationally on privacy issues with other countries and in multinational groups such as the United Nations or the Organisation for Economic Co-operation and Development (OECD).
- The U.S. Department of Commerce (DOC) plays a leading role in federal privacy policy development and administers the Privacy Shield Framework between the United States and the EU.[2]
- The U.S. Department of Transportation (DOT) is the agency responsible for transportation companies under its jurisdiction and for enforcing violations of the Privacy Shield Framework between the U.S. and the EU for some transportation companies. Within DOT, the Federal Aviation Administration (FAA) has recently played an increasing role for drones. The National Highway Traffic Safety Administration (NHTSA), also within DOT, addresses privacy and security issues for connected cars.
- The U.S. Office of Management and Budget (OMB) is the lead agency for interpreting the Privacy Act of 1974, which applies to federal agencies and private-sector contractors to those agencies. The OMB also issues guidance to agencies and contractors on privacy and information security issues, such as data breach disclosure and privacy impact assessments.

- The Internal Revenue Service (IRS) is subject to privacy rules concerning tax records, including disclosures of such records in the private sector. Other parts of the Department of Treasury are also involved with financial records issues, including compliance with money-laundering rules at the Financial Crimes Enforcement Network.
- The U.S. Department of Homeland Security (DHS) faces numerous privacy issues, such as the E-Verify program for new employees, rules for air traveler records (Transportation Security Administration), as well as immigration and other border issues (Immigration and Customs Enforcement).
- As new technologies emerge, additional agencies become involved in privacy. For instance, the development of the smart grid is making privacy an important issue for the electric utility system, thus involving the Department of Energy. The increased use and surveillance implications of unmanned aerial vehicles, or drones, have raised privacy issues for the FAA. In short, almost every agency in the federal government is or may soon become involved with privacy in some manner within that agency's jurisdiction.

DOJ is the sole federal agency to bring criminal enforcement actions, which can result in imprisonment or criminal fines. Some statutes, such as HIPAA, provide for both civil and criminal enforcement. In such cases, procedures exist for the roles of both HHS and DOJ.[3]

3.3 FTC Jurisdiction

The FTC was founded in 1914 to enforce antitrust laws, and its general consumer protection mission was established by a statutory change in 1938.[4] The FTC navigates both roles today, and privacy and computer security issues have become an important part of its work. The FTC is an independent agency instead of falling under the direct control of the president.[5]

Section 5 of the FTC Act is perhaps the single most important piece of U.S. privacy law. Section 5 notably says that "unfair or deceptive acts or practices in or affecting commerce, are hereby declared unlawful," although it does not mention privacy or information security.[6] The application of Section 5 to privacy and information security, however, is clearly established today. The FTC has enforced privacy violations for decades, beginning with the Fair Credit Reporting Act of 1970. During the 1990s, the FTC began bringing privacy enforcement cases under its powers to address unfair and deceptive practices. Congress added privacy-related responsibilities to the FTC over time, such as those under the Children's Online Privacy Protection Act (COPPA) of 1998 and the Controlling the Assault of Non-Solicited Pornography and Marketing (CAN-SPAM) Act of 2003. Among other authoritative powers, Section 6 of the FTC Act vests the commission with the authority to conduct investigations and to require businesses to submit investigatory reports under oath.[7]

Section 5 of the FTC Act applies to unfair and deceptive practices "in commerce," and does not apply to nonprofit organizations. The commission's powers also do not extend to certain industries, including banks, other federally regulated financial institutions, and common carriers such as the transportation and communications industries.[8]

In addition to the authority granted under Section 5, the FTC retains separate and specific authority over privacy and security issues under other federal statutes. Until the creation of the CFPB, the FTC issued rules and guidance for the Fair Credit Reporting Act, as amended by the Fair and Accurate Credit Transactions Act of 2003 and the Gramm-Leach-Bliley Act of 1999. The CFPB now has authority to issue rules for those areas and shares enforcement authority with the FTC for financial institutions that are not covered by a separate financial regulator.

The FTC is the rule-making and enforcement agency for COPPA. With the FCC, it shares rule-making and enforcement power under the Telemarketing Sales Rule and the CAN-SPAM Act. The FTC also shares rule-making and enforcement power with HHS for data breaches related to medical records under the Health Information Technology for Economic and Clinical Health (HITECH) Act of 2009. These laws are discussed in more detail later in this chapter.

The FTC has general authority in theory to issue regulations to implement protections against unfair and deceptive acts and practices.[9] Such regulations, however, are not promulgated under the usual procedures of the APA. Instead, any such regulation must comply with the complex and lengthy procedures under the Magnuson-Moss Warranty Federal Trade Commission Improvement Act of 1975.[10] As of the date of writing, the FTC had not put forth any privacy or information security regulation under its Magnuson-Moss authority. The FTC has supported congressional proposals to provide the FTC with APA rule-making authority; such proposals have not been successful to date, in part due to opposition from companies that are against increased regulation.

3.4 FTC Enforcement Process and Consent Decrees

The typical FTC enforcement action begins with a claim that a company has committed an unfair or deceptive practice or has violated a specific consumer protection law. The need for an enforcement action can be brought to the FTC's attention in numerous ways such as press reports covering questionable practices or complaints from consumer groups or competitors. If the violation is minor, the FTC may work with the company to resolve the problem without launching a formal investigation. If the violation is more significant or there is a pattern of noncompliance, the FTC may proceed to full enforcement.

The FTC has broad investigatory authority, including the authority to subpoena witnesses, demand civil investigation and require businesses to submit written reports under oath.[11] Following an investigation, the commission may initiate an enforcement action if it has reason to believe a law is being or has been violated.[12] The commission issues a complaint, and an administrative trial can proceed before an ALJ. If a violation is found, the ALJ can enjoin the company from continuing the practices that caused the violation. The decision of the ALJ can be appealed to the five commissioners. That decision, in turn, can be appealed to federal district court.

An order by the commission becomes final 60 days after it is served on the company. Although the FTC lacks the authority to assess civil penalties, if an FTC ruling is ignored, as of the writing of this book, the FTC can seek civil penalties in federal court of up to $40,654 per violation and can seek compensation for those harmed by the unfair or deceptive practices.[13] Each violation of such an order is treated as a separate offense and each day the violator fails to comply with the order is considered a separate offense. The court can also order redress for consumers harmed by the act or practice. Additional penalties can be assessed if a company does not respond to a complaint or order. The court can also mandate an injunction against a violator.[14]

In practice, FTC privacy enforcement actions have usually been settled through consent decrees and accompanying consent orders. In a consent decree, the respondent does not admit fault, but promises to change its practices and avoids further litigation on the issue. Consent decrees are posted publicly on the FTC's website, and the details of these decrees provide guidance about what practices the FTC considers inappropriate. Once an individual or company has agreed to a consent decree, any violation of that decree can lead, following an FTC investigation, to enforcement in the federal district court, including civil penalties, as discussed above. The federal court can also grant injunctions and other forms of relief. The FTC's Enforcement Division, within the Bureau of Consumer Protection, monitors and litigates violations of consent decrees in cooperation with DOJ.

Consent decree terms vary depending on the violation. Usually, the consent decree states what affirmative actions the respondent needs to take, and which practices the respondent must refrain from engaging in. Consent decrees often require the respondent to maintain proof of compliance with the decree and to inform all related individuals of the consent decree obligations. The respondent is also usually required to provide the FTC with confirmation of its compliance with the decree and must inform the FTC if company changes will affect the respondent's ability to adhere to its terms. Respondents may also face civil penalties. Increasingly, in privacy cases, companies are subject to periodic outside audits or reviews of their practices, or they may be required to adopt and implement a comprehensive privacy program. Over time, consent decrees have become more specific in nature.

Both the company and the FTC have incentives to negotiate a consent decree rather than proceed with a full adjudication process. The company avoids a prolonged trial, as well as negative, ongoing publicity. It also avoids having the details of its business practices exposed to the public. The FTC (1) achieves a consent decree that incorporates good privacy and security practices, (2) avoids the expense and delay of a trial and (3) gains an enforcement advantage because monetary fines are much easier to assess in federal court if a company violates a consent decree than if no decree is in place. Under the FTC's "Sunset Policy," administrative orders such as consent decrees are imposed for up to 20 years.

3.5 Privacy Policies and Notices and Early FTC Enforcement Actions

Long before the FTC began to use consent decrees in privacy cases, its Bureau of Consumer Protection negotiated such decrees for other consumer protection issues such as false advertising or unfair debt collection practices under Section 5 of the FTC Act. Review of nonprivacy decrees can be instructive for lawyers or others who seek to understand the FTC's approach to and priorities for consumer protection consent decrees.

As commercial activity on the Internet became significant in the mid-1990s, the FTC, along with the DOC, began convening public workshops and conducting other activities to highlight the importance of privacy protection on websites.[15] Importantly, organizations began to post clearly stated privacy notices on their websites. These privacy notices helped inform consumers about how their personal information was being collected and used. The privacy notices were also important for enforcement purposes. If a company promised a certain level of privacy or security on its website or elsewhere and did not fulfill its promise, then the FTC considered that breach of promise a "deceptive" practice under Section 5 of the FTC Act.[16]

Although there is no omnibus federal law requiring companies to have public privacy notices, certain sector-specific statutes such as HIPAA, Gramm-Leach-Bliley, and COPPA do impose notice requirements. Also, as discussed in Chapter 8, California requires companies and organizations doing in-state business to post privacy policies on their websites.

By 2000, the vast majority of commercial websites posted privacy notices even in the absence of a legal requirement.[17] By then, privacy notices had become a standard feature of legitimate commercial websites. In addition, the absence of a privacy notice is easily visible—any consumer advocate or regulator visiting the site can tell whether a notice is posted. In practice today, most commercial websites are expected to post a privacy notice.

As companies began to post privacy notices, the FTC started to investigate whether they adhered to their own policies. If a company did not, the FTC would bring an enforcement action for deceptive trade practices. Important early consent decrees can be found in the IAPP reference text, *The Information Privacy Case Book: A Global Survey of Privacy and Security Enforcement Actions with Recommendations for Reducing Risk.*[18]

Two early cases provided insights on the FTC's early focus on privacy policies. The first FTC Internet privacy enforcement action was In the Matter of GeoCities, Inc. in 1999.[19] GeoCities operated a website that provided an online community through which users could maintain personal home pages. To register and become a member of GeoCities, users were required to fill out an online form that requested certain personal information, with which Geocities created an extensive information database. Geocities promised on its website that the collected information would not be sold or distributed without user consent. The FTC alleged that GeoCities misrepresented how it would use information collected from its users by reselling the information to third parties, which violated its privacy notice. GeoCities settled the action and the FTC issued a consent order, which required GeoCities to post and adhere to a conspicuous online privacy notice that disclosed to users how it would collect and use personal information.

In 2002 the FTC brought an enforcement against Eli Lilly and Company, a pharmaceutical manufacturer that maintained a website where users could provide personal information for messages and updates reminding them to take their medication.[20] The website included a privacy notice that made promises about the security and privacy of the information provided. When Eli Lilly decided to end the program, it sent subscribers an email announcement, inadvertently addressed to and revealing the email addresses of all subscribers. The FTC enforcement action against Eli Lilly resulted in settlement terms, which required Eli Lilly to adhere to representations about how it collects, uses and protects user information. It also required, for the first time in an online privacy and security case, that Eli Lilly develop and maintain an information privacy and security program. Before this case, the FTC had only required companies to stop current unfair and deceptive practices. After the settlement, it became clear that the scope of settlement terms had expanded to include implementation and evaluation of company programs for processing personal information.

3.6 Enforcement Actions and Deceptive Trade Practices

These early enforcement actions have evolved into multiple privacy and security "deceptive" practices cases in a typical year.[21] For a practice to be deceptive, it must involve a material statement or omission that is likely to mislead consumers who are acting reasonably under the circumstances.[22] Deceptive practices include false promises, misrepresentations, and failures to comply with representations made to consumers, such as statements in privacy policies and Safe Harbor or Privacy Shield certifications.[23] Some cases from 2014-2015 highlight current practices.

3.6.1 In the Matter of Nomi

Nomi provided a service to brick-and-mortar businesses whereby Nomi placed sensors in these retail businesses to detect the MAC addresses of mobile devices that are searching for Wi-Fi service.[24] Nomi used the information that it collected to provide analytics reports to its business clients about their customers' retail traffic patterns. According to the FTC, Nomi misled consumers about the ability to opt out of their service and failed to inform these consumers about the location of stores where the tracking was taking place. The consent order that Nomi entered into with the FTC restricted the company from continuing to engage in these business practices for 20 years.[25]

3.6.2 In the Matter of Snapchat

Snapchat promised its customers that its app provided a private, short-lived messaging service, known as a "snap." According to the company, the consumer set a timer for the snap to be viewed, and after that time expired the snap disappeared "forever." In addition, Snapchat's app included a feature to "Find Friends" that appeared to the user as the only means to choose to provide information to the company about individuals the user knew. According to the FTC, the company was aware of numerous methods that could be employed to save chats indefinitely, and it was actually collecting the names and phone numbers of all contacts in the user's mobile device address book. Further, Snapchat failed to adequately secure the Find Friends feature. Because of the lax security measures, hackers managed to compile a database of millions of user names and phone numbers and subjected these individuals to spam, phishing, and other unsolicited communications. The company entered into a consent order with the FTC in 2014 agreeing that it would not engage in these business practices for the next 20 years.[26]

3.6.3 In the Matter of TRUSTe, Inc.

TRUSTe, Inc. (now doing business as TrustArc) is a business that provides certifications to companies regarding privacy issues. The business has provided a seal to companies that have privacy practices in compliance with standards such as COPPA and the U.S.-EU Safe Harbor Framework. According to the FTC, TRUSTe failed to conduct annual recertifications in more than 1,000 instances from 2006 to January 2013, despite claiming to conduct recertifications every year on its website. In the settlement agreement with the FTC, TRUSTe was required to maintain comprehensive records for 10 years related to its certifications and to pay a $200,000 civil penalty.[27]

3.7 Enforcement Actions and Unfair Trade Practices

As discussed above, early privacy and security enforcement actions focused on deceptive practices. By 2004, the FTC began to enforce "unfair" practices as well. Unfair claims can exist even where the company has not made any deceptive statements if the injury is substantial, lacks offsetting benefits, and cannot be easily avoided by consumers.[28] Each step involves a detailed, fact-specific analysis that must undergo careful consideration by the commission.[29]

The FTC has sanctioned companies for unfair practices when they failed to implement adequate protection measures for sensitive personal information or when they provided inadequate disclosures to consumers.[30] The scope of the term *unfairness* was clarified in a 1980 policy statement,[31] in 1994 amendments to the FTC Act[32] and most recently in the court case of FTC v. Wyndham Worldwide Corp.[33] In 2015, the federal appellate court determined that the company does not act appropriately "when it publishes a privacy policy to attract customers who are concerned about data privacy, fails to make good on that promise by investing inadequate resources in cybersecurity, exposes its unsuspecting customers to substantial financial injury, and retains the profits for their business."[34]

3.7.1 In the Matter of Wyndham Worldwide Corp.

The FTC's unfairness authority was upheld in the federal courts in litigation against Wyndham Worldwide Corporation, a hotel company that suffered three hacks to its systems from 2008 to 2009. Based on these breaches to its systems, the FTC investigated Wyndham for unfair and deceptive trade practices. The FTC asserted that Wyndham:

- Stored credit card information in unencrypted text
- Permitted passwords for property management systems to be easily guessable
- Failed to use firewalls between individual hotels, corporate systems and the Internet
- Allowed out-of-date operating systems to run on property management systems and failed to update these computers with timely security updates
- Failed to adequately control computer access by third-party vendors
- Did not have unauthorized access detection measures in place
- Failed to add security measures after they suffered known breaches

When the FTC sought to sanction Wyndham, the company initially chose not to settle the case. In 2012, the FTC filed suit against the company in U.S. District Court. Wyndham challenged the FTC's authority to require the company to meet more than the minimum standards set forth in Section 5 of the FTC Act. The federal district court ruled for the FTC.

The Third Circuit Court of Appeals, on appeal, affirmed the ruling for the FTC. The court stated that the FTC's longstanding authority to regulate "unfair methods of competition in or affecting commerce" under Section 5 of the FTC Act extended to regulation of cyberspace practices that are harmful to consumers.[35]

In 2015, after the Third Circuit's decision, Wyndham agreed to enter into a consent order with the FTC.[36] Wyndham agreed to maintain a comprehensive information security program, which include a formal risk assessment process. The company also consented to cardholder data assessments, which required annual security audits of its information security programs to ensure compliance with the Payment Card Industry Data Security Standard (PCI DSS). In the event of a future breach affecting more than 10,000 payment card numbers, Wyndham agreed to obtain an assessment of the breach within six months and to provide the assessment to the FTC. The requirements in the stipulated consent order will remain in effect until 2035.

3.7.2 In the Matter of LabMD, Inc.

LabMD is another company that chose to litigate against the FTC rather than agree to a consent decree. LabMD was significantly hacked on two separate occasions in 2009 and 2012. According to the FTC's complaint, sensitive patient information for thousands of LabMD customers was taken in the 2009 hack, and placed on a peer-to-peer file-sharing network. The types of information included names, Social Security numbers, birth dates, health insurance provider information, and standardized medical treatment codes. The second hack, in 2012, resulted in at least 500 customer names and Social Security numbers being found in the possession of identity thieves.[37]

In 2013, the FTC brought an enforcement action against LabMD under Section 5 of the FTC Act claiming that the company engaged in unfair trade practices by failing to take appropriate measures to prevent unauthorized disclosure of sensitive data on its network. Rather than enter into a consent order with the FTC, LabMD chose to proceed with an administrative hearing before an ALJ.

The ALJ dismissed the action against LabMD. As to the 2009 incident, the ALJ decided that the FTC failed to establish that there was actual harm to the customers, as required under the legal test for unfairness. Notably, the ALJ stated that consumer's "embarrassment or other emotional harm" from exposure of sensitive information on a peer-to-peer network was not sufficient to be a basis to sanction LabMD.[38] With regard to the 2012 incident, the ALJ determined that the FTC failed to introduce evidence that LabMD was the source of the information found with the identity thieves.

The FTC reversed the decision by the ALJ, and issued a Final Order requiring the company to implement a comprehensive security program. LabMD appealed the FTC's Final Order to the Eleventh Circuit Court of Appeals, a federal appellate court. LabMD also requested a stay of the Final Order, meaning that it asked not to have to implement the security program while the appeal was pending. The Court granted the request for a stay. At the time of the writing of this book, the appeal is pending.[39] The outcome of the case promises to provide additional guidance on the FTC's powers in the area of data privacy and data security.

3.7.3 In the Matter of LifeLock, Inc.

The LifeLock case illustrates the ongoing consequences for a company operating under an FTC consent decree. In 2006, LifeLock began an advertising campaign claiming that it could prevent all identity theft in exchange for consumers paying a monthly fee for its services. Prominent in the LifeLock ads was the Social Security number of the company's CEO. In the 2010 FTC enforcement action against the company, the Commission asserted that LifeLock's business practice was deceptive because its approach to protecting customers against identity theft addressed only certain forms of identity theft.[40] In addition, the FTC alleged that LifeLock failed to encrypt its customers' data or to properly restrict access to data held by the company, putting the data it held at risk.[41]

In 2010, LifeLock agreed to a settlement with the FTC and the states. LifeLock agreed to pay $11 million to the FTC.[42] Each of the two cofounders of LifeLock agreed to pay $10,000 to the FTC. As part of the settlement, LifeLock agreed to maintain a comprehensive information security program to protect its customers' sensitive personal data that would be assessed every two years for compliance with security requirements, and to cease deceptive advertising practices. These requirements of this consent order remained in effect until 2026.[43]

In 2015, the FTC filed a contempt action against LifeLock for failure to comply with the 2010 consent order. According to the documents filed with the court, LifeLock failed to maintain a comprehensive information security program to protect customers' sensitive data and engaged in deceptive advertising about the protection it offered to customers. The resulting court order required the company to deposit $100 million with the court. Of this money, $68 million was to be used to repay monthly premiums to former clients who had filed a class-action lawsuit. The remaining money was to be paid either to the state attorneys general or to the federal government.[44]

3.7.4 In the Matter of DesignerWare, LLC

The DesignerWare case illustrated FTC unfairness concerns that go beyond data breach. DesignerWare licensed software to rent-to-own companies to help them track and recover rented computers. Unbeknownst to customers, the software could log key strokes, capture screen shots, and take photographs using a computer's webcam. Data gathered by DesignerWare and provided to rent-to-own stores revealed sensitive information about computer users: user names and passwords; Social Security numbers; medical and financial records; and webcam pictures of children, partially undressed individuals, and intimate activities. In addition, DesignerWare used geolocation tracking software without obtaining the permission of the computer users. The DesignerWare system also presented a fake software program registration screen on the users' computer that tricked the individuals into providing their personal contact information.

The FTC alleged in its enforcement action that DesignerWare and the seven rent-to-own companies involved engaged in the unfair practices of surreptitiously collecting webcam photos and consumer information and inappropriately using geolocation information, as well as the deceptive practice of using fake software registration. In the consent order entered into with the FTC, these companies agreed not to engage in these practices for 20 years.[45]

3.8 Future of Federal Enforcement

Important guidance about the future of federal privacy enforcement comes from a series of reports, including the Obama administration's proposed Consumer Privacy Bill of Rights and FTC reports on data brokers and enforcement actions to date. FTC reports on Big Data and the Internet of Things are discussed in Chapter 13.

3.8.1 Federal 2012 Privacy Reports

In 2012, the Obama administration issued a report titled "Consumer Data Privacy in a Networked World: A Framework for Protecting Privacy and Promoting Innovation in the Global Digital Economy" (hereafter referred to as "White House Report").[46] The FTC issued a report striking many of the same themes, titled "Protecting Consumer Privacy in an Era of Rapid Change: Recommendations for Businesses and Policymakers" ("FTC Report").[47] Together, the two reports provide insights into how current enforcement priorities have evolved from earlier approaches.

The FTC' primary method of enforcement under Chairman Robert Pitofsky in the late 1990s is sometimes referred to as the "notice and choice approach." During that period, companies were encouraged to provide privacy notices on their websites and to offer choice to consumers about whether information would be shared with third parties. Enforcement actions were based on deception and the failure to comply with a privacy promise rather than specific, tangible harm to consumers.[48]

From 2001 to 2009, FTC Chairs Timothy Muris and Deborah Platt Majoris emphasized the "harm-based model" approach to enforcement. The FTC led efforts to address the harms consumers suffer due to identity theft. This approach placed enforcement emphasis on addressing substantial injury, as required under the FTC's unfairness authority.

Under Chairman Jon Leibowitz, appointed in 2009, the FTC began to include the requirement of a comprehensive privacy program in consent decrees, and expanded its privacy and security efforts further, beyond instances where there was tangible financial harm to consumers. This more comprehensive approach to privacy enforcement is reflected in the 2012 White House and FTC reports.

The White House Report contains a preface signed by President Obama and defines the "Consumer Privacy Bill of Rights" based on traditional fair information practices. The report states that these rights should apply to commercial uses of personal data:

1. **Individual control.** Consumers have a right to exercise control over what personal data companies collect from them and how they use it.
2. **Transparency.** Consumers have a right to easily understandable and accessible information about privacy and security practices.
3. **Respect for context.** Consumers have a right to expect that companies will collect, use, and disclose personal data in ways that are consistent with the context in which consumers provide the data.
4. **Security.** Consumers have a right to secure and responsible handling of personal data.
5. **Access and accuracy.** Consumers have a right to access and correct personal data in usable formats, in a manner that is appropriate to the sensitivity of the data and the risk of adverse consequences to consumers if the data is inaccurate.
6. **Focused collection.** Consumers have a right to reasonable limits on the personal data that companies collect and retain.
7. **Accountability.** Consumers have a right to have personal data handled by companies with appropriate measures in place to assure they adhere to the Consumer Privacy Bill of Rights.

The report recommends that these rights be included in federal legislation, with use of multistakeholder processes to develop enforceable codes of conduct until legislation is passed. The report emphasizes the importance of achieving international interoperability, including trans-border cooperation on privacy enforcement. It also emphasizes the role and expertise of the FTC for privacy enforcement.

The FTC Report, issued shortly after the White House Report, states many of the same themes. In its summary, the FTC emphasizes three areas:

1. **Privacy by design.** Companies should promote consumer privacy throughout their organizations and at every stage in the development of their products and services. They should incorporate substantive privacy protections into their practices, such as data security, reasonable collection limits, sound retention and disposal practices, and data accuracy.
2. **Simplified consumer choice.** Companies should simplify consumer choice. They do not need to provide choice before collecting and using consumer data for practices that are consistent with the context of the transaction or the company's relationship with the consumer, or are required or specifically

authorized by law. For practices requiring choice, companies should offer the choice at a time and in a context in which the consumer is making a decision about his or her data. Companies should obtain affirmative express consent before (1) using consumer data in a materially different manner than claimed when the data was collected or (2) collecting sensitive data for certain purposes.

3. **Transparency.** Privacy notices should be clearer, shorter and more standardized to enable better comprehension and comparison of privacy practices. Companies should provide reasonable access to the consumer data they maintain; the extent of access should be proportionate to the sensitivity of the data and the nature of its use. All stakeholders should expand their efforts to educate consumers about commercial data privacy practices.

The FTC also announced five priority areas for attention:

1. **Do Not Track mechanism.** The FTC has encouraged industry to create a mechanism for consumers to signal if they do not wish to be tracked for online behavioral advertising purposes.
2. **Mobile.** The FTC encourages greater self-regulation in the swiftly evolving area of location- and other mobile-related services.
3. **Data brokers.** The FTC supports targeted legislation to provide consumers with access to information held about them by data brokers who are not already covered by the FCRA.
4. **Large platform providers.** The FTC is examining special issues raised by very large online companies that may do what the FTC calls "comprehensive" tracking.
5. **Promotion of enforceable self-regulatory codes.** The FTC will work with the multistakeholder processes that are being facilitated by the DOC.

Taken together, the White House Report and FTC Report indicate a significantly more comprehensive approach to privacy protection and enforcement than the FTC's earlier approaches to enforcement.

3.8.2 Privacy and Data Security: 2015 Update

In its 2015 Privacy and Data Security Update, the FTC states that reasonable data security practices include at least five principles: (1) companies should be aware of what consumer information they have and who has legitimate access to this data; (2) companies should limit the information they collect and maintain for their legitimate business purposes; (3) companies should protect the information they maintain by assessing risk and by implementing procedures for electronic security, physical security, employee training and vendor management; (4) companies should properly dispose of information they no longer need; and (5) companies should have a plan in place to respond to security incidents, in case they occur.[49]

The FTC conducts data security investigations to determine whether a company's data security measures are reasonable in light of the volume and sensitivity of consumer information it holds, the complexity and breadth of its data operations, and the cost of tools available to reduce vulnerabilities and improve security.[50]

Along with the cases discussed above, the FTC entered into consent orders with the following companies:

- ASUS failed to address security issues with routers, and hackers exploited these security flaws to gain unauthorized access to the storage units of 12,900 customers.[51]
- TRENDnet failed to secure live video feeds from 700 customers, allowing hackers to post links to these live video feeds.[52]

These last two actions are significant in that the FTC did not challenge the companies' own data security practices; it charged that the companies were allegedly selling products that were not safe enough and thus caused product users to expose their personal data to risks that seemed unfair.

According to the 2015 Report, one recent trend by the FTC has involved bringing enforcement actions against companies for "unfair practices" when they unreasonably and unnecessarily exposed consumers' personal data to unauthorized access. After customer information has been hacked or customers' computers have suffered the effects of malware, the FTC investigates the companies to determine whether they took reasonable steps to ensure that they were not inadvertently enabling third parties to harm consumers.[53]

3.8.3 Privacy and Data Security: 2016 Update

The 2016 Report discusses more than 40 general privacy cases, 130 spam and spyware cases, and 60 data security cases the FTC has brought.[54] Examples of recent cases include:

- Singapore-based mobile advertising company InMobi was fined almost one million for allegedly deceiving hundreds of millions of consumers, including children, concerning tracking their locations. Even when the consumers denied permission to access their location for geo-tracking advertising, the company collected this information.[55]

- Turn, Inc., a mobile ad network, settled charges with the FTC that it deceived consumers into believing they could reduce the amount of tracking by the company both online and on their mobile phones. Instead, the company allegedly utilized a Verizon Wireless program that allowed them to track millions of customers, even after the consumers took steps to delete cookies or reset identifiers on their phones.[56]
- Technology company Vulcan settled charges that it unfairly replaced "Running Fred," a popular web browser game, with a program that directly installed apps onto the consumers' smart phones. Vulcan's program bypassed the permissions process in the phones' operating systems.[57]

In addition to these cases, the FTC issued a letter of warning to 12 app developers concerning software that can be used to activate a device's microphone to listen for audio beacons emitted by televisions. According to the FTC, these beacons cannot be heard by consumers, but can be detected by the software. Monitoring these beacons could produce a detailed log of consumers' television use. That information could then be used for targeted ads as well as for analytics. In the letters, the FTC cautioned that if the statements related to these apps assert or imply that television data is not being collected and transmitted when it is, then such activities could be the basis of a violation of Section 5 of the FTC Act.[58]

The report notes that the FTC hosted a three-part event to examine new technologies that raise important consumer protection issues. The three issues addressed include:

- **Smart TVs**—The ability to track consumer viewing habits was discussed, as well as the implications of such tracking for consumer privacy
- **Drones**—In addition to focusing on privacy and security concerns raised by the use of drones, the event also examined the practical issues of providing choice and transparency
- **Ransomware**—The focus was steps businesses can take to prevent infiltration as well as to limit impact[59]

For privacy professionals, these recent focus areas by the FTC may provide insight into future enforcement efforts.

3.9 State Enforcement

Each state has a law roughly similar to Section 5 of the FTC Act. These laws are commonly known as Unfair and Deceptive Acts and Practices, or UDAP statutes. In addition to covering unfair and deceptive practices, some statutes allow enforcement against "unconscionable" practices, a contract law term for a range of harsh seller practices.[60] UDAP laws are enforced by state attorneys general, who serve as the chief legal officers of each state.

Some federal statutes, such as CAN-SPAM, also allow state attorneys general to bring enforcement actions along with the relevant federal agency. Several states allow private rights of action under their state UDAP laws, so individuals can bring suit against violators.[61]

State enforcement of information security lapses has been especially prominent, driven by data breach notifications. Since California enacted the first breach notification law in 2002, almost every state has passed a similar breach notification law. Many of these laws, as discussed in Chapter 6, require organizations to furnish the state attorney general with reports about breaches when they occur. These laws also often confer enforcement authority on state attorneys general if the breach notification reveals the implementation of inadequate security controls.

States have many other specialized statutes protecting privacy. These exist for the medical, financial, workplace and other sectors, as discussed in the relevant chapters of this book.[62] As with federal law, new issues arise with changing technology. State public utilities commissions, for instance, have started to set rules for personal information collected in connection with the smart grid.[63]

Apart from statutes, state common law is an additional source of privacy enforcement. Plaintiffs can sue under the privacy torts, which traditionally have been categorized as intrusion upon seclusion, appropriation of name or likeness, publicity given to private life, and publicity placing a person in false light.[64] Plaintiffs may also sue under a contract theory in certain situations, such when a physician, financial institution or other entity holding sensitive information breaches a promise of confidentiality and causes harm.

The National Association of Attorneys General Consumer Protection Project helps coordinate the work of state attorneys general. The project "works to improve the enforcement of state and federal consumer protection laws by State Attorneys General, as well as supports multistate consumer protection enforcement efforts."[65] The project also "promotes information exchange among the states with respect to investigations, litigation, consumer education, and both federal and state legislation."[66]

One example of the efforts by states is California's work related to mobile apps. California's attorney general created a special Privacy Task Force that reached an important agreement on standardization of easily understandable privacy permissions with app platform providers. California's attorney general has brought several actions against companies for failure to provide timely data security breach notifications, to obtain consent for call monitoring, and to provide required data privacy notices.[67] California's actions in this area are particularly important and influential, due to the size of the state's economy and given that California has jurisdiction over the country's largest technology companies and platform providers.

3.10 Self-Regulation and Enforcement

The term *self-regulation* refers to a variety of approaches to privacy protection. Self-regulation, similar to government regulation, can occur through the three separation-of-powers components: legislation, enforcement and adjudication.[68] Legislation refers to the question of who should define appropriate rules for protecting privacy. Enforcement refers to the question of who should initiate enforcement actions. Adjudication refers to the question of who should decide whether a company has violated the privacy rules, and with what penalties.

For enforcement under Section 5 of the FTC Act or state UDAP laws, self-regulation only occurs at the quasi-legislation stage (i.e., voluntary industry rule-making). A company writes its own privacy policy, or an industry group drafts a code of conduct that companies agree to follow. Under Section 5, the FTC can then decide whether to bring an enforcement action, and adjudication can occur in front of an ALJ, with appeal to federal court. Referring to this approach as self-regulation is somewhat confusing, because a government agency is involved at the enforcement and adjudication stage.

Other self-regulatory systems engage in all three roles without the involvement of a government agency. For example, the PCI DSS provides an enforceable security standard for payment card data. The rules were drafted by the PCI DSS Council, which built on previous rules written by the various credit card companies. Except for small companies, compliance with the standard requires hiring a third party to conduct security assessments and detect violations. Failure to comply can lead to exclusion from Visa, MasterCard or other major payment card systems, as well as penalties of $5,000 to $100,000 per month.[69]

Third-party privacy seal and certification programs play an important role in providing assurances that companies are complying with self-regulatory programs. Services offered by TrustArc, the Better Business Bureau and others provide methods for third parties to oversee compliance. Companies may demonstrate compliance and thus improve consumer confidence by displaying a trust mark in the form of a seal, logo or certification showing that the company is part of a certification program. It can serve as a way to comply with legal requirements. For instance, the Privacy Shield requires participating companies to name a compliance third party. COPPA authorizes the FTC to confirm that certification programs are in compliance with the law. Companies are deemed to meet compliance requirements through their participation in that certification program.

One prominent self-regulatory effort involves the Digital Advertising Alliance (DAA), a coalition of media and advertising organizations. The DAA helped develop an icon program, intended to inform consumers about how they can exercise choice with respect to online behavioral advertising.[70] The AdChoices system allows users to click on an icon near an ad or to visit the AdChoices website and choose to what extent the user will view behavioral ads from participating advertisers.

It is important to note that self-regulation is controversial. Privacy advocates and supporters of the European approach to data protection often express concern that industries are not strict enough when creating, adhering to and enforcing privacy rules or codes of conduct. European regulators, for instance, say that privacy is a fundamental human right, and data protection authorities should be involved in defining and protecting that right. Supporters of self-regulation tend to emphasize the fact that industry has greater expertise about how their systems operate and therefore should lead the creation, establishment and enforcement of those rules.

Since the 2012 White House and FTC reports, there has been increased attention on new self-regulatory efforts. The White House Report stressed the importance of engaging in a multistakeholder privacy self-regulatory process, with the DOC facilitating these efforts. This process has important similarities to earlier self-regulatory efforts, in terms of industry experts working together to craft enforceable rules. One important difference, however, is that consumer groups and other stakeholders are explicitly included in the process, instead of industry alone defining the rules.

By the end of the Obama administration, the DOC convened self-regulatory efforts for mobile phone notices and drones. The National Telecommunications and Information Administration (NTIA) issued a report of best practices from its multistakeholder process concerning privacy, transparency, and accountability issues for drones. The voluntary best practices include: inform others of the use of the drone; show care when operating the drone or collecting and storing data; limit the use and sharing of data; secure data; and monitor and comply with evolving federal, state and local laws related to drones.[71]

3.11 Cross-border Enforcement Issues

As the volume of cross-border data transfers increases, privacy enforcement increasingly involves companies and government agencies in more than one jurisdiction. Key issues include cooperation between enforcement agencies, conflicts between privacy laws and laws seeking to compel disclosure, and cross-border enforcement.

3.11.1 Cooperation Between Enforcement Agencies

One trend in cross-border enforcement is for enforcement agencies in different countries to engage in closer cooperation. In 2007, the OECD adopted the Recommendation on Cross-Border Co-operation in the Enforcement of Laws Protecting Privacy.[72] The recommendation focuses on the need to address common privacy issues on a global scale, rather than focusing on country-by-country differences in law or enforcement power. The recommendation calls for member countries to:

- Discuss the practical aspects of privacy law enforcement cooperation
- Share best practices in addressing cross-border challenges
- Work to develop shared enforcement priorities
- Support joint enforcement initiatives and awareness campaigns[73]

In response to the recommendation, the FTC, along with enforcement authorities from around the world, established the Global Privacy Enforcement Network (GPEN) in 2010. The GPEN aims to promote cross-border information sharing as well as investigation and enforcement cooperation among privacy authorities around the world.[74]

Another cross-border enforcement cooperation effort is the Asia-Pacific Economic Cooperation (APEC). The APEC Cross-border Privacy Enforcement Arrangement (CPEA) aims to establish a framework for participating members to share information and evidence in cross-border investigations and enforcement actions in the Asia-Pacific region.[75] The CPEA also will facilitate cooperation and communication between APEC and non-APEC members. The FTC is a CPEA participant.

3.11.2 Conflicts Between Privacy and Disclosure Laws

Conflicts can arise when the privacy laws in one country prohibit disclosure of information, but laws in a different country compel disclosure. For instance, the United States generally permits a greater range of discovery in litigation than European courts, with a party to the litigation in the United States potentially facing fines or contempt of court if it does not produce records. By contrast, laws in the EU, under the General Data Protection Regulation (GDPR)[76] may prohibit disclosure of the same records. Although U.S. courts have found ways to resolve such disputes, concerns persist.[77]

In 2012, the International Chamber of Commerce released a policy statement entitled "Cross-border Law Enforcement Access to Company Data—Current Issues Under Data Protection and Privacy Law."[78] The statement highlights problems that may arise when law enforcement compliance requirements conflict with data protection and privacy commitments. It provides analysis of these issues as well as recommendations for law enforcement bodies that face these challenges.[79]

These issues have become more complex over time. The section entitled "Global Perspective" in Chapter 4 provides more detailed discussion.

3.12 Conclusion

Over the years, the FTC's enforcement has evolved from focusing on deceptive practices to a more comprehensive approach—moving beyond the mere punishment of violators to requiring the implementation of best practices in privacy and security.

This chapter has also highlighted, however, the large number of other agencies and actors that are now involved in U.S. privacy enforcement. Enforcement efforts come from other federal agencies, the states, self-regulatory regimes, and organizations and countries outside of the United States. Privacy professionals must be aware of both domestic enforcement authorities and potential enforcement authorities in other countries.

Endnotes

1 APA, https://www.archives.gov/federal-register/laws/administrative-procedure/ (accessed November 2017).

2 This topic is discussed in Chapter 4. EU-U.S. Privacy Shield, Commerce.gov, https://www.commerce.gov/tags/eu-us-privacy-shield (accessed November 2017).

3 42 U.S.C. 1320d–6(a), https://www.law.cornell.edu/uscode/text/42/1320d-6 (accessed November 2017).

4 J. Howard Beales III, "The FTC's Use of Unfairness Authority: Its Rise, Fall, and Resurrection," FTC, https://www.ftc.gov/public-statements/2003/05/ftcs-use-unfairness-authority-its-rise-fall-and-resurrection (accessed November 2017).

5 *See* Chris Jay Hoofnagle, *Federal Trade Commission Privacy Law and Policy* (2016); Andrew Serwin, *The Federal Trade Commission and Privacy: Defining Enforcement and Encouraging Adoption of Best Practices*, 48 San Diego L. Rev. 809 (2011).

6 15 U.S.C. § 45(a)(1), https://www.law.cornell.edu/uscode/text/15/45 (accessed November 2017).

7 15 U.S.C. §§ 46(a)-(b), https://www.law.cornell.edu/uscode/text/15/46 (accessed November 2017).

8 15 U.S.C. § 45, https://www.law.cornell.edu/uscode/text/15/45 (accessed November 2017).

9 15 U.S.C. § 57A, https://www.law.cornell.edu/uscode/text/15/57a (accessed November 2017).

10 15 U.S.C. § 45, https://www.law.cornell.edu/uscode/text/15/45 (accessed November 2017).

11 15 U.S.C. § 46, 49, 57b-1, https://www.law.cornell.edu/uscode/text/15/45 (accessed November 2017); https://www.law.cornell.edu/uscode/text/15/49; and https://www.law.cornell.edu/uscode/text/15/57b-1 (accessed November 2017).

12 "A Brief Overview of the Federal Trade Commission's Investigative and Law Enforcement Authority," FTC, https://www.ftc.gov/about-ftc/what-we-do/enforcement-authority (accessed July 2016).

13 16 C.F.R. § 1.98(d), https://www.law.cornell.edu/cfr/text/16/1.98 (accessed November 2017); 15 U.S.C. § 45(m)(1)(A), https://www.law.cornell.edu/uscode/text/15/45 (accessed November 2017). "FTC enforcement actions just got a lot more expensive," *ZwillGen blog*, http://blog.zwillgen.com/2016/06/30/ftc-enforcement-actions-just-got-lot-expensive/ (accessed November 2017).

14 15 U.S.C. § 53, https://www.law.cornell.edu/uscode/text/15/53 (accessed November 2017).

15 Peter P. Swire, "Trustwrap: The Importance of Legal Rules for E-commerce and Internet Privacy," *Hastings Law Journal* 54 (2003): 847 (discussing the history), http://home.uchicago.edu/mferzige/Trustwrap%20-%20privacy.pdf (accessed November 2017).

16 "Gateway Learning Settles FTC Privacy Charges," FTC, https://www.ftc.gov/news-events/press-releases/2004/07/gateway-learning-settles-ftc-privacy-charges (accessed November 2017).

17 "Privacy Online: Fair Information Practices in the Electronic Marketplace, A Report to Congress" (2000), FTC, https://www.ftc.gov/reports/privacy-online-fair-information-practices-electronic-marketplace-federal-trade-commission (accessed November 2017).

18 Margaret Eisenhauser, *The Information Privacy Case Book: A Global Survey of Privacy & Security Enforcement Actions with Recommendations for Reducing Risk*, International Association of Privacy Professionals 2009.

19 In the Matter of Geocities, Inc., FTC, https://www.ftc.gov/enforcement/cases-proceedings/982-3015/geocities (accessed November 2017).

20 In the Matter of Eli Lilly & Co., FTC, https://www.ftc.gov/enforcement/cases-proceedings/012-3214/eli-lilly-company-matter (accessed November 2017).

21 2015 FTC Privacy and Security Update, FTC, https://www.ftc.gov/reports/privacy-data-security-update-2015 (accessed November 2017).

22 FTC Policy Statement on Deception, FTC, https://www.ftc.gov/public-statements/1983/10/ftc-policy-statement-deception (accessed July, 2016); *see Big Data: A Tool for Inclusion? Understanding the Issues*, FTC, https://www.ftc.gov/reports/big-data-tool-inclusion-or-exclusion-understanding-issues-ftc-report (accessed November 2017).

23 *Essentially Equivalent: A comparison of the legal orders for privacy and data protection in the European Union and United States*, Sidley Austin, www.sidley.com/~/media/publications/essentially-equivalent---final.pdf (accessed November 2017).

24 MAC is an acronym for "media access control" and refers to a 12-digit identifier that is unique to a particular device.

25 "FTC approves final order in Nomi Technologies case," FTC, https://www.ftc.gov/news-events/press-releases/2015/09/ftc-approves-final-order-nomi-technologies-case (accessed November 2017).

26 "Snapchat settles FTC charges that promises of disappearing messages were false," FTC, https://www.ftc.gov/news-events/press-releases/2014/05/snapchat-settles-ftc-charges-promises-disappearing-messages-were (accessed November 2017).

27 "TRUSTe settles FTC charges it deceived customers through its privacy seal program," FTC, https://www.ftc.gov/news-events/press-releases/2014/11/truste-settles-ftc-charges-it-deceived-consumers-through-its (accessed November 2017).

28 15 U.S.C. § 45(n), https://www.law.cornell.edu/uscode/text/15/45 (accessed November 2017). FTC Policy on Unfairness, FTC, https://www.ftc.gov/public-statements/1980/12/ftc-policy-statement-unfairness (accessed November 2017). *See Big Data: A Tool for Inclusion? Understanding the Issues.*

29 J. Howard Beales III, "The FTC's Use of Unfairness Authority: Its Rise, Fall, and Resurrection," FTC, https://www.ftc.gov/public-statements/2003/05/ftcs-use-unfairness-authority-its-rise-fall-and-resurrection (accessed November 2017).

30 *Essentially Equivalent: A comparison of the legal orders for privacy and data protection in the European Union and United States.*

31 The Unfairness Policy Statement was published in International Harvester Co., 104 F.T.C. 949, 1070 (1984).

32 15 U.S.C. § 45(n), https://www.law.cornell.edu/uscode/text/15/45 (accessed November 2017).

33 FTC v. Wyndham Worldwide Corporation, 799 F.3d 236 (3rd Cir. 2015), http://harvardlawreview.org/2016/02/ftc-v-wyndham-worldwide-corp/ (accessed November 2017).

34 The United States Court of Appeals for the Third Circuit ruling in FTC v. Wyndham Worldwide Corporation, 799 F.3d 236 (2015), http://harvardlawreview.org/2016/02/ftc-v-wyndham-worldwide-corp/ (accessed November 2017).

35 "FTC held to have authority to regulate cybersecurity practices under Section 5 of the FTC Act," Chadbourne, http://www.nortonrosefulbright.com/files/chadbourne/publications/160101_ftcheldauthorityregulatecybersecuritypractices_privacycybersecurity.pdf (accessed November 2017).

36 Because there was a pending case before a federal court between the FTC and Wyndham related to this enforcement action, this consent order (unlike those most of the consent orders with the FTC) had to be approved by the federal court. "Wyndham settles FTC charges it unfairly placed consumers' payment card information at risk," FTC, https://www.ftc.gov/news-events/press-releases/2015/12/wyndham-settles-ftc-charges-it-unfairly-placed-consumers-payment (accessed November 2017).

37 Initial decision of Administrative Law Judge in the case of In the Matter of LabMD, https://www.ftc.gov/system/files/documents/cases/151113labmd_decision.pdf (accessed November 2017).

38 Specifically, Section 5(n) defines an "unfair" practice as one that "causes or is likely to cause substantial injury to consumers." https://www.law.cornell.edu/uscode/text/15/45 (accessed November 2017).

39 Rita Heimes, "US appeals court narrows FTC's 'unfair' standard in LabMD case," Privacy Bar Section, IAPP (November 14, 2016), https://iapp.org/news/a/us-appeals-court-narrows-ftcs-unfair-standard-in-labmd-case/ (accessed November 2017); *see* Angelique Carson, "LabMD argues 'matter of principle' in FTC data security appeal," The Privacy Advisor, IAPP (June 26, 2017), https://iapp.org/news/a/11th-circuit-hears-arguments-in-labmd-v-ftc-appeal/# (accessed November 2017). It is worth noting that, during the enforcement action by the FTC, LabMD has gone out of business. The company, however, continues its legal fight against the agency. *See* Dune Lawrence, "A Leak

Wounded This Company. Fighting the Feds Finished It Off," *Bloomberg*, April 25, 2016, https://www.bloomberg.com/features/2016-labmd-ftc-tiversa/ (accessed November 2017); Cheryl Conner, "When the Government Closes Your Business," *Forbes*, February 1, 2014, https://www.forbes.com/sites/cherylsnappconner/2014/02/01/when-the-government-closes-your-business/#48e190041435 (accessed November 2017).

40 Complaint filed by the FTC against LifeLock, https://www.ftc.gov/sites/default/files/documents/cases/2010/03/100309lifelockcmpt.pdf (accessed November 2017).

41 "LifeLock will pay $12 million to settle charges by the FTC and 35 states that identify theft prevention and data security claims," FTC, https://www.ftc.gov/news-events/press-releases/2010/03/lifelock-will-pay-12-million-settle-charges-ftc-35-states (accessed November 2017).

42 At the same time as the FTC action, 35 state attorneys general's offices conducted investigations regarding similar concerns of LifeLock's business practices. The FTC and state attorneys general claims were decided in the same court order, with an additional $1 million split between the states.

43 Final Order in FTC v. LifeLock (2010), https://www.ftc.gov/sites/default/files/documents/cases/2010/03/100309lifelockstip.pdf (accessed November 2017).

44 "LifeLock to pay $100 million to consumers to settle FTC charges it violated 2010 order," FTC, https://www.ftc.gov/news-events/press-releases/2015/12/lifelock-pay-100-million-consumers-settle-ftc-charges-it-violated (accessed November 2017).

45 "FTC approves final order settling charges against software and rent-to-own companies accused of computer spying," FTC, https://www.ftc.gov/news-events/press-releases/2013/04/ftc-approves-final-order-settling-charges-against-software-and (accessed November 2017).

46 "Consumer Data Privacy in a Networked World: A Framework for Protecting Privacy and Promoting Innovation in the Global Digital Economy," White House Report, https://obamawhitehouse.archives.gov/sites/default/files/privacy-final.pdf (accessed November 2017).

47 "Protecting Consumer Privacy in an Era of Rapid Change: Recommendations for Businesses and Policymakers," FTC, https://www.ftc.gov/reports/protecting-consumer-privacy-era-rapid-change-recommendations-businesses-policymakers (accessed November 2017).

48 In re Cliffdale Assoc., 103 F.T.C. 110 (1984).

49 2015 FTC Privacy and Security Update, https://www.ftc.gov/news-events/blogs/business-blog/2016/01/2015-privacy-data-security-update (accessed November 2017).

50 "Emerging Threats in the Online Advertising Industry," Prepared Statement of the Federal Trade Commission Before the Committee on Homeland Security and Governmental Affairs Permanent Subcommittee on Investigations, United States Senate, https://www.ftc.gov/public-statements/2014/05/prepared-statement-federal-trade-commission-emerging-threats-online (accessed November 2017).

51 "ASUS settles FTC charges that insecure home routers and 'cloud' services put consumers' privacy at risk," FTC, https://www.ftc.gov/news-events/press-releases/2016/02/asus-settles-ftc-charges-insecure-home-routers-cloud-services-put (accessed November 2017).

52 "FTC approves final order settling charges against TRENDnet, Inc.," FTC https://www.ftc.gov/news-events/press-releases/2014/02/ftc-approves-final-order-settling-charges-against-trendnet-inc (accessed November 2017).

53 Data Security, FTC, https://www.ftc.gov/datasecurity (accessed July 2016); *see* "Emerging Threats in the Online Advertising Industry," Prepared Statement of the Federal Trade Commission Before

the Committee on Homeland Security and Governmental Affairs Permanent Subcommittee on Investigations, U.S. Senate, https://www.ftc.gov/public-statements/2014/05/prepared-statement-federal-trade-commission-emerging-threats-online (accessed November 2017).

54 2016 FTC Privacy and Security Update, FTC, https://www.ftc.gov/reports/privacy-data-security-update-2016 (accessed November 2017).

55 In the Matter of InMobi Pte Ltd., FTC (June 22, 2016), https://www.ftc.gov/enforcement/cases-proceedings/152-3203/inmobi-pte-ltd (accessed November 2017).

56 In the Matter of Turn, Inc., FTC (April 21, 2017), https://www.ftc.gov/enforcement/cases-proceedings/152-3099/turn-inc-matter (accessed November 2017).

57 In the Matter of General Workings Inc., also doing business as Vulcan, FTC (May 10, 2016), https://www.ftc.gov/enforcement/cases-proceedings/152-3159/general-workings-inc-also-doing-business-vulcun-matter (accessed November 2017).

58 "FTC Issues Warning Letters to App Developers Using 'Silverpush' Code," FTC (March 17, 2016), https://www.ftc.gov/news-events/press-releases/2016/03/ftc-issues-warning-letters-app-developers-using-silverpush-code (accessed November 2017).

59 2016 FTC Privacy and Security Update, FTC, https://www.ftc.gov/reports/privacy-data-security-update-2016 (accessed November 2017).

60 HI § 480-2, www.capitol.hawaii.gov/hrscurrent/vol11_ch0476-0490/hrs0480/hrs_0480-0002.htm (accessed November 2017). A detailed definition of "unconscionable" is contained in 13 Ohio Revised Code § 1345.03, http://codes.ohio.gov/orc/1345 (accessed November 2017).

61 California Business and Professions Code § 17200-17210, http://leginfo.legislature.ca.gov/faces/codes_displayText.xhtml?lawCode=BPC&division=7.&title=&part=2.&chapter=5.&article= (accessed November 2017).

62 Robert Ellis Smith, *Compilation of State and Federal Privacy Laws* (Providence: Privacy Journal, 2012).

63 For example, Decision and Order, Adopting Rules to Protect the Privacy and Security of the Electricity Usage Data, https://www.smartgrid.gov/document/decision_adopting_rules_protect_privacy_and_security_electricity_usage_data_customers_pacif.html (accessed November 2017) and 4CCR 723-3, Colorado Department of Regulatory Agencies, https://www.colorado.gov/dora/puc (accessed November 2017).

64 Restatement (Second) of Torts, § 652A-E, www.tomwbell.com/NetLaw/Ch05/R2ndTorts.html (accessed November 2017).

65 Consumer Protection, National Association of Attorneys General, www.naag.org/CFPB_protection.php (accessed November 2017).

66 *See generally* Daniel Citron, "The Privacy Policymaking of State Attorneys General," Notre Dame Law School (2016), http://scholarship.law.nd.edu/ndlr/vol92/iss2/5/ (accessed November 2017).

67 *See* Lothar Determann, *California Privacy Law - Practical Guide and Commentary,* Chapter 6 (2016).

68 Peter P. Swire, "Markets, Self-Regulation, and Government Enforcement in the Protection of Personal Information," in U.S. Department of Commerce, *Privacy and Self-Regulation in the Information Age* (1997), http://ssrn.com/abstract=11472 (accessed November 2017).

69 PCI Compliance Guide, PCI FAQs, https://www.pcicomplianceguide.org/pci-faqs-2/ (accessed July, 2016).

70 DAA Self-Regulatory Program, www.aboutads.info/ (accessed November 2017).

71 Multistakeholder Process: Unmanned Aircraft System, NTIA, https://www.ntia.doc.gov/other-publication/2016/multistakeholder-process-unmanned-aircraft-systems (accessed November 2017).

72 "OECD Recommendation on Cross-Border Co-operation in the Enforcement of Laws Protecting Privacy," www.oecd.org/dataoecd/43/28/38770483.pdf (accessed November 2017).

73 *Id.*

74 Global Privacy Enforcement Network, www.privacyenforcement.net/ (accessed November 2017).

75 APEC CPEA, www.apec.org/Groups/Committee-on-Trade-and-Investment/Electronic-Commerce-Steering-Group/Cross-border-Privacy-Enforcement-Arrangement.aspx (accessed November 2017).

76 GDPR is discussed in Chapter 4. *See* GPDR Portal: Site Overview, EUGDPR.org, www.eugdpr.org (accessed November 2017).

77 Volkswagen, A.G. v. Valdez, 909 S.W. 2d 900 (Tex. 1995) (avoiding conflict with German data protection law), www.leagle.com/decision/19951809909SW2d900_11725/VOLKSWAGEN,%20A.G.%20v.%20VALDEZ (accessed November 2017).

78 "Cross-border Law Enforcement Access to Company Data—Current Issues Under Data Protection and Privacy Law," International Chamber of Commerce, https://iccwbo.org/publication/icc-policy-statement-on-cross-border-law-enforcement-access-to-company-data-current-issues-under-data-protection-and-privacy-law/ (accessed November 2017).

79 *See* generally Cross-Border Requests for Data Project, Institute for Information Security & Privacy, Georgia Institute of Technology, www.iisp.gatech.edu/cross-border-data-project (accessed November 2017).

CHAPTER 4

Principles of Information Management

The first three chapters discussed the legal framework and legal privacy concepts. This chapter will focus on principles of information management. In most organizations, information management requires a combination of skills, including legal, marketing, sales, human resources, public and government relations, and information technology. In large organizations, privacy professionals may be part of a team that draws on a mix of these skill sets.

This chapter begins by examining some major benefits and risks of using personal information (PI) in the private sector. Next, it discusses best practices for developing an information management program that addresses privacy and other information management concerns, including security. The chapter includes a discussion of a preliminary task for this undertaking, which is to perform a data inventory of an organization's data storage and transfers. This permits the organization to achieve benefits and mitigate risks based on the results of that inventory.

The chapter then turns to management issues connected to the prominent fair information practices of notice, choice and access, and concludes with a discussion of contract and vendor management. The chapter concludes with an overview of key global issues related to data traveling to or from the United States.

This material should be read in the context of more detailed discussions of legal rules in the other chapters of this book. Considerable discussion of information security issues is provided in Chapter 5. The important information management issues associated with data breach and incident response are examined in Chapter 6.

4.1 The Role of the Privacy Professional

Privacy professionals need to appreciate both the benefits and the risks of using personal information. PI is essential to most businesses—every organization with employees or even volunteers manages PI. Organizations may collect consumer PI for many purposes, both directly from prospective and existing customers and indirectly through enhanced data available from public and private sources. Organizations may disclose information to service providers, affiliates, business partners and government agencies for a wide range of purposes. At the same time, as discussed in this book, many risks can arise from the collection, use and disclosure of PI.

Perceptions of acceptable privacy practices vary, creating challenges for privacy professionals. Decades of opinion surveys show that people can be categorized in three groups: the "privacy fundamentalists" (people with a strong desire to protect privacy), the "privacy unconcerned" (people with low worries about privacy), and the "privacy pragmatists" (people whose concern about privacy varies with context and who are willing to give up some privacy in exchange for benefits).[1] Perceptions about privacy risks not only vary within the population, but they also shift over time. Sometimes the shift is toward greater privacy protection. For example, Social Security numbers used to be visible through the envelope window of millions of Social Security and Supplemental Security Income checks mailed by the U.S. Treasury. With rising fears of identity theft, that practice was abolished in 2000.[2] Sometimes the shift is toward less privacy protection. For example, the modern world is filled with people who post intimate details of their lives on widely adopted social networks.[3] Sometimes the target of privacy concerns shifts— Edward Snowden's 2013 revelations about National Security Agency (NSA) surveillance practices raised concerns about privacy from government surveillance.[4]

Established techniques exist for information security, such as installing firewalls or using industry-standard encryption for communications.[5] For many privacy issues, there is less consensus about good practice. Laws vary across jurisdictions and industry sectors, and views about good practice often differ, both within an organization and as defined by external norms.[6] One role for privacy professionals is to alert their organizations to these often-divergent perspectives.

Privacy professionals also help their organizations manage a range of risks that can arise from processing personal information, and do so in a manner consistent with meeting the organization's growth, profitability and other goals. Privacy professionals can help the organization to identify areas where compliance is difficult in practice, and design policies to close gaps between stated policies and actual operations.

4.2 Risks of Using PI Improperly

In designing and administering a privacy program, an organization should consider and balance four types of risks.

1. **Legal risks.** The organization must comply with applicable state, federal and international laws regarding its use of information or potentially face litigation or regulatory sanctions such as consent decrees, which may last for many years.[7]

The company must also comply with its contractual commitments, privacy promises and commitments to follow industry standards, such as the Payment Card Institute Data Security Standard (PCI DSS).[8]

2. **Reputational risks.** The organization can face reputational harm if it announces privacy policies but does not carry them out;[9] it may also face enforcement actions—particularly from the Federal Trade Commission (FTC).[10] An organization should seek to protect its reputation as a trusted institution with respected brands.
3. **Operational risks.** The organization must ensure that its privacy program is administratively efficient. If a privacy program is too heavy-handed, it may interfere with relationships and inhibit uses of PI that benefit the organization and its customers, such as for personalization or risk management.[11]
4. **Investment risks.** The organization must be able to receive an appropriate return on its investments in information, information technology and information-processing programs in light of evolving privacy regulations, enforcement and expectations.

4.3 Developing an Information Management Program

Over time, PI management has become vital to a large range of organizations. It is now increasingly common for companies to develop an information management program that seeks a holistic approach to the risks and benefits of processing PI. The program, in turn, helps create policies and practices for important parts of the organization's activities. Common activities for such policies include maintaining preference lists for direct marketing, developing appropriate security for human resources data, executing proper contracts to authorize international data flows and publishing online privacy notices when data is collected.

As a matter of terminology, statements on a company website are often called either "privacy notices" or "privacy policies." This book uses the term *privacy policy* when referring to the internal organization statement of policies designed to communicate what practices to follow to those inside the organization, and *privacy notice* for external communications. In practice, however, privacy policy is often used to refer to statements made for both external and internal audiences.

In creating the information management program, privacy leaders help their organizations develop privacy policies in an organized way, meeting policy goals as well as preserving business flexibility. Privacy professionals seek to understand and anticipate future changes both in the regulatory environment and in their companies' business needs. To achieve these objectives, companies should take four distinct steps.

4.3.1 Four Basic Steps for Information Management

The four steps—discover, build, communicate and evolve—are summarized below. A closer look at each phase follows.

1. Discover
    - Issue identification and self-assessment
    - Determination of best practices
2. Build
    - Procedure development and verification
    - Full implementation
3. Communicate
    - Documentation
    - Education
4. Evolve
    - Affirmation and monitoring
    - Adaptation

4.3.1.1 Phase 1: Discover

Before drafting or updating a privacy policy, consider the company's environment, information goals and corporate culture. What laws regulate the company's collection or use of information? Does the company wish to be aggressive in its use of information? Does the company instead plan to be more cautious in its use of PI to reduce legal and reputational risks or perhaps to achieve a competitive advantage as a privacy-sensitive leader? How do the company's information policy objectives mesh with those of its competitors, customers and business partners? The answers to these questions can help an organization define its information policy goals. These goals serve as the foundation upon which the company's policies are built.

In addition to the many state, federal and international laws that regulate the collection, use and/or disclosure of personal information, many industry groups have promulgated self-regulatory guidelines. Some of these standards are mandatory for members of the specific industry group.

Useful privacy guidance for an organization depends on an accurate understanding of the company's actual data practices as well as its intended data use. The successful privacy professional forges honest and open relationships with individuals across departments and at different levels in the organization's hierarchy. The participation of a range of departments, including legal compliance, customer service, marketing, IT, human resources and sales, is often beneficial in the creation of an information plan. The team should have the knowledge base and influence in the organization to determine and articulate the company's current practices and future goals.

Figure 4-1. Sample Organization Chart for Privacy and Data Protection Activities

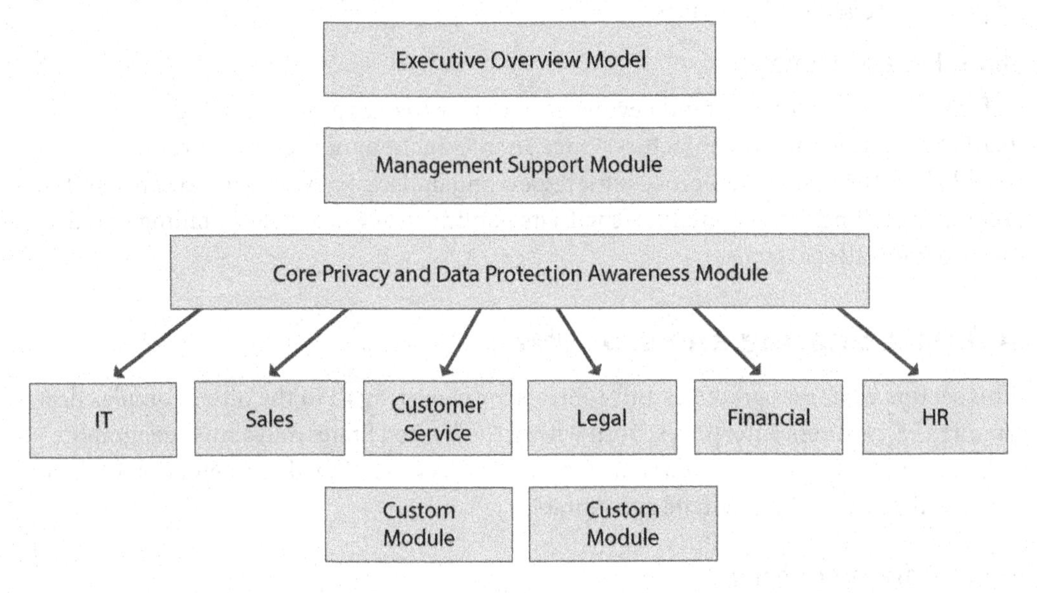

4.3.1.2 Phase 2: Build

Armed with an accurate assessment of the organization's practices and goals, the privacy professional can help determine how best to meet those goals by both facilitating and restricting flows of PI where appropriate. Successful building of the information management program requires close coordination between those writing the policies (whose expertise may include legal compliance and protection of reputation) and IT experts and others who actually work in the various departments that must comply with the policies.

4.3.1.3 Phase 3: Communicate

Along with developing and implementing the information management program, the organization must ensure effective communication to internal and external audiences. Internal audiences must be trained on policies and procedures, with individual accountability for compliance. Specific policies and more general goals should be communicated clearly to the organization's decision makers and consumer-facing employees so they can shape appropriate messages to relevant audiences.

Transparency is also critical. A written privacy notice must accurately reflect the company's practices to external audiences. As discussed further below, companies over time have increasingly used a layered privacy notice approach—placing a summary form that highlights key terms of the policy on top of a longer, more detailed statement of privacy and security practices.[12]

4.3.1.4 Phase 4: Evolve

Information practices constantly evolve in response to changing technology, laws, market conditions and other factors. Once an information management program is established, there must be a process for review and update. Failure to do so can result in a company falling out of compliance with its public privacy promises or failing to meet other organizational goals.

4.4 Data Sharing and Transfer

This section examines practices and controls for managing PI in the often-complex flows among U.S. business enterprises, both within the United States and across geographic boundaries. It also addresses data inventory, data classification, documentation of data flows and determination of data accountability.

4.4.1 Data Inventory

It is important for an organization to undertake an inventory of the PI it collects, stores, uses or discloses—whether within the organization or to outside entities. This inventory should include both customer and employee data records. It should document data location and flow as well as evaluate how, when and with whom the organization shares such information—and the means for data transfer used.

This sort of inventory is legally required for some institutions, such as those covered by the Gramm-Leach-Bliley Act (GLBA) Safeguards Rule discussed in Chapter 8. The benefits of the inventory apply more generally, because it identifies risks that could affect reputation or legal compliance. If a problem subsequently occurs, current enforcement practices indicate penalties are likely to be less severe if the company has an established system of recording and organizing this inventory. The organization's inventory should be reviewed and updated on a regular basis.

4.4.2 Data Classification

After completing an inventory, the next step is to classify data according to its level of sensitivity. The data classification level defines the clearance of individuals who can access or handle that data, as well as the baseline level of protection appropriate for that data.

Most organizations handle different types of PI, such as personnel and customer records, as well as other information the organizations treats as sensitive, such as trade secrets and business plans. Data that is more sensitive generally requires greater protection than other information held by the organization. It may be segregated from less sensitive data, for instance, through access controls that enable only authorized individuals to retrieve the data, or even kept in an entirely separate system. If all data is held in the same system, temporary or lower-level employees might gain access to sensitive data. Holding all data in one system can increase the consequences of a single breach.

In the United States, classification is often important for compliance purposes because of sector-specific privacy and security laws. As discussed throughout this book, different rules apply to financial services information, medical information, and numerous other categories. An effective data classification system helps an organization address compliance audits for a particular type of data, respond to legal discovery requests without producing more information than necessary, and use storage resources in a cost-effective manner.

4.4.3 Documenting Data Flows

Once data has been inventoried and classified, data flows should be examined and documented. An organization chart can be useful to help map and document the systems, applications and processes for handling data. Documenting data flows helps identify areas for compliance attention.

4.4.4 Determining Data Accountability

Privacy professionals often have significant responsibility within an organization for ensuring compliance with privacy laws and policies. Here are some helpful questions for privacy professionals when doing due diligence and for an organization to consider as it addresses privacy risks:

- ***Where, how and for what length of time is the data stored?***
  Data breach laws have focused increasing attention on where and how an organization stores PI.[13] The organization needs policies to address potential risks of data lost from laptops as well as centralized computer centers. An organization should also have retention policies that limit the time PI is stored. A limited retention period reduces the risk from data breach—no breach will occur once the data is removed from the system. Some laws require data to be deleted after a certain period or after the reason for collection has ceased to be relevant.[14]

- ***How sensitive is the information?***
  As discussed above, data should be classified according to its level of sensitivity. Though the data management cycle includes many participants—from the data owner to the privacy professional, the information security professional, the vendor (if applicable), the auditor (if applicable) and the end user—ultimately, the data owner is responsible for assigning the appropriate sensitivity level or classification to the information based on company policy. Common categories include confidential, proprietary (i.e., property of the organization), sensitive, restricted (i.e., available to select few) and public (i.e., generally available).

- ***Should the information be encrypted?***
  Under many breach notification laws, no notice is required if the lost PI is sufficiently encrypted or protected by some other effective technical protection. Such laws have encouraged greater use of encryption for stored data, and good security practices have included a wider use of encryption over time.[15] Encryption in transit has become far more widespread, including for emails and communications over the web that use HTTPS (the secure version of the widely used HTTP web protocol). On the other hand, encryption can be difficult to implement correctly and may reduce function in some applications. IT professionals should be consulted about how to take advantage of encryption while achieving other organizational goals.

- ***Will the information be transferred to or from other countries, and if so, how will it be transferred?***
  Because different countries have significantly different privacy laws, an organization should familiarize itself with the privacy requirements of both origination and destination countries for transborder data flows.

- ***Who determines the rules that apply to the information?***

U.S. privacy professionals have increasingly used some terms that are included in the European Union (EU) privacy regime—for example, a *controller* is an entity who "determines the purposes and means of the processing of personal data" and a *processor* is an entity that "processes personal data on behalf of the controller."[16] Similar terms for processor in the U.S. include *business associate* under the Health Insurance Portability and Accountability Act (HIPAA) or *service provider* under GLBA. Privacy professionals should assess which organization determines the rules that apply to the processing of data. If an organization stores data on behalf of another, the organization should expect to be required to meet the privacy policy guarantees of the other entity (the controller) in the use and storage of such data. Most likely, a storing company (or processor) will be required to sign a contract to this effect.

- ***How is the information to be processed, and how will these processes be maintained?***
  The processes through which personal information is processed also must be defined. Steps should be taken to train staff members involved in the processes, and computers on which the information will be processed should be secured appropriately to minimize the risk of data leak or breach. Physical transfer of the data also should be secured.

- ***Is the use of such data dependent upon other systems?***
  If the use of personal data depends on the working condition of other systems, such as a cloud provider or specialized computer programs, the condition of those systems must also be evaluated and updated if necessary. A system that is outdated may call for developing a new method or program for using the relevant data.

4.5 Privacy Policies and Disclosure

Privacy policies are central to information management programs. They inform relevant employees about how PI must be handled, and in some cases made public, in the form of a privacy notice for the purpose of transparency. As discussed in the previous chapter on enforcement, they also are important as legal documents. If an organization violates a promise made in a privacy policy that is also communicated in the privacy notice, then the FTC or state attorney general may bring an enforcement action for a deceptive practice.

4.5.1 Decision: One or Multiple Privacy Policies?

An organization must determine whether to have one privacy policy that applies globally to all its activities, or multiple policies. One policy will work if an organization has a consistent set of values and practices for all its operations. Multiple policies may make sense for a company that has well-defined divisions of lines of business, especially if each division uses customer data in very different ways, does not typically share PI with other divisions, and is perceived in the marketplace as a different business.

Sometimes separate corporations decide to use a common privacy policy. For financial holding companies, the same corporate name may be used by multiple subsidiaries and affiliates, and a single privacy policy can avoid complications in handling PI. For example, mutual funds and their advisors are separate corporations, but may decide to adopt a joint privacy policy and a joint form of notice.[17] All the mutual funds in a corporate "family" may use joint notices.

Conversely, using multiple policies can create complications. One division's privacy policy may be more stringent in a particular way than another division's, preventing sharing of customer information between two parts of the same company. Where multiple policies are used, it makes sense to align policies as closely as possible so as not to hinder cooperation between divisions.

4.5.2 Policy Review and Approval

An organization should not finalize a privacy policy without legal consultation followed by executive approval. If the policy is not strict enough, then consumers, regulators, and the press may criticize the company for its failure to protect privacy. If a policy is too strict, then open-ended statements or overly ambitious security promises can result in legal penalties or reputational problems if the organization cannot satisfy its promises.

If a privacy policy is revised, the organization should announce the change first to employees, then to both current and former customers through its privacy notice. Both in a 2012 report and in a 2015 update, the FTC stated that companies should obtain express affirmative consent (opt-in) before making material retroactive changes to privacy representations. The FTC stated that a "material" change "at a minimum includes sharing consumer information with third parties after committing at the time of collection not to share the data.[18]

4.5.3 Communication of Privacy Policy Through a Notice

The content of privacy notices is based on fair information practices such as the Organisation for Economic Co-operation and Development (OECD) Guidelines and Asia-Pacific Economic Cooperation (APEC) Principles. The easiest method to communicate an organization's privacy notice, as well as to review the privacy notices of competitors or business partners, is to review the relevant organizations' websites.

Organizations may use multiple methods to communicate privacy notices to consumers and other external stakeholders.

1. **Make the notice accessible online.** The websites of most organizations, even those primarily involved in offline commerce, today contain the privacy notice. It is standard to have a link from the company's front page.
2. **Make the notice accessible in places of business.** Clearly post the organization's privacy notice at the location of business in areas of high customer traffic and in legible form. Organization staff also should have ready access to copies of the up-to-date company privacy policy in case a customer wishes to obtain a copy for review.
3. **Provide updates and revisions.** For financial institutions, GLBA requires that customers receive the privacy notice annually, with clear notice of the customer's right with respect to opt-outs.[19] For institutions without this sort of required updating, provide good notice when the privacy policy is revised, with express customer consent for material changes and a clear opportunity to opt out for smaller changes.
4. **Ensure that the appropriate personnel are knowledgeable about the policy.** Organization staff who interact with PI should receive training in the organization's privacy policy. HIPAA creates specific training requirements for all employees of covered entities.[20] Especially for employees working with sensitive data, organizations should provide regular training and keep records of which employees have been trained.

As one type of appropriate training, customer service representatives (CSRs), such as in customer call centers, should receive a summary statement or script that describes the privacy notice and can be used to answer customer questions. CSRs should have a full copy of the privacy notice in their standard reference material and should retain the ability to send or direct customers to a copy of the privacy notice that they can review in detail. They should know how to escalate privacy issues or incidents once observed.

4.5.4 Policy Version Control

An organization's privacy policy will need to be updated as its information collection, use and transfer needs evolve. As such changes occur, a new version of the privacy policy must be drafted to replace the older version. Replacement of the policy must occur systematically across all areas of posting (physical and electronic) to reduce the risk that representations made under different versions of the policy will be implemented. Privacy policies should reflect the policy revision date along with a version number, if used.

For compliance purposes, it is useful to save and store older versions of the privacy policy and its associated notice. These earlier versions may be useful internally, for example, to show what representations have been made in connection with which customer transactions. The earlier versions may also be useful in the event of an enforcement action, to reduce the risk that the company will be held to an incorrect set of representations. Data should only be used in compliance with the policy notice in effect at the time the data was collected, unless the data subject later agrees to the terms of a revised notice.

4.6 Managing User Preferences and Access Requests

In following their privacy policies, organizations can face management challenges on topics including how to manage user preferences and respond to requests for access and correction. Legal rules may set basic requirements for what must be done, but privacy professionals must often choose options within those requirements and ensure that implementation occurs correctly. The discussion here illustrates major areas where user preferences are handled through opt-in, opt-out or no option, and then examines management issues for handling user preferences and customer access and redress requests.

4.6.1 Opt-in, Opt-out and No Option

Privacy professionals should become aware of situations that call for different approaches to user preferences, notably an opt-in (also called affirmative or express consent), an opt-out, or no option for the consumer.

Some U.S. privacy laws require **affirmative consumer consent**, or **opt-in**, before data is used or collected. For instance, COPPA requires express consent from a parent before a child's PI is collected.[21] HIPAA requires opt-in consent before personal health information is disclosed to third parties, subject to important exceptions.[22] The Fair Credit Reporting Act (FCRA) requires opt-in before a consumer's credit report may be provided to an employer, lender or other authorized recipient.[23] As discussed above, the FTC believes that opt-in consent should occur before PI collected under one privacy notice is processed under a materially changed privacy notice.

Some industry segments commonly employ opt-in, such as email marketers who send a confirmation email requiring a response from the subscriber before the subscriber receives actual marketing emails. This email approach is sometimes called "double opt-in" or "confirmed opt-in," because a consumer first indicates interest in the mailing list and then confirms that interest in response to the follow-up email. In addition, the EU takes a general position that opt-in consent is the appropriate way for marketing to occur, and this position is underscored in the General Data Protection Regulation (GDPR). Opt-in is often the preferred consent mechanism when collecting sensitive information such as a customer's geolocation data.

On the other extreme, **no consumer choice**, or **no option**, is expected in a range of situations. The 2010 preliminary FTC staff report, "Protecting Consumer Privacy in an Era of Rapid Change," called these situations "commonly accepted practices." In such situations, an organization has been given implied authority to share PI. For example, a consumer who orders a product online expects her PI to be shared with the shipping company, the credit card processor and others who are engaged in fulfilling the transactions. The consumer does not expect to have to sign an opt-in or be offered an opt-out option for the shipping company to learn the address. In addition to product fulfillment, other examples provided by the FTC include "internal operations such as improving services offered, fraud prevention, legal compliance and first-party marketing" by the seller to the customer.[24] The FTC received public comments that the term *commonly accepted practices* would not work well for companies providing innovative services. The final report, in 2012, addressed the same issue by saying: "Companies do not need to provide choice before collecting and using consumers' data for practices that are consistent with the context of the transaction, consistent with the company's relationship with the consumer, or as required or specifically authorized by law."[25]

It is common practice for companies to offer an **opt-out**, sometimes referred to as **consumer choice**, before customer information is sold or shared with third parties. This privacy notice creates an enforceable promise. If an individual sells the information for individuals who have opted out, the FTC or state enforcers may bring suit under the unfair and deceptive trade practices laws.

Some U.S. statutes require that a company provide at least an opt-out. For example, GLBA requires an opt-out before transferring the PI of a customer of a financial institution to an unaffiliated third party for the latter's own use. The Video Privacy Protection Act requires an opt-out before covered movie and other rental data is provided to a third party. The CAN-SPAM Act requires email marketers to provide an opt-out. The Do Not Call rules provide the opportunity to opt out of telemarketing phone calls, both in general or on a company-by-company basis.

Opt-outs are required for companies that subscribe to any of a number of self-regulatory systems. For instance, the Data & Marketing Association has long operated an opt-out system for consumers who do not wish to receive commercial mail sent to their homes.[26] The Network Advertising Initiative,[27] TrustArc,[28] and the Digital Advertising Alliance[29] operate opt-out systems in connection with online advertising.

4.6.2 Managing User Preferences

Effective management of user preferences can become quite challenging, especially for organizations that interact with their customers with multiple channels and for multiple products. The following are some of these challenges:

1. The **scope** of an opt-out or another user preference can vary. As mentioned above, financial institutions must provide an opt-out by law prior to sharing personal information with third parties, but sharing with affiliates can be done without offering such an opt-out. An organization must decide how broadly an opt-out or another user preference will apply. Some opt-out rules are by channel, such as specific limits on phone calls or commercial emails.

2. The **mechanism** for providing an opt-out or another user preference can also vary. A good rule of thumb is that the channel for marketing should be the channel for exercising a user preference. This rule is written into law for the CAN-SPAM Act, where an email solicitation must be exercisable by the consumer through an online mechanism; it is not acceptable under the law to require customers to mail or call in their opt-out.[30] Similarly, if communication with a customer is done via a website, good practice is to enable user preferences to be expressed through a web channel, and not to insist on mailing or a phone call.

3. **Linking** a user's interactions through multiple channels, including in person, by phone, by email or by web, can be a management challenge when customers interact with an organization. Good practice is for the organization to implement the opt-out or other user preference across channels and platforms. Under GLBA a bank receiving an opt-out request from a customer must comply across all communications regardless of the media used to communicate the request.[31]

4. The **time period** for implementing user preferences is sometimes provided by law. For instance, the CAN-SPAM Act and Telemarketing Sales Rules mandate specific time periods for processing customer preferences.[32]

5. **Third-party vendors** often process PI on behalf of the company that has the customer relationship. In such instances, the user preferences expressed to the first organization should be honored by the vendor.[33]

4.6.3 Customer Access and Redress

Some U.S. laws provide consumers with clear rights to access the PI held about them. For instance, individuals have the right to access their credit reports under FCRA and rectify incorrect data.[34] Patients can access their medical records under HIPAA, with records that the patient believes are incorrect noted as such in the patient files.[35] Where customer access is not required under a specific statute, access is included in statements of fair information practices such as the OECD Guidelines and the APEC Principles, and in the EU-U.S. Privacy Shield agreement and the EU Data Protection Directive.[36] Under the Judicial Redress Act of 2015, the United States expressly extended the right to a civil action against a U.S. government agency for qualifying non-U.S. individuals to obtain access to covered records, as well as rectification of incorrect records.[37]

The APEC Principles, which provide guidance on the proper scope of access requests and appropriate exceptions to providing access, provide a good baseline to determine when access requests should be granted.[38]

> *Individuals should be able to:*
>
> a. *obtain from the personal information controller confirmation of whether or not the personal information controller holds personal information about them;*
>
> b. *have communicated to them, after having provided sufficient proof of their identity, personal information about them;*
>
> i. *within a reasonable time;*
>
> ii. *at a charge, if any, that is not excessive;*
>
> iii. *in a reasonable manner; and*
>
> iv. *in a form that is generally understandable;*

c. *challenge the accuracy of information relating to them and, if possible and as appropriate, have the information rectified, completed, amended or deleted.*

Such access and opportunity for correction should be provided except where:

i. *the burden or expense of doing so would be unreasonable or disproportionate to the risks to the individual's privacy in the case in question;*

ii. *the information should not be disclosed due to legal or security reasons or to protect confidential information; or*

iii. *the information privacy of persons other than the individual would be violated.*

If a request under (a) or (b) or a challenge under (c) is denied, the individual should be provided with reasons why and be able to challenge such denial.

4.7 Contract and Vendor Management

Many U.S. organizations elect to outsource information processing to an outside vendor or plan to sell the collected information to a third party. Specific precautions must be taken if a company plans to share personal data with a third-party data processor.[39]

4.7.1 Vendor Contracts

Companies are responsible for the actions of vendors with whom they contract to collect, analyze, catalog or otherwise provide data management services on the company's behalf. The claims in a privacy policy also apply to third parties when they are working with an organization's data. To ensure the responsibility and security of data once it is in the hands of a contractor or vendor, precautions to consider incorporating in written contracts include:

1. **Confidentiality provision.** Contractors and vendors involved in personal information collection for an organization—or with whom an organization shares data—should be required to sign a contract containing a confidentiality provision before engaging in business that uses the information.

2. **No further use of shared information.** The contract with the vendor managing personal information on the organization's behalf should specify that the data be used only for the purposes contracted.
3. **Use of subcontractors.** If the vendor intends to use subcontractors in the collection, use, or processing of personal information, the contractor organization should require all subcontractors to follow the privacy and security protection terms in the vendor's contract (which, in turn, should be consistent with the organization's own privacy protection terms). Vendor contracts should also address whether the data can flow across borders to ensure that the organization's policy on this issue is not violated.
4. **Requirement to notify and to disclose breach.** An organization should require prompt notification in the event of a data breach or breach of contract. Details of the breach should be disclosed promptly and in detail.
5. **Information security provisions.** Contracts may include provisions concerning specific security controls; encryption of data in transit, on media and on portable devices; network security; access controls; segregation of data; employee background checks; audit rights and so on.

4.7.2 Vendor Due Diligence

A procuring organization may have specific standards and processes for vendor selection. A prospective vendor should be evaluated against these standards. Standards for selecting vendors may include:

1. **Reputation.** A vendor's reputation with other companies can be a valuable gauge of the vendor's appropriate collection and use of personal data. Requesting and contacting references can help determine a vendor's reputation.
2. **Financial condition and insurance.** The vendor's finances should be reviewed to ensure the vendor has sufficient resources in the case of a security breach and subsequent litigation. A current and sufficient insurance policy can also protect the procuring organization in the event of a breach.
3. **Information security controls.** A service provider should have sufficient security controls in place to ensure the data is not lost or stolen.
4. **Point of transfer.** The point of transfer between the procuring organization and the vendor is a potential security vulnerability. Mechanisms of secure transfer should be developed and maintained.

5. **Disposal of information.** Appropriate destruction of data and/or information in any format or media is a key component of information management—for both the contracting organization and its vendors. As discussed in Chapter 8, the Disposal Rule under the Fair and Accurate Credit Transactions Act of 2003 sets forth required disposal protections for financial institutions. The Disposal Rule requirements provide a good baseline for disposal of PI more generally.
6. **Employee training and user awareness.** The vendor should have an established system for training its employees about its responsibilities in managing personal or sensitive information.
7. **Vendor incident response.** Because of the potentially significant costs associated with a data breach, the vendor should clearly explain in advance its provisions for responding to any such breach, with required cooperation to meet the organization's business and legal needs.
8. **Audit rights.** Organizations should be able to monitor the vendor's activities to ensure it is complying with contractual obligations. Audit needs can sometimes be satisfied through periodic assessments or reports by independent trusted parties regarding the vendor's practices.

4.8 Global Perspective

Governments around the world vary in their approach to privacy law, policy, and regulation—as was discussed in Chapter 1. Today, more than 100 nations globally have enacted significant privacy laws that apply to companies doing business within their borders (including e-commerce) and with their citizens. As of the writing of this book, the greatest attention has focused on the legal responsibility of companies, including those based in the United States, to comply with the comprehensive EU privacy requirements of the GDPR. Fines for violations of GDPR are based on a company's worldwide revenues, making sanctions significant enough to garner the attention of even the top management in businesses. The EU requirements apply broadly—to companies with assets and employees in the EU, to those who sell to individuals in the EU, as well as to data that has been stored in the EU. The evolving privacy rules outside of the U.S. will often impact business practices that relate to privacy.

4.8.1 General Data Protection Regulation

Key new provisions introduced in the GDPR include: (1) notification of security breaches, (2) new requirements for processors (contractors who act on behalf of data controllers), (3) designation of data protection officers, (4) accountability obligations, (5) rules for international transfers and (6) sanctions of up to four percent of worldwide revenues.[40] The GDPR provides extensions of individual rights, including the right to be forgotten, the right to data portability, and implementation of principles of data protection by design and data protection by default.[41] Under the broad definition in the EU of what companies are covered by the GDPR, companies doing business in the EU have the legal obligation to comply with these comprehensive privacy requirements, subject to potentially very large fines.

4.8.2 Privacy Shield and Other Lawful Bases for Data Transfer

As of the writing of this book, the legal authorization to transfer data between the EU and the United States has transformed from a stable process to one that is in flux. Until 2015, many U.S. companies that did business in the EU participated in the U.S.–EU Safe Harbor program to provide a lawful basis for EU data to be transferred to the United States. In the case of Schrems v. Data Protection Commission, the European Court of Justice struck down the Safe Harbor program in significant part based on U.S. government surveillance concerns raised by the 2013 Snowden disclosures.[42]

As of the writing of this text, the primary lawful bases for transfer of data between the EU and the United States include: (1) the Privacy Shield Framework, (2) Standard Contract Clauses (SCCs) and (3) Binding Corporate Rules (BCRs).[43] As explained below, commentators warn that these methods of data transfer are subject to the same sorts of concerns as those expressed in the Safe Harbor case.[44]

In July 2016, after extensive negotiations, the EU-U.S. Privacy Shield was finalized after its formal adoption by the EU.[45] The agreement sets forth: (1) commitments by U.S. companies, (2) detailed explanations of U.S. laws, and (3) commitments by U.S. authorities. U.S. companies wishing to import personal data from the EU under the Privacy Shield accept obligations on how that data can be used, and those commitments are legally binding and enforceable. The U.S. government, through the Department of Justice and the Office of the Director of National Intelligence, ensures that access for law enforcement and national security purposes is subject to safeguards and oversight mechanisms. An ombudsman will follow up on complaints and inquiries by EU individuals. EU individuals who believe their data has been misused will have several avenues of redress, including cost-free alternative dispute resolution.[46] In 2017, the Privacy Shield passed its first review by EU and U.S. officials.[47]

Other mechanisms exist for lawful transfers of personal data from the EU to the United States. The most widely used have been SCCs, where a company contractually promises to comply with EU law and submit to the supervision of an EU privacy supervisory agency.[48] BCRs are an additional basis for transferring data, providing that a multinational company can transfer data between countries after certification of its practices by an EU privacy supervisory agency.[49]

A pending lawsuit regarding the lawfulness of standard contract clauses (along with litigation about the Privacy Shield[50]) could have a major impact on future mechanisms for data transfers between the EU and the United States.[51] In a case dubbed Schrems II, the legality of SCCs has been challenged in the EU, again based largely on the fact that the U.S. government can conduct national security surveillance on data that enters the country.[52] At the time of this writing, the case has been referred to the EU's highest court, the European Court of Justice, to determine whether SCCs may be used to transfer data to the United States.[53] The implications of the decision could be staggering if the EU's highest court decides to limit flows of personal data based on the existence of U.S. surveillance practices.[54] In essence, the court's opinion could invalidate all legal bases for transfer of data to the United States, as well as to all countries outside of the EU who provide less protections against government surveillance than the United States.[55]

4.9 Conclusion

Effective information management addresses legal and reputational risks while using information appropriately to meet the organization's goals. Protection of privacy requires far more than the writing of policies that comply with applicable law; actual implementation must occur within the fast-paced and demanding setting of modern business. By designing and implementing a good information management program, privacy professionals can play a vital role in helping their companies achieve both business success and good privacy practices. For companies doing business outside of the United States, an increasingly important aspect of information management is ensuring compliance with the laws in non-U.S. countries, and specifically with rules governing international data flows.

Endnotes

1 Ponnurangam Kumaraguru and Lorrie Faith Cranor, *Privacy Indexes: A Survey of Westin's Studies*, Carnegie Mellon University, Institute for Software Research International, (2005), www.casos.cs.cmu.edu/publications/papers/CMU-ISRI-05-138.pdf (accessed November 2017).

2 "Treasury Announces Steps to Increase Privacy Protections," U.S. Treasury Department, (2000), https://www.treasury.gov/press-center/press-releases/Pages/ls859.aspx (accessed November 2017).

3 According to Statista.com, the global social network penetration was 31 percent in 2016. In the U.S., the rate was 78 percent. https://www.statista.com/topics/1164/social-networks/ (accessed November 2017).

4 Lee Rainie, "The State of Privacy in Post-Snowden America," Pew Research Center (September 21, 2016), www.pewresearch.org/fact-tank/2016/09/21/the-state-of-privacy-in-america/ (accessed November 2017).

5 The National Institute of Standards and Technology's (NIST) Cybersecurity Framework is a guide for best practices. Cybersecurity Framework, NIST, https://www.nist.gov/cyberframework (accessed November 2017).

6 The NIST Cybersecurity Framework is an example of a voluntary standard developed in partnership between the U.S. federal government and the private sector. Cybersecurity Framework, NIST, https://www.nist.gov/cyberframework (accessed December 2016). An example of mandatory requirements can be found in the EU, where recently approved rules impose security and reporting obligations on companies, which are implemented through national legislation. "The Directive on Security of Network and Information Systems," EU, https://ec.europa.eu/digital-single-market/en/network-and-information-security-nis-directive (accessed November 2017).

7 The consent orders entered into between the FTC and various companies have placed compliance and reporting requirements on the companies for 20 years. *See* In the Matter of Facebook, https://www.ftc.gov/sites/default/files/documents/cases/2011/11/111129facebookagree.pdf (accessed November 2017); United States of America v. InMobi Pte Ltd., https://www.ftc.gov/system/files/documents/cases/160622inmobistip.pdf (accessed November 2017).

8 PCI Security, https://www.pcisecuritystandards.org/pci_security/ (accessed November 2017).

9 Cara McGoogan, "WhatsApp Met with Backlash After Giving Users' Data to Facebook," *The Telegraph,* August 26, 2016, www.telegraph.co.uk/technology/2016/08/26/whatsapp-met-with-backlash-after-giving-users-data-to-facebook/ (accessed November 2017).

10 A detailed analysis of enforcement actions can be found in Chapter 3.

11 *Realising Opportunities with Personal Information in a Privacy Friendly Way,* New Zealand Government, https://www.ict.govt.nz/assets/GCPO/Privacy-Realising-opportunities-with-personal-information.pdf (accessed November 2017).

12 Mehmet Munur, Sarah Branam and Matt Mkrobrad, "Best Practices in Drafting Plain-Language and Layered Privacy Policies" (2012), https://iapp.org/news/a/2012-09-13-best-practices-in-drafting-plain-language-and-layered-privacy/ (accessed November 2017).

13 The requirements of state laws in the U.S. vary considerably. A listing can be found at the website maintained by the National Conference of State Legislatures (NCSL). Security Breach Notification Laws, NCSL, www.ncsl.org/research/telecommunications-and-information-technology/security-breach-notification-laws.aspx (accessed November 2017). For a detailed discussion of the topic, see Chapter 6.

14 For example, the FCRA requires delinquent debts to be removed from credit reports after seven years and bankruptcies to be removed from credit reports after ten years. "Consumer Reports: What Information Furnishers Need to Know," FTC, https://www.ftc.gov/tips-advice/business-center/guidance/consumer-reports-what-information-furnishers-need-know (accessed November 2017).

15 Peter Swire, *From Real-Time Intercepts to Stored Records: Why Encryption Drives the Government to Seek Access to the Cloud* (2012), http://ssrn.com/abstract=2038871.

16 EU Data Protection Directive 95/46/EC, Article 2, http://eur-lex.europa.eu/legal-content/en/ALL/?uri=CELEX:31995L0046 (accessed November 2017). The General Data Protection Regulation addresses these issues and replaces Directive 95/46/EC. GDPR 2016/679, Article 4, http://eur-lex.europa.eu/legal-content/EN/TXT/?uri=uriserv:OJ.L_.2016.119.01.0001.01.ENG&toc=OJ:L:2016:119:TOC (accessed November 2017).

17 Robert G. Bagnall, *Investment Company Regulation and Compliance Conference: Privacy*, SJ095 ALI-ABA 209 (2004).

18 "Protecting Consumer Privacy in an Era of Rapid Change: Recommendations for Businesses and Policy Makers," FTC (March 2012), https://www.ftc.gov/sites/default/files/documents/reports/federal-trade-commission-report-protecting-consumer-privacy-era-rapid-change-recommendations/120326privacyreport.pdf (accessed November 2017); "Merger and Privacy Promises," FTC (March 25, 2015), https://www.ftc.gov/news-events/blogs/business-blog/2015/03/mergers-privacy-promises (accessed November 2017).

19 GLBA, https://www.gpo.gov/fdsys/pkg/PLAW-106publ102/pdf/PLAW-106publ102.pdf (accessed November 2017).

20 45 C.F.R. § 164.530(b)(1), https://www.law.cornell.edu/cfr/text/45/164.530 (accessed November 2017).

21 Children's Online Privacy Protection Act, http://www.columbia.edu/~mr2651/ecommerce3/2nd/statutes/ChildrenOnlinePrivacyProtectionAct.pdf (accessed November 2017).

22 HIPAA, https://www.gpo.gov/fdsys/pkg/PLAW-104publ191/pdf/PLAW-104publ191.pdf (accessed November 2017).

23 FCRA, https://www.consumer.ftc.gov/articles/pdf-0111-fair-credit-reporting-act.pdf (accessed November 2017).

24 "Protecting Consumer Privacy in an Era of Rapid Change, A Proposed Framework for Businesses and Policymakers," FTC, Preliminary Staff Report, (2010), vi, www.ftc.gov/os/2010/12/101201privacyreport.pdf.

25 "Protecting Consumer Privacy," FTC, (2012), iv.

26 Give your mailbox a makeover, Data & Marketing Association, DMAchoice.org (accessed October 2017).

27 Opt Out of Interest-Based Adverting, Network Advertising Initiative, www.networkadvertising.org/choices/ (accessed November 2017).

28 Your Advertising Choices, TrustArc, https://preferences-mgr.truste.com/ (accessed November 2017).

29 User's Current IBA Status, Digital Advertising Alliance, www.aboutads.info/choices/ (accessed November 2017).

30 CAN-SPAM Act, https://www.ftc.gov/sites/default/files/documents/cases/2007/11/canspam.pdf (accessed November 2017).

31 How to Comply with the Privacy Consumer Financial Information Rule of the Gramm-Leach-Bliley Act, FTC, https://www.ftc.gov/tips-advice/business-center/guidance/how-comply-privacy-consumer-financial-information-rule-gramm (accessed November 2017).

32 CAN-SPAM Act: A Compliance Guide for Business, Federal Trade Commission, https://www.ftc.gov/tips-advice/business-center/guidance/can-spam-act-compliance-guide-business (accessed November 2017).

33 D. Reed Freeman Jr. and Maury Riggan, "A Primer on FTC Expectations for Your Partner and Vendor Relationships: Enforcement Shows You Are Your Brother's Keeper," *Bloomberg BNA*, May 4, 2015, https://www.bna.com/primer-ftc-expectations-n17179926099/ (accessed November 2017).

34 FCRA, https://www.consumer.ftc.gov/articles/pdf-0111-fair-credit-reporting-act.pdf (accessed November 2017).

35 Your Medical Records, HHS.gov, https://www.hhs.gov/hipaa/for-individuals/medical-records/index.html?language=es (accessed November 2017).

36 EU-U.S. Privacy Shield, https://www.commerce.gov/tags/eu-us-privacy-shield (accessed November 2017); EU Data Protection Directive 95/46/EC, http://eur-lex.europa.eu/legal-content/en/ALL/?uri=CELEX:31995L0046 (accessed November 2017). The General Data Protection Regulation replaces Directive 95/46/EC, addressing these issues. Directive 95/46/EC, addressing these issues. General Data Protection Regulation 2016/679, http://eur-lex.europa.eu/legal-content/EN/TXT/?uri=uriserv:OJ.L_.2016.119.01.0001.01.ENG&toc=OJ:L:2016:119:TOC (accessed November 2017).

37 Judicial Redress Act of 2015, codified at 5 U.S.C. § 552a, https://www.congress.gov/114/plaws/publ126/PLAW-114publ126.pdf (accessed November 2017).

38 APEC Privacy Framework, https://www.apec.org/Publications/2017/08/APEC-Privacy-Framework-(2015) (accessed November 2017).

39 Peter Swire, "Vendor Management by Banks: How Law Firms are Affected," ABA Antitrust Meeting, Spring 2016, http://peterswire.net/speeches_post/vendor-management-banks-law-firms-affected/ (accessed November 2017).

40 EU Data Protective Directive, http://eur-lex.europa.eu/legal-content/EN/TXT/?uri=celex:31995L0046 (accessed November 2017).GDPR, http://eur-lex.europa.eu/legal-content/EN/TXT/?uri=uriserv:OJ.L_.2016.119.01.0001.01.ENG&toc=OJ:L:2016:119:TOC (accessed November 2017). For a discussion of the regime in the EU, view Protection of Personal Data, http://ec.europa.eu/justice/data-protection/ (accessed November 2017). GDPR replaces the EU's Data Protection Directive; *see* Jan Dhont, Delphine Charlot and Jon Filipek, "The EU General Data Protection Regulation – Europe Adopts Single Set of Privacy Rules," *Alston & Bird Privacy & Data Security Blog*, www.alstonprivacy.com/the-eu-general-data-protection-regulation-europe-adopts-single-set-of-privacy-rules/ (accessed November 2017).

41 Věra Jourová, "How Does the Data Protection Reform Strengthen Citizens' Rights?" EU (January 2016), http://ec.europa.eu/justice/data-protection/document/factsheets_2016/factsheet_dp_reform_citizens_rights_2016_en.pdf (accessed November 2017).

42 "The Court of Justice Declares that the Commission's US Safe Harbour Decision is Invalid," Court of Justice of the EU (October 6, 2015), https://curia.europa.eu/jcms/upload/docs/application/pdf/2015-10/cp150117en.pdf (accessed November 2017). Even though Edward Snowden's revelations focused on U.S. government surveillance, many countries operate similar programs yet have lesser privacy protections in their constitutions and legal systems. See Global Surveillance Law Comparison Guide, Baker & McKenzie (April 2016), www.bakermckenzie.com/QRGGlobalSurveillanceLawApr16/ (accessed November 2017); Lothar Determann and Karl-Theodor zu Guttenberg, "On War and Peace in Cyberspace: Security, Privacy, Jurisdiction," 41 *Hastings Constitutional Law Quarterly* 1, 4 (2014), https://www.americanbar.org/content/dam/aba/events/labor_law/2015/march/tech/war-peace_in_cyberspace.authcheckdam.pdf (accessed November 2017).

43 Although consent can be a basis to transfer data from the EU to the U.S., valid consent under the GDPR is difficult to obtain. Dr. Detlev Gabel and Tim Hickman, "Chapter 7: Lawful Basis for Processing – Unlocking the EU General Data Protection Regulation," Detailed Analysis Chart, White & Case (July 22, 2016), https://www.whitecase.com/publications/article/chapter-7-lawful-basis-processing-unlocking-eu-general-data-protection (accessed November 2017); *see* Dr. Detlev Gabel and Tim

Hickman, "Chapter 8: Consent—Unlocking the General Data Protection Regulation," Detailed Analysis Chart, White & Case (July 22, 2016), https://www.whitecase.com/publications/article/chapter-8-consent-unlocking-eu-general-data-protection-regulation (accessed November 2017).

44 *See* Peter Swire, "Essay 5: Broader Implications of the Standard Contract Clause Case," Alston & Bird, https://www.alston.com/en/resources/peter-swire-irish-high-court-case-testimony (accessed November 2017); Jones Day, "Looming Ruling on EU Data Transfer Rules Carries Potentially Serious Implications," *JDSupra*, October 17, 2017, https://www.jdsupra.com/legalnews/looming-ruling-on-eu-data-transfer-58017/ (accessed November 2017).

45 Aaron Souppouris, "The EU-US Privacy Shield is up, but its future is in doubt," engadget (July 12, 2016), https://www.engadget.com/2016/07/12/eu-us-privacy-shield-data-protection/ (accessed November 2017).

46 "Privacy Shield Finalized—How Everyone Can Take Advantage of the New European Data Transfer Framework," Bryan Cave (July 15, 2016), https://www.bryancave.com/en/thought-leadership/privacy-shield-finalized-how-everyone-can-take-advantage-of-the.html (accessed November 2017).

47 Swapna Krishna, "US-Europe privacy agreement passes its yearly review," engadget (September 22, 2017), https://www.engadget.com/2017/09/22/privacy-shield-first-year-review/ (accessed November 2017).

48 "Model Contracts for the Transfer of Personal Data to Third Countries," European Commission, http://ec.europa.eu/justice/data-protection/international-transfers/transfer/index_en.htm (accessed November 2017).

49 "Overview of Binding Corporate Rules," European Commission, http://ec.europa.eu/justice/data-protection/international-transfers/binding-corporate-rules/index_en.htm (accessed November 2017).

50 Dr. Detlev Gabel, Robert Blamires and Tim Hickman, "EU-US Privacy Shield challenged," White & Case (November 2, 2016), https://www.whitecase.com/publications/alert/eu-us-privacy-shield-challenged (accessed November 2017).

51 Elaine Edwards, "All You Need to Know in the Max Schrems-Facebook Case," *The Irish Times*, February 6, 2017, www.irishtimes.com/business/technology/all-you-need-to-know-in-the-max-schrems-facebook-case-1.2965482 (accessed November 2017). For a detailed discussion of the case, view "Update on Litigation Involving Facebook Maximilian Schrems," Data Protection Commission, https://www.dataprotection.ie/docs/16-03-2017-Update-on-Litigation-involving-Facebook-and-Maximilian-Schrems/1598.htm (accessed November 2017).

52 *See* Schrems v. Data Protection Commissioner, epic.org, https://epic.org/privacy/intl/schrems/ (accessed November 2017).

53 Natasha Lomas, "Challenge to data transfer tool used by Facebook will go to Europe's highest court," *techcrunch*, October 3, 2017, https://techcrunch.com/2017/10/03/challenge-to-data-transfer-tool-used-by-facebook-will-go-to-europes-top-court/ (accessed November 2017).

54 *See* Peter Swire, "EU Judges US Surveillance Law," *Lawfare*, September 11, 2017, https://www.lawfareblog.com/eu-judges-us-surveillance-law (accessed November 2017).

55 *See* Peter Swire, "Essay 5: Broader Implications of the Standard Contract Clause Case"; Jones Day, "Looming Ruling." A team of Oxford researchers found that the U.S. legal system of foreign intelligence law contains "much clearer rules on the authorization and limits on the collection, use, sharing, and oversight of data relating to foreign nationals than the equivalent laws of almost all EU Member States." Ian Brown, Morton H. Halperin, Ben Hayes, Ben Scott and Mathias Vermeulen,

CHAPTER 5

Online Privacy

Using Personal Information on Websites and Other Internet Technologies

This chapter discusses different facets of online privacy. It begins with an overview of web technologies to provide the technical vocabulary that will enable better understanding of the other topics. The chapter next delves into a range of privacy considerations for online technology, including specialized regimes for children's online privacy and commercial emails. The chapter then looks at online privacy notices and related methods of communication before examining specific mechanisms for the collection and use of electronic data. The chapter concludes with a discussion of digital advertising.

Commercial activity on the Internet began to develop in the mid-1990s and has continued to grow and evolve ever since. Although the technical vocabulary can seem daunting to new privacy professionals, the complexity becomes more manageable as the professional learns to trace personal information from collection, through its various uses, to possible dissemination to third parties, and ultimately to archiving or deletion. These stages in the lifecycle of personal information remain consistent over time even as the precise technologies evolve.

5.1 Overview of Web Technologies

The Internet is a global system of interconnected networks that links billions of computers and devices around the world and can be accessed by computers and other electronic devices anywhere, instantaneously.

The precursor to the Internet we know today was the ARPAnet, a military computer network developed in the early 1960s by the U.S. Advanced Research Projects Agency (ARPA). The ARPAnet established a secure means for the exchange of military information and expanded to scientific research when the National Science Foundation became involved with the network in the early 1970s.[1] Distant in time and size from its origins, the Internet today has the same basic architecture as when it was first designed. Data on the vast network is transferred by shuttling small pieces of information known as data "packets" from one computer to the next. Data is disassembled into packets on transmission, scattered through the network while in transit and then dynamically reassembled upon arrival at the destination computer. The open and dynamic nature of the Internet enables its speed, functionality and continued growth but—as will be described later in this chapter—also exposes it to certain information privacy vulnerabilities.

5.1.1 The World Wide Web

The World Wide Web is an information-sharing model that is built on top of the physical Internet. It was first designed to facilitate the exchange not just of text-based information—as the Internet primarily did originally—but also graphic images, interactive document files and other, "richer" information formats.

5.1.1.1 Historic Development of the Web

By the late 1980s, millions of computers had been connected through the Internet, but it was difficult for these computers to share information. In 1989, an emerging technology called hypertext was used to develop the web.[2]

The web historically functioned based on two key technologies:

1. **Hypertext transfer protocol (HTTP)**, an application protocol that manages data communications over the Internet, defines how messages are formatted and transmitted over a TCP/IP network (defined below) for websites. Further, it defines what actions web servers and web browsers take in response to various commands.

2. **Hypertext markup language (HTML)** is a content-authoring language used to create web pages. The web browser interprets the HTML markup language within a web page to determine how the content on the page should be rendered. Document "tags" can be used to format and lay out a web page's content and to "hyperlink"—connect dynamically—to other web content. Forms, links, pictures and text may all be added with minimal commands. Headings are also embedded into the text and are used by web servers to process commands and return data with each request.[3]

Sir Tim Berners-Lee, a British physicist working out of the Switzerland-based particle physics laboratory known as CERN, developed the HTML authoring language in the early 1990s. Berners-Lee recognized the inherent limitations of the early Internet and advanced the HTML language as a means for research scientists such as himself to dynamically tie documents and files together—a capability he referred to as hyperlinking.

At approximately the same time, the U.S.-based National Center for Supercomputing Applications (NCSA) developed the first web browser application, Mozilla. This browser software offered, for the first time, a user-friendly interface through which the ever-evolving web documents and websites could be viewed from a personal computer. Mark Andreessen, an NCSA student and young author of Mozilla, went on to form Netscape Communications and create the browser that became known as Netscape, a derivative of the earlier Mozilla.

5.1.1.2 Developments in the Technology of the Web

Numerous advancements have occurred since the web's creation. The development of Hyper Text Transfer Protocol Secure (**HTTPS**) allows the transfer of data from a browser to a website over an encrypted connection.[4] By early 2016, HTTPS traffic became greater than HTTP traffic.[5]

HTML has continually evolved since it was first developed in the 1990s. Today, many browsers support features of **HTML5**, the fifth and most recent version of the HTML standard. HTML5 has new capabilities and features, such as the ability to run video, audio and animation directly from websites without the need for a plug-in (a piece of software that runs in the browser and renders media such as audio or video). HTML5 had significant implications for the rapidly expanding mobile ecosystem, as many mobile devices do not support Flash (discussed further below).[6] One important aspect of HTML5 is that it increases security.[7] Another feature of HTML5 is the ability to store information offline, in web applications that can run when not connected to the Internet.[8]

Extensible markup language (XML) is another language that facilitates the transport, creation, retrieval and storage of documents. Like HTML, XML uses tags to describe the contents of a web page or file. HTML describes the content of a web page in terms of how it should be displayed. Unlike HTML, XML describes the content of a web page in terms of the data that is being produced, enabling automatic processing of data in large volumes and necessitating attention to privacy issues.[9]

The web browser software is considered a "web client" application in that it is used by the computer or other device (the "client") to navigate the web and retrieve web content from web servers for viewing. Some web server firewalls also function as a web client.[10] To protect the inner system, the firewall will interact with the inner web proxy as a client and then relay the same request out to the web server. By forcing a two-step process, the inner system never has a direct network connection to the external web.

Two of the more common web-browser-level functions are uniform resource locators (URLs) and hyperlinks.

- A **URL** is the address of documents and other content that are located on a web server. An example of a URL is "https://iapp.org." This URL contains: (1) an HTTPS prefix to indicate its use of the protocol; "www" to signify a location on the World Wide Web, (3) a domain name (e.g., "iapp") and (4) an indicator of the top-level domain (e.g., "com" for a commercial organization, "org" for an organization,"gov" for government,"edu" for an educational institution, or a two-letter country code, such as "uk" for United Kingdom or "jp" for Japan).[11] A URL can also include a "deep link" to a specific page within the domain, such as "news" in "https://iapp.org/news.
- A **hyperlink** is used to connect an end user to other websites, parts of websites, and/or web-enabled services. The URL of another site is embedded in the HTML code of a site so that when a user clicks on the link in the web browser, the end user is transported to the destination website or page.

5.1.2 Web Infrastructure

The web is built from a conglomeration of hardware and software technologies that include server computers, client applications (such as browsers, discussed above) and various networking protocols.

- A **web server** is a computer that is connected to the Internet, hosts web content and is configured to share that content. Documents that are viewed on the web are actually located on individual web servers and accessed by a browser.
- A **proxy server** is an intermediary server that provides a gateway to the web. Employee access to the web often goes through a proxy server. A proxy server typically masks what is happening behind the organization's firewall, so that an outside website sees only the IP address and other characteristics of the proxy server, and not detailed information about which part of an organization is communicating with the outside website. A proxy server generally logs each user interaction, filters out malicious software downloads, and improves performance by caching popular, regularly fetched content.
- **Virtual private networks (VPNs)** are an important category of proxy server, widely used in the United States for employee web access, but not nearly as widely used by consumers. VPNs encrypt the information from the user to the

organization's proxy server, thus masking from the ISP both the content and web destinations of that user.

- **Caching** occurs when web browsers and proxy servers save a local copy of the downloaded content, reducing the need to download the same content again from the web server. To protect privacy, pages that display personal information should be set to prohibit caching.
- A **web server log** is sometimes automatically created when a visitor requests a web page. Examples of the information automatically logged include the IP address of the visitor, the date and time of the web page request, the URL of the requested file, the URL visited immediately prior to the web page request, and the visitor's web browser type and computer operating system. Depending on how the web server is configured, it is possible for personal information such as a user name to appear in web server logs. IP addresses themselves, and thus web server logs containing them, are considered personal information by some regulators but not by others.

The following additional terms are essential to understanding the online privacy concepts to be addressed in this chapter.

- **The Internet protocol (IP)** specifies the format of data packet that travels over the Internet and also provides the appropriate addressing protocol. An IP address is a unique number assigned to each connected device—it is similar to a phone number because the IP address shows where data should be sent from the website.
- An **Internet service provider (ISP)** often assigns a new IP address on a session-by-session basis. When the IP address used by an individual thus shifts with each session, this approach is referred to as a "dynamic" IP address. Conversely, "static" IP addresses have become more common in recent years. A static IP address remains the same over time for a particular device. In such cases, a website can use the static IP address as a way to recognize a device that returns to the site.[12] This persistent link to a device is the basis for the European Union (EU) and some other regulators considering an IP address as personal information, because of the greater likelihood that data can be linked to a specific user.[13] The next generation of the Internet protocol, IPv6, has additional privacy concerns because the address of the computing device is by default based on hardware characteristics of the device's networking interface, allowing for easier tracking of computing devices as they move between networks.[14]

- **Transmission control protocol (TCP)** enables two devices to establish a stream-oriented reliable data connection. A combination of TCP and IP is used to send data over the Internet. Data is sent in the form of packets, which contain message content and a header that specifies the destination of the packet.
- **Transport layer security (TLS)** is a protocol that ensures privacy between a user and a web server. When a server and client communicate, TLS secures the connection to ensure that no third party can eavesdrop on or corrupt the message. TLS is a successor to secure sockets layer (SSL).
- **Javascript** is a scripting language used to produce a more interactive and dynamic website. Javascript has vulnerabilities and problems interacting with some programs and systems.[15] A common malicious practice is cross-site scripting (XSS), which is discussed later in this chapter. Simple additions to coding such as an infinite loop can overwhelm the memory and impose a denial of service attack.[16] Information security professionals should examine the risks that can arise from the use of Javascript.
- **Cascading style sheets (CSS)** is the language used to describe the presentation of web pages. This includes colors, layout and font. This language allows for adaptation of the web page to different types of devices. CSS and HTML are independent of each other.[17]
- **Flash** is a bandwidth-friendly interactive animation and video technology that has been widely used to enliven web pages and advertisements. Compatibility and security problems, however, have led to a decrease in use. Some security experts now discourage users from installing Flash.[18] As HTML5 becomes more widely adopted, and as the mobile computing environment grows, use of external plug-ins such as Flash may diminish.[19] As of the writing of this book, Flash is used in less than 10 percent of websites.[20]

5.2 Privacy Considerations for Online Information

When individuals provide information about themselves through the Internet—whether through a social networking site, online shopping transaction, or otherwise—they reasonably expect this information to be protected. The global nature of the networked technologies today, however, inherently places this information at risk of unauthorized access and use. It is critical that organizations familiarize themselves with common threats to online privacy in order to identify and mitigate these risks.

5.2.1 Threats to Online Privacy

Some threats to online privacy come from **unauthorized access** to a website or other computer system. This access may be criminal behavior, such as fraudulent use of identity credentials and related financial information. **Malware** is a term for software that is designed for malicious purposes, for instance, to provide an attacker unauthorized control over a remote computer. **Phishing** is a term for emails or other communications that are designed to trick a user into believing that he or she should provide a password, account number or other information. The user then typically provides that information to a website controlled by the attacker. **Spear phishing** is a phishing attack that is tailored to the individual user, for example, when an email appears to be from the user's boss instructing the user to provide information.

Social engineering is a general term for how attackers can try to persuade a user to provide information or create some other sort of security vulnerability. The social engineer is intent on gaining access to private information and targets an individual or group within an organization that may have such access. Techniques include using an assumed identity in communications, eavesdropping on private conversations or calls, or impersonating an employee or hired worker.[21]

Social engineering contrasts with a wide array of **technically based attacks** such as structured query language (SQL) injection, cookie poisoning or use of malware. In these attacks, the attacker exploits a technical vulnerability or inserts malicious code. One technical but common threat to online privacy is XSS. XSS is code injected by malicious web users into web pages viewed by other users. Often, the unauthorized content resulting from XSS appears on a web page and looks official, so the users are tricked into thinking the site is legitimate and uncorrupted. XSS is the basis for many convincing phishing attacks and browser exploits.[22]

Other threats to online privacy can come in the ordinary course of an organization's use of personal information. For instance, a website may collect more information about visitors' behavior than is permitted by law, or may misuse information within the organization, in violation of the organization's privacy policies. As technology has evolved, there have been ongoing public debates about the extent of information that is lawful and appropriate to collect when users visit websites.

5.2.2 Online Security

Security administrators and hackers alike use software scripts to probe websites for security vulnerabilities—though with markedly different agendas. A security administrator should use tools to identify system weaknesses so that these can be addressed and rectified. An attacker can, however, use similar tools to exploit weaknesses to gain unauthorized access to the web server.[23] In many respects, this has led to an "arms race" of technical weapons and tactics that pits "white hats" (security practitioners) against "black hats" (hackers and exploit artists).[24]

The web facilitates information exchange between computers. While this provides further communication capability, it also exposes web servers and computers to greater risks. An organization should ensure that proper precautions are taken when it connects its computers to the Internet and the web. To take a familiar example, passwords should not be dictionary words but rather a combination of letters, symbols and numbers that hackers cannot easily guess.

The discussion here addresses who gains access to data collected from the web, the increasing expectation that data be encrypted in transit, issues of authentication and protecting online identity, verification and certification of compliance with the organization's stated practices, and issues of email security.

5.2.2.1 Web Access

An organization should have a comprehensive defense plan and a procedure in place to effectively address information security threats. A wide range of the employees of the organization should be trained in security and aware of the organization's policies, and the overall security plan should extend to multiple areas and combat a variety of attack types. Also, the organization should anticipate that an attacker will utilize more than one method, so the design should have both the depth and the breadth to withstand sophisticated attacks.

These information security principles apply to an organization's website infrastructure. In many respects, websites are more vulnerable to compromise—both internal and external. Websites by design are externally facing and easily accessible through the use of a standard web browser application. This sort of easy external visibility underscores the need for strict technical security and web access policies. The more sensitive the website, the stronger the website authentication should be—requiring more than one form of access credential (e.g., two-factor authentication such as manual password plus token or ID card). Further, consider deploying web forms that use the "password field" in HTML. This approach displays characters such as asterisks and bullets as text is entered, masking the actual characters entered.

Despite their use by website operators as identification mechanisms, web cookies offer imprecise means for authenticating and authorizing end-user access. Cookies can be deleted or blocked by the user. This form of identification also lacks an accurate means of differentiating individual users of a single machine, which occurs when a device is used by multiple people in a household or by different scientists in a research laboratory.

5.2.2.2 Data in Transit—Transport Layer Security

Increasingly, the norm is that data should be encrypted in transit. TLS, mentioned earlier in this chapter, is a standard method for encrypting the transmission of personally identifiable information over the web—including the verification of end user information required for website access.[25] It has replaced SSL, which is no longer considered secure. [26] TLS is widely used for handling transmission of sensitive online data such as passwords or bank account numbers between web computers.

5.2.2.3 Protecting Online Identity

Ultimately, individual end users have considerable responsibility for keeping their information private—and not disclosing it without appropriate consideration. Even if every website offers impeccable security, human error can lead to identity theft or data leaks. The following are standard practices to protect the privacy of information transmitted over the web:

- **Login/password/PINs.** Individuals should use unique passwords whenever possible, change passwords regularly, decline to set a system to "remember my password," and memorize passwords or keep them in secure storage rather than documenting them on paper or conveying them to others. Security professionals suggest the use of a password manager (secure storage for passwords) where the user's passwords are stored locally on his or her machine or smartphones or remotely in a secure cloud.[27]
- **Software.** Individuals should use antivirus and firewall software. In addition, the computer and server operating system and application software should be kept current by installing patches on a consistent basis.
- **Wireless networks (Wi-Fi)** and Bluetooth. Wireless communications are prone to interception by receivers near a Wi-Fi network or Bluetooth connection. In the cat-and-mouse game between attackers and computer security, there have been periods when attackers have been able to listen in on wireless conversations. When deploying these technologies, keep current on the known vulnerabilities.
- **File sharing.** BitTorrent has been used since its development in 2001 for audio peer-to-peer sharing. For those who use BitTorrent and similar services, it is important to use the options available to restrict what files and directories can be accessed by the website and services.[28]

- **Public computers (e.g., in libraries, universities, airline lounges, hotel lobbies).** Individuals should be cautious of the information provided through devices used by others, since they are not personally aware of: (1) how these machines have been configured, (2) who has used them previously or (3) what software (suspect or legitimate) they may host.
- **Public charging stations.** Individuals should be cautious about using public charging stations, because mobile devices that are connected to a USB port are generally programmed to sync, which makes the devices susceptible to malware.[29]
- **Personal information on websites**. Individuals should be cautious about providing personal information unless they know the website is secure.

As identity theft has become more common and companies face legal liability for breaches of inadequately protected databases, more organizations are developing standards for the secure storage of personal information, whether the data is stored internally or via third parties such as subsidiaries and vendors.[30]

5.2.2.4 Online Verification and Certification

Verifying and certifying privacy protections is one way to enhance users' level of trust in online activity. The verification or certification can be done by third-party organizations, known as accreditation or assurance services, or trust seal providers. The third parties evaluate activities, such as the privacy notices of a website, or confirm the absence of viruses or spyware from a software download. The activities are evaluated against predefined industry standards and best practices. Where compliance exists, the third parties then grant the certification. For instance, the third party's name and seal may appear on a website or next to the download link for software.

TrustArc, Norton, and BBBOnline are three examples of third parties that provide online verification and certification services. Each offers an accreditation that sets standards for receiving a trust mark and also provides an independent dispute resolution process in the event of a privacy abuse alleged by an online consumer.[31]

Other self-regulatory regimes include the Network Advertising Initiative, the Data & Marketing Association (formerly Direct Marketing Association), JIPDEC (formerly Japan Information Processing Development Center), European Privacy Seal (EuroPriSe), the Health Information Trust Alliance (HITRUST), and American Institute of Certified Public Accountants.[32]

5.2.2.5 Email Security

The principles of confidentiality, integrity and availability are as important in protecting email as in any other area of web security or information security generally. Confidentiality of email requires protecting it from unauthorized access. Integrity of email involves a guarantee that it has not been modified or destroyed by an unauthorized individual. Availability of email requires that mail servers remain online and able to service the user community.[33]

Some of the common features in email security products today include content filtering services such as antivirus, antispam, HTML tag removal, script removal, blocking of attachments by file type, scanning of inappropriate content, confidentiality checks and disclaimer enforcement.[34] Antispam methods supported by most products include real-time blackhole lists (RBLs), heuristics, confirmation process, Bayesian filtering, open relay protection, size and bandwidth control, and encryption.[35] Many organizations train their employees on how to avoid phishing and spear-phishing attacks.[36]

5.2.3 Online Attacks on Users

Internet users face attacks such as spam, phishing and malware. Many organizations train their staff to identify these attacks to help curb their impact.[37]

5.2.3.1 Spam Email

Spam is unsolicited commercial email. The name is that of a packaged meat product and was first used in the early 1990s in response to an online mass marketing campaign by a U.S. immigration law firm. The firm distributed its message promoting the firm's legal services to thousands of Internet users. Because the Internet in that early period was not used for commercial activity, Internet users responded very negatively. The term they used has become synonymous with unsolicited commercial messages online.

One obvious concern with spam is its sheer volume. Experts estimated that between 100 and 200 billion spam emails were sent globally each day in 2015, constituting approximately 50 percent of global email.[38] Spam clogs user inboxes, taking up the user's time and potentially overflowing available storage and bandwidth. In addition, spam emails can contain software viruses and other malicious code.

In response to this problem, email providers and system operators today deploy sophisticated spam filters. Such filters often examine the content of emails to block messages containing known viruses and other malicious code. Where the sender or content of the email seems likely to indicate spam, the filter can block delivery to the user entirely, or send such emails to a separate "likely spam" folder, which the user can review as desired. Spam filters are often configurable to different levels of strictness, and organizations or individual users can often "train" the spam filter over time to distinguish more accurately between spam and emails that users wish to receive.

Specific laws work together with such technical measures. In the United States, the CAN-SPAM Act requires a commercial email to have a clear and conspicuous way for the user to unsubscribe from future emails. Since the enactment of CAN-SPAM in 2003, commercial companies are required to provide an easy way for users to prevent future emails from that company. Enforcement actions under CAN-SPAM have resulted in high fines and even jail sentences, pushing spammers to countries outside of the United States.

Many business groups have codes of conduct and self-regulatory frameworks in place for commercial email. Common commercial email principles include:

- No false or misleading header information
- No deceptive subject lines
- Opt-out mechanism in each message
- Notification that the message contains an advertisement or promotional information
- Information about the sending organization[39]

5.2.3.2 Phishing

Phishing is the practice of sending a spam email or using a fake website to fraudulently capture sensitive personal information. These emails or websites appear to originate from legitimate organizations—such as recognized banks or retailers—and may include seemingly legitimate trademarks, colors, logos or other corporate signatures. Users are asked to share their account number, credit card details or other sensitive or personal information. The perpetrators can then resell the personal information or use it for illegal activities such as bank fraud or identity theft.[40]

Phishing to perpetrate theft is a crime, and not simply an annoyance or technical threat. Sending an email costs a fraction of a cent, and creating a fake website is fairly inexpensive. This means, for the most part, that a phishing attack is easy and cheap to engineer as well as extremely hard to trace. Even if only a small percentage of recipients respond to requests for personal information, the return on investment can be very high.[41] Phishing has been attractive to criminals because minimal response can result in high returns.[42]

Early phishing attacks were often crudely done, containing typographic and syntactic errors and bad imitations of famous logos. Over time, the quality of the fake emails has improved, so even a sophisticated recipient might believe that the email is from a genuine source.[43]

Spear phishing is a more sophisticated variation on the earlier type of phishing. With spear phishing, the perpetrator crafts an email that specifically targets the recipient—instead of a phishing "net" that scoops up a lot of victims, the spear phishing attack is pointed at a particular victim. For instance, the message may appear to come from the recipient's coworker, or from someone who has recently been in a meeting with the recipient. **Whaling** is a specialized type of spear phishing that is targeted at C-suite executives, celebrities, and politicians. The aim is the same as spear phishing—to use an email or website to obtain personal and/or sensitive information from the victim. The inappropriately obtained information is then used for fraud or other criminal activity.[44]

5.2.3.3 Malware

Malware is a term used to describe malicious software that is designed to disrupt or damage a computer, a network or an electronic device. As mobile devices become increasingly popular, mobile malware has also become more prevalent. Examples of malware include viruses, worms, spyware, and ransomware.[45]

Spyware is software that is downloaded covertly, without the understanding or consent of the end user. Spyware is used to fraudulently collect and use sensitive personal information such as bank account credentials and credit card numbers. Some spyware, for instance, can report each keystroke by a user back to the entity that controls the spyware. Other spyware can take control of the device's camera or microphone, creating audio or video streams without the user's knowledge. Spyware is often installed by "drive-by downloads," where the user never provides consent to the download or is tricked into downloading the software. For example, spyware may be bundled with other software that the user wishes to download.[46] (See Figure 5-1 for an example of a fraudulent spyware message.)

Figure 5-1: False Security Warning

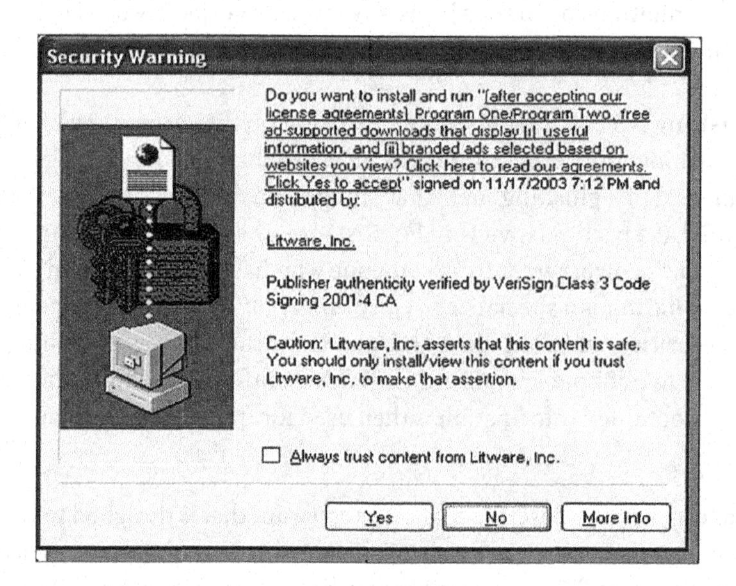

It is important to understand that defining software as spyware is dependent in large part on the intent and knowledge of the user, and whether it is reasonable to believe the user wished to have the information transmitted back to the remote location. There is no simple distinction between illegal or inappropriate spyware and legitimate software that performs user activity monitoring as intended. Spyware cannot be defined simply by the technical act of sending personal information from the user's computer to a remote computer. For instance, a user might wish to have software that allows someone at a remote location to read what is on the screen, for instance, when a computer user receives technical help from a technician who can see the user's screen or each keystroke.

Ransomware is a type of malware with which the malicious actor either (1) locks a user's operating system, restricting the user's access to their data and/or device, or (2) encrypts the data so that the user is prevented from accessing his or her files. As the name implies, the victim is then told to pay a ransom to regain access. For victims who choose to pay the ransom, access may or may not be returned.[47]

By 2016, the annual number of users who had encountered ransomware rose to more than two million.[48] The average amount of ransom paid by a victim has risen to over $500 per attack.[49] The financial impact of ransomware, including both ransoms paid and productivity lost, topped $75 billion per year.[50]

5.2.4 Mobile Online Privacy

Use of mobile devices, often connected to the Internet, has expanded enormously in recent years. Mobile devices such as smartphones, cell phones and tablet computers empower individuals, bringing the advantages of the Internet to daily life.[51] Users have rapidly become accustomed to previously unimaginable capabilities, from accessing real-time maps while driving to asking questions of search engines during social or business events. Today's mobile devices are powerful and complex machines capable of running operating systems and applications that previously were available to individuals primarily through desktop computers.

Mobile devices also present new privacy and security challenges. There are challenging issues regarding how to provide notice on the small screens typical of mobile devices, as discussed below. Geolocation data is a particularly important privacy issue related to mobile devices. Individuals often carry their mobile phones and tablet computers with them during the day. These devices enable tracking of the user's movements at a level of detail rarely available previously. It is notably difficult to anonymize location data—people return often to their homes and workplaces, allowing linkage of location data with identity.

Another set of privacy issues concerns the proper rules for collection, use and storage of location data by mobile phone companies, operating system and application developers, or others who may be authorized to know the location of the device in order to provide mobile service. An additional set of privacy issues concerns the ability of other parties to access that location data or to pay those with location data to place advertisements. Analysts expect location-based services (LBS) to expand rapidly in the coming years. LBS informs users about activities they can do or purchase close to their current location. LBS also present new business opportunities for local businesses and for the intermediaries that link users to businesses, but privacy and security best practices will need to be developed for this evolving industry.[52]

5.2.5 Children's Online Privacy

Many children access the Internet from an early age, raising privacy issues distinct from the data collection and use issues relevant for adults. First, young children may not understand what data is being collected about them and how it is used. Second, even for children who might understand data collection and use, they cannot give meaningful consent to these activities as an adult can. In most countries, children cannot sign binding contracts, and thus meaningful consent to the collection and use of data must be obtained from parents or guardians. Third, children can easily fall victim to criminal behavior online. Unsuspecting young web users might reveal to an online "friend" seemingly innocuous information such as details about their appearance, the name of their schools or the location of their homes—but a malicious web user can appropriate such information to criminal advantage.

One important source of protection for children is for parents to install filtering software on the household computer to block access to certain websites. Limits on a child's access also come from websites themselves. Many websites not designed for children require the user to be of a certain minimum age to access the site. For example, online retailers, app developers, and adult entertainment sites can put restrictions on the ability of minors to access their products or services by requiring credit card information or proof of sufficient age.

In the United States, the Children's Online Privacy Protection Act (COPPA) was passed specifically to protect children's use of the Internet—particularly websites and services targeted toward children. COPPA requires website operators to provide clear and conspicuous notice of the data collection methods employed by the website, including functioning hyperlinks to the website privacy policy on every web page where personal information is collected. It also requires consent by parents prior to collection of personal information for children under the age of 13.

Recognizing that teenagers between the ages of 13 and 18 are not protected under COPPA, states have made efforts to address privacy issues for this age group.[53] As early as the 2000s, state attorneys general have focused their attention on the privacy rights of middle school and high school students. In one multistate enforcement action, more than two-thirds of the states in the country alleged that a company named "Educational Research Center of America" had engaged in a deceptive trade practice when it requested middle school and high school students to fill out surveys that appeared to be meant for colleges or universities when, in fact, the personal information of the students was collected for advertisers. In the settlement, the company agreed to reform its practices, to pay a civil penalty, and to be subject to monitoring.[54] In addition, at least two states have adopted legislation to address online privacy of teenagers.[55] Under California's Privacy Rights for California Minors in the Digital World, individuals under the age of 18 have the right to request removal of information posted online. The statute prohibits online advertising to minors related to products that these consumers are not legally permitted to buy and also restricts certain online advertising practices based on the minors' personal information.[56] Delaware's Online and Personal Privacy Protection Act contains similar categories of restrictions related to advertising to minors.[57]

In countries with comprehensive data protection regimes, there have often been no specific laws governing collection and use of personal information from children. In such settings, general rules about "legitimate" processing of information may lead to more restrictive data practices concerning children.[58]

Neither the safeguards described throughout this book nor relevant privacy laws, however, will completely prevent abuse of children's personal information online. Parents are advised to discuss web "dos and don'ts" with their children. Similarly, parents should become engaged in their children's online activities as well as be cognizant of emerging online threats.

5.3 Online Privacy Notices and Methods for Communication

Online privacy notices play an important role in consumer privacy. An effective online privacy notice provides consumers with easy-to-follow guidance about how their information is being accessed, used and protected. Notices vary in form and length, and are often used together with other indices of certified privacy protection. Notices should be drafted carefully, as regulators and courts often treat them as enforceable promises made by a company.

5.3.1 Web Privacy Notices

A comprehensive privacy statement is the standard mechanism for organizations to articulate their various information practices and communicate them to the public. Such a statement is commonly—though not exclusively—made available on the organization's website. This statement covers:

- Effective date
- Scope of notice
- Types of personal information collected (both actively and passively)
- Information uses and disclosures
- Choices available to the end user
- Methods for accessing, correcting or modifying personal information or preferences
- Methods for contacting the organization or registering a dispute
- Processes for how any policy changes will be communicated to the public

The online trust verification service TrustArc recommends that organizations include the following practices when developing a basic website privacy statement:

- Say what the organization does and do what is stated
- Tailor disclosures to the actual business operations model
- Do not treat privacy statements as disclaimers
- Revisit the privacy statement frequently to ensure it reflects current business and data collection practices
- Communicate these privacy practices to the entire company[59]

Trustmarks

Trustmarks are images or logos that are displayed on websites to indicate that a business is a member of a professional organization or to show that it has passed security and privacy tests. They are designed to give customers confidence that they can safely engage in e-commerce transactions. TrustArc, Norton and the Better Business Bureau are examples of trustmarks.

Consumers have the right to know if their information can be shared with another company or used for a purpose beyond the scope of their relationship with the primary organization.

This principle applies to information gathering that is conducted online. If consumers are aware that the information will be adequately safeguarded, they can make informed decisions about allowing the secondary use of their information.[60] Limiting secondary use of personal information—unless consent is obtained—is one of the fair information practices that were first developed in 1973.[61] These practices are embodied in many national laws, such as the Privacy Act in the United States[62] and the national laws implementing the EU Data Protection Directive,[63] and also in international agreements such as the Organisation for Economic Co-operation and Development (OECD) Guidelines.[64]

5.3.2 Layered Notices

As data practices online have evolved and become more complex, many privacy notices have become quite lengthy. Privacy notices have often been criticized for being written in "legalese"— dense prose, written by lawyers to reduce the risk of enforcement actions and difficult to understand. There is clear evidence that users rarely read these lengthy privacy notices.

- **Layered notices** are a response to problems with a single long notice. The basic idea is to offer "layers" that provide the key points on top in a short notice, but give users the option to read a detailed notice or click through to greater detail on particular parts of the notice.
- The **short notice** is the top layer. Often using a standard format, it summarizes the notice scope as well as basic points about the organization's practices for personal information collection, choice, use and disclosure. Details for contacting the organization on information privacy matters are also included along with links to the full notice.
- The **full notice** is the bottom layer. Often referenced from the short notice via a hyperlink, it is a comprehensive information disclosure that articulates the organization's privacy notice in its entirety. The full notice is thus available for end users who are interested. The full notice also guides an organization's employees on permitted data practices and can be used for accountability by enforcement agencies or the general public.

Organizations help facilitate meaningful choice by using a "just in time" notice, which follows the principle of notice "at or before the point of information collection" or before a user accepts a service or product. Many websites choose to provide a link on every page to cover passive information collection. The best choice is an easy-to-find location, in a font that is no less prominent than other links on the page.

5.3.3 Mobile Privacy Notices

Numerous privacy challenges arise in the mobile environment because of the vast amount of personalized information available on mobile devices. Privacy issues concerning geo-location data were discussed above. Other categories of data are created more often on mobile devices than on traditional computers, including text messages, metadata from telephone calls, medical monitoring, and other information generated by the numerous apps users download.

The small screens available on most mobile devices make notice an especially challenging issue. Small screens make it difficult to convey the amount of information previously provided in privacy notices to laptops and desktops.[65] Because of the complexity of the issues regarding privacy in the mobile environment, the Federal Trade Commission (FTC) has recommended best practices for platforms, advertising networks, app developers, and app developer networks.[66] Overarching principles to address privacy and security in the mobile environment include privacy by design (or even privacy by default), transparency, and simplification of consumer choices.[67]

5.3.4 Customer Access to Information

A privacy notice should lay out what sort of notice customers will receive, and when and how they can access their records. For companies constructing defensible online disclosure schemes, awareness of who has access to web-based information, when they can access it, and why are all important considerations.

The methods for providing access should be accomplished while keeping in mind the possibility that the access request may be made by an unauthorized person for nefarious purposes such as to carry out identity fraud. Methods for triggering access could include requiring the same information as the account (account name and password) and requiring additional information about activity. The information could then be sent to the account or the user could receive a one-time access code to the account.[68]

Some global variation exists in defining the scope of individuals' right to access information about themselves. Data protection and privacy professionals thus should consider which laws and policies apply to an individual's request for access. In the United States, there is no general legal right for individuals to access or correct personal information held about them. Such rights do exist for personal health information covered by the Health Insurance Portability and Accountability Act (HIPAA) medical privacy rule.[69] The Fair Credit Reporting Act (FCRA) also contains detailed access and correction provisions to prevent credit, employment or similar decisions being made based on incorrect personal information.[70] The EU Data Protection Directive implements what the EU considers the data subject's fundamental right to access and correct personal information about the data subject."[71] The Privacy Shield, as an example of a lawful basis for transferring personal data from the EU to the U.S., includes specific provisions about access and correction, as does the Asia-Pacific Economic Cooperation (APEC) Privacy Framework.[72] The latter affirms the basic access principle that individuals should be able to obtain confirmation of whether the data controller holds personal information about them, and should gain access within a reasonable time and in a reasonable manner.[73] The framework sets forth exceptions to the access and correction rights, with language similar to that in the Privacy Shield agreement:

Such access and opportunity for correction should be provided except where:

i. *the burden or expense of doing so would be unreasonable or disproportionate to the risks to the individual's privacy in the case in question;*

ii. *the information should not be disclosed due to legal or security reasons or to protect confidential commercial information; or*

iii. *the information privacy of persons other than the individual would be violated.*[74]

In the event of a denial of access or correction request, the individual should be provided with reasons why and be able to challenge the denial.

5.4 Collection and Use of Electronic Data

The Internet allows the collection of information about consumers' purchasing patterns as well as the ability to target ads based on their searches concerning everything from politics to sports and medical ailments. (Big Data will be discussed in detail in Chapter 13.) With this collection comes both legal and ethical responsibilities.

5.4.1 Online Data Collection

For consumers, the most visible mechanism for capturing end user information online is through the use of web forms, as shown in Figure 5-2.

Figure 5-2: Web Form Soliciting User Information

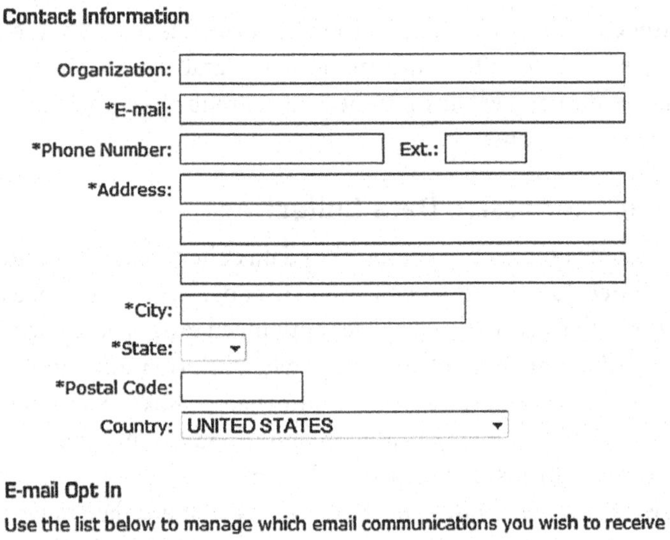

Contact Information

Organization:

*E-mail:

*Phone Number: Ext.:

*Address:

*City:

*State:

*Postal Code:

Country: UNITED STATES

E-mail Opt In

Use the list below to manage which email communications you wish to receive

A **web form** is a portion of a web page that contains blank fields, text boxes, check boxes or other input areas that end users complete by providing data (which may or may not include personal information).

- **One-line** text boxes are used to capture specific pieces of information such as name, city, credit card number or search terms. A label requesting a clear-cut entry is typically present. An important privacy consideration is that limitations should be placed on one-line text boxes to ensure they are used only as intended (e.g., a maximum of 14 characters for a first name). Failure to set such limits can result in security vulnerabilities.
- **Scrolling text boxes** are used to capture a sentence or more of text. These are frequently used when an unspecified answer is desired. For instance, a common use is a request for support. Scrolling text boxes should be used with caution since little control exists over what information a user submits.
- **Checkboxes and radio buttons** are used to collect answers to structured questions. Check boxes allow multiple answers to be selected out of a list of items, while radio buttons limit the user to one answer. Both options are more secure than fields that require the user to type text—the input is limited to the given options, and the content of the answer is not communicated over the web.

When the user completes and submits the web form, it is sent to a web server that processes and stores the submitted information in a database. This information may subsequently be used to process any number of user requests such as site entry, search queries or online transactions.

5.4.2 Active Versus Passive Data Collection

Web forms commonly employ two methods of data collection: active and passive.

Active data collection occurs when the end user deliberately provides information to the website through the use of one of the input mechanisms described above.

Conversely, **passive data collection** occurs when information is gathered automatically— often without the end user's knowledge—as the user navigates from page to page on a website. This is typically accomplished through the use of web cookies or other types of mechanisms that identify a device.

To maximize privacy and reduce exposure in the event of a data breach, web forms should be designed to require only the information that is genuinely needed and should make it clear to the end user what, if anything, is optional. The end user may then provide only the personal information necessary for the transaction.

Further, the form input should be accompanied by a functioning link to the privacy statement (known formally as "notice at the point of collection"). The privacy statement should give the user a clear idea of how the data is used and who will have access to the information. The process that users must undergo to view their data should be clear and explicit. One important consideration is that collection of sensitive personal information should be protected by use of secure transmission (e.g., TLS).

The autocomplete function of most web form submission processes should be disabled (or at least masked with asterisks or other obscuring characters) so that sensitive personal information is not exposed on shared computers (such as a machine used jointly by multiple family members for surfing the web). To protect against account access by an unauthorized person, passwords should not be prepopulated in the web form.

A single sign-on service allows one universal service to confirm user authentication.[75] Only one sign-on is required per web session. This practice is risky if the user is on a public computer. Should he or she leave his or her station, another party could access information without proper authorization. A session should be set to time out automatically to reduce this risk.

5.4.3 Desktop Products with Web Interfaces

Today, client software applications enable web-friendly capabilities such as active file types that support live sound and video. "Privacy by design," an approach to systems engineering that takes privacy into account throughout the whole engineering process, should be built into these products at the development phase so the applications can be used safely and appropriately.

- **Office productivity applications** (e.g., word processors and spreadsheets) for many years resided principally on an individual's personal computer. Today, they are also provided through online cloud services such as Google Docs. These products must ensure that the transmission to and from the cloud does not allow the data to leak into unprotected areas and risk capture by unauthorized persons.

- **Media player applications** allow music and video files to be played on a computer or mobile device. The player software must be discriminating in terms of the file formats and sources it imports and stores. For example, a past vulnerability allowed a false music file to be played that created a buffer overflow. Another concern has been the extent to which players allow the unauthorized copying and distribution of copyrighted material.[76]

- **Financial software** and services contain substantial amounts of confidential information. Such services are especially prone to attacks by criminals seeking to take money from accounts. Consequently, their protection is essential. When investigating reports of financial leaks in the past, the U.S. Government Accounting Office has evaluated features a company might use to control financial data. These include the ability to protect data and application programs from unauthorized access; prevent the introduction of unauthorized changes to application and system software; provide segregation of duties involving application programming, system programming, computer operations, information security and quality assurance; ensure recovery of computer processing operations in case of a disaster or other unexpected interruption; and ensure an adequate information security management program.[77]

5.4.4 Third-Party Interactions

The boundaries between websites are becoming blurred through the emergence of syndicated content, web services, co-branded online ventures, widgets, and online advertising networks.[78]

Privacy professionals need to understand these third-party interactions and ensure that the appropriate privacy protections are in place. To the extent technically feasible, it should be clear to end users which entities are capturing or receiving personal information in each of these scenarios—and that such entities accept accountability and fulfill their obligations under contract and applicable law.

Syndicated content is not actually created by the host site, but rather is developed by and/or purchased or licensed from outside sources such as news organizations. One concern with such content is that it might contain malicious code that is then unwittingly incorporated into the organization's own website source code. For example, XSS allows attackers to inject scripts into web pages for malicious purposes, taking advantage of the trust users have for a given site.[79] The users' browsers may have settings that accept cookies or downloads from certain sites and not from others, but attacks such as XSS can smuggle code from such other sites.

Web services facilitate direct communication between computers.[80] They make it possible for organizations to interconnect with their suppliers online, or for users to get content from a site that has contracted with the site the user has selected to visit. The linking organizations need to be particularly conscious of the information that is flowing between the computers, however, as the complexity of the system places both ends of the communication at a greater risk.

Co-branded sites are online partnerships between two or more content or service providers. Sharing of information between the partners is often allowed on co-branded sites as long as it is disclosed in the privacy notice.

Web widgets are applications that can be installed on a web page, blog, social profile or other HTML page. Typically they are executed by the third party, although they appear on the page itself. The application can be executed by the owner of the page to deliver new website features or increased functionality. Widgets are frequently used as tools or content to make the site more dynamic.

Online advertising networks connect online advertisers with web publishers that host advertisements on their sites. The networks enable media buyers to coordinate ad campaigns across sites. Through these targeted campaigns, advertisers can reach broad or focused audiences. Ad networks themselves vary in focus and size. Online advertising is discussed in more detail later in this chapter.

Agent and vendor contracts present a unique set of issues, which are discussed in more detail in Chapter 4. Language in contracts holding software vendors liable for problems that lead to security breaches is becoming more common. Similarly, the contracts may contain provisions that require notification of breaches that occur or patches that are available to repair the software.

5.4.5 Onward Transfers

A final consideration in online data collection is onward transfer of information from the original organization that holds the data to a third party. The organizations that receive the data can be placed in three categories: (1) those who process data on behalf of the original organization; (2) those who receive data related to the original data collection for a distinct reason, such as to ensure payment; and (3) those who receive the data and determine how it shall be used.

The term *processors* comes from EU law, where processors act on behalf of, and are subject to, the direction of the controller. Terms that are similar to processor include *business associate* for hospitals and other entities covered by HIPAA or *service provider* for banks and other financial institutions regulated under The Gramm-Leach-Bliley Act (GLBA). For instance, the original website (under European terminology, the "controller") hires accountants and may use a cloud service to store the data. The accountants and cloud service are processors, who act under the direction of the controller and should not use the data for purposes other than the controller's. The processors are able to use the data for their normal internal processes, such as their own management systems, but may not use the data for other purposes, such as marketing to individuals. In most cases, controllers hire processors without the need to get consent from the individual data subject.

To complete the transaction, secondary organizations may receive and use data about the individual data subjects. Examples related to online commerce include a website's payment processor and a company that delivers packages to customers. Similar to processors, organizations that complete the transaction generally cannot use the individuals' data for their own marketing purposes. In most cases, these organizations are hired by the website without the need for consent from the individual data subject.

Where other third parties receive data to do their own marketing, or further their other purposes, they become controllers as well. For instance, a third party may receive data to conduct a sweepstakes or target marketing to the individuals. In many jurisdictions, including the EU, the original controller remains responsible for proper handling by third parties who receive personal information through onward transfer.[81] In the United States, the FTC considers onward transfer to be the responsibility of the host website—not the third party—and has issued guidance and brought enforcement actions toward this end. Onward transfer of EU data by U.S. companies is addressed as part of the Privacy Shield.[82]

Protection of personal information must be assured—contractually and in practice—in data transfers between an organization's website and such third parties. Moreover, standard practice in many settings is for consumers to be explicitly notified when such transfers occur that (a) their personal information will be in the custody of a third party engaged by the host site and (b) they have the ability to make a choice, typically by opting out, if they desire to prevent the onward transfer.[83]

5.5 Digital Advertising

In recent years, digital advertising—with its industry-specific privacy concerns—has become integral to any discussion of marketing. In 2015, companies spent $182.78 billion on media advertising; $67.27 billion of this amount was spent on digital advertising,[84] with most of the remaining amount spent on TV ads. In 2016, spending on digital advertising comprised 36.7 percent of all U.S. dollars spent on advertising, surpassing that of TV advertising; by the end of 2021, it is predicted that this figure will increase to 51.3 percent.[85]

Digital advertising is composed of desktop/laptop advertising and mobile advertising. An increasingly large portion of the total digital advertising ecosystem is made up of mobile advertising, and this proportion is projected to continue to grow in the near future. In 2014, spending on desktop/laptop advertising amounted to $30.54 billion, while mobile advertising spending lagged behind at $19.15 billion.[86] By

2015, the amount spent on mobile advertising outpaced that spent on desktop/laptop advertising—with advertisers spending $31.59 billion on mobile advertising and only $28.02 billion on desktop/laptop advertising. The projections for 2021 are that mobile advertising will top $65 billion while desktop/laptop advertising will lag behind at less than $29 billion.[87]

Many websites rely on online advertising to fund their services to customers. As technology has evolved, there have been extensive public debates about the proper rules and procedures for targeted online advertising.[88] Proponents of targeted advertising emphasize how it provides value to both the web user and the website operator. Users benefit by seeing more relevant content and advertising; higher ad revenues support a wider range of free content on the Internet. Targeted advertisements support the websites themselves as well as the ecosystem of advertising and other companies that provide support services for websites.[89]

On the other hand, privacy advocates and some regulators have expressed concerns about targeted online advertising. Concerns include the fact that individuals receive unclear notice and often do not know how to choose whether to receive targeted advertisements. When individuals visit a website, they are often unaware that their browsing habits may be tracked by third-party advertising networks. Significant concerns have also been raised about cross-device tracking, a practice that involves advertisers mapping users as they move between devices such as laptops and smartphones, and cross-context tracking, a practice where advertisers also gather information as users move among different online environments such as search engines and social media sites.[90]

Although industry has provided mechanisms for opting out of such networks, regulators have questioned the effectiveness of current mechanisms. The FTC and others have suggested a "Do Not Track" approach, which would allow individuals to make a single choice not to be subjected to targeted online advertising.[91] A prominent self-regulatory effort involves the Digital Advertising Alliance, a coalition of media and advertising organizations that has developed an icon program users can access to obtain information on how to exercise choice with respect to online behavioral advertising.[92] In Europe, Directive 2009/136/EC, also known as the EU Cookie Directive, requires that users give consent before having cookies placed on their computers, thereby preventing cookie tracking of their online activities if they do not opt in.[93]

In addition to advertising techniques such as pop-up ads and "adware," much online advertising has depended on technologies such as cookies, which help a website or advertising network track a user's browsing activities, potentially across multiple websites visited.

Pop-up ads are advertising messages that appear to the end user in a separate browser window in response to browsing behavior or viewing of a site. Pop-up ads were a major advertising technique early in the development of online commerce, but are less prominent today, in part because major web browsers block pop-up ads by default or through easy-to-use controls. Pop-up ads have also sometimes been a symptom of greater problems, such as spyware or other malware.[94]

Adware is software that is installed on a user's computer, often bundled with freeware (free software), such as online games. It monitors the end user's online behavior so that additional advertising can be targeted to that person based on his or her specific interests and behaviors. Unless there is clear consent by users to this monitoring, however, such adware may be considered spyware by privacy enforcement agencies.[95]

5.5.1 Web Cookies

The word *cookie* comes from "magic cookie," a term in programming languages for a piece of information shared between cooperating pieces of software. Cookies are widely used on the Internet to enable someone other than the user to link a computing device to previous web actions by the same device. The standard cookie, or HTML, cookie is a small text file that a web server places on the hard drive of a user's computer. Cookies enable a range of functions, including authentication of web visitors, personalization of content and delivery of targeted advertising. There have been ongoing privacy debates, however, about what constitutes appropriate notice and choice for users for cookies placed on their hard drives.

For purposes of privacy compliance, an ongoing issue has been when and whether information contained in cookies should be considered personal information. In some usage cases, the information clearly is personal information; for instance, a website has an identified transaction with a user, such as a credit card purchase that shows the user's name. If that credit card purchase is linked in the company's database with the information collected through cookies, then all of the information is identifiable. In other settings, however, no name is directly linked to a cookie. The cookie might indicate that a particular computer has visited the same website on several occasions, or show that the same computer has visited a list of different websites. The organization that sets the cookie, however, may have no indication of the name or other identifying information associated with that computer.

The EU, in its Electronic Privacy Directive of 2002, has taken the position that information stored in cookies is generally personal data, so that individual consent is needed before the cookie can be placed on a user's hard drive.[96] How and when to implement such consent has been the topic of ongoing uncertainty, including for websites that operate outside of the EU but have EU visitors. As of the writing of this book, the EU is considering revisions to the E-Privacy Directive.

In recognition of possible privacy issues related to cookies, web browsers have created user controls for cookies. Individuals can thus choose when to have explicit notice that a cookie is being set, can view cookies stored on their hard drive, and can choose whether or not to permit cookies to be set by default. Users can also delete the cookies stored on their hard drive.

From a best practices standpoint, web cookies should:

- Not store unencrypted personal information
- Provide adequate notice of their usage
- Use a persistent variation only if the need justifies it (see below)
- Not set long expiration dates
- Disclose the involvement of a third-party cookie provider (if applicable) as well as an opt-out (or in Europe, an opt-in) mechanism for delivery from that third party

Several varieties of the standard web cookie files, also known as HTML cookies, are used widely on the web. These include session-based and persistent cookies (relating to the time and duration of cookie deployment) as well as first-party and third-party cookies (relating to the organization that originated the cookie file delivery).

A **session cookie** is stored only while the user is connected to the particular web server—the cookie is deleted when the user closes the web browser. Session cookies address a basic problem—a website has no way to know automatically that it is the same device, operated for the same user, that asks for one page after another. For instance, session cookies are used in online shopping carts—the software that enables a user to select items from an online store, pay for them, and arrange for delivery. Without a cookie, the website has no easy and effective way to know that each item in the shopping cart is for the same user, and to list the contents of the shopping cart, when complete, for payment. Other common uses of session cookies include managing chat sessions (to ensure that the same device sends and receives messages for each user name) and supporting interactive opinion surveys conducted by market research organizations. Because session cookies expire when the browser closes, they do not identify a device over time, and so have not been the subject of most privacy debates about cookies.

A **persistent cookie** is set to expire at some point in the future, from a few minutes to days or even years from initial delivery. Until expiration, the organization that set the cookie can recognize that it is the same cookie on the same device, and thus often the same user, that earlier visited the website.

The use of persistent cookies has expanded significantly over time. They are the standard mechanisms for authenticating return visitors to websites where a user has an account, including social networking sites, music sites, e-commerce sites and many other sites. Persistent cookies enable personalization, so the website displays different content or a different format based on an individual's prior interactions with that site. For instance, a news site might be personalized to feature news about a person's favorite sports teams or other topics of interest. Persistent cookies are also used by online advertising networks to recognize when the same device has visited one of the websites that has a contract with that network. The advertising network may keep a history of what ads have previously been sent to that device and can tailor subsequent ads based on this history.

A **first-party cookie** is set and read by the web server hosting the website the user is visiting. For instance, an online retailer or government agency can set a first-party cookie on the hard drive of a user who chooses to visit the retailer's or agency's site.

Conversely, a **third-party cookie** is set and read by or on behalf of a party other than the web server that is providing a service. (The second party is understood to be the user who is surfing the web.) Online advertising networks set third-party cookies, as do companies that provide analytics of web usage across sites. Some websites enable widgets or other software that appears on the first party's website but interacts with a third party, which may set a third-party cookie.

A **Flash cookie** is a different technology. Flash cookies are stored and accessed by Adobe Flash, a browser plug-in historically used by many Internet sites. While online, an individual's Internet browser collects and stores information from sites visited in the form of cache, or cookies.

Traditional HTML cookies, as previously discussed in this chapter, can be deleted. A Flash cookie, however, is stored outside the Internet browser's control, meaning individuals cannot delete the Flash cookies directly through the browser. Additionally, individuals are not notified when Flash cookies are stored, and these cookies do not expire. Flash cookies can be used to track an individual's actions and to store the same information stored in a normal HTML cookie. Thus, when an individual deletes the HTML cookie, websites can use the Flash cookies to "respawn" the information that was stored in the HTML cookie. This raises serious privacy implications for individuals, who under current technology have little control over the use of such cookies, and whose privacy choices about cookies can thus be circumvented.[97]

5.5.2 Web Beacons

Another online identification mechanism is called a web beacon. Known also as a web bug, pixel tag or clear GIF, a web beacon is a clear, one-pixel-by-one-pixel graphic image that is delivered through a web browser or HTML-compliant email client application to an end user's computer—usually as part of a web page request or in an HTML email message, respectively.

The web beacon operates as a tag that records an end user's visit to a particular web page. It is also often used in conjunction with a web cookie and provided as part of a third-party tracking service. Web beacons provide an ability to produce specific profiles of user behavior in combination with web server logs. Common usage scenarios for web beacons include online ad impression counting, file download monitoring and ad campaign performance management (e.g., clickthrough rates, ad frequency limitation). Web beacons also can report to the sender about which emails are read by recipients.

Privacy considerations for web beacons are similar to those for cookies, notably how to meet a jurisdiction's requirements. Some sort of notice is important because the clear pixel of a web beacon is quite literally invisible to the end user.

5.5.3 Digital Fingerprinting

Digital fingerprinting can identify a device based on information revealed to the website by the user. When a web page is requested, there is no automatic identification of who is seeking to download the content. The web server, though, typically receives certain information connected to the request, and maintains logs, which are used for security and system maintenance purposes. These log files generally include the IP address of the visitor, the date and time stamp of the page request, the URL of the requested page or file, the URL of the page the visitor came from immediately before the visit (i.e., the referrer URL), the visitor's web browser type version, and the web user's computer operating system.

The website also receives more detailed information, such as the particular fonts used by the requesting computer, which can in some cases be used to "fingerprint" a device. This more detailed information varies enough among computing devices that two devices are unlikely to be the same. This digital fingerprinting has been used as a security technique by financial and other institutions so that an account holder is asked for additional security assurances before logging on from a new device. In contrast to this security benefit, some privacy enforcement agencies have questioned what would constitute sufficient notice and consent for digital fingerprinting techniques to be used for targeted advertising.

5.5.4 Search Engines

Specific issues about search engine privacy have been raised by regulators and privacy advocates. The use of personal information in connection with search engines is important because of the central role search engines perform in determining how people access information on the Internet. When using cookies or other tracking techniques, the issues concerning search engines are generally similar to those for cookies, as discussed above.

Some privacy issues, however, are more specific to search engines. The content of the search may give clues about a searcher's identity, for instance through "vanity" searches (where users look up their own names), as may search patterns around a person's address or workplace. The content of searches may also include information considered sensitive for privacy purposes in a particular country, such as medical information or a person's political views. To address such concerns, major search engines have adopted measures to encrypt searches and to anonymize them after a defined period such as an agreed-upon number of months.

5.5.5 Online Social Networking

Online social networks are services or platforms that build on and expand traditional social networks established in everyday life. These websites establish forums for connecting with friends, family, colleagues and others. Popular social networks include Facebook, LinkedIn, Twitter and WhatsApp.

While their technological features are similar, the cultures of different social networks are varied. Some sites enhance preexisting social networks; others allow strangers to connect based on shared interests or views. Some social networks, such as Facebook, cater to large and diverse populations. Others are targeted at specific audiences with similar interests or affiliations. Many sites incorporate communication tools, file- and media-sharing capability, and blogging features and allow for mobile access.

Social networks have grown recently and rapidly. For instance, Facebook opened to the general public in 2006, but by 2016 had over 1.79 billion users globally.[98] Online social networks are valuable for facilitating the exchange of information and increasing global connectivity and have become platforms for online games, specialized marketing campaigns, and an increasing array of activities.

These new activities, however, carry with them privacy concerns. The individual has tools for controlling his or her visibility on these networks; however, privacy control mechanisms are not consistent and are still evolving.[99] Privacy vulnerabilities include the transmission of personal information (by the individual, friends, or others) to unwanted third parties, such as potential employers, law enforcement, or strangers. Information can potentially be passed on or sold to advertisers and intruders may steal passwords or other unencrypted data. Privacy and security standards and best practices are likely to evolve with the continued rapid expansion of online social networks.

5.5.6 Desktop/Laptop Advertising Ecosystem

In the desktop/laptop advertising ecosystem, one of the most common ways advertisers are able to track users' devices and serve targeted advertisements is through the use of cookies.[100] Cookies are used to track the activities of devices as they visit particular web pages, allowing advertisers to build profiles of a device's online activities; these profiles can then be used to create targeted advertising tailored to the user of that device. The greater the amount of data an advertiser has about a user, the more detailed the user's profile will be, thereby leading to more relevant advertising. Data about the user's online activity is combined and analyzed to predict an online behavioral pattern for the user, classifying users into online demographics.

When online advertising began in the 1990s, the desktop/laptop advertising ecosystem was relatively simple. The two principle actors were the advertiser (buying the ad) and the publisher (selling the ad). As the ecosystem to deliver online behavioral advertising has become more complex, additional players have entered the market:

- Supply-side platforms help publishers optimize the yield for each ad space by making inventory available to ad exchanges.
- Demand-side platforms help marketers find their target audience at the best price. They typically do this through real-time bidding across ad exchanges.
- Ad exchanges are online platforms for the buying and selling of ads. Real-time bidding can happen across different ad exchanges.[101]

The desktop/laptop advertising ecosystem has evolved into a complex system with numerous players. Although the system is much more elaborate today, it still does the same basic job of matching supply (publishers) and demand (advertisers) but in a way that now includes verification, management of publishers' inventory and flexibility for advertisers when buying advertisements.[102]

5.5.7 Mobile Advertising Ecosystem

In 2016, industry experts estimated that the average digital consumer owned more than two mobile devices, including smartphones, tablets, and other Internet-connected devices; that number is expected to climb dramatically over the next few years.[103]

With regard to marketing to digital consumers, it is important to understand two key components that differentiate the mobile advertising ecosystem from the better known cookie-based desktop/laptop advertising ecosystem: app-based usage and mobile browser settings. In a mobile operating system, each individual application is run in a separate, secure sandbox. Whereas a mobile browser can use cookies to identify a user across different websites and visits, each mobile app has to create its identifier for a user. This means a single user on three different apps on the same device will appear as three different users.

The sandboxing environment means that a cookie set in one app cannot interact with any other app on the device, making the automatic linking of these cookies difficult. Default mobile browser settings that block third-party cookies automatically also make mobile operating systems more difficult for cookie tracking. Even when those cookies are able to load in a mobile browser, the browser itself is an individual application on a mobile device, in its own sandbox,

Another important aspect of mobile devices is that, compared with nonmobile devices, they can be a rich source of detailed location data. Nearly all mobile devices include a GPS receiver, which is turned on by default. These receivers can be turned off by the user for access by apps, but some location tracking is always enabled for emergency services. GPS data is accurate within a radius of about 10 feet. The permissions for apps to access location information have varied over time and between different operating systems such as Android and iOS.

Location information enables very precise advertising targeting. Location data can also augment search-based advertisements, highlighting ads for nearby businesses during a relevant search. Bluetooth beaconing can even be used to target ads to users in a specific part of a store, or to users who spend a predetermined amount of time in front of a product.[104] A targeted coupon at that moment may be enough to result in a purchase, which is only available due to the location data from the user's device.

Mobile devices can send location data through the device's Wi-Fi receiver. When enabled, the Wi-Fi receiver is continuously searching for available networks in range. Every router in range of the device returns the available network name (or SSID) and the router's device identifier (or MAC address). An advertising tracking company can purchase commercial databases mapping each of these known MAC addresses to their location. That database, combined with the MAC addresses viewed by a mobile device, in effect transmits location data back to the advertising tracking company.

The different identifiers available from a mobile device, combined with location data, allow advertisers to more accurately target ads and collect a broader set of data on devices. For example, once a mobile advertising tracking company can coordinate all its app-specific device IDs, it now has insight into a greater percentage of the device's total complete history of Internet activity. Similarly, these trackers can give information on how often an app is accessed, how long it is used, as well as when a user clicks on a mobile ad. This rich data set is valuable to data analysis, as well as to ad publishers seeking to increase user interaction.[105]

Importantly, mobile device tracking is valuable because mobile devices are rarely shared among users. Unlike a traditional desktop or laptop, which may be shared among the various members of a family, mobile devices are rarely shared in the United States. Therefore, once the device is identified, by default, so is the device's user.[106]

5.5.8 Cross-Device Tracking

Cross-device tracking is a tool an advertising tracking company deploys for combining information about each of a user's devices to track as close to 100 percent of that individual's history of Internet activity as possible. As an individual uses an increasing assortment of Internet-connected devices throughout his or her typical day, each device constitutes a percentage of that user's complete history of Internet activity. Advertisers today are mapping users as they move between devices.

For purposes of building cross-device tracking company's device map, a user who logs in from a new device enables the company to link any unique device identifier, such as a smartphone ID or a static IP address, to the user. The ability of a company to connect a user's devices via login is sometimes called deterministic tracking,[107] because the identical login provides a basis for determining that it is the same user.[108]

Logged-in cross-device tracking can also create a device map around a known identity, rather than just a known account. Social network accounts often include a user's real name, verifiable information on personal details, and other identity-tied data points. Retailers can often connect devices when the same user purchases from both a mobile device and a laptop. Other companies offer a suite of services to logged-in users, so that a login to one service can be linked to the devices used to log in for other services.

A cross-device tracking company can also build a device map without login information based on inferences from other data available from the company. This approach is sometimes called probabilistic tracking, because the links are based on assessments of probabilities rather than deterministically from the same log-in information.

Non-logged-in device maps are still built around an individual user, but without an attached user name account. Instead, the cross-device tracking company will look at all the data it collected and access and use a proprietary algorithm to determine, with some degree of certainty, which devices it believes belongs to the user.

A cross-device tracking company may create a device map to use with its own advertising business or as a commodity to sell to other companies in the advertising ecosystem.[109]

5.6 Conclusion

The continued growth and success of the Internet is due largely to its increasing pervasiveness as a platform for electronic communications, commerce and information exchange. Not surprisingly, privacy and security considerations abound. Web consumers accustomed to submitting information to various service providers in order to obtain desired features and services must be more vigilant about the release of such information. Website operators have a number of legal and practical obligations to ensure that they are capturing personal information for reasonable business purposes and with appropriate notice and choice to the consumer. Legislators and privacy advocates will continue to press for more controls on what information is tracked on the Internet, with the ability for users to make a conscious choice on what information is collected on them, by whom and for what purposes.

Endnotes

1 Jack L. Brock Jr. and Keith A. Rhodes, Testimony Before the Permanent Subcommittee on Investigations, Committee on Governmental Affairs, U.S. Senate, Information Security: Computer Hacker Information Available on the Internet, www.gao.gov/archive/1996/ai96108t.pdf (accessed November 2017).

2 History of the Web, World Wide Web Foundation, https://webfoundation.org/about/vision/history-of-the-web/ (accessed November 2017).

3 "Web Accessibility Best Practices from NASA Webmaster Community," NASA, https://www.hq.nasa.gov/webmaster/accessibility/ (accessed November 2017).

4 "Intro to HTTPS," https://https.cio.gov/faq/ (accessed November 2017).

5 Peter Swire, Justin Hemmings and Alana Kirkland, "Online Privacy and ISPs: ISP Access to Consumer Data is Limited and Often Less than Access by Others," p. 28 (February 29, 2016), www.iisp.gatech.edu/sites/default/files/images/online_privacy_and_isps.pdf (accessed November 2017).

6 HTML5 Introduction, www.w3schools.com/html/html5_intro.asp (accessed November 2017).

7 William West and S. Monisha Pulimood, "Analysis of Privacy and Security in HTML5 Web Storage," https://dl.acm.org/citation.cfm?id=2038791 (accessed November 2017).

8 Recommendations for HTML 5.1 were released in June 2016. "HTML 5.1 expected for release in September 2016," WhatPixel, http://whatpixel.com/html51-expected-release-rc-2016/ (accessed

November 2017); HTML 5.1 W3C Recommendation, https://www.w3.org/TR/html51/ (accessed November 2017).

9 Paul Madsen and Carlisle Adams, XML.com, "Privacy and XML," Part I, April 17, 2002, www.xml.com/pub/a/2002/04/17/privacy.html (accessed November 2017).

10 *Technology Assessment: Cybersecurity for Critical Infrastructure Protection*, General Accounting Office, May 2004, 151,www.gao.gov/new.items/d04321.pdf (accessed November 2017).

11 The International Corporation for Assigned Names and Numbers (ICANN) controls the creation of top-level domains. (The application can be viewed at ICANN's website, www.icann.org.) As of October 2016, Public Technical Identifiers is responsible for the operation of IANA (Internet Assigned Numbers Authority) functions, namely domain names. https://pti.icann.org/ (accessed November 2017).

12 "What is the difference between a static and dynamic IP address?" IP Location, https://www.iplocation.net/static-vs-dynamic-ip-address (accessed November 2017).

13 *See* Lindsey Tonsager, "FTC's Jessica Rich Argues IP Addresses and Other Persistent Identifiers Are 'Personally Identifiable,'" Covington's Inside Privacy (April 29, 2016), https://www.insideprivacy.com/united-states/ftcs-jessica-rich-argues-ip-addresses-and-other-persistent-identifiers-are-personally-identifiable/ (accessed November 2017).

14 "Security versus privacy with IPv6 deployment," *ZDNet*, www.zdnet.com/article/security-versus-privacy-with-ipv6-deployment/ (accessed November 2017); World IPv6 Launch, www.worldipv6launch.org/infographic/ (accessed November 2017).

15 Avinash Kak, "Lecture Notes for Lecture 28: Web Security: Cross-Site Scripting and Other Browser-Side Exploits," Purdue University (April 18, 2017), https://engineering.purdue.edu/kak/compsec/NewLectures/Lecture28.pdf (accessed November 2017).

16 An infinite loop is a piece of coding with a set of instructions that are repeated endlessly, often the result of a coding error. Infinite Loop, *TechTarget*, WhatIs.com, http://whatis.techtarget.com/definition/infinite-loop-endless-loop (accessed November 2017).

17 HTML & CSS, *W3C*, https://www.w3.org/standards/webdesign/htmlcss (accessed November 2017).

18 Matteo Campofiorito, "Pwn2Own 2010—interview with Charlie Miller," *pmi.it* (blog), March 1, 2010, http://blog.pmi.it/01/03/2010/interview-with-charlie-miller-pwn2own/ (accessed November 2017).

19 TRUSTe (now TrustArc), "TRUSTe Guidance on Model Website Disclosures," www.chnm.gmu.edu/digitalhistory/links/pdf/chapter6/6.24c.pdf (accessed November 2017).

20 "Flash is used by 5.5% of all websites." *W3Techs*, https://w3techs.com/technologies/details/cp-flash/all/all (accessed January 2018).

21 George Hulme and Joan Goodchild, "Social Engineering: The basics," *CSO* (August 3, 2017), https://webfoundation.org/about/vision/history-of-the-web/ (accessed November 2017).

22 *See* SebastianZ, "Security 1:1 – Part 2 – Trojans and Other Security Threats," Symantec, December 26, 2013, https://www.symantec.com/connect/articles/security-11-part-2-trojans-and-other-threats (accessed November 2017); SebastianZ, "Security 1:1 – Part 3- Various Types of Network Attacks," Symantec, December 27, 2013, https://www.symantec.com/connect/articles/security-11-part-3-various-types-netwo rk-attacks (accessed November 2017).

23 "Email Security Threats," *SANS.org*, https://www.sans.org/reading-room/whitepapers/email/email-security-threats-1540 (accessed November 2017).

24 In addition, "gray hats" fall into the middle ground, such as by selling or disclosing technical exploits to governments. Kim Zetter, "Hacker Lexicon: What are white hat, grey hat, and black hat hackers?," *Wired*, April 12, 2016, https://www.wired.com/2016/04/hacker-lexicon-white-hat-gray-hat-black-hat-hackers/ (accessed November 2017).

25 Transport Layer Security, https://hpbn.co/transport-layer-security-tls/ (accessed November 2017).

26 In 2015, the Payment Card Industry Security Standards Council (PCI SSC) announced that it no longer considered the SSL protocol to be an acceptable method to protect payment card information. Jeffrey Man, "PCI SSC Announces the End of SSL Usage for the Payment Card Industry," *Tenable Network Security* (blog, February 16, 2015), https://www.tenable.com/blog/pci-ssc-announces-the-end-of-ssl-usage-for-the-payment-card-industry (accessed November 2017).

27 Sharon Profis, "The Guide to Password Security and Why Should You Care," *CNET*, January 1, 2016, https://www.cnet.com/how-to/the-guide-to-password-security-and-why-you-should-care/ (accessed November 2017).

28 Rick Falkvinge, "BitTorrent is fifteen years old. What would a file sharing technology developed today look like?" *Privacy News Online*, https://www.privateinternetaccess.com/blog/2016/07/bittorrent-fifteen-years-old-file-sharing-technology-developed-today-look-like/ (accessed November 2017).

29 Liz Klimas, "Could Your Privacy Be Compromised by Using Public Charging Stations?" the blaze, August 19, 2011, www.theblaze.com/stories/2011/08/19/could-your-privacy-be-compromised-by-using-public-charging-stations/ (accessed November 2017).

30 For additional information on privacy and vendor management, *see* Peter Swire, "Vendor Management by Banks: How Law Firms are Affected," ABA Antitrust Spring Meeting (2016), http://peterswire.net/speeches_post/vendor-management-banks-law-firms-affected/ (accessed November 2017).

31 TrustArc, https://www.trustarc.com/consumer-resources/ (accessed November 2017); Norton, https://www.symantec.com/page.jsp?id=seal-transition# (accessed November 2017); BBBOnline, www.bbb.org/council/for-businesses/national-partnerships/bbbs-industry-self-regulation-solutions/bbbs-online-trustmark-program/ (accessed November 2017).

32 Network Advertising Initiative, www.networkadvertising.org/ (accessed November 2017); Data & Marketing Association, https://thedma.org/ (accessed November 2017); JIPDEC, https://english.jipdec.or.jp/ (accessed November 2017); EuroPriSe, https://www.european-privacy-seal.eu/EPS-en/Home (accessed November 2017); Health Information Trust Alliance, https://hitrustalliance.net/ (accessed November 2017); American Institute of CPAs, https://www.aicpa.org/ (accessed November 2017).

33 "Confidentiality, Integrity, and Availability (CIA triad)," *TechTarget*, http://whatis.techtarget.com/definition/Confidentiality-integrity-and-availability-CIA (accessed November 2017).

34 "Email Security: The Challenges of Network Security," International Journal on Recent and Innovation Trends in Computing and Communication, www.ijritcc.org/download/1434184002.pdf (accessed November 2017).

35 Patrick McDaniel, "Computer and Network Authentication," September 18, 2006, www.patrickmcdaniel.org/pubs/mcdaniel-netauth.pdf (accessed November 2017).

36 Knowledge Base, "What are phishing scams and how can I avoid them?" Indiana University, https://kb.iu.edu/d/arsf (accessed November 2017); "Spear Phishing 101: What is Spear Phishing?" Trend Micro, www.trendmicro.com/vinfo/us/security/news/cyber-attacks/spear-phishing-101-what-is-spear-phishing (accessed November 2017).

37 For an example, view "How to Avoid Being Phished," Georgia Tech, https://security.gatech.edu/how-avoid-being-phished (accessed November 2017).

38 *Internet Security Threat Report*, Symantec, p. 27 (April 2017), https://www.symantec.com/content/dam/symantec/docs/reports/istr-22-2017-en.pdf (accessed November 2017); *Statistics—Proportion of Spam in Email Traffic*, Securelist (First Quarter 2017), https://securelist.com/analysis/quarterly-spam-reports/78221/spam-and-phishing-in-q1-2017/ (accessed November 2017).

39 Jedidiah Bracy, "Will Industry Self-Regulation Be Privacy's Way Forward?" IAPP Privacy Advisor (June 24, 2014), https://iapp.org/news/a/will-industry-self-regulation-be-privacys-way-forward/ (accessed November 2017).

40 Phishing, Consumer Information, FTC (July 2017), https://www.consumer.ftc.gov/articles/0003-phishing (accessed November 2017).

41 Anthony Elledge, "Phishing: An Analysis of a Growing Threat," SANS Institute (May 2004 with an update in January 2007), https://www.sans.org/reading-room/whitepapers/threats/phishing-analysis-growing-problem-1417 (accessed November 2017).

42 Julia Angwin, "Stealthy Tracking Tools Raise Questions About Self-Regulation," *Wall Street Journal*, August 18, 2011, https://blogs.wsj.com/digits/2011/08/18/stealthy-tracking-tools-raise-questions-about-self-regulation/ (accessed November 2017).

43 See "Enterprise Phishing Susceptibility and Resiliency Report," PhishMe (2016), https://phishme.com/enterprise-phishing-susceptibility-report (accessed November 2017).

44 Whaling, Search Security, *TechTarget*, http://searchsecurity.techtarget.com/definition/whaling (accessed November 2017).

45 For a detailed discussion of malware threats, view the Association of Certified Fraud Examiners' training on malware-related threats, www.acfe.com/course_samples/PAECR/presentation_html5.html (accessed November 2017).

46 Jason Glassberg, "What You Need to Know about 'Drive By' Cyber Attacks," *FoxNews*, www.foxbusiness.com/features/2015/02/04/what-need-to-know-about-drive-by-cyber-attacks.html (accessed November 2017). Drive-by downloads can also occur when auto-run software vulnerabilities are exploited. "How AutoRun Malware Became a Problem on Windows, and How it was (Mostly) Fixed," How-To Geek, www.howtogeek.com/203522/how-autorun-malware-became-a-problem-on-windows-and-how-it-was-mostly-fixed/ (accessed November 2017).

47 Sherisse Pham, "What is Ransomware?" *CNNTech*, May 15, 2017, http://money.cnn.com/2017/05/15/technology/ransomware-wannacry-explainer/ (accessed November 2017). For an in-depth discussion of ransomware, view Symantec's White Paper on the subject at /www.symantec.com/content/en/us/enterprise/media/security_response/whitepapers/ISTR2016_Ransomware_and_Businesses.pdf (accessed November 2017).

48 For a detailed discussion, view the report by Kaspersky Lab. *KSN Report: Ransomware in 2014-2016*, https://securelist.com/files/2016/06/KSN_Report_Ransomware_2014-2016_final_ENG.pdf (accessed November 2017).

49 Jonathan Crowe, "Ransomware by the Numbers: Must-Know Ransomware Statistics 2016," Barkly, https://blog.barkly.com/ransomware-statistics-2016 (accessed November 2017).

50 Adam Chandler, "How Ransomware Became a Billion-Dollar Nightmare for Businesses," *The Atlantic*, www.theatlantic.com/business/archive/2016/09/ransomware-us/498602/ (accessed November 2017). The FBI urges businesses to report incidents of ransomware. FBI Public Service Announcement, https://www.ic3.gov/media/2016/160915.aspx (accessed November 2017).

51 By 2015, 92 percent of adults in the U.S. had cell phone, 68 percent owned smartphones, and 45 percent had tablets. *Technology Device Ownership: 2015*, Pew Research Center,www.pewinternet.org/2015/10/29/technology-device-ownership-2015/ (accessed November 2017).

52 Privacy Tracker, "The Next Privacy Frontier: Geolocation," https://iapp.org/news/a/the-next-privacy-frontier-geolocation/ (accessed November 2017). For a more detailed analysis of the issue of geolocation, *see* Peter Swire, Justin Hemmings and Alana Kirkland, "Online Privacy and ISPs," pp. 66-80.

53 Danielle Keats Citron, "The Privacy Policymaking of State Attorneys General," *Notre Dame Law Review* (2016), p. 775-76, http://ndlawreview.org/wp-content/uploads/2017/02/NDL205.pdf (accessed November 2017).

54 In the Matter of Educational Research Center of America, Inc., Assurance of Discontinuance/Assurance of Voluntary Compliance (2008), www.nj.gov/oag/newsreleases08/pr20081030b-ERCA-Settlement.pdf (accessed November 2017).

55 The National Conference of State Legislatures (NCSL) maintains an up-to-date list of state laws related to Children's Online Privacy. State Laws Related to Internet Privacy, NCSL (June 20, 2017), www.ncsl.org/research/telecommunications-and-information-technology/state-laws-related-to-internet-privacy.aspx (accessed November 2017).

56 Calif. Bus. & Prof. Code §§ 22580-22582, http://leginfo.legislature.ca.gov/faces/codes_displayText.xhtml?lawCode=BPC&division=8.&chapter=22.1. (accessed November 2017).

57 Del. Code § 1204C, http://delcode.delaware.gov/title6/c012c/index.shtml (accessed November 2017).

58 The General Data Protection Regulation (GDPR) requires parental permission for the processing of personal data about children. Gabe Maldoff, "Top 10 Operational Impacts of the GDPR: Part 3 – Consent," IAPP (January 12, 2016), https://iapp.org/news/a/top-10-operational-impacts-of-the-gdpr-part-3-consent/ (accessed November 2017).

59 Janlori Goldman, Health Privacy Project, Testimony Before the U.S. House of Representatives Subcommittee on Government Management, Information, and Technology of the Committee on Government Reform and Oversight on "The Consumer Protection and Medical Record Confidentiality Act of 1998," May 14, 1998.

60 Privacy Act of 1974, 5 U.S.C. §552a, (1974), https://www.justice.gov/opcl/privacy-act-1974 (accessed November 2017).

61 "Fair Information Practices" are a set of guidelines for handling, storing, and managing data with privacy, security, and fairness in an information society that is rapidly evolving. Pam Dixon, "A Brief Introduction to Fair Information Practices," World Privacy Forum, https://www.worldprivacyforum.org/2008/01/report-a-brief-introduction-to-fair-information-practices/ (accessed November 2017). To view the code itself, see Code for Fair Information Practices, EPIC, https://www.epic.org/privacy/consumer/code_fair_info.html (accessed November 2017).

62 Privacy Act of 1974, 5 U.S.C. §552a, (1974), https://www.justice.gov/opcl/privacy-act-1974 (accessed November 2017).

63 EU Data Protection Directive, http://eur-lex.europa.eu/legal-content/EN/TXT/?uri=celex:31995L0046 (accessed November 2017). General Data Protection Regulation, http://eur-lex.europa.eu/legal-content/EN/TXT/?uri=uriserv:OJ.L_.2016.119.01.0001.01.ENG&toc=OJ:L:2016:119:TOC (accessed November 2017). For a discussion of the regime in the EU, view Protection of Personal Data, http://ec.europa.eu/justice/data-protection/ (accessed November 2017).

64 The OECD Privacy Framework, https://www.oecd.org/internet/ieconomy/privacy-guidelines.htm (accessed November 2017).

65 Mark Brennan, "Mobile App Privacy Considerations," *Lexis Practice Advisor Journal*, https://www.lexisnexis.com/lexis-practice-advisor/the-journal/b/lpa/archive/2016/11/08/mobile-app-privacy-considerations.aspx (accessed November 2017).

66 "Mobile Privacy Disclosures: Building Trust Though Transparency," FTC, https://www.ftc.gov/sites/default/files/documents/reports/mobile-privacy-disclosures-building-trust-through-transparency-federal-trade-commission-staff-report/130201mobileprivacyreport.pdf (accessed November 2017).

67 *Id.*

68 For a discussion of these concepts, view Sean Price, "Protecting Customer Privacy Information," *IT Today*, www.ittoday.info/Articles/Protecting_Customer_Privacy_Information.htm#.WF2jd1UrKM8 (accessed November 2017).

69 HIPAA Privacy Rule, https://www.hhs.gov/hipaa/for-professionals/privacy/ (accessed November 2017).

70 "Disputing Errors on Credit Reports," FTC, https://www.consumer.ftc.gov/articles/0151-disputing-errors-credit-reports (accessed November 2017).

71 EU Data Protective Directive, http://eur-lex.europa.eu/legal-content/EN/TXT/?uri=celex:31995L0046 (accessed December 2016). General Data Protection Regulation, http://eur-lex.europa.eu/legal-content/EN/TXT/?uri=uriserv:OJ.L_.2016.119.01.0001.01.ENG&toc=OJ:L:2016:119:TOC (accessed November 2017). For a discussion of the regime in the EU, view Protection of Personal Data, http://ec.europa.eu/justice/data-protection/ (accessed November 2017).

72 Guide to EU-U.S. Privacy Shield, EU, http://ec.europa.eu/justice/data-protection/document/citizens-guide_en.pdf (accessed November 2017).

73 APEC Privacy Framework, https://www.apec.org/Publications/2017/08/APEC-Privacy-Framework-(2015)(accessed November 2017).

74 *Id.* at p. 23.

75 "RealNetworks Patches Media-Player Vulnerabilities: After Confirming Three Flaws Uncovered in U.K.," *TechBuilder.org*, February 6, 2004, www.technewsworld.com/story/32797.html (accessed November 2017).

76 "Information Security: Weak Controls Place Interior's Financial and Other Data at Risk," GAO, July 3, 2001, 14, www.iwar.org.uk/comsec/resources/gao/d01615.pdf (accessed November 2017).

77 *PHP Security Guide*, PHP Security Consortium, November 14, 2004, 14, http://shiflett.org/php-security.pdf (accessed November 2017).

78 For an in-depth discussion of the online advertising ecosystem, *see* "Chapter 6: Interest-Based Advertising ("IBA") and Tracking" in Peter Swire, Justin Hemmings and Alana Kirkland, *Online Privacy and ISPs*, pp. 82-88.

79 Usha Ladkani, "Prevent cross-site scripting attacks by encoding HTML responses," IBM DeveloperWorks (July 30, 2013), https://www.ibm.com/developerworks/library/se-prevent/ (accessed November 2017).

80 Daren Lewis, "The Recent Drop in Global Spam Volumes—What Happened?" Symantec.com, October 6, 2010, www.symantec.com/connect/blogs/recent-drop-global-spam-volumes-what-happened.

81 Frequently Asked Questions Relating to Transfers of Personal Data from the EU/EEA to Third Countries, http://ec.europa.eu/justice/policies/privacy/docs/international_transfers_faq/international_transfers_faq.pdf (accessed November 2017).

82 Kelley Drye, "What you need to know about Privacy Shield: An Overview of the New Transatlantic Framework," July 14, 2016, www.kelleydrye.com/publications/client_advisories/1058 (accessed November 2017).

83 This issue is handled differently outside of the U.S. For example, in the EU, transfers to third parties for the latter's purposes are generally prohibited, unless the data subject affirmatively chooses to opt-in to the sharing. Arent Fox, "What the new EU General Data Protection Regulation means for business," *Lexology*, www.lexology.com/library/detail.aspx?g=79064754-96c1-41a2-861d-84dd2a99cd7e (accessed November 2017).

84 This figure includes $7.66 billion in digital video adverting. *Digital video advertising* is a term that refers to advertising that appears on desktops, laptops, and mobile devices before, during and after digital video content in a video player.

85 US Ad Spending: eMarketer's Updated Estimates and Forecast for 2017, *eMarketer*, https://www.emarketer.com/Report/US-Ad-Spending-eMarketers-Updated-Estimates-Forecast-2017/2002134 (accessed November 2017).

86 "US digital display ad spending to surpass search ad spending in 2016," *eMarketer*, www.emarketer.com/Article/US-Digital-Display-Ad-Spending-Surpass-Search-Ad-Spending-2016/1013442 (accessed November 2017).

87 US Ad Spending: eMarketer's Updated Estimates and Forecast for 2017 *eMarketer*, https://www.emarketer.com/Report/US-Ad-Spending-eMarketers-Updated-Estimates-Forecast-2017/2002134 (accessed November 2017).

88 "Protecting Consumer Privacy in an Era of Rapid Change," FTC, Preliminary Staff Report, December 2010, www.ftc.gov/os/2010/12/101201privacyreport.pdf (accessed November 2017).

89 For a detailed discussion of the online advertising ecosystem, view Peter Swire, Justin Hemmings and Alana Kirkland, *Online Privacy and ISPs*, pp. 82-88.

90 For a detailed discussion of cross-device tracking and cross-context tracking, view Peter Swire, Justin Hemmings and Alana Kirkland, *Online Privacy and ISPs*, pp. 101-107, 116-121.

91 Jerry Berman, Center for Democracy and Technology, Testimony Before the Senate Committee on Commerce, Science, and Transportation Subcommittee on Communications on the SPY BLOCK Act, March 23, 2004, https://www.globalsecurity.org/security/library/congress/2004_h/040323-berman.pdf (accessed November 2017). The State of California has a Do Not Track requirement. *Making Your Privacy Practices Public*, https://oag.ca.gov/sites/all/files/agweb/pdfs/cybersecurity/making_your_privacy_practices_public.pdf (accessed November 2017).

92 Frequently Asked Questions about the Digital Advertising Alliance and Its Consumer Choice Tools, www.aboutads.info/how-interest-based-ads-work#about (accessed November 2017).

93 Directive 2009/136/EC, http://eur-lex.europa.eu/legal-content/EN/TXT/?uri=celex%3A32009L0136 (accessed November 2017).

94 Kim Komando, "Five signs your computer is infected," *USA Today*, May 31, 2013, https://www.usatoday.com/story/tech/columnist/komando/2013/05/31/computer-infection-messages-computer/2366835/ (accessed November 2017).

95 "What is Adware?" Kaspersky, https://usa.kaspersky.com/internet-security-center/threats/adware#.WFzZR1UrKM8 (accessed November 2017).

96 Directive 2002/58/EC, http://eur-lex.europa.eu/LexUriServ/LexUriServ.do?uri=CELEX:32002L0058:en:HTML (accessed November 2017).

97 Cleaning Flash cookies, Piriform, https://www.piriform.com/docs/ccleaner/ccleaner-settings/cleaning-flash-cookies (accessed November 2017).

98 "The Top 20 Valuable Facebook Statistics—Updated December 2016," Zephoria, https://zephoria.com/top-15-valuable-facebook-statistics/ (accessed November 2017).

99 An example is the experience of Adam Ghetti that led him to found the data security company, Ionic Security. Ghetti was frustrated that Facebook changed the setup of its privacy settlings, meaning that Ghetti as a user had to manually reset his privacy preferences. Sean Kerner, "Ionic Security Raises $40.1 Million for Enterprise Security Data," *eWeek*, January 13, 2015, www.eweek.com/security/ionic-security-raises-40.1-million-for-enterprise-data-security.html (accessed November 2017).

100 Cookies are small text files that are downloaded onto a user's web browser as the user browses the Internet. Cookies generally do not contain the name of a user, but instead contain a string of text or a unique identifier that is correlated with a particular device.

101 For additional information, view The Display Advertising Technology Landscape, http://www.displayadtech.com/the_display_advertising_technology_landscape#the-display-landscape (accessed November 2017).

102 For a detailed discussion on the desktop/laptop ecosystem, view Peter Swire, Justin Hemmings and Alana Kirkland, *Online Privacy and ISPs.*

103 Although laptops are included in the statistic provided by globalwebindex, these devices have been removed from the quoted number because laptops are discussed in the advertising ecosystem analysis in section 7.1. "Digital consumers own 3.64 connected devices," globalwebindex, www.globalwebindex.net/blog/digital-consumers-own-3.64-connected-devices (accessed November 2017). Predictions suggest there will be four devices per person by 2020. "Four connected devices per person by 2020," *MobileMarketing*, http://mobilemarketingmagazine.com/four-connected-devices-per-person-worldwide-by-2020/ (accessed November 2017).

104 By knowing the three closest cell towers a mobile device is currently accessing, it is possible to calculate the current location of the device through a process known as triangulation. Cell tower triangulation can also provide location information, accurate within a 100-foot radius in urban areas and a greater distance outside of cities. Generally, this information is available to the device's ISP and the operating system, but not to any individual app on the device. This form of mobile-device tracking is more relevant in relation to government actions, discussed in Chapter 12.

105 For a related analysis of personal data gathered by mobile apps, view "Who Knows About Me? A Survey of Behind the Scenes Personal Data Sharing to Third Parties," *Technology Science*, http://techscience.org/a/2015103001/ (accessed November 2017).

106 For a detailed discussion on the mobile advertising ecosystem, view Peter Swire, Justin Hemmings and Alana Kirkland, *Online Privacy and ISPs.*

107 For a PowerPoint presentation discussing cross-device tracking, view "Event Material," FTC, at https://www.ftc.gov/news-events/events-calendar/2015/11/cross-device-tracking (accessed November 2017).

108 Although there is some possibility that more than one person could log into an account, for most practical purposes the same login indicates the same user. For advertising purposes, identities may be considered deterministic even though they are not 100 percent verified.

109 For a detailed discussion on cross-device tracking, view Peter Swire, Justin Hemmings and Alana Kirkland, *Online Privacy and ISPs.*

CHAPTER 6

Information Security and Data Breach Notification Laws

- *Forbes*, January 10, 2014: "Target data breach spilled info on as many as 70 million customers."[1]
- *USA Today*, February 5, 2015: "As many as 80 million customers of the nation's second-largest health insurance company, Anthem Inc., have had their account information stolen.... The hackers gained access to Anthem's computer system and got information including names, birthdays, medical IDs, Social Security numbers, street addresses, email addresses, and employment information, including income data."[2]
- *CNN Money*, September 23, 2016: "Yahoo says 500 million accounts stolen.... The account information may have included names, email addresses, telephone numbers, date of births, hashed passwords, and, in some cases, encrypted or unencrypted security questions and answers."[3]
- *Fortune*, October 2, 2017: "Equifax has revised its estimate for the number of people potentially affected by its recent massive data breach to a total of 145.5 million people, 2.5 million more than it initially reported.... From mid-May through July, an as yet unidentified hacker group gained access to a large swathe of this data—including names, birthdates, street addresses, credit card numbers, and Social Security numbers.[4]

As these examples show, evolving technologies in an interconnected society have created not only new uses of data, but also huge data pools containing personal information. This chapter provides an overview of the information security concepts and laws to which companies must adhere in order to protect this ever-expanding amount of data, as well as data breach notification laws that are triggered when this data is unlawfully accessed. Because a large data breach in an organization can bring privacy professionals into direct contact with the most senior leaders in the organization, understanding data breaches and how to reduce the risks related to them is an important task for many of them.

6.1 Information Security

Information security (IS) is the protection of information for the purpose of preventing loss, unauthorized access or misuse. Information security requires ongoing assessments of threats and risks to information and of the procedures and controls to preserve the information, consistent with three key attributes:

1. **Confidentiality**—access to data is limited to authorized parties
2. **Integrity**—assurance that the data is authentic and complete
3. **Availability**—knowledge that the data is accessible, as needed, by those who are authorized to use it

Information security is achieved by implementing controls, which need to be monitored and reviewed, to ensure that organizational security objectives are met. It is vital to both public and private sector organizations.

Security controls are mechanisms put in place to prevent, detect, or correct a security incident. The three types of security controls are:

1. **Physical controls**—such as locks, security cameras, and fences
2. **Administrative controls**—such as incident response procedures and training
3. **Technical controls**—such as firewalls, antivirus software, and access logs

Information security is different from information privacy. Generally, information security is the protection of personal or other types of information from unauthorized access, use and disclosure. Information privacy notably includes deciding what sorts of use and disclosure of personal information should be authorized. Despite this distinction, the two concepts are similar and overlap in certain respects. Information security is a necessary component of privacy protection—if security is breached, then privacy controls will not be effective. Information privacy and information security both include the use and confidentiality of and access to personal information. Information privacy, however, also involves the data subject's right to control the data, which includes rights to notice and choice.

6.2 Information Security Laws

Although no federal legislation directly imposes information security standards across all industries, the healthcare and financial sectors have federally imposed information security provisions, as will be discussed in Chapter 7 and Chapter 8, respectively. In addition, as discussed in Chapter 3, the Federal trade Commission (FTC) uses its Section 5 power (under the FTC Act) to bring actions against companies misrepresenting their information security practices (as a deceptive trade practice) or failing to provide reasonable procedures to protect personal information (as an unfair trade practice).

6.2.1 State Laws on Information Security Measures

In the absence of comprehensive federal requirements, some state legislatures have passed laws requiring companies to take information security measures to protect citizens' sensitive information. California, a recognized innovator in consumer protection laws, enacted the first state security breach notification law in 2003 and a year later enacted Assembly Bill 1950 (AB 1950) to "encourage businesses that own or license personal information about Californians to provide reasonable security."[5] Specifically, the law requires a business "that owns or licenses personal information about a California resident" to "implement and maintain reasonable security procedures and practices appropriate to the nature of the information, to protect the personal information from unauthorized access, destruction, use, modification, or disclosure."[6] Furthermore, the bill requires businesses using unaffiliated third-party data processors to contractually mandate similar security procedures.

In the security portion of California's law, "personal information" is defined as an individual's name in combination with any one or more of (1) Social Security number, (2) driver's license number or California identification card number, (3) financial account number or credit or debit card number "in combination with any required security code, access code or password that would permit access to an individual's financial account," (4) medical information, (5) health insurance information, and (6) data collected from automated license plate recognition systems.[7] Personal information that is publicly available or encrypted is excluded from the law.

Companies already subject to greater information security requirements such as the Gramm-Leach-Bliley Act, (GLBA) or Health Insurance Portability and Accountability Act (HIPAA) are exempt from the law. Although California's AB 1950 provides no guidance as to what constitutes "reasonable security procedures and practices," California's attorney general issued a report in 2016 that identifies the Center for Internet Security's Critical Security Controls (formerly SANS Top 20) as the minimum level of security needed to comply with the statute.[8] Since California implemented its information security law in 2003, numerous other states have similar laws. [9] To better explain the various requirements found in these laws, this chapter highlights provisions from New York, Massachusetts and Washington.

Although in 2017 New York issued new regulations applying to financial services companies that may become the new standard for strictest state law, the Massachusetts state security law, 201 CMR 17.00, has generally been considered the most prescriptive in the nation.[10] The Massachusetts law establishes detailed minimum standards to "safeguard . . . personal information contained in both paper and electronic records."[11] The law goes beyond breach notification by requiring businesses holding "personal information" (defined as a Massachusetts resident's name plus a sensitive data element, such as a Social Security number) to:

1. Designate an individual who is responsible for information security
2. Anticipate risks to personal information and take appropriate steps to mitigate such risks
3. Develop security program rules
4. Impose penalties for violations of the program rules
5. Prevent access to personal information by former employees
6. Contractually obligate third-party service providers to maintain similar procedures
7. Restrict physical access to records containing personal information
8. Monitor the effectiveness of the security program
9. Review the program at least once a year and whenever business changes could impact security
10. Document responses to incidents[12]

From a technical perspective, 201 CMR 17.00 mandates user authentication, access controls, encryption, monitoring, firewall protection, updates and training. The law came into effect in 2010.

The Washington state security law, House Bill 1149, also took effect in 2010.[13] Along with states including Minnesota and Nevada, Washington is part of a growing trend to incorporate the Payment Card Industry Data Security Standard (PCI DSS) into statute to ensure the security of credit card transactions and related personal information.[14] Washington's HB 1149 permits financial institutions to recover the costs associated with reissuance of credit and debit cards from large processors whose negligence in the handling of credit card data is the proximate cause of the breach. Processors are not liable if the data were encrypted at the time of the breach or had been certified as PCI-compliant within one year of the breach.

6.2.2 Laws Limiting Use of Social Security Numbers

A majority of states have laws limiting businesses' right to use Social Security numbers.[15] California law, for example, prohibits businesses as well as state and local agencies from using Social Security numbers for a variety of purposes including public posting, printing on mailings (unless mandated by federal law) and printing on ID or membership cards.[16] Additionally, this law prohibits businesses from requiring that customers transmit their Social Security number over an unencrypted Internet connection. The federal government has a variety of limits on disclosure of Social Security numbers,[17] including prohibition on having the numbers be visible through the window of Treasury-disbursed check envelopes.[18]

6.3 Types of Data Breach Incidents

Laws that impose security requirements on businesses that process personal information, such as those discussed above, provide some protection of personal information. But even in organizations with extensive security controls, data breaches can occur.

In chronicling data breaches since 2005, the Privacy Rights Clearinghouse lists eight types of incidents:

1. **Unintended disclosure**—sensitive information posted publicly on a website, mishandled or sent to the wrong party via email, fax or mail
2. **Hacking or malware**—electronic entry by an outside party, malware and spyware
3. **Payment card fraud**—fraud involving debit and credit cards that is not accomplished via hacking; for example, skimming devices at point-of-service terminals
4. **Insider**—someone with legitimate access, such as an employee or contractor, intentionally breaching information
5. **Physical loss**—lost, discarded or stolen nonelectronic records such as paper documents;
6. **Portable device**—e.g., lost, discarded or stolen laptop, PDA, smartphone, portable memory device, CD, hard drive, data tape
7. **Stationary device**—lost, discarded or stolen stationary electronic device such as a computer or server not designed for mobility
8. Unknown or other[19]

According to the Identity Theft Resource Center, nearly 40 percent of the data breaches in 2015 were hacking incidents.[20] From 2005 to 2016, the Center tracked more than 6,000 reported breaches affecting more than 860 million records containing personal information.

6.4 Fundamentals of Incident Management for Data Breaches

Regardless of the incident, the privacy professional must be prepared to support, and often lead, company efforts to detect, contain, report and prevent breaches of personal information. Accordingly, the privacy professional must also be familiar with the specific data breach notification requirements of the states in which his or her organization does business or in which it has customers. Data breach notification laws are also spreading outside of the United States, notably including for the European Union, where breach notifications are promptly required for EU customers under the General Data Protection Regulation (GDPR).[21]

The first step in incident management is determining whether a breach has actually occurred.[22] This may be fairly obvious for certain types of breaches, such as a lost laptop containing personal information or a misdirected file. For other breaches, which may be made by attackers testing a system or gaining entry for later use, the existence of a breach can be harder to detect. Evidence of a possible breach could be multiple failed log-in attempts, the sudden use of long-dormant access accounts, or the use of information systems during off-hours. IT managers should be alert for the presence of unknown programs, files, devices or users. Unfortunately, some of the largest breaches can occur as a result of advanced persistent threats that compromise the entire corporate network but are difficult to detect and to evaluate in terms of the personal information that may have been taken.

Once a breach is discovered, **the second step is containment and analysis of the incident.** The steps that need to be taken vary greatly with the nature of the breach. For example, if media or devices are lost, the organization should take whatever steps it can to recover the items. If a file is misdirected, the company should reach out to the actual recipient to confirm that the information has been deleted without use or further disclosure. For a network intrusion, the organization should shut down the infiltrated system or systems and revoke physical access to the area, if applicable. Forensic support may be needed to determine what files were accessed or acquired by the intruder. A full system audit should be performed to ensure that vulnerabilities are not reinstated when the system is back and running. After containment, organizations should engage in careful analysis and documentation of the incident, which can help in later stages of incident management, such as negotiations and litigation.

The third step in incident management is to notify affected parties. Affected individuals and government authorities may need to be notified, as required by laws and regulations, depending on the type of information compromised and the jurisdiction(s) in which the affected individuals reside. A number of states have specific requirements for notification letter contents.[23] These letters should include information on the risks (if any) posed to the individual as a result of the breach along with steps that can be taken to mitigate the harm. In addition, an organization may have contractual obligations to notify impacted third parties consistent with the terms of their agreements with those parties. The timing for notification is critical—there may be specific deadlines for notice upon discovery of an incident (notice is often required without "undue delay"), but premature notice with inaccurate or incomplete facts can exacerbate an already challenging situation.[24] Privacy professionals need to help organizations navigate these risks when providing notice.

Finally, for organizational learning and prevention, **organizations should implement effective follow-up methods**, such as additional training, internal self-assessments and third-party audits where needed. These assessments should analyze the breach itself as well as the response plan and should identify deficiencies. Monitoring or "data loss prevention" systems can also be implemented or expanded to help prevent and mitigate future data breaches.

Organizations may adopt different approaches in their incident response practices, but the fundamentals are generally the same, and practices should be tailored to meet particular business and legal obligations, address likely scenarios and facilitate a methodical and defensible response.

In 2017, the Executive Office of the President's Office of Management and Budget (OMB) updated requirements for federal agencies preparing for and responding to breaches of personally identifiable information (PII).[25] This detailed, public guidance can be a useful template for organizations that are looking for best practices in the development of a security breach plan.[26] The OMB set forth the following framework for a security breach plan:

- Designate the members who will make up a breach response team[27]
- Identify applicable privacy compliance documentation[28]
- Share information concerning the breach to understand the extent of the breach[29]
- Determine what reporting is required[30]

- Assess the risk of harm for individuals potentially affected by the breach[31]
- Mitigate the risk of harm for individuals potentially affected by the breach[32]
- Notify the individuals potentially affected by the breach[33]

OMB policies also focused on the issue of contracts with vendors. From a best-practices perspective, organizations should ensure that vendors are contractually required to do the following: provide training to their employees on identifying and reporting a breach, properly encrypt PII, report suspected or confirmed breaches; participate in the exchange of information in case of a breach, cooperate in the investigation of a breach, and make staff available to participate in the breach response team.[34]

6.5 Lack of Federal Data Breach Law

With massive, high-profile data breaches making the front pages, calls for a uniform federal data breach law have continued.[35] These discussions began at the national level in 2003, when Senator Diane Feinstein of California introduced the first federal breach notification bill. In 2015, President Obama proposed the Personal Data Notification Act,[36] which he said would correct the "patchwork problem" of laws that are said to be confusing for consumers and for companies.[37] The proposal was criticized by state attorneys general and privacy advocates because it would preempt stricter state laws. As of the writing of this book, no federal legislation has been enacted.[38] Reaching consensus on such a law is difficult—privacy advocates have generally supported approaches that would match federal law to the strictest state laws, while businesses have generally supported a federal law with fewer regulatory requirements as well as preemption of stricter state laws.

6.6 State Breach Notification Laws

In the absence of a federal law, states have taken the lead in setting requirements related to data breaches. California enacted the first state-level breach notification law in 2003.[39] As of 2017, 48 of the 50 states, the District of Columbia, Puerto Rico and the U.S. Virgin Islands have enacted state breach notification laws.[40] These laws create important incentives for companies to develop good information security practices. Some states statutes, such as the Massachusetts law described earlier in this chapter, directly require businesses to implement information security controls. Most other state laws do not specifically require information security controls, but instead create an incentive for effective controls—reduce the costs on the company of public disclosure of the breach.[41]

Companies who operate nationally are faced with compliance with all the state data breach laws. When examining these state laws, it is important to realize that state data breach notification laws generally contain the same basic topics:

- The definition of personal information, meaning the specific data elements that trigger reporting requirements
- The definition of what entities are covered
- The definition of a "security breach" or "breach of the security of a system"
- The level of harm requiring notification
- Whom to notify
- When to notify
- What to include in the notification letter
- How to notify
- Exceptions that may exist to the obligation to notify (or when notification may be delayed)
- Penalties and rights of action[42]

We will examine each of these topics, with special reference to the Connecticut law as an example.[43] We will focus on the similarities as well as point out key differences.

6.6.1 Definition of Personal Information

An example of the typical definition of "personal information" is Connecticut's, which defines it as "an individual's first name or first initial and last name in combination with any one, or more, of the following data: (1) Social Security number,[44] (2) driver's license number or state identification card number or (3) account number, credit or debit card number, in combination with any required security code, access code or password that would permit access to an individual's financial account."[45]

These data are part of the definition of personal information in all state data breach notification laws, although more than half contain additional elements.[46] For example, Arkansas, California, Florida, Illinois, Missouri, Montana, Nevada, New Hampshire, North Dakota, Oregon, Rhode Island, Texas, Virginia and Wyoming include medical and healthcare information. The laws in Connecticut, Oregon, Wisconsin and

Wyoming apply to any federal or state identification number, which serves as a catchall for passport numbers, Drug Enforcement Agency (DEA) numbers and other tax identification numbers. Connecticut, Illinois, Iowa, Nebraska, New Mexico, North Carolina, Oregon, Wisconsin and Wyoming include unique biometric data (i.e., a fingerprint, retina or iris image, or other unique physical representation or digital representation of biometric data[47]). Wisconsin specifically lists a DNA profile;[48] Puerto Rico includes tax information and work-related evaluations;[49] and North Dakota adds mother's maiden name (often used as a security question), employee number and digital signature.[50] Numerous state laws focus on both computerized and written material,[51] with Illinois specifically listing both.[52] Laws in other states, such as California, apply only to computerized data.

Almost all states exclude publicly available information, defined often to include information "lawfully made available to the general public from federal, state or local government records or widely distributed media."[53] There are, however, some outliers such as Idaho, Louisiana and Michigan, which do not include such an exception in their laws.[54] Ohio specifically expands its exclusion of publicly available information to include "any news, editorial or advertising statement published in any bona fide newspaper, journal, or magazine, or broadcast over radio or television, or any type of media similar in nature; any gathering or furnishing of information or news by any bona fide reporter, correspondent, or news bureau to any bona fide newspaper, journal, magazine, radio or television news media, or any type of media similar in nature; or any publication designed for and distributed to members of any bona fide association or charitable or fraternal nonprofit corporation, or any type of media similar in nature."[55]

6.6.2 Definition of Covered Entities

Connecticut describes the covered entities subject to its notification law as "any person who conducts business in this state, and who, in the ordinary course of such person's business, owns, licenses or maintains computerized data that includes personal information."[56] Some states limit the definition of covered entities to those that conduct business in that state.[57] Note, however, that some state laws are narrower; the Georgia law, for instance, applies only to information brokers.[58] Texas law specifically requires notification to be sent to residents of other states that do not have a similar law requiring notification.[59]

6.6.3 Harm and Definition of Security Breach

Connecticut defines a "breach" of security as "unauthorized access to or acquisition of electronic files, media, databases or computerized data containing personal information, when access to the personal information has not been secured by encryption or by any other method or technology that renders the personal information unreadable or unusable."[60] In California, a "breach of the security of [a] system" occurs when there is unauthorized acquisition of the personal information that "compromises the confidentiality, security or integrity" of the information.[61] Virtually every state contains similar language, although some laws require the compromised information to be "material" (e.g., in Florida[62]), and several states define breach as an event that causes or is likely to cause identity theft or other material harm (Kansas[63] and South Carolina,[64] for example). Connecticut, California and other states do not have any similar requirement of harm for a defined breach to occur.[65]

6.6.4 Whom to Notify

The primary recipients of a breach notification are state residents who are at risk because their personal information has potentially been exposed based on the level of unauthorized access or harm. The Texas law requires Texas companies that experience a data breach to notify not only Texas residents but also residents of states lacking a data protection notification law.[66]

More than half of the states require entities who detected a data breach to notify the state attorney general (AG) and/or other state agencies:[67]

- California entities must notify the AG if more than 500 California residents are affected. For a medical information breach, the California Department of Health Services must be notified no later than 5 days after the breach. Iowa and Florida have similar laws, although Florida allows 30 days to notify the AG of the breach.
- In Idaho, state agencies suffering a data breach must notify the AG within 24 hours of incident detection. Several other states take a similar approach with somewhat longer time periods for entities to notify the AG: Illinois (5 business days); Louisiana (10 days); and Puerto Rico (10 days to notify the Puerto Rico Department of Consumer Affairs).
- In North Dakota and Oregon, entities must notify the AG of breaches involving more than 250 state residents at one time. In Rhode Island, notification is not required until 500 state residents have been affected by a breach. In Hawaii, Missouri, South Carolina and Virginia, entities must notify the AG if more than 1,000 state residents are affected.

- In Connecticut and Washington, notification to the AG is required no later than when the affected residents are notified. Maryland, New Jersey and New York require AG notification prior to sending notices to affected data subjects. In Montana, entities are required to notify the AG simultaneously with sending notice to individuals. Vermont requires notification to the AG after the notice of a breach has been sent to consumers.
- Alaska requires notification to the AG if the entity determines, after an investigation into the breach, that the breach does not create a reasonable likelihood that harm to the consumers has or will result. Entities in Indiana, Maine, Massachusetts, New Hampshire, New York and North Carolina must also report to the state AG.

At least 28 states require that entities notify nationwide Credit Reporting Agencies (CRAs) of a data breach, but there are different provisions:[68]

- Minnesota requires notification if more than 500 Minnesota residents are affected
- Alaska, Colorado, the District of Columbia, Florida, Hawaii, Indiana, Kansas, Kentucky, Maine, Maryland, Michigan, Missouri, Nevada, New Jersey, North Carolina, Ohio, Oregon, Pennsylvania, South Carolina, Tennessee, Vermont, Virginia, West Virginia and Wisconsin require notification if more than 1,000 state residents are affected
- Maine and New Hampshire require notification if a breach affects more than 1,000 consumers at one time, regardless of whether all are state residents
- In New York, entities must notify CRAs if more than 5,000 New York residents are affected
- In Georgia, information brokers must notify CRAs if more than 10,000 Georgia residents are affected
- In Texas, entities must notify CRAs if more than 10,000 individuals (Texas residents or residents of states without data breach notification laws) are affected
- Montana requires entities to coordinate notification with CRAs

In addition, all data breach state laws require third-party notification. The Connecticut law, for example, states: "Any person that maintains computerized data that includes personal information that the person does not own shall notify the owner or licensee of the information of any breach of the security of the data immediately following its discovery, if the personal information was, or is reasonably believed to have been accessed by an unauthorized person."[69]

6.6.5 When to Notify

All states with data breach notification laws use similar language to describe the required timing of notifications. The most common phrase used in conjunction with timing is *the most expeditious time possible and without unreasonable delay.*[70] Legislators, however, recognize the need for the affected entity to conduct a "reasonable investigation in order to determine the scope of the breach and to restore the reasonable integrity of the data system."[71] As of 2017, only Florida, New Mexico, Ohio, Rhode Island, Tennessee, Vermont, Washington and Wisconsin specify a limit to expeditious time—typically no later than 45 days after the discovery of the breach.[72]

When a data breach is suspected to be the result of criminal activity, most states also allow delays "for a reasonable period of time if a law enforcement agency determines the notification will impede a criminal investigation and such law enforcement agency has made a request that the notification be delayed."[73] The entity is, however, expected to issue the notification as soon as possible after such an investigation is complete or the law enforcement agency decides that notification will not compromise the criminal investigation.

As noted above, Puerto Rico requires notification of the Department of Consumer Affairs within 10 days, and within 24 hours the department makes the breach public, making Puerto Rico arguably the most stringent data breach notification law in the country (at least in terms of speed of public exposure).[74]

6.6.6 What to Include

Most states do not specify the contents of the notification to the data subject, but California, Hawaii, Illinois, Iowa, Maryland, Massachusetts, Michigan, Missouri, Montana, New Hampshire, New York, North Carolina, Oregon, Vermont, Virginia, Washington, West Virginia, Wisconsin and Wyoming do.[75] North Carolina's requirements, for example, are among the most extensive, including:

- A description of the incident in general terms
- A description of the type of personal information that was subject to the unauthorized access and acquisition
- A description of the general acts of the business to protect the personal information from further unauthorized access

- A telephone number for the business that the person may call for further information and assistance, if one exists
- Advice that directs the person to remain vigilant by reviewing account statements and monitoring free credit reports
- The toll-free numbers and addresses for the major consumer reporting agencies
- The toll-free numbers, addresses and website addresses for the FTC Commission and the North Carolina attorney general's office, along with a statement that the individual can obtain information from these sources about preventing identity theft[76]

Oregon's requirements include "advice to the individual to report suspected identity theft to law enforcement,"[77] while Massachusetts and West Virginia require the notification to specify how an individual can obtain a police report and request a credit freeze.[78] Massachusetts law also prohibits including a description of the nature of the breach in the notification or the number of residents affected by the breach, while laws in other states require the notification to include a general description of the incident.[79] Privacy professionals residing in states that do not specify notification contents can use the requirements of those that do as guidance.

6.6.7 How to Notify

States generally provide notification options, but a written notice to the data subject is always required first. Telephonic and electronic messages are typical alternatives, but usually only if the data subject has previously explicitly chosen one of those as the preferred communication method.

Most legislation recognizes that data breach notifications involving thousands or millions of impacted data subjects could place an undue financial burden on an organization and therefore allow substitute notification methods. In Connecticut, for example: "Substitute notice shall consist of the following: (A) Electronic mail notice when the person, business or agency has an electronic mail address for the affected persons; (B) conspicuous posting of the notice on the web site of the person, business or agency if the person maintains one; and (C) notification to major state-wide media, including newspapers, radio and television."[80]

Notification to attorneys general and regulators may be sent via letter or email. Some states (notably California, New York and North Carolina) have specific online forms that must be used for this reporting.[81] The CRAs have established email addresses to receive breach notification reports.

6.6.8 Exceptions to Notification

There are three basic exceptions for providing data breach notification. The first and most common exception allowed by states is for entities subject to other, more stringent data breach notification laws. This includes HIPAA-covered entities and financial institutions subject to and in compliance with the GLBA Safeguards Rule, discussed in Chapter 8.

Second, most states allow exceptions for entities that already follow breach notification procedures as part of their own information security policies as long as these are compatible with the requirements of the state law. Connecticut's relevant language is:

> *Any person that maintains such person's own security breach procedures as part of an information security policy for the treatment of personal information and otherwise complies with the timing requirements of this section, shall be deemed to be in compliance with the security breach notification requirements of this section, provided such person notifies subject persons in accordance with such person's policies in the event of a breach of security. Any person that maintains such a security breach procedure pursuant to the rules, regulations, procedures or guidelines established by the primary or functional regulator, as defined in 15 USC 6809(2), shall be deemed to be in compliance with the security breach notification requirements of this section, provided such person notifies subject persons in accordance with the policies or the rules, regulations, procedures or guidelines established by the primary or functional regulator in the event of a breach of security of the system.*[82]

Ohio similarly allows exceptions for preexisting contracts.

Third, in most states, a safe harbor exists for data that was encrypted, redacted, unreadable or unusable.[83] The specific requirements vary by state and are subject to change. Some states exclude encrypted data from the definition of breach. In other states, the notification requirement is avoided if the data is encrypted based on the idea that there has not been a compromise (or, more pointedly, there is no risk of harm).[84]

Encryption is the process of encoding information so that only the sender and intended recipients can access it. Encryption systems often use a public key, available to the public, and a private key, which allows only the intended recipient to decode the message.[85] Most states exempt individuals and businesses from data breach notification and disclosure requirements if the data was encrypted when lost. Together, these laws help motivate many organizations to use encryption to protect data and thus avoid the burden of providing notice of breaches, as well as the embarrassment and potential brand damage of a public data breach. The encryption exception, however, typically applies only when the key remains secure. Most states make this explicit by stating that the exception does not apply when the decryption key is breached along with the encrypted data.

In 2010, Massachusetts adopted a more prescriptive encryption rule. The Massachusetts Personal Information Security Regulation states that all parties that "own or license" personal information pertaining to Massachusetts residents must encrypt all personal information stored on laptops or other portable devices, as well as wireless transmissions and transmissions sent over public networks.[86] As with the California data breach law, the level and type of encryption required is not specified.

While some state data breach statutes, such as in Massachusetts, mention encryption specifically, others contain more technology-neutral language. These states may stipulate that notification requirements do not apply when there is no "reasonable likelihood of harm to customers" after reasonable investigation, or similar language.[87]

More importantly, if the data is effectively encrypted, the breach did not "compromise the confidentiality, security and integrity" of the information—therefore it is not a breach under the laws with that compromise standard. Connecticut is the only state that doesn't have this compromise language. Many other statutes only require notice in a smaller range of situations, but if the data is effectively encrypted, there is no risk of harm, and the compromise requirement thus has not been met.

In the wake of recent massive data breaches, this safe-harbor approach to encrypted data is being re-examined by at least some states. In 2016, Tennessee removed provisions from its data breach notification that exempted encrypted data from the notification requirement. According to news accounts, this made Tennessee the first state in the country to broadly require notification regardless of whether the information was encrypted.[88] Later that year, California changed its data breach notification law to require notice that a breach occurred related to: (1) both encrypted data and the encryption key or (2) encrypted data when the business has a reasonable belief that the encryption key or security credentials can be obtained by the hacker.[89] In 2017, Tennessee again amended its statute. The change clarified that encrypted data receives the protection of the safe harbor, unless the encryption key is also acquired in the breach.[90] For businesses who are engaged in business across the country, this trend regarding how state laws handle encrypted data may significantly impact how these businesses approach their handling of data. Commentators warn that companies can no longer operate under the presumption that state data breach laws are not triggered when personal information was encrypted at the time that the breach occurred.[91]

6.6.9 Penalties and Right of Action

The Connecticut law reserves enforcement, as many states do, to the state attorney general,[92] and some states specify penalties. In Missouri, for example, "The attorney general shall have exclusive authority to bring an action to obtain actual damages for a willful and knowing violation of this section and may seek a civil penalty not to exceed one hundred fifty thousand dollars per breach of the security of the system or series of breaches of a similar nature that are discovered in a single investigation."[93] Louisiana, Michigan, Rhode Island, Texas and Virginia also specify civil penalties.

The data breach notification laws of Alaska, California, the District of Columbia, Louisiana, Maryland, Massachusetts, Nevada, New Hampshire, North Carolina, Oregon, South Carolina, Tennessee, Texas, Virginia and Washington also grant a private right of action to individuals harmed by disclosure of their personal information to recover damages.[94]

6.7 State Data Destruction Laws

As of 2017, at least 32 states have data destruction laws.[95] These requirements are sometimes incorporated in data breach laws. Most of the laws have common elements describing to whom the law applies (government and/or private businesses), the required notice, exemptions, for example, GLBA, HIPAA, Fair Credit Reporting Act (FCRA), the covered media (electronic and/or paper), and the penalties.

North Carolina's law,[96] for example, applies to "any business that conducts business in North Carolina and any business that maintains or otherwise possesses personal information of a resident of North Carolina." It requires such entities to take "reasonable measures" to safeguard against unauthorized access to personal information "in connection with or after its disposal."

North Carolina provides a three-fold description of required reasonable measures:

1. Implementing and monitoring compliance with policies and procedures that require the burning, pulverizing or shredding of papers containing personal information so that information cannot be practicably read or reconstructed
2. Implementing and monitoring compliance with policies and procedures that require the destruction or erasure of electronic media and other nonpaper media containing personal information so that the information cannot practicably be read or reconstructed
3. Describing procedures relating to the adequate destruction or proper disposal of personal records as official policy in the writings of the business entity

The law allows businesses to subcontract with record destruction businesses "after due diligence," which requires reviewing an independent audit of the business' operations, reviewing references and requiring independent certification of the business and/or personally evaluating "the competency and integrity of the disposal business."

North Carolina exempts financial institutions subject to GLBA, health insurers or healthcare facilities subject to HIPAA, and consumer reporting agencies subject to FCRA. The law does not specify damages but denies a right of public action in the absence of personal injury.

Most other state laws are essentially the same as North Carolina's, although variations exist among the laws. For example, the Arizona law applies only to paper records. Alaska specifically authorizes a right to private action. New Mexico requires "shredding, erasing or otherwise modifying the personal identifying information contained in the records to make the personal identifying information unreadable or undecipherable."[97] California requires destruction such that records are "unreadable or undecipherable through *any* means" (emphasis added). Illinois and Utah apply only to government entities. Massachusetts stipulates steep penalties of "not more than $100 per data subject affected, provided said fine shall not exceed $50,000 for each instance of improper disposal."[98]

It is also worth noting that the FTC's Disposal Rule contains requirements for proper disposal of consumer reports and information derived from consumer reports.[99]

6.8 Conclusion

The spread of state data breach laws since 2003 has had a major impact on private-sector information security practices. When breaches occur, top management often focuses intensively on information management practices; in many instances, the budget and visibility increases for information security activities in the wake of a breach. Similarly, concerns about the possibility of data breaches, with the resulting negative publicity, financial penalties and other effects, provides an important incentive for companies to develop strong information security practices. While significant differences remain among the state laws, the end result today is that entities processing personal data in the United States are compelled to disclose data breaches in an expeditious manner, and the data breach requirements spread to the EU with the implementation of the GDPR.

Data breach laws, combined with information security laws in Massachusetts and other jurisdictions, have thus become an important component of protection of personal data in the United States. The United States lacks comprehensive private-sector information security and data breach notification statutes, leading some observers to suggest the nation is less stringent about protection of personal data than other jurisdictions, notably Europe. In practice to date, the intensive attention to data breaches in the United States has quite often led to more rigorous information security programs than has existed in other jurisdictions.[100]

Endnotes

1 "Target Data Breach Spilled Info on as Many as 70 Million Customers," *Forbes,* January 10, 2014, https://www.forbes.com/sites/maggiemcgrath/2014/01/10/target-data-breach-spilled-info-on-as-many-as-70-million-customers/#5b46fd64e795 (accessed November 2017).This breach resulted in a multimillion-dollar legal settlement with affected customers. "Target settles for $39 million over data breach," *CNN Money,* December 2, 2015, http://money.cnn.com/2015/12/02/news/companies/target-data-breach-settlement/ (accessed November 2017). For a searchable listing of data breaches, see the database maintained by Privacy Rights Clearinghouse. Data Breaches, Privacy Rights Clearinghouse, https://www.privacyrights.org/data-breaches?title=&org_type%5B%5D=259&taxonomy_vocabulary_11_tid%5B%5D=2434&taxonomy_vocabulary_11_tid%5B%5D=2257&taxonomy_vocabulary_11_tid%5B%5D=2122 (accessed November 2017).

2 "Anthem hack exposes data on 80 million; experts warn of identity theft," *Los Angeles Times,* February 5, 2015, www.latimes.com/business/la-fi-anthem-hacked-20150204-story.html (accessed October 2017). Anthem reached a $115 million class-action settlement with individuals affected by the breach. "Record Data Breach Settlement in Anthem Class Action," *Hunton & Williams* (blog, June 26, 2017), https://www.huntonprivacyblog.com/2017/06/26/record-data-breach-settlement-anthem-class-action/ (accessed November 2017).

3 "Yahoo says 500 million accounts stolen," *CNN Money,* September 23, 2016, http://money.cnn.com/2016/09/22/technology/yahoo-data-breach/ (accessed November 2017). Numerous class-action lawsuits were filed in the wake of the public learning about the breach. "Yahoo facing lawsuits in the wake of massive data breach," *CNN Money,* September 23, 2016, http://money.cnn.com/2016/09/23/news/companies/yahoo-sued-data-breach/ (accessed November 2017).

4 "Equifax Underestimated by 2.5 Million the Number of Potential Breach Victims," *Fortune,* October 2, 2017, http://fortune.com/2017/10/02/equifax-credit-breach-total/ (accessed November 2017). As of the writing of this text, more than 70 class-action breaches have been filed related to the Equifax breach. *See* Kevin McCoy, "Do you want to sue Equifax over the cyberbreach? Winning a lawsuit may not be so easy," CNBC (September 22, 2017), https://www.cnbc.com/2017/09/22/do-you-want-to-sue-equifax-over-the-cyberbreach-winning-a-lawsuit-may-not-be-so-easy.html (accessed November 2017).

5 Cal. Civil Code § 1798.81.5, https://leginfo.legislature.ca.gov/faces/codes_displaySection.xhtml?lawCode=CIV§ionNum=1798.81.5 (accessed November 2017). In 2013, California became the first state to expand this definition to include email addresses or user names in combination with a password or security question and answer that would allow access to an online accounts. Since that time, numerous states, including Florida and Georgia, have adopted this approach. "States in which definition of 'personal information' is broader than the general definition," *Data Breach Charts,* BakerHostetler (October 2017), https://www.bakerlaw.com/files/Uploads/Documents/Data%20Breach%20documents/Data_Breach_Charts.pdf (accessed November 2017).

6 Cal. Civil Code § 1798.81.5, https://leginfo.legislature.ca.gov/faces/codes_displaySection.xhtml?lawCode=CIV§ionNum=1798.81.5 (accessed November 2017).

7 Cal. Civil Code § 1798.81.5, https://leginfo.legislature.ca.gov/faces/billNavClient.xhtml?bill_id=201520160AB2828 (accessed November 2017).

8 California Data Breach Report (February 2016), https://oag.ca.gov/sites/all/files/agweb/pdfs/dbr/2016-data-breach-report.pdf (accessed November 2017). For a discussion of the security aspects of the Attorney General's Data Breach Report, view "California Data Breach Report Defines 'Reasonableness' Standard for Data Protection," Ballard Spahr, www.ballardspahr.com/alertspublications/legalalerts/2016-03-02-ca-data-breach-report-defines-reasonableness-standard-for-data-protection.aspx (accessed November 2017). To learn more about Center for Internet Security's Critical Security Controls, *see* "Welcome to the CIS Controls," https://www.cisecurity.org/critical-controls.cfm (accessed November 2017).

9 *See* "Ten years later: The legacy of SB 1386 compliance on data privacy laws," *TechTarget*, http://searchsecurity.techtarget.com/opinion/Ten-years-later-The-legacy-of-SB-1386-compliance-on-data-privacy-laws (accessed November 2017). A list of states with data security laws for the private sector and those with laws for the public sector can be found at National Conference of State Legislatures. *See* Data Security Laws—Private Sector, NCSL (January 16, 2017), www.ncsl.org/research/telecommunications-and-information-technology/data-security-laws.aspx (accessed November 2017); Data Security Laws—Public Sector, NCSL (January 16, 2017), www.ncsl.org/research/telecommunications-and-information-technology/data-security-laws-state-government.aspx (accessed November 2017).

10 "Cybersecurity Requirements for Financial Services Companies," New York State Department of Financial Services, 23 NYCRR 500, www.dfs.ny.gov/legal/regulations/adoptions/dfsrf500txt.pdf (accessed November 2017).

11 201 CMR 17.00, www.mass.gov/ocabr/docs/idtheft/201cmr1700reg.pdf (accessed November 2017).

12 *Id.*

13 Wash. Rev. Code 19.255.010, http://apps.leg.wa.gov/rcw/default.aspx?cite=19.255.010 (accessed November 2017).

14 "FAQ on Washington State's PCI Law," Information Law Group, www.infolawgroup.com/2010/03/articles/payment-card-breach-laws/faq-on-washington-states-pci-law/ (accessed November 2017).

15 "Security in Numbers: SSNs and ID Theft," FTC, https://www.ftc.gov/sites/default/files/documents/reports/security-numbers-social-security-numbers-and-identity-theft-federal-trade-commission-report/p075414ssnreport.pdf (accessed November 2017).

16 Cal. Civ. Code § 1798.85, http://leginfo.legislature.ca.gov/faces/codes_displaySection.xhtml?lawCode=CIV§ionNum=1798.85. (accessed November 2017). For a summary of the California statute on the confidentiality of Social Security numbers, see the California Attorney General's website. Social Security Number Confidentiality, California Law—General Privacy Laws, Privacy Laws, Office of the Attorney General, State of California Department of Justice, https://oag.ca.gov/privacy/privacy-laws (accessed November 2017).

17 GN 03325.002, Disclosure of Social Security Numbers (SSN) Without Consent, Program Operations Manual System (POMS), Social Security, https://secure.ssa.gov/apps10/poms.nsf/lnx/0203325002 (accessed November 2017).

18 "President Signs the Social Security Number Confidentiality Act of 2000," Social Security (November 17, 2000), https://www.ssa.gov/legislation/legis_bulletin_111700.html (accessed November 2017).

19 "Chronology of Data Breaches: Security Breaches 2005 - Present," Privacy Rights Clearinghouse, www.privacyrights.org/data-breach (accessed November 2017). This site keeps an up-to-date list of data breaches that is searchable by type of breach, by type of organization and by year.

20 The Identity Theft Resource Center identifies similar categories of data loss methods: insider theft, hacking/skimming/phishing, data on the move, subcontractor/third party/business associate, employee error/negligence/improper disposal/lost, accidental web/Internet exposure, and physical theft. www.idtheftcenter.org/id-theft/data-breaches.html (accessed November 2017).

21 Reform of EU Data Protection Rules, EU, http://ec.europa.eu/justice/data-protection/reform/index_en.htm (accessed November 2016). For a discussion of GDPR, view "The EU General Data Protection Regulation—EU Adopts Single Set of Privacy Rules," *Alston & Bird Privacy & Data Security Blog*, www.alstonprivacy.com/the-eu-general-data-protection-regulation-europe-adopts-single-set-of-privacy-rules/ (accessed November 2017).

22 Under the GDPR and some state laws, there is a requirement to inform the government entities within a certain time period of becoming aware of the breach, even if that is prior to determining whether a breach has occurred. See Article 33, GDPR ("without undue delay, and where feasible, not later than 72 hours after having become aware" of the breach), https://gdpr-info.eu/ (accessed November 2017); State of Connecticut (requiring five-day notification to the insurance department for breaches by licensees), www.ct.gov/cid/lib/cid/Bulletin_IC_25_Data_Breach_Notification.pdf (accessed November 2017); State of Washington (requiring two-day notification to insurance commissioner for breaches by licensees), https://www.insurance.wa.gov/sites/default/files/documents/taa-security-breaches.pdf (accessed November 2017); *see* also Alex Reynolds, "GDPR matchup: US state data breach laws," IAPP (May 10, 2017), https://iapp.org/news/a/gdpr-match-up-u-s-state-data-breach-laws/ (accessed November 2017).

23 For information on state coordination of multistate data breach investigations, *see* the discussion of the National Association of Attorney Generals (NAAG) Privacy Working Group in Danielle Citron's article entitled, "Privacy Enforcement Pioneers: The Role of State Attorney Generals in the Development of Privacy Law," http://papers.ssrn.com/sol3/papers.cfm?abstract_id=2733297 (accessed November 2017).

24 Chart, State Data Breach Notification Laws, Foley & Lardner LLP (October 5, 2017), https://www.foley.com/state-data-breach-notification-laws/ (accessed November 2017).

25 Preparing for and Responding to a Breach of Personally Identifiable Information, Memorandum for Heads of Executive Departments and Agencies, Executive Office of the President's Office of Management and Budget (OMB), M-17-12 (January, 3, 2017), https://obamawhitehouse.archives.gov/sites/default/files/omb/memoranda/2017/m-17-12_0.pdf (accessed November 2017). For an overview of the memo, *see* "OMB Publishes Memorandum on Responding to Data Breaches," *Hunton & Williams* (January 5, 2017), https://www.huntonprivacyblog.com/2017/01/05/omb-publishes-memorandum-responding-data-breaches/ (accessed November 2017).

26 Today, the U.S. government is increasingly targeted for breaches by actors who want to sell PII for criminal uses or who seek the information for other malicious purposes. For more than a decade, the federal government has implemented policies to prepare for and respond to these breaches. A recent example of a significant government breach occurred in 2015 when the records of approximately 5 million people who had applied for or received security clearances were exposed after the Office of Personnel Management networks were compromised. "US Government Hack Stole 5.6 Million Federal Employees," *The Guardian*, September 23, 2015, https://www.theguardian.com/technology/2015/sep/23/us-government-hack-stole-fingerprints (accessed November 2017).

27 Preparing for and Responding to a Breach of Personally Identifiable Information, Memorandum for Heads of Executive Departments and Agencies, Executive Office of the President's Office of Management and Budget, M-17-12 (January, 3, 2017), pp. 16-18, https://obamawhitehouse.archives.gov/sites/default/files/omb/memoranda/2017/m-17-12_0.pdf (accessed November 2017).

28 *Id.* at 18.

29 *Id.*

30 *Id.* at 19-20.

31 *Id.* at 20-27.

32 *Id.* at 27-29.

33 *Id.* at 29-34.

34 *Id.* at 11-13.

35 For a timeline of major data breaches, view World's Biggest Data Breaches, Information is Beautiful (September 10, 2017), www.informationisbeautiful.net/visualizations/worlds-biggest-data-breaches-hacks/ (accessed November 2017).

36 John Seiver and Bryan Thompson, "President Obama Proposes National Data Breach Law, Unveils New Consumer and Student Privacy Initiatives," *Privacy & Security Law Blog* (January 15, 2015), https://www.privsecblog.com/2015/01/articles/dataprotection/president-obama-proposes-national-data-breach-law-unveils-new-consumer-and-student-privacy-initiatives/ (accessed November 2017).

37 "Fixing the patchwork: Will Congress enact a federal data breach law?" *Westlaw Journal,* https://www.weil.com/~/media/files/pdfs/wlj_cmp_3226_commentary_weil.pdf (accessed November 2017).

38 Morgan Chalfant, "Five Takeaways from Equifax's Brutal Week," (in wake of Equifax breach, "support is growing for a national data breach standard"), http://thehill.com/policy/cybersecurity/354252-five-takeaways-from-equifaxs-brutal-week (accessed November 2017); "Federal data-breach bill would replace dozens of stronger state laws," *Los Angeles Times,* www.latimes.com/business/la-fi-lazarus-20150421-column.html (accessed November 2017).

39 Choi Chow, "California Updates Its Data Breach Notification Law," Corodata (March 18, 2016) https://corodata.com/california-updates-its-data-breach-notification-law (accessed November 2017).

40 Security Breach Notification Laws," National Conference of State Legislatures, www.ncsl.org/research/telecommunications-and-information-technology/security-breach-notification-laws.aspx (accessed November 2017). At the time of publication, only Alabama and South Dakota have yet to enact some form of state breach notification law. Even if a breach occurs in one of these two states, consumers residing in other states who are affected by the breach may be entitled to notice of the breach under their respective state laws.

41 For details on the various states' approaches, view Steptoe's "Comparison of US State and Federal Security Breach Notification Laws," https://www.steptoe.com/assets/htmldocuments/SteptoeDataBreachNotificationChart.pdf (accessed November 2017).

42 For state-by-state analysis, view "State Data Security Breach Notification Laws," https://www.mintz.com/newsletter/2007/PrivSec-DataBreachLaws-02-07/state_data_breach_matrix.pdf (accessed November 2017).

43 Conn. Gen. Stat. § 36a-701b, https://www.cga.ct.gov/current/pub/chap_669.htm#sec_36a-701b (accessed November 2017). Connecticut is considered to be at the forefront of data breach

policy. Sarah Breitenbach, "States and Feds disagree on data breach proposals," *Stateline*, June 16, 2015, www.governing.com/topics/public-justice-safety/states-at-odds-with-feds-on-data-breach-proposals-1.html (accessed November 2017).

44 Nevada specifically excludes the last four digits from the definition of PI. Nevada's Security of Personal Information Act, www.leg.state.nv.us/NRS/NRS-603A.html (accessed November 2017).

45 Connecticut's Act Improving Security and Agency Effectiveness, https://www.cga.ct.gov/2015/act/pa/2015PA-00142-R00SB-00949-PA.htm (accessed November 2017). Effective October 1, 2015, Connecticut expanded its definition of "personal information" to include protected health information and unique biometric data such as a fingerprint, a voice print, a retina or an iris image, or other unique physical representations.

46 "States in which definition of 'personal information' is broader," Data Breach Charts, BakerHostetler.

47 Wis. Stat. §134.98, http://docs.legis.wisconsin.gov/statutes/statutes/134/98 (accessed November 2017).

48 *Id.*

49 10 Laws of Puerto Rico §§ 4051 et seq., www.schwartzandballen.com/ImportedDocs/Puerto%20Rico%20security%20breach.pdf (accessed June 2016).

50 N.D. Cent. Code §§ 51-30-01 et seq., www.legis.nd.gov/cencode/t51c30.pdf?20150408094101 (accessed November 2017).

51 "States where the statute is triggered by a breach of security in electronic and/or paper records," Data Breach Charts, BakerHostetler (October 2017), https://www.bakerlaw.com/files/Uploads/Documents/Data%20Breach%20documents/Data_Breach_Charts.pdf (accessed November 2017).

52 815 ILCS §§ 530/1 to 530/25, www.ilga.gov/legislation/ilcs/ilcs3.asp?ActID=2702&ChapAct=815 ILCS 530/&ChapterID=67&ChapterName=BUSINESS+TRANSACTIONS&ActName=Personal+Information+Protection+Act (accessed November 2017).

53 Conn. Gen. Stat. § 36a-701b, https://www.cga.ct.gov/current/pub/chap_669.htm#sec_36a-701b (accessed November 2017).

54 Idaho Stat. §§ 28-51-104 to -107, https://legislature.idaho.gov/statutesrules/idstat/title28/t28ch51/sect28-51-104/ (accessed November 2017); La. Rev. Stat. §§ 51:3071 et seq., https://legis.la.gov/Legis/Law.aspx?p=y&d=322027 (accessed November 2017); Mich. Comp. Law §§ 445.63, 445.72, www.legislature.mi.gov/(S(bsn1zcb2xa324ubku4tw0eoc))/mileg.aspx?page=GetObject&objectname=mcl-445-63 (accessed November 2017).

55 Ohio Rev. Code § 1347.12, http://codes.ohio.gov/orc/1347.12 (accessed November 2017).

56 Conn. Gen. Stat. § 36a-701b, https://www.cga.ct.gov/current/pub/chap_669.htm#sec_36a-701b (accessed November 2017).

57 The majority of state data breach notification laws contain this requirement. To view a sampling, *see* Ariz. Rev. Stat. tit. 44, Ch. 32, § 44-7501, http://az.elaws.us/ars/44-7501 (accessed November 2017); Conn. Gen Stat. § 36a-701(b), https://www.cga.ct.gov/current/pub/chap_669.htm#sec_36a-701b (accessed June 2016); Del. C., Tit. 6, Ch. § 12B-102, http://delcode.delaware.gov/title6/c012b/index.shtml (accessed November 2017); and Fl. Stat. § 501.171, www.leg.state.fl.us/statutes/index.cfm?App_mode=Display_Statute&Search_String=&URL=0500-0599/0501/Sections/0501.171.html (accessed November 2017).

58 Ga. Code § 10-1-910 to -912, www.lexisnexis.com/hottopics/gacode/Default.asp (accessed November 2017).

59 Tex. Bus. & Com. Code §§ 521.002, 521.053,www.statutes.legis.state.tx.us/Docs/BC/htm/BC.521.htm#521.002 (accessed November 2017).

60 Conn. Gen. Stat. § 36a-701b, https://www.cga.ct.gov/current/pub/chap_669.htm#sec_36a-701b (accessed November 2017).

61 Cal. Civil Code § 1798.29 and § 1798.82, https://leginfo.legislature.ca.gov/faces/codes_displaySection.xhtml?lawCode=CIV§ionNum=1798.82 (accessed November 2017).

62 Fl. Stat. § 501.171,www.leg.state.fl.us/statutes/index.cfm?App_mode=Display_Statute&Search_String=&URL=0500-0599/0501/Sections/0501.171.html (accessed November 2017).

63 Kan. Stat. § 50-7a01 et seq., www.kslegislature.org/li_2014/b2013_14/statute/050_000_0000_chapter/050_007a_0000_article/ (accessed November 2017).

64 S.C. Code § 39-1-90, www.scstatehouse.gov/code/t39c001.php (accessed November 2017).

65 For a summary of different states' approaches to harm analysis, view "States That Require a Risk of Harm Analysis in Determining When Notification is Triggered," Data Breach Charts, BakerHostetler (October 2017), https://www.bakerlaw.com/files/Uploads/Documents/Data%20Breach%20documents/Data_Breach_Charts.pdf (accessed November 2017).

66 Tex. Bus. & Com. Code §§ 521.002, 521.053, www.statutes.legis.state.tx.us/Docs/BC/htm/BC.521.htm#521.002 (accessed November 2017).

67 "4. What Form of Notice is Permitted?" in State Data Breach Notification Laws – Overview of Requirements for Responding to a Data Breach Updated April 2017, Keller and Heckman (April 28, 2017), https://www.khlaw.com/State-Data-Breach-Notification-Laws---Overview-of-Requirements-for-Responding-to-a-Data-Breach-Updated-April-2017 (accessed November 2017). Additional state information can be located at "States that Require Notice to Attorney General or State Agency," Data Breach Charts, BakerHostetler (October 2017), https://www.bakerlaw.com/files/Uploads/Documents/Data%20Breach%20documents/Data_Breach_Charts.pdf (accessed November 2017).

68 "6. When is Notification to CRAs Required?" in State Data Breach Notification Laws – Overview of Requirements for Responding to a Data Breach Updated April 2017, Keller and Heckman (April 28, 2017), https://www.khlaw.com/State-Data-Breach-Notification-Laws---Overview-of-Requirements-for-Responding-to-a-Data-Breach-Updated-April-2017 (accessed November 2017).

69 Conn. Gen. Statute § 36a-701b, https://www.cga.ct.gov/current/pub/chap_669.htm#sec_36a-701b (accessed November 2017).

70 State attorneys general have developed a rule of thumb that notice should proceed on a rolling basis. Danielle Citron, "The Privacy Policymaking of State Attorney Generals," p. 768, *Notre Dame Law Review* (2016), http://scholarship.law.nd.edu/cgi/viewcontent.cgi?article=4693&context=ndlr (accessed November 2017).

71 La. Rev. Stat. §§ 51:3071, https://legis.la.gov/Legis/Law.aspx?d=322030 (accessed November 2017).

72 Florida provides for a 30-day time frame, while New Mexico, Ohio, Rhode Island, Tennessee, Vermont, Washington and Wisconsin mandate a 45-day time frame. "States that Require Notification within a Specific Time Frame," Data Breach Charts, BakerHostetler (October 2017), https://www.bakerlaw.com/files/Uploads/Documents/Data%20Breach%20documents/Data_Breach_Charts.pdf (accessed November 2017). Maryland's requirement for notification within 45 days went into effect on January 1, 2018. *See* Privacy and Data Security Group, "Maryland Amends Data Breach Notification Law," Ballard Spahr LLP (August 3, 2017), www.ballardspahr.com/alertspublications/legalalerts/2017-08-03-maryland-amends-data-breach-notification-law.aspx (accessed November 2017).

73 "3. When Must Notice to Individuals be Given?" in State Data Breach Notification Laws – Overview of Requirements for Responding to a Data Breach Updated April 2017, Keller and Heckman (April 28, 2017), https://www.khlaw.com/State-Data-Breach-Notification-Laws---Overview-of-Requirements-for-Responding-to-a-Data-Breach-Updated-April-2017 (accessed November 2017).

74 10 L.P.R.A. § 4051, www.schwartzandballen.com/ImportedDocs/Puerto%20Rico%20security%20breach.pdf (accessed November 2017).

75 "5. What Must be Included in Breach Notices to Individuals Under Statute?" in State Data Breach Notification Laws – Overview of Requirements for Responding to a Data Breach Updated April 2017, Keller and Heckman (April 28, 2017), https://www.khlaw.com/State-Data-Breach-Notification-Laws---Overview-of-Requirements-for-Responding-to-a-Data-Breach-Updated-April-2017 (accessed November 2017).

76 N.C. Gen. Stat. § 75-65, www.ncga.state.nc.us/EnactedLegislation/Statutes/HTML/BySection/Chapter_75/GS_75-65.html (accessed November 2017).

77 Oregon Rev. Stat. § 646A.600 to .628, https://www.oregonlegislature.gov/bills_laws/lawsstatutes/2015orLaw0357.pdf (accessed November 2017).

78 Mass. Gen. Laws § 93H-1 et seq., https://malegislature.gov/Laws/GeneralLaws/PartI/TitleXV/Chapter93H/Section3 (accessed November 2017); W.V. Code §§ 46A-2A-101 et seq., www.legis.state.wv.us/WVCODE/Code.cfm?chap=46a&art=2A#2A (accessed November 2017).

79 Massachusetts' prohibition may have repercussions on the idea of treating all breach victims the same if the breach cross state lines, which can be addressed by working with the authorities in Massachusetts. Compare Mass. Gen. Laws § 93H-1 et seq., https://malegislature.gov/Laws/GeneralLaws/PartI/TitleXV/Chapter93H/Section3 (accessed November 2017) with California's notification requirements, Cal. Civil Code § 1798.29 and § 1798.82, https://leginfo.legislature.ca.gov/faces/codes_displaySection.xhtml?lawCode=CIV§ionNum=1798.82 (accessed November 2017). Details of current state notification requirements can be found at Summary of U.S. State Data Breach Notification Statutes (Davis Wright Tremain, LLP 2017), www.dwt.com/statedatabreachstatutes/ (accessed November 2017).

80 Conn. Gen. Stat. § 36a-701b, http://law.justia.com/codes/connecticut/2012/title-36a/chapter-669/section-36a-701b (accessed November 2017).

81 California Attorney General breach notification form, https://oag.ca.gov/ecrime/databreach/report-a-breach (accessed November 2017); New York Incident Reporting, https://its.ny.gov/incident-reporting (accessed November 2017); North Carolina breach notification form, www.ncdoj.gov/getdoc/81eda50e-8feb-4764-adca-b5c47f211612/Report-a-Security-Breach.aspx (accessed November 2017).

82 Conn. Gen. Stat. § 36a-701b, http://law.justia.com/codes/connecticut/2012/title-36a/chapter-669/section-36a-701b (accessed November 2017).

83 Chart, State Data Breach Notification Laws, Foley & Lardner LLP (October 5, 2017), https://www.foley.com/state-data-breach-notification-laws/ (accessed November 2017).

84 "States with an Encryption Safe Harbor," Data Breach Charts, BakerHostetler (October 2017), https://www.bakerlaw.com/files/Uploads/Documents/Data%20Breach%20documents/Data_Breach_Charts.pdf (accessed November 2017). As of January 1, 2017, the safe harbor for encryption no longer exists in California law. *See* AB-2828 Personal Information: Privacy Breach, http://leginfo.legislature.ca.gov/faces/billNavClient.xhtml?bill_id=201520160AB2828 (accessed November 2017).

85 For an explanation of encryption, *see* Lee Bell, "Encryption explained: how apps and sites keep your private data safe (and why that's important)," *Wired,* (June 5, 2017), www.wired.co.uk/article/encryption-software-app-private-data-safe (accessed November 2017).

86 Mass. Gen. Laws Ch. 93I, § 2, https://malegislature.gov/Laws/GeneralLaws/PartI/TitleXV/Chapter93i/Section2 (accessed November 2017).

87 For example, *see* Alaska Stat. § 45.48.010, www.legis.state.ak.us/basis/folioproxy.asp?url=http://wwwjnu01.legis.state.ak.us/cgi-bin/folioisa.dll/stattx09/query=[JUMP:%27AS4548010%27]/doc/{@1}?firsthit (accessed November 2017).

88 Tennessee's SB 2005, Act to Amend Tennessee Code Annotated Title 47 relative to release of personal information, https://www.workplaceprivacyreport.com/wp-content/uploads/sites/162/2016/03/dBP.pdf (accessed November 2017); *see* Tennessee Amends Breach Notification Statute, *The National Law Review* (March 24, 2016), https://www.natlawreview.com/article/tennessee-amends-breach-notification-statute (accessed November 2017).

89 California's AB 2828, https://leginfo.legislature.ca.gov/faces/billNavClient.xhtml?bill_id=201520160AB2828 (accessed November 2017); *see* Tiffany Quach, "California Amends Data Breach Notification Law to Require Notification of Breach of Encrypted Personal Information When Encryption Key Has Been Leaked," *Privacy Law Blog*, Proskauer (November 8, 2016), https://www.workplaceprivacyreport.com/wp-content/uploads/sites/162/2016/03/dBP.pdf (accessed November 2017). For a discussion of the impacts to business, *see* Robert Braun, "AB 2828—California Updates its Breach Disclosure Laws," Cybersecurity Lawyer Forum (October 6, 2016), https://cybersecurity.jmbm.com/2016/10/06/ab-2828-california-updates-breach-disclosure-law/ (accessed November 2017).

90 Thomas Ritter, "Tennessee Amends its Breach Notification Law (AGAIN) and Reinserts the Encryption Safe Harbor," Cybersecurity Law, Thompson Burton (March 29, 2017), https://thompsonburton.com/cybersecurity-law/2017/03/29/tennessee-amends-its-breach-notification-law-again-and-reinserts-the-encryption-safe-harbor/ (accessed November 2017).

91 Joseph Lazzarotti, "California Amends Its Data Breach Notification Law … Again," *The National Law Review*, November 10, 2016, https://www.natlawreview.com/article/california-amends-its-data-breach-notification-law-again (accessed November 2017).

92 Conn. Gen. Stat. § 36a-701b, http://law.justia.com/codes/connecticut/2012/title-36a/chapter-669/section-36a-701b (accessed November 2017).

93 Mo. Rev. Stat. § 407.1500, www.moga.mo.gov/mostatutes/stathtml/40700015001.html (accessed November 2017).

94 "States That Permit a Private Right of Action," Data Breach Charts, BakerHostetler (October 2017), https://www.bakerlaw.com/files/Uploads/Documents/Data%20Breach%20documents/Data_Breach_Charts.pdf (accessed November 2017).

95 *See* Data Disposal Laws, National Conference of State Legislatures (December 1, 2016), www.ncsl.org/research/telecommunications-and-information-technology/data-disposal-laws.aspx (accessed November 2017).

96 N.C. Gen. Stat. § 75-64, www.ncleg.net/EnactedLegislation/Statutes/HTML/BySection/Chapter_75/GS_75-64.html (accessed November 2017).

97 In 2017, New Mexico enacted its data breach law, H.B. 15. In addition to data breach notification requirements, the law requires those who own or license data of a New Mexico resident to maintain reasonable data security measures. New Mexico's H.B. 15, Data Breach Notification Act (2017),

https://www.nmlegis.gov/Sessions/17%20Regular/bills/house/HB0015JCS.pdf (accessed November 2017).

98 Mass. Gen. Laws Ch. 93I, § 2, https://malegislature.gov/Laws/GeneralLaws/PartI/TitleXV/Chapter93i/Section2 (accessed June, 2016); *see* Data Disposal Laws, National Conference of State Legislatures (December 1, 2016), www.ncsl.org/research/telecommunications-and-information-technology/data-disposal-laws.aspx (accessed November 2017).

99 Disposing of Consumer Report Information? Rule Tells How, FTC, https://www.ftc.gov/tips-advice/business-center/guidance/disposing-consumer-report-information-rule-tells-how (accessed November 2017).

100 *See* Eric Langland, "Survey of data security requirements in multistate breach settlements," IAPP (October 26, 2017), https://iapp.org/news/a/survey-of-data-security-requirements-in-multi-state-breach-settlements/ (accessed November 2017).

CHAPTER 7

Medical Privacy

Special privacy protections for healthcare date back thousands of years. The modern Hippocratic Oath states, "I will respect the privacy of my patients, for their problems are not disclosed to me that the world may know."[1] There are several reasons why relatively strict privacy laws exist for healthcare. First, at the most basic level, medical information is related to the inner workings of one's body or mind. One's individual sense of self may be violated if others have unfettered access to this information. Second, most doctors believe that patients will be more open about their medical conditions if they have assurance that embarrassing medical facts will not be revealed. Third, medical privacy protections can protect employees from the risk of unequal treatment by employers. For instance, a person who uses birth control, has had an abortion, contracted a sexually transmitted disease, been treated for a substance abuse issue, or has undergone psychiatric treatment could potentially be fired if a prejudiced employer gained access to this information. Health insurers and employers may also have incentives to avoid employing or insuring workers who suffer from expensive medical conditions or who may be at higher risk for such conditions based on their genetic background.

Despite the existence of strict laws protecting medical information within the healthcare industry, modern insurance and medical practices often use patient medical information quite extensively. For example, information about medical procedures is frequently used to assure accurate payment for those services. Doctors in one location may wish to access records about a patient's medical treatment in other cities in order to treat the patient appropriately. Researchers also use medical information, sometimes de-identified, in trying to find new patterns as they seek to develop cures for illnesses and promote public health. Records of many patients' outcomes may be used to evaluate healthcare providers on the overall quality of care.

This chapter begins with a discussion of the federal protections for records relating to treatment for alcohol and drug abuse that have been in place since the 1970s, currently found in the 2017 version of the Confidentiality of Substance Use Disorder Patients Records Rule. Next, the chapter explains the basic privacy and security provisions of the Health Insurance Portability and Accountability Act of 1996 (HIPAA), as updated by the Health Information Technology for Economic and Clinical Health Act of 2009 (HITECH). State healthcare privacy laws are not discussed here in detail, but it is important to know that HIPAA does not preempt stricter state privacy laws and the California Medical Information Privacy Act (CMIA), for example, expands health information privacy protection duties to providers of software, hardware and online services.[2] The chapter then discusses the Genetic Information Nondiscrimination Act of 2008 (GINA). The chapter ends with a summary of the privacy protections included in the 21st Century Cures Act.

One potential source of confusion is that an individual's health-related information in the United States is legally protected in some settings but not others. For example, HIPAA applies to "covered entities," notably including healthcare providers and insurers as well as "business associates" who receive data from covered entities. By contrast, health information in the hands of other entities is not protected by HIPAA. Suppose, for instance, that an individual buys a book about a rare form of cancer. That book purchase, along with other book purchases, is covered by the bookstore's privacy policy (if one exists). A California bookstore would also be covered by California's Reader Privacy Act,[3] but would not be covered by HIPAA. Similarly, the records of a website that provides detailed information about this form of cancer may show that the same user has come back repeatedly with questions about the disease. This website is likely outside the scope of HIPAA, yet potentially covered by California's Medical Information Privacy Act.[4] Companies such as the website can publicly agree, as part of self-regulation, to comply with the requirements of HIPAA in relation to any self-reported medical information. Violation of such a pledge would make the company subject to enforcement as a deceptive trade practice under Section 5 of the Federal Trade Commission Act.[5] Because U.S. privacy law and self-regulatory efforts varies by sector, the privacy professional should examine carefully whether personal information, including health-related information, is covered by HIPAA or some other sector-specific law.[6]

7.1 Confidentiality of Substance Use Disorder Patient Records Rule

Several decades before passage of HIPAA,[7] Congress began its foray into the arena of medical privacy. This federal action was prompted by concern that individuals might not seek medical care for alcohol and substance abuse problems unless the privacy of this information was strictly protected. In 1970, Congress passed the Comprehensive Alcohol Abuse and Alcoholism Prevention, Treatment and Rehabilitation Act. Two years later, Congress enacted the Drug Abuse Prevention, Treatment and Rehabilitation

Act.[8] These confidentiality requirements are implemented in the Confidentiality of Substance Use Disorder Patient Records Rule.[9]

Scope. The scope of the Rule covers the disclosure and use of "patient identifying" information by treatment programs for alcohol and substance abuse.[10] Patient-identifying information is any and all information that could reasonably be used to identify, directly or indirectly, a person who has been diagnosed with a substance abuse issue or has undergone alcohol or substance abuse treatment.[11] In addition, the Rule restricts use of any information, whether written or verbal, that could lead to or substantiate criminal charges against a patient concerning their alcohol or drug usage.[12]

Applicability. The law applies to any program that receives federal funding. For purposes of the Rule, the term *program* means any one of the following:

1. "an individual or entity (other than a general medical facility) who holds itself out as providing, and provides," alcohol or substance abuse diagnosis, treatment, or referral for treatment"
2. "an identified unit within a general medical facility that holds itself out as providing, and provides," alcohol or substance abuse diagnosis, treatment, or referral for treatment
3. "medical personnel or other staff in a general medical facility whose primary function is provision of" the alcohol or substance abuse diagnosis, treatment, or referral for treatment[13]

Other entities may become subject to the regulation in either of the following ways: (1) a state licensing agency requires them to comply or (2) the clinician uses controlled substances for detoxification, requiring licensing through the U.S. Drug Enforcement Administration (DEA).[14]

Disclosure. The program must obtain written patient consent before disclosing information subject to the Rule. The consent form may include a general designation that allows disclosure to either individuals or entities so long as those entities have a treating provider relationship with the patient. Upon request, the patient who signs a consent form with a general designation may receive a list of entities to which his or her information has been disclosed. In addition, the consent form must explicitly describe the type of information that is to be disclosed related to alcohol or drug abuse treatment.[15]

Redisclosure. Redisclosing information obtained from a program is prohibited when that information would "identify, directly or indirectly, an individual as having been diagnosed, treated, or referred for treatment."[16]

Exceptions to consent requirements. Exceptions to the Rule that allow disclosures without consent include:

- Medical emergencies[17]
- Scientific research[18]
- Audits and evaluations[19]
- Communications with a qualified service organization (QSO) related to information needed by the organization to provide services to the program[20]
- Crimes on program premises or against program personnel[21]
- Child abuse reporting[22]
- Court order[23]

Security of records. An entity lawfully holding patient-identifying information must have formal policies and procedures in place to protect the security of this information. There are separate requirements for paper and electronic records.[24]

Violations of the Confidentiality of Patient Records for Alcohol and Other Drug Treatment Rule are criminal. The first violation results in a fine of not more than $500. Each subsequent offense is fined not more than $5,000. These violations are reported to the U.S. Attorney's Office.[25]

Entities subject to this rule are likely to also be subject to the HIPAA Privacy Rule.[26] In many areas, these two requirements will have parallel requirements.[27] Privacy practitioners should review both the rule and HIPAA to fully understand when the two do not converge.[28] Also, the rule is similar to HIPAA—it does not preempt state laws that include stricter protections for disclosures than those at the federal level.[29]

7.2 The Health Insurance Portability and Accountability Act of 1996

Although the protections found in HIPAA are broader than those covered by the earlier laws concerning alcohol and substance abuse treatments records, the initial reason for HIPAA was not to protect privacy and security. Instead, Congress was seeking to meet other goals, including improving the efficiency of healthcare delivery. To improve efficiency, HIPAA required entities receiving federal healthcare payments such as Medicare and Medicaid to shift reimbursement requests to electronic formats. At the same time, Congress realized that the shift from paper to electronic reimbursements posed a threat to privacy and security. Accordingly, HIPAA required the U.S.

Department of Health and Human Services (HHS) to promulgate regulations to protect the privacy and security of healthcare information.

Protected health information (PHI) is defined as any individually identifiable health information that: is transmitted or maintained in any form or medium; is held by a covered entity or its business associate; identifies the individual or offers a reasonable basis for identification; is created or received by a covered entity or an employer; and relates to a past, present or future physical or mental condition, provision of health care or payment for health care to that individual.[30]

Electronic protected health information (ePHI) is any PHI that is transmitted or maintained in electronic media (such as computer hard drives, magnetic tapes or disks, or digital memory cards, all of which are considered electronic storage media). Paper records, paper-to-paper fax transmissions, and voice communications (e.g., telephone) are not considered transmissions via electronic media.[31]

This statutory link to electronic reimbursements helps clarify which healthcare information is covered under HIPAA. Entities that are directly covered under HIPAA ("covered entities") include:[32]

- Healthcare providers (e.g., a doctors' offices, hospitals) that conduct certain transactions in electronic form
- Health plans (e.g., health insurers)
- Healthcare clearinghouses (e.g., third-party organizations that host, handle or process medical information)[33]

It is important to understand that HIPAA applies to these covered entities, but not to other healthcare providers and services. For instance, some doctors accept only cash or credit cards and do not bill for insurance.[34] They are not covered by HIPAA. More broadly, individuals reveal medical information in a wide variety of settings, ranging from conversations with friends and colleagues, to purchasing books about healthcare, to surfing on healthcare websites and even posting medical information online. These sorts of healthcare information are outside the scope of HIPAA.[35]

Before the HITECH update, business associates were not subject to HIPAA but became subject to privacy and security protections under the written contracts they signed with covered entities. Under HITECH, however, HIPAA privacy and security rules are codified and apply directly to business associates.[36]

Beyond covered entities, HIPAA creates important obligations for business associates, including, for example, cloud storage providers that handle PHI knowingly or unknowingly.[37] Under the Privacy Rule, a business associate is any person or organization, other than a member of a covered entity's workforce, that performs services and activities for, or on behalf of, a covered entity, if such services or activities involve the use or disclosure of PHI.[38] Business associates may provide services and activities such as claims processing, data analysis, utilization review and billing as well as legal, actuarial, accounting, consulting, data aggregation, management, administrative, accreditation and/or financial services.

Before the release of HHS' final rule, under HITECH, when a covered entity engaged another entity to provide the activities and services described above, the Privacy Rule required that the covered entity enter into a business associate agreement (a contract) with that other entity.[39] This contract would include provisions that passed the privacy and security standard down to the contracting entity. Also, the business associate agreement had to be in writing, although it could be signed electronically as long as such signatures are valid as "written signatures" under the applicable state's contract laws. Modifications to the Security Rule in HITECH, however, now require business associates and covered entities to implement reasonable, appropriate safeguards to protect PHI (in addition to signing a business associate agreement).[40] As such, covered entities and business associates should implement security practices that, on the whole, comply with the Security Rule.[41]

7.2.1 The HIPAA Privacy Rule

In August 2000, HHS promulgated the regulations on standard electronic formats for healthcare transactions, known as the "Transactions Rule." This was followed in December 2000 by rules to protect the privacy of personal health information, known as the "Privacy Rule."[42] The initial HIPAA Privacy Rule was revised somewhat in 2002.[43] In February 2003, HHS promulgated the final "Security Rule." In January 2013, the Privacy and Security Rules were modified to implement statutory amendments under HITECH, which is discussed fully below. The definition of "covered entity" is the same for all three rules.

7.2.1.1 The Privacy Rule and the Fair Information Privacy Practices

Compared with other U.S. privacy laws, HIPAA provides perhaps the most detailed implementation of the Fair Information Privacy Practices, including requirements concerning privacy notices, authorizations for use and disclosure of PHI, limits on use and disclosure to the minimum necessary, individual access and accounting rights, security safeguards, and accountability through administrative requirements and enforcement. There are also important exceptions to the HIPAA rules. The following are some of the key privacy protections.

- **Privacy notices.** The Privacy Rule generally requires a covered entity to provide a detailed privacy notice at the date of first service delivery. There are some defined exceptions to the notice requirements. For example, a privacy notice does not have to be provided when the healthcare provider has an "indirect treatment relationship" with the patient or in the case of medical emergencies. The rule is quite specific about elements that must be included in the notice, including detailed statements about individuals' rights with respect to their PHI.
- **Authorizations for uses and disclosures.** Consistent with the statutory goal of improving efficiency in the healthcare system, HIPAA itself authorizes the use and disclosure of PHI for essential healthcare purposes: treatment, payment and operations (collectively, TPO), as well as for certain other established compliance purposes. Other uses or disclosures of PHI require the individual's opt-in authorization. An authorization is an independent document that specifically identifies the information to be used or disclosed, the purposes of the use or disclosure, the person or entity to which a disclosure may be made, and other information. A covered entity may not require an individual to sign an authorization as a condition of receiving treatment or participating in a health plan. Additional, strict rules apply for authorizations to use or disclose psychotherapy notes.[44]

  Specific rules define when the opt-in is required for marketing purposes. For instance, face-to-face communications by a covered entity to an individual are not considered "marketing."
- **"Minimum necessary" use or disclosure.** Other than for treatment, covered entities must make reasonable efforts to limit the use and disclosure of PHI to the minimum necessary in order to accomplish the intended purpose. As discussed more fully below, covered entities may disclose PHI to a business associate (such as a billing company, third-party administrator, attorney or consultant) only if the covered entity ensures that the business associate is bound by all of the obligations applicable to the covered entity, including the minimum necessary standards.
- **Access and accountings of disclosures.** Under the Privacy Rule, individuals have the right to access and copy their own PHI from a covered entity or a business associate. The right applies to PHI kept in a "designated record set," which is a fairly broad definition including a patient's medical records and billing records, or other records used by the covered entity to make decisions

about individuals. Only fairly narrow exceptions exist to this right of access. Additionally, individuals have a right to receive an accounting of certain disclosures of their PHI that have been made. A reasonable charge may be assessed to cover the costs of providing access.

Individuals also have the right to amend PHI possessed by a covered entity. If the covered entity denies the request to amend the PHI, the individual may file a statement that must then be included in any future use or disclosure of the information.

- **Safeguards.** The Privacy Rule requires that covered entities implement administrative, physical and technical safeguards to protect the confidentiality and integrity of all PHI. The HIPAA Security Rule requires both covered entities and business associates to implement administrative, physical and technical safeguards only for ePHI. Like the Privacy Rule, the HIPAA Security Rule aims to prevent unauthorized use or disclosure of PHI. However, the Security Rule also aims to maintain the integrity and availability of ePHI. Accordingly, the Security Rule addresses data backup and disaster recovery, among other related issues. These are discussed further below.
- **Accountability.** To foster compliance, covered entities are subject to a set of administrative requirements. Covered entities must designate a privacy official who is responsible for the development and implementation of privacy protections. Personnel must be trained, and complaint procedures, along with other procedures, must be in place.

Accountability is furthered by a range of enforcement agencies. The primary enforcer for the Privacy Rule in HHS is the Office of Civil Rights (OCR), which processes individual complaints and can assess civil monetary penalties of up to approximately 1.6 million per year per type of violation, as of the writing of this book.[45] The OCR has assessed substantial penalties under HIPAA in recent years. For example, WellPoint agreed to pay a civil penalty of $1.7 million in 2013 to settle allegations that it violated HIPAA when it did not adequately implement policies and procedures to protect the ePHI of 612,402 customers.[46] In 2016, Feinstein Institute for Medical Research agreed to pay $3.9 million to settle claims that it violated the Family Educational Rights and Privacy Act (FERPA) when the ePHI of 13,000 patients and research participants was stolen in a laptop taken from an employee's vehicle.[47] The OCR has started to regularly audit a select number of covered entities and business associates to ensure HIPAA compliance.[48]

The U.S. Department of Justice (DOJ) has criminal enforcement authority, with prison sentences of up to 10 years.[49] For the many companies within its jurisdiction, the FTC can bring enforcement actions for unfair and deceptive practices, even for entities covered by HIPAA. State attorneys general can also bring enforcement for unfair and deceptive practices, or pursuant to any applicable state medical privacy law.

7.2.1.2 Limits on and Exceptions on the Privacy Rule

In issuing the Privacy Rule, HHS stressed the dual goals of protecting PHI while also improving the efficiency of the healthcare system. As mentioned above, the rule does not require authorizations for the major categories of treatment, payment and healthcare operations. Other limits on the scope of the rule include de-identified information and medical research.

- **De-identification.** The Privacy Rule does not apply to information that has been "de-identified"—information that does not actually identify an individual and where there is no reasonable basis to believe that the information can be used to identify an individual.[50] The Privacy Rule provides two methods for de-identifying data: (1) remove all of at least 17 data elements listed in the rule, such as name, phone number and address; or (2) have an expert certify that the risk of re-identifying the individuals is very small.[51]
- **Research.** The Privacy Rule has detailed provisions for how PHI is used for medical research purposes. Research can occur with the consent of the individual, or without consent if an authorized entity such as an institutional review board approves the research as consistent with the Privacy Rule and general rules covering research on human subjects. Research is permitted on de-identified information, and rules are more flexible if only a limited data set is released to researchers.[52]
- **Other exceptions.** The Privacy Rule contains other exceptions under which PHI may be used without consent.[53] These include information used for public health activities; to report victims of abuse, neglect or domestic violence; in judicial and administrative proceedings; for certain law enforcement activities; and for certain specialized governmental functions. A covered entity is required to release PHI to the individual to whom it pertains or to the person's representative (see "Access and Accountings of Disclosures," discussed above), and to the secretary of HHS to investigate compliance with the privacy rules.

7.2.2 The HIPAA Security Rule

The HIPAA Security Rule[54] was finalized in February 2003 and modified in January 2013. It establishes minimum security requirements for PHI that a covered entity receives, creates, maintains or transmits in electronic form.[55] The Security Rule is designed to require covered entities to implement "reasonable" security measures in a technology-neutral manner. The goal is for all covered entities to implement "policies and procedures to prevent, detect, contain, and correct security violations."

The Security Rule is comprised of "standards" and "implementation specifications," which encompass administrative, technical and physical safeguards. Some of the implementation specifications are required, while others are considered "addressable." This means that the covered entity must assess whether it is an appropriate safeguard for the entity to adopt. If not, the covered entity must document why it is not reasonable, and, if appropriate, adopt an alternative measure.

The HIPAA Security Rule requires covered entities and business associates to:

1. Ensure the confidentiality, integrity and availability of all ePHI the covered entity creates, receives, maintains or transmits
2. Protect against any reasonably anticipated threats or hazards to the security or integrity of the ePHI
3. Protect against any reasonably anticipated uses or disclosures of such information that are not permitted or required under the Privacy Rule
4. Ensure compliance with the Security Rule by its workforce[56]

As noted above, the Security Rule strives for a reasonable level of security. Accordingly, the rule permits a covered entity to "use any security measures that allow the covered entity or business associate to reasonably and appropriately implement the standards and implementation specifications."[57] As it develops its security program, each covered entity must consider the following factors:

1. The size, complexity and capabilities of the covered entity
2. The covered entity's technical infrastructure, hardware and software security capabilities
3. The costs of security measures
4. The probability and criticality of potential risks to electronic protected health information[58]

The HIPAA Security Rule also requires that:

1. Each covered entity must identify an individual who is responsible for the implementation and oversight of the Security Rule compliance program.[59] (This may be the same person who oversees the Privacy Rule compliance program.)
2. Each covered entity must conduct initial and ongoing risk assessments. In particular, the covered entity must "conduct an accurate and thorough assessment of the potential risks and vulnerabilities to the confidentiality, integrity, and availability of electronic protected health information held by the covered entity."[60] This assessment should identify potential risks and vulnerabilities, each of which must be addressed.
3. Each covered entity must implement a security awareness and training program for its workforce. Additionally, individual workers must be disciplined if they fail to comply with the policies and procedures.[61]

For the privacy professional, it is important to remember that HIPAA does not preempt state laws that provide more protection than the federal law. In practice, reviewing applicable state laws will be important for ensuring compliance. Topics that should be of particular concern in this review include: (1) additional patient rights, (2) added uses or disclosures for PHI, and (3) shortened deadlines for action.[62]

7.3 The Health Information Technology for Economic and Clinical Health Act

HITECH was enacted as part of the American Recovery and Reinvestment Act of 2009 to promote the adoption and meaningful use of health information technology. HITECH codified and funded the Office of the National Coordinator for Health Information Technology and provided $19 billion in incentives for healthcare providers to adopt electronic health records and develop a national electronic health information exchange. HITECH also strengthened HIPAA to address the privacy impacts of the expanded use of electronic health records.[63]

7.3.1 Notice of Breach

In the event of unauthorized acquisition, access, use or disclosure of information, a breach is presumed to have occurred, unless the covered entity demonstrates through a risk assessment that there is a low probability that the security or privacy of the information has been compromised.[64] This language provides that covered entities and business associates have the burden of proof that an impermissible use or disclosure did not constitute a breach.[65] If there is a high probability that the security or privacy of the information (financial, reputational or other) has been compromised, a covered entity must notify individuals within 60 days of discovery.[66] If a business associate discovers a breach it must notify the covered entity.[67] If the breach affects more than 500 people, the covered entity must notify HHS immediately, and if the breach affects 500 or more in the same jurisdiction, it must notify the media.[68] All breaches requiring notice must be reported to HHS at least annually. A breach applies only to "unsecured" information, and a covered entity can avoid liability if it utilizes encryption software to secure information.[69]

7.3.2 Increased Penalties

HHS has issued a final rule pursuant to HITECH that allows for penalties of up to $1.5 million for the most willful violations and extends criminal liability to individuals who misuse PHI.[70] The enforcement rules provide for penalties even if the covered entity did not know of the violation.[71]

7.3.3 Limited Data

All disclosures by a covered entity should attempt to comply with the definition of a limited data set, and if this is not feasible, data disclosed must be the minimum amount necessary. The term *limited data set* refers to protected health information that includes direct identifiers of the individual.[72] Furthermore, patients who directly pay their provider for medical care may restrict their PHI from being disclosed to a health plan unless the disclosure is otherwise required by law.[73]

7.3.4 Electronic Health Records

The $19 billion in funding in HITECH created important incentives for health providers to use Electronic Health Records (EHRs) more extensively. Providers who make "meaningful use" of EHRs can qualify for these funds.[74] In local markets, more practice groups have linked their EHRs with local hospitals. For broader geographic regions, there has been increased sharing of medical information toward the HHS goal of having a National Health Information Network.[75] Sharing of PHI is generally permitted under HIPAA to the extent necessary for treatment, payment or healthcare operations. Compliance issues become more important if information shared through EHRs is used for other purposes or with other entities, and such sharing can lawfully be done only with patient consent or under some other provision of HIPAA. Compliance also can become considerably more complex where the laws of different states apply to the same EHR system.

HITECH itself, along with providing funding for greater use of EHRs, made certain changes to HIPAA's legal treatment of EHRs. Covered entities must provide individuals with a copy of their EHR on request and must account for all non-oral disclosures made within three years on the request.[76] Additionally, covered entities may not sell EHRs without the consent of the patient and covered entities cannot receive payment for certain marketing plans.[77]

7.4 Genetic Information Nondiscrimination Act of 2008

GINA created new national limits on the use of genetic information in health insurance and employment.[78] In considering GINA, Congress found that genetic testing, before symptoms appeared, would allow individuals to take steps to reduce the likelihood of ultimately developing a disease or disorder. At the same time, such testing could create the risk of misusing that information for health insurance or employment.[79] Concerns about misuse were supported by historical examples of genetic discrimination, such as sterilization programs aimed at those with disorders that were perceived to be genetic, programs aimed at mandating sickle cell testing for African Americans, and pre-employment genetic screening of federal employees.[80] Generally, GINA prohibits health insurance companies from discriminating on the basis of genetic predispositions in the absence of manifest symptoms or from requesting that applicants receive genetic testing, and prohibits employers from using genetic information in making employment decisions.[81]

GINA amended a variety of existing pieces of legislation including, among others, the Employee Retirement Income Security Act (ERISA), the Social Security Act and the Civil Rights Act. The amendments to ERISA prohibit group health plan providers from adjusting premiums or other contribution schemes on the basis of genetic information, absent a manifestation of a disease or disorder.[82] GINA also amended ERISA to prohibit group health plan providers from requesting or requiring genetic testing in connection with the offering of group health plans, although an exception is carved out for requests for voluntary testing in connection with research.[83] For the research exception to apply, providers must notify the HHS secretary and make clear that compliance is voluntary, that noncompliance will have no effect on enrollment or contributions, and that no genetic information will be used for underwriting purposes.[84] The amendments to ERISA also allow for governmental enforcement.[85] A statutory penalty is set at $100 for each day of noncompliance (inclusive of the beginning date and date of rectification) with respect to each plan participant or beneficiary, although minimum penalties can rise to $15,000 in certain circumstances.[86] Some liability, however, may be avoided under this section if the grounds for liability could not have been discovered by exercising reasonable diligence.[87]

Similar provisions revise the Public Health Service Act and apply to participants in the individual health insurance market to prohibit adjustments to premiums or other contribution schemes on the basis of genetic information absent the manifestation of disease or disorder.[88] These revisions prohibit insurers from using a genetic predisposition to find an excludable preexisting condition.[89] Once again, the revisions allow for governmental enforcement against violators. Amendments to the Social Security Act extend similar provisions to the providers of Medicare supplemental insurance policies.[90] GINA also directs the secretary of HHS to revise HIPAA regulations such that genetic information is considered health information,[91] and the disclosure of such information may not be disclosed by covered entities, pursuant to HIPAA.[92]

Aside from health care insurance, GINA also takes aim at the possibility of employment discrimination based on genetic information in the absence of the manifestation of a disease or disorder.[93] Additionally, the employment-related sections of GINA prohibit discrimination against individuals because they have a family member who has manifested a disease.[94] These sections of GINA revised the Civil Rights Act and apply coextensively with that act.[95] Along with expressly prohibiting discrimination on the basis of genetic information, these portions of GINA prohibit employers from requiring, requesting or purchasing such genetic information about employees or family members unless an express exception applies.[96] Exceptions are provided for instances where: (1) such a request is inadvertent, (2) the request is part of an employer-offered wellness program that the employee voluntarily participates in with written authorization, (3) the request is made to comply with the Family and Medical Leave Act of 1993, (4) an employer purchases commercially and publicly available materials that include the information, (5) the information is used for legally required genetic monitoring for toxin exposure in the workplace if the employee voluntarily participates with written authorization or (6) the employer conducts DNA analysis for law enforcement purposes and requests the information for quality-control purposes (i.e., to identify contamination).[97] These parts of GINA not only apply to employers, but also prohibit unions and training programs from excluding or expelling individuals on the basis of such information.[98]

GINA does recognize that employers or unions may have legitimate reasons for possessing such information (e.g., as part of a toxin exposure monitoring program or company-sponsored wellness program).[99] Accordingly, if an employer possesses such information, it must be kept on separate forms in separate medical files, and such files must be treated as confidential employee medical records.[100]

GINA itself does not provide for a private right of action, but—depending on the violation—private rights of action may be available under the federal laws that it revises, as well as under similar state laws.[101] To ensure regulation keeps up with technology, GINA mandates the creation of a commission to review the developments in the science of genetics and make recommendations as to whether to establish a disparate impact cause of action under GINA.[102]

7.5 The 21st Century Cures Act of 2016

The purpose of the 21st Century Cures Act ("Cures Act") is to expedite the research process for new medical devices and prescription drugs, quicken the process for drug approval, and reform mental health treatment.[103] Although the initial version of the bill raised concerns that pharmaceutical companies would be able to purchase individually identifiable health information that was deemed to have research or public health purposes, the final bill addressed these potential pitfalls. The Cures Act has numerous privacy-related provisions, and seeks a balance between the protection of personal data and the public interest in the appropriate utilization of this information.[104]

Privacy provisions in the Cures Act include:

Certain individual biomedical research information exempted from disclosure under Freedom of Information Act. To the extent that individual biomedical research information could reveal individual identity, the Cures Act exempts this information from mandatory disclosure under the Freedom of Information Act.[105]

Researchers permitted to remotely view PHI. The Cures Act provides a clarification to existing law that allows medical researchers to remotely review PHI. This remote access must meet minimum safeguards consistent with HIPAA's Privacy and Security Rules.[106]

Information blocking prohibited but HIPAA's protection of PHI remains. The Cures Act prohibits providers, health information technology (HIT) providers, health information exchanges (HIEs), or networks from *information blocking*, a term meant to describe unreasonable conduct that is likely to interfere with the exchange of electronic health information. This requirement must be balanced with HIPAA's requirements concerning PHI.[107]

"Certificates of confidentiality" for research. The Cures Act provides stronger privacy protections for those participating in research, particularly those with alcohol and substance abuse issues. The Cures Act requires certificates of confidentiality to be issued by the National Institutes of Health (NIH) for any federally funded research, and permits the NIH to issue such certificates at its discretion for research that is not federally funded. These certificates ensure that the research material cannot be used in any legal or administrative proceeding without the consent of the individual involved.[108]

"Compassionate" sharing of mental health or substance abuse information with family or caregivers. The Cures Act requires HHS to issue guidance to HIPAA regarding the circumstances under which a health care provider or a covered entity is permitted to discuss with family members or caregivers the treatment of an adult with a mental health disorder or an alcohol or substance abuse disorder.[109]

A violation of the information blocking provision of the Cures Act can result in a fine up to $1 million.[110]

7.6 Conclusion

U.S. law about medical and genetic privacy reflects the view that such personal information is particularly sensitive. This chapter has described the Confidentiality of Substance Use Disorder Patient Records Rule, the comprehensive HIPAA privacy and security rules as updated by the HITECH Act, GINA's comprehensive rules prohibiting discrimination based on genetic personal information, as well as the privacy protections found in the 21st Century Cures Act. That said, there are also compelling reasons to use these categories of personal information. HIPAA notably enables use and disclosure of protected health information for treatment, payment and healthcare operations, as well as for medical research. Similarly, there is great interest in the promise of medical and genetic research. The 21st Century Cures Act aims to balance these often-conflicting goals. Privacy professionals who work with health data need to be aware not only that strong protections are required, but also that such data is often used as permitted by the regulations.

Endnotes

1 Peter Tyson, "The Hippocratic Oath: Modern Version," WGBH Educational Foundation, 2001, www.pbs.org/wgbh/nova/body/hippocratic-oath-today.html (accessed November 2017).

2 For additional information on preemption, view "Does the HIPAA Privacy Rule Preempt State Laws?" HHS, www.hhs.gov/hipaa/for-professionals/faq/399/does-hipaa-preempt-state-laws/index.html (accessed November 2017). For more information on health information privacy laws in California in the context of HIPAA and GINA, *see* Lothar Determann, California Privacy Law—Practical Guide and Commentary, Chapters 2-9 (2016).

3 *See* Cal. Civ. Code §§ 1798.90–1798.90.05.

4 Cal. Civ. Code §§ 56-59. The website could be covered under HIPAA if it is the website of a covered entity and it collects protected health information as defined under HIPAA.

5 *See* Compliance with Other Laws, Regulations and Codes, DMA Ethical Guidelines, Data & Marketing Association, https://thedma.org/accountability/ethics-and-compliance/dma-ethical-guidelines/laws-codes-and-regulations/#health (accessed October 2017).

6 For additional information on medical information that is not protected by HIPAA, view Robert Gellman, "Personal Health Records: Why Many PHRs Threaten Privacy," World Privacy Forum, February 20, 2008), www.worldprivacyforum.org/wp-content/uploads/2012/04/WPF_PHR_02_20_2008fs.pdf (accessed November 2017).

7 HIPAA is discussed in Section 7.2 of this chapter.

8 *The Confidentiality of Alcohol and Drug Abuse Patient Records Regulation and the HIPAA Privacy Rule: Implications for Alcohol and Substance Abuse Programs*, HHS (June 2004), https://www.samhsa.gov/sites/default/files/part2-hipaa-comparison2004.pdf (accessed October 2017). The rule-making authority relating to confidentiality that is granted by these statutes is now codified in 42 U.S.C. § 290dd-2. 42 U.S.C. § 290dd-2 (2006), https://www.law.cornell.edu/uscode/text/42/290dd-2 (accessed October 2017).

9 Confidentiality of Substance Use Disorder Patient Records Rule, 42 C.F.R. Part 2 (2017) [*formerly* Confidentiality of Alcohol and Drug Abuse Patient Records], https://www.federalregister.gov/documents/2017/01/18/2017-00719/confidentiality-of-substance-use-disorder-patient-records (accessed October 2017); see Final Rule: 42 CFR Part 2, Confidentiality of Substance Use Disorder Patient Records, American Psychiatric Society, https://www.psychiatry.org/psychiatrists/practice/practice-management/hipaa/42-cfr-part-2 (accessed October 2017).

10 The term used by the Rule is *substance use disorder* treatment programs. Section 2.11, Confidentiality of Substance Use Disorder Patient Records Rule, 42 C.F.R. Part 2 (2017), https://www.federalregister.gov/documents/2017/01/18/2017-00719/confidentiality-of-substance-use-disorder-patient-records (accessed October 2017).

11 Section 2.11, Confidentiality of Substance Use Disorder Patient Records Rule, 42 C.F.R. Part 2 (2017), https://www.federalregister.gov/documents/2017/01/18/2017-00719/confidentiality-of-substance-use-disorder-patient-records (accessed October 2017); Final Rule: 42 CFR Part 2, Confidentiality of Substance Use Disorder Patient Records, American Psychiatric Society, https://www.psychiatry.org/psychiatrists/practice/practice-management/hipaa/42-cfr-part-2 (accessed October 2017); *see* The Confidentiality of Alcohol and Drug Abuse Patient Records Regulation and the HIPAA Privacy Rule: Implications for Alcohol and Substance Abuse Programs, HHS (June 2004), https://www.samhsa.gov/sites/default/files/part2-hipaa-comparison2004.pdf (accessed October 2017).

12 Section 2.12, Confidentiality of Substance Use Disorder Patient Records Rule, 42 C.F.R. Part 2 (2017), https://www.federalregister.gov/documents/2017/01/18/2017-00719/confidentiality-of-substance-use-disorder-patient-records (accessed October 2017).

13 Section 2.11, Confidentiality of Substance Use Disorder Patient Records Rule, 42 C.F.R. Part 2 (2017), https://www.federalregister.gov/documents/2017/01/18/2017-00719/confidentiality-of-substance-use-disorder-patient-records (accessed October 2017); *see Final Rule: 42 CFR Part 2, Confidentiality of Substance Use Disorder Patient Records*, "Comparison Chart—1987 rule, 2017 updated final rule, and HIPAA," American Psychiatric Society (February 23, 2017), https://www.psychiatry.org/File%20Library/Psychiatrists/Practice/Practice-Management/42-CFR-Part-Standards-Comparison.pdf (accessed October 2017).

14 Susan Awad, "Confused on Confidentiality? A Primer on 42 CFR Part 2," Resources— American Society of Addiction Medicine (August 15, 2013), https://www.asam.org/resources/publications/

magazine/read/article/2013/08/15/confused-by-confidentiality-a-primer-on-42-cfr-part-2 (accessed October 2017).

15 Section 2.31, Confidentiality of Substance Use Disorder Patient Records Rule, 42 C.F.R. Part 2 (2017), https://www.federalregister.gov/documents/2017/01/18/2017-00719/confidentiality-of-substance-use-disorder-patient-records (accessed October 2017); *see* Final Rule: *42 CFR Part 2*, Confidentiality of Substance Use Disorder Patient Records, American Psychiatric Society, Comparison Chart—1987 rule, 2017 updated final rule, and HIPAA (February 23, 2017), https://www.psychiatry.org/File%20Library/Psychiatrists/Practice/Practice-Management/42-CFR-Part-Standards-Comparison.pdf (accessed October 2017).

16 Section 2.32, Confidentiality of Substance Use Disorder Patient Records Rule, 42 C.F.R. Part 2 (2017), https://www.federalregister.gov/documents/2017/01/18/2017-00719/confidentiality-of-substance-use-disorder-patient-records (accessed October 2017); *see* Final Rule: 42 CFR Part 2, Confidentiality of Substance Use Disorder Patient Records, American Psychiatric Society, Comparison Chart—1987 rule, 2017 updated final rule, and HIPAA (February 23, 2017), https://www.psychiatry.org/File%20Library/Psychiatrists/Practice/Practice-Management/42-CFR-Part-Standards-Comparison.pdf (accessed October 2017).

17 Section 2.51, Confidentiality of Substance Use Disorder Patient Records Rule, 42 C.F.R. Part 2 (2017), https://www.federalregister.gov/documents/2017/01/18/2017-00719/confidentiality-of-substance-use-disorder-patient-records (accessed October 2017).

18 Section 2.52, Confidentiality of Substance Use Disorder Patient Records Rule, 42 C.F.R. Part 2 (2017), https://www.federalregister.gov/documents/2017/01/18/2017-00719/confidentiality-of-substance-use-disorder-patient-records (accessed October 2017). Disclosures for scientific research must meet certain requirements related to protections for human research. *See* Mark Moran, "Rule Governing Confidentiality of Substance Use Data Updated," *Psychiatric News*, American Psychiatric Association, February 23, 2017, http://psychnews.psychiatryonline.org/doi/full/10.1176/appi.pn.2017.3a4 (accessed October 2017).

19 Section 2.53, Confidentiality of Substance Use Disorder Patient Records Rule, 42 C.F.R. Part 2 (2017), https://www.federalregister.gov/documents/2017/01/18/2017-00719/confidentiality-of-substance-use-disorder-patient-records (accessed October 2017).

20 *Id.* at Section 2.12(c)(4).

21 *Id.* at Section 2.12(c)(5).

22 *Id.* at Section 2.12(c)(6).

23 *Id.* at Section 2.61-2.67.

24 *Id.* at Section 2.16.

25 (Name Redacted) Specialist in Health Policy, "Privacy Protections for Individuals with Substance Abuse Disorders: The Part 2 Final Rule in Brief," pp. 4-5, Congressional Research Service (March 17, 2017). https://www.everycrsreport.com/files/20170317_R44790_9f35e7a104d6d5dc1eef64d245f1bf62fcc0f0b0.pdf (accessed October 2017); see Section 2.3-2.4, Confidentiality of Substance Use Disorder Patient Records Rule, 42 C.F.R. Part 2 (2017), https://www.federalregister.gov/documents/2017/01/18/2017-00719/confidentiality-of-substance-use-disorder-patient-records (accessed October 2017).

26 HIPAA's Privacy Rule is discussed in Section 7.2.1 of this chapter.

27 *The Confidentiality of Alcohol and Drug Abuse Patient Records Regulation and the HIPAA Privacy Rule: Implications for Alcohol and Substance Abuse Programs*, HHS (June 2004), https://www.samhsa.gov/sites/default/files/part2-hipaa-comparison2004.pdf (accessed October 2017).

28 Comparison charts are available at Final Rule: 42 CFR Part 2, Confidentiality of Substance Use Disorder Patient Records, American Psychiatric Society, Comparison Chart—1987 rule, 2017 accessed final rule, and HIPAA (February 23, 2017), https://www.psychiatry.org/File%20Library/Psychiatrists/Practice/Practice-Management/42-CFR-Part-Standards-Comparison.pdf (accessed October 2017) and (Name Redacted) Specialist in Health Policy, "Privacy Protections for Individuals with Substance Abuse Disorders: The Part 2 Final Rule in Brief," pp. 4-5, Congressional Research Service (March 17, 2017) https://www.everycrsreport.com/files/20170317_R44790_9f35e7a104d6d5dc1eef64d245f1bf62fcc0f0b0.pdf (accessed October 2017).

29 *Confidentiality of Patient Records for Alcohol and Other Drug Treatment*, Technical Assistance Publication, Series 13, DHHS Publication No. (SMA) 95-3018, HHS (1994), http://adaiclearinghouse.org/downloads/tap-13-confidentiality-of-patient-records-for-alcohol-and-other-drug-treatment-103.pdf (accessed October 2017).

30 45 C.F.R. § 160.103, located at www.ecfr.gov/cgi-bin/text-idx?tpl=/ecfrbrowse/Title45/45cfr160_main_02.tpl (accessed November 2017).

31 *Id.*

32 "Are You a Covered Entity?" Centers for Medicare & Medicaid Services, https://www.cms.gov/Regulations-and-Guidance/Administrative-Simplification/HIPAA-ACA/AreYouaCoveredEntity.html (accessed November 2017).

33 A healthcare clearinghouse means a public or private entity, including a billing service, repricing company, community health management information system or community health information system, and value-added networks and switches that does either of the following functions:

- Processes or facilitates the processing of health information received from another entity in a nonstandard format or containing nonstandard data content into standard data elements or a standard transaction
- Receives a standard transaction from another entity and processes or facilitates the processing of health information into nonstandard format or nonstandard data content for the receiving entity https://www.law.cornell.edu/cfr/text/45/160.103 (accessed November 2017).

34 "New Rule Protects Patient Privacy, Secures Health Information," HHS, http://www.girardslaw.com/library/HHS_Press_Release_about_New_HIPAA_Rules_2013.pdf (accessed November 2017).

35 "Medical Privacy: When Is Medical Information Not Covered by HIPAA?" Electronic Frontier Foundation, https://www.eff.org/issues/medical-privacy (accessed November 2017).

36 42 U.S.C. § 17921(2), https://www.law.cornell.edu/uscode/text/42/17921 (accessed November 2017); 45 C.F.R. § 160.103, www.hhs.gov/hipaa/for-professionals/privacy/guidance/business-associates/index.html (accessed November 2017).

37 *See* Lothar Determann and Oliver Zee, "Cloud Provider Obligations as Business Associates under HIPAA," 30 *Computer & Internet Lawyer* 6, 1 (2013).

38 Please note that, in order to be a "business associate" under HIPAA, the person or organization must process PHI. Entities that do not process PHI (or whose access to PHI is truly incidental) are not business associates. Covered entities can themselves be business associates of other covered entities.

39 The HIPAA Privacy Rule only applies to covered entities, not their business associates. The Privacy Rule permits covered entities to disclose protected health information to their business associates if the covered entities obtain satisfactory assurances that the business associate will use the information only for the purposes for which it was engaged by the covered entity, will safeguard the information, and will help the covered entity to comply with some of its duties under the Privacy Rule. "Business Associates," HHS.com, www.hhs.gov/hipaa/for-professionals/privacy/guidance/business-associates/ (accessed November 2017).

40 The sample business associate contract provided by HHS on its website includes 10 requirements. "Business Associate Contracts," HHS.com, www.hhs.gov/hipaa/for-professionals/covered-entities/sample-business-associate-agreement-provisions/index.html (accessed November 2017). For insight from HHS, view "Summary of the HIPAA Security Rule," HHS.com, www.hhs.gov/hipaa/for-professionals/security/laws-regulations/ (accessed November 2017).

41 45 C.F.R. § 160.102(b), www.hhs.gov/sites/default/files/ocr/privacy/hipaa/administrative/combined/hipaa-simplification-201303.pdf (accessed April 2016). The detailed changes in the rule can be found at https://www.gpo.gov/fdsys/pkg/FR-2013-01-25/pdf/2013-01073.pdf (accessed November 2017).

42 This HIPAA statute, Transaction Rule, Privacy Rule (with all the amendments), Security Rule, and publNovember 2017April 2016). The combined regulation text of all these rules can be found at www.hhs.gov/hipaa/for-professionals/privacy/laws-regulations/combined-regulation-text/index.html (accessed November 2017).

43 For additional information, view Summary of the HIPAA Privacy Rule, HHS, www.hhs.gov/hipaa/for-professionals/privacy/laws-regulations/index.html (accessed November 2017).

44 For additional information on mental health and substance abuse records, view www.ncbi.nlm.nih.gov/books/NBK19829/ (accessed November 2017).

45 "Annual Civil Monetary Penalties Inflation Adjustment," Federal Register, https://www.federalregister.gov/documents/2017/02/03/2017-02300/annual-civil-monetary-penalties-inflation-adjustment (assessed January 2018)

46 "WellPoint pays HHS $1.7 million for leaving information accessible over the Internet," HHS, https://www.hhs.gov/hipaa/for-professionals/compliance-enforcement/examples/wellpoint/index.html (accessed November 2017).

47 "Improper disclosure of research participants' protected health information results in $3.9 million HIPPA settlement," HHS, https://www.hhs.gov/hipaa/for-professionals/compliance-enforcement/agreements/feinstein/index.html (accessed November 2017).

48 HIPAA Privacy, Security, and Breach Notification Audit Program, HHS (December 1, 2016), www.hhs.gov/hipaa/for-professionals/compliance-enforcement/audit/ (accessed October 2017).

49 42 U.S.C. § 1320d-6, located at https://www.law.cornell.edu/uscode/text/42/1320d-6 (accessed November 2017); *see* United States v. Zhou, United States Court of Appeals (9th Cir. 2012) (appeal of misdemeanor conviction for violation of 42 U.S.C. § 1320d-6), http://cdn.ca9.uscourts.gov/datastore/opinions/2012/05/10/10-50231.pdf (accessed November 2017).

50 45 C.F.R. § 164.502(d), located at https://www.law.cornell.edu/cfr/text/45/164.502 (accessed November 2017).

51 45 C.F.R. § 164.514, https://www.law.cornell.edu/cfr/text/45/164.514 (accessed November 2017). For guidance on methods of de-identification, view www.hhs.gov/hipaa/for-professionals/privacy/special-topics/de-identification/index.html (accessed November 2017).

52 45 C.F.R. § 164.512(i), https://www.law.cornell.edu/cfr/text/45/164.512 (accessed November 2017).

53 45 C.F.R. § 164.512, https://www.law.cornell.edu/cfr/text/45/164.512 (accessed November 2017).

54 For additional information, view Summary of the HIPAA Security Rule at www.hhs.gov/hipaa/for-professionals/security/laws-regulations/index.html (accessed April 2016). In addition, the National Institute of Standards and Technology provides a HIPAA Security Rule kit that can be accessed at https://scap.nist.gov/hipaa/ (accessed November 2017).

55 HHS considered extending the Security Rule to nonelectronic PHI, so that the provisions mirror the scope of protection offered by the Privacy Rule. *See* http://nationalacademies.org/hmd/~/media/files/activity%20files/research/hipaaandresearch/hipaabackground.pdf (accessed November 2017). (Note that the financial services counterpart, the Gramm-Leach-Bliley Act (GLBA), does not limit applicability of its Safeguards Rule to electronic data. For health insurers subject to HIPAA and GLBA, the security program must encompass paper as well as electronic records.)

56 45 C.F.R. § 164.306(a)(1-4), https://www.law.cornell.edu/cfr/text/45/164.306 (accessed November 2017).

57 45 C.F.R. § 164.306(b)(1), https://www.law.cornell.edu/cfr/text/45/164.306 (accessed November 2017).

58 45 C.F.R. § 164.306(b)(2), https://www.law.cornell.edu/cfr/text/45/164.306 (accessed November 2017).

59 45 C.F.R. § 164.308(a)(2), https://www.law.cornell.edu/cfr/text/45/164.308 (accessed November 2017).

60 45 C.F.R. § 164.308(a)(1)(ii)(A), https://www.law.cornell.edu/cfr/text/45/164.308 (accessed November 2017).

61 45 C.F.R. § 164.308(a)(5)(i), https://www.law.cornell.edu/cfr/text/45/164.308 (accessed November 2017).

62 David Craig, "What You Need to Know about HIPAA and Your State's Privacy Law," *Spruce Blog* (October 10, 2016), https://blog.sprucehealth.com/need-know-hipaa-states-laws/ (accessed October 2017); *see* The Law and Medical Privacy, Electronic Freedom Foundation, https://www.eff.org/issues/law-and-medical-privacy (accessed October 2017). Numerous states have made guides or commentary available about the particulars of their state law requirements. *See*, e.g., Deven McGraw, Alice Leiter and Christopher Rasmussen, *Rights and Requirements: A Guide to Privacy and Security of Health Information in California*, California Healthcare Foundation (October 2013), www.chcf.org/~/media/MEDIA%20LIBRARY%20Files/PDF/PDF%20P/PDF%20PrivacySecurityGuide.pdf (accessed October 2017); State and Federal Health Privacy Laws, Texas Attorney General, https://www.texasattorneygeneral.gov/cpd/state-and-federal-health-privacy-laws (accessed October 2017).

63 42 U.S.C. § 17921, https://www.law.cornell.edu/uscode/text/42/17921 (accessed November 2017).

64 45 CFR 164.402, https://www.law.cornell.edu/cfr/text/45/164.402 (accessed November 2017).

65 *Id.* For additional insight, view "Final Rule: Modified Definition of Breach," hipaa.com, https://www.hipaa.com/final-rule-modified-definition-of-breach/ (accessed November 2017).

66 42 U.S.C. § 17932, https://www.law.cornell.edu/uscode/text/42/17932 (accessed November 2017).

67 42 U.S.C. § 17932, https://www.law.cornell.edu/uscode/text/42/17932 (accessed November 2017). 42 U.S.C. § 17932(h), https://www.law.cornell.edu/uscode/text/42/17932 (accessed November 2017).

68 42 U.S.C. § 17932(e)(2)-(3), https://www.law.cornell.edu/uscode/text/42/17932 (accessed November 2017). 42 U.S.C. § 17932(h), https://www.law.cornell.edu/uscode/text/42/17932 (accessed November 2017).

69 42 U.S.C. § 17932(h), https://www.law.cornell.edu/uscode/text/42/17932 (accessed November 2017).

70 "HITECH Act Enforcement Interim Rule," HHS, www.hhs.gov/hipaa/for-professionals/special-topics/HITECH-act-enforcement-interim-final-rule/index.html (accessed November 2017).

71 42 U.S.C. § 17320d-5, https://www.law.cornell.edu/uscode/text/42/1320d-5 (accessed November 2017).

72 42 U.S.C. § 17935(a)-(b), https://www.law.cornell.edu/uscode/text/42/17935 (accessed November 2017). 45 CFR § 164.522(a)(1)(vi)(A)-(B), https://www.law.cornell.edu/cfr/text/45/164.522 (accessed April 2016); see 45 CFR § 164.514(e) (limited data set), https://www.law.cornell.edu/cfr/text/45/164.514 (accessed November 2017).

73 45 CFR § 164.522(a)(1)(vi)(A)-(B), https://www.law.cornell.edu/cfr/text/45/164.522 (accessed November 2017). For an in-depth discussion, view "Overview of HIPAA/HITECH Act Omnibus Final Rule, Alston & Bird, www.alston.com/files/publication/16f88170-1cf1-4676-be7c-cb0f4a769843/presentation/publicationattachment/81794b42-2bcc-4d74-94e5-be33385227bd/13-066%20hipaa-hitech-omnibus-finalrule.pdf (accessed November 2017).

74 42 CFR §§ 412, 413, 422, 495; 45 CFR § 170.32. https://www.law.cornell.edu/cfr/text/42/part-412; https://www.law.cornell.edu/cfr/text/42/part-413; https://www.law.cornell.edu/cfr/text/42/part-422; https://www.law.cornell.edu/cfr/text/42/part-495; https://www.law.cornell.edu/cfr/text/45/part-170 (accessed November 2017). For a detailed discussion of Stage 3 of the incentive program, view https://www.federalregister.gov/articles/2015/03/30/2015-06685/medicare-and-medicaid-programs-electronic-health-record-incentive-program-stage-3 (accessed November 2017) and https://www.cms.gov/Regulations-and-Guidance/Legislation/EHRIncentivePrograms/index.html?redirect=/ehrincentiveprograms (accessed November 2017).

75 www.nhinwatch.com/ (accessed November 2017).

76 42 U.S.C. § 17935(c), https://www.law.cornell.edu/uscode/text/42/17935 (accessed November 2017).

77 42 U.S.C. § 1936, https://www.law.cornell.edu/uscode/text/42/17936 (accessed November 2017).

78 Pub. L. 110-233, 122 Stat. 881 (2008), https://www.gpo.gov/fdsys/pkg/PLAW-110publ233/pdf/PLAW-110publ233.pdf (update November 2017). For a summary, view https://www.genome.gov/pages/policyethics/geneticdiscrimination/ginainfodoc.pdf (accessed November 2017).

79 *Id.* at § 2.

80 *Id.*

81 *See generally id.* at §§ 101, 104, 200.

82 *Id.* at § 101.

83 *Id.*

84 *Id.*

85 *Id.*

86 *Id.*

87 *Id.*

88 *Id.* at § 102.

89 *Id.*

90 *Id.* at § 104.

91 As described in 42 U.S.C. § 1171(4)(B) (2006); https://aspe.hhs.gov/report/health-insurance-portability-and-accountability-act-1996#1171 (accessed November 2017).

92 *Id.* at § 105.

93 *Id.* at tit. II.

94 *Id.* at § 202.

95 *Id.* at §§ 202-205.

96 *Id.* at § 202.

97 *Id.*

98 *Id.* at §§ 203-205.

99 *Id.* at § 206.

100 *Id.* Such medical records should be kept in a manner consistent with the practices mandated for employee entrance exams under 42 U.S.C. § 12112(d)(3)(B), https://www.law.cornell.edu/uscode/text/42/12112 (accessed November 2017).

101 For example, a private right of action for employment discrimination may be available under Title VII of the Civil Rights Act. https://www.eeoc.gov/laws/statutes/titlevii.cfm (accessed November 2017). Additionally, 35 states and the District of Columbia have private rights of action for genetic discrimination. https://www.genome.gov/27552194/ (accessed November 2017).

102 GINA, at § 208.

103 Russell Berman, "Congress Nears a Breakthrough on Medical Research Funding," *The Atlantic*, December 1, 2016, https://www.theatlantic.com/politics/archive/2016/12/cures-act-compromise-elizabeth-warren/509228/ (accessed October 2017). The law can be found at Public Law 114-255 (December 13, 2016), https://www.congress.gov/114/plaws/publ255/PLAW-114publ255.pdf (accessed October 2017). For a chart of provisions of the Cures Act that are relevant to data sharing, view Mary Majumder, Christi Guerrini, Juli Bollinger, Robert Cook-Deegan and Amy McGuire, "Sharing Data under the 21st Century Cures Act, Table 1: 21st Century Cures Act provisions relevant to data sharing," *Genetics in Medicine—The Official Journal of the American College of Medical Genetics and Genomics*, https://www.nature.com/articles/gim201759.epdf (accessed October 2017).

104 Kirk Nahra, "Privacy and Security Impacts of the 21st Century Cures Legislation," IAPP Privacy Tracker (December 19, 2016), https://iapp.org/news/a/privacy-and-security-impacts-of-the-21st-century-cures-legislation/ (accessed October 2017).

105 21st Century Cures Act (Public Law 114-255), Sections 2012 and 2013, *SciPol*, http://scipol.duke.edu/content/21st-century-cures-act-public-law-114-255 (accessed October 2017); *see* Kathy Hudson and Dr. Francis Collins, "The 21st Century Cures Act—A View from the NIH," *The New England Journal of Medicine*, January 12, 2017, www.nejm.org/doi/full/10.1056/NEJMp1615745#t=article (accessed October 2017).

106 Jim Gearhart, "The 21st Century Cures Act—"What's In It for Researchers and IRBs?" Important Cures Act Sections for Researchers and the Ethics Community, Section 2063: Assessing, Sharing, and Using Health Data for Research Purposes," *Quorum*, January 10, 2017, https://www.quorumreview.com/the-21st-century-cures-act-whats-in-it-for-researchers-and-irbs/ (accessed October 2017); *see* Dena Feldman, "Twenty-First Century Cures Act Includes HIPAA

Provisions," Covington Digital Health (December 23, 2016), https://www.covingtondigitalhealth.com/2016/12/twenty-first-century-cures-act-includes-hipaa-provisions/ (accessed October 2017).

107 "Fact Sheet on 21st Century Cures Act's biomedical innovation provisions," Faster Cures – A Center of the Milken Institute, www.fastercures.org/programs/r-and-d-policy/21st-century-cures/ (accessed October 2017). There is a concern that this provision of the Cures Act could conflict with HIPAA's protections concerning the disclosure of PHI. At present, it is unknown how the Office of Civil Rights (OCR) of HHS, the entity that enforces HIPAA, and the Inspector General of the HHS, the designated enforcement officer for the Cures Act, will view the interaction of these two laws. Bass, Berry & Sims, LLP, "21st Century Cures Act – HIPAA & Other Privacy Considerations," *Lexology*, December 16, 2016, https://www.lexology.com/library/detail.aspx?g=dae83798-6229-47a7-9e68-283c0da27d18 (accessed October 2017).

108 21st Century Cures Act; *see* Bass, Berry & Sims, LLP, "21st Century Cures Act."

109 William Maruca, "21st Century Cure for a 'Broken' Mental Health System Includes HIPAA Clarification," Fox Rothschild (December 30, 2016), https://hipaahealthlaw.foxrothschild.com/tags/mental-health/ (accessed November 2017); *see* "Compassionate Communication and Mental Health," *The HIPAA E-Tool Blog*, January 4, 2017, https://www.thehipaaetool.com/blog/2017/1/4/compassionate-communication-and-mental-health (accessed October 2017); Dena Feldman, "21st Cures Act."

110 21st Century Cures Act (Public Law 114-255), Section 3022(b)(2)(A), *SciPol*, http://scipol.duke.edu/content/21st-century-cures-act-public-law-114-255 (accessed October 2017); *see* Vasilios Kalogredis and Katherine LaDow, "21st Century Cures Act Imposes High Penalties Upon Healthcare Providers for Electronic Information Blocking," Lamb McErlane (January 31, 2017), https://www.lambmcerlane.com/articles/21st-century-cures-act-imposes-high-penalties-upon-healthcare-providers-electronic-information-blocking/ (accessed October 2017).

CHAPTER 8

Financial Privacy

Banking and other financial records have long been treated with high levels of confidentiality. Medieval and early modern banks often kept the identity of their borrowers secret and would not reveal intimate financial details of their customers. One reason for this confidentiality was to encourage borrowers to report honestly to the lender about their other debts and ability to pay. Another priority in the financial sector is to ensure security—thieves and fraudsters can target individuals or transactions if they have access to these details.

This chapter focuses on restrictions on how financial services firms may collect, use and disclose personal information. Financial institutions are also subject to a variety of special rules about when they must disclose personal information. For instance, banks and other financial institutions have a variety of reporting obligations under the anti-money-laundering laws. These required disclosures are discussed in Section 8.5.

The chapter begins with the Fair Credit Reporting Act (FCRA), which was enacted in 1970 and substantially updated by the Fair and Accurate Credit Transactions Act of 2003 (FACTA). It next discusses the privacy and security portions of the Gramm-Leach-Bliley Act of 1999 (GLBA), which supplies the general framework for confidentiality of records in the financial services sector. It concludes with the relevant portions of the Dodd-Frank Wall Street Reform and Consumer Protection Act of 2010. That law, passed in the wake of the financial crisis that struck in 2008, created a new regulatory agency, the Consumer Financial Protection Bureau (CFPB). The CFPB now has rule-making authority for the FCRA, as updated by FACTA, as well as for most financial institutions under GLBA, and shares enforcement authority for these with the FTC and banking regulators.[1]

8.1 The Fair Credit Reporting Act

The United States began regulation of credit reporting during the early days of commercial data processing by computers.[2] The Fair Credit Reporting Act (FCRA) was enacted in 1970 to regulate the consumer reporting industry and provide privacy rights in consumer reports. Specifically, FCRA mandates accurate and relevant data collection, provides consumers with the ability to access and correct their information, and limits the use of consumer reports to defined permissible purposes.[3]

The origins of the FCRA can be traced to the rise of consumer credit in the United States. In the post-World War II era, merchants began to share more in-depth customer data in order to facilitate lending to households. By the 1960s, consumer credit was critical, but increasingly, individuals were being harmed by inaccurate information that they could neither see nor correct. In response, Congress passed the FCRA, the first federal law to regulate the use of personal information by private businesses.[4]

FCRA amendments in 1996 strengthened consumer access and correction rights and included provisions for non-consumer-initiated transactions (also known as "prescreening"). The FCRA was further amended by FACTA, with provisions related to identity theft and other subjects.[5]

The FCRA regulates any "consumer reporting agency" (CRA) that furnishes a "consumer report," which is used primarily for assisting in establishing consumer's eligibility for credit.[6] A CRA is any person or entity that compiles or evaluates personal information for the purpose of furnishing consumer reports to third parties for a fee.[7] Three well-known examples of CRAs are Experian, Equifax and TransUnion, which are leading providers of credit information and credit scores. There are thousands of smaller CRAs that compile personal records, such as criminal records or driving histories, for other consumer reporting purposes, such as preemployment screening.[8]

A consumer report is any communication by a CRA related to an individual that pertains to the person's:

- Creditworthiness
- Credit standing
- Credit capacity
- Character
- General reputation
- Personal characteristics
- Mode of living

and that is used in whole or in part for the purpose of serving as a factor in establishing a consumer's eligibility for credit, insurance, employment or other business purpose.

Users of consumer reports must meet four main requirements under the FCRA:

1. Third-party data for substantive decision making must be appropriately accurate, current and complete

2. Consumers must receive notice when third-party data is used to make adverse decisions about them
3. Consumer reports may be used only for permissible purposes
4. Consumers must have access to their consumer reports and an opportunity to dispute them or correct any errors

Additionally, users of consumer reports must comply with other requirements, such as record keeping, providing certifications to the CRAs and securely disposing of the consumer report data.

The FCRA also specifically requires CRAs to:

- Provide consumers with access to the information contained in their consumer reports, as well as the opportunity to dispute any inaccurate information
- Take reasonable steps to ensure the maximum possible accuracy of information in the consumer report
- Not report negative information that is outdated; in most cases this means account data more than seven years old or bankruptcies more than 10 years old
- Provide consumer reports only to entities that have a permissible purpose under the FCRA
- Maintain records regarding entities that received consumer reports
- Provide consumer assistance as required by FTC rules

As discussed below, the FCRA imposes obligations on organizations that are not CRAs, including "users" (lenders, insurers, employers and others who use consumer reports) and "furnishers" (lenders, retailers, and others who furnish credit history or other personal information to the CRAs). Additionally, as also discussed below, companies that extend credit to consumers, even if they do not use consumer reports to make credit decisions, are now required to implement a "Red Flag" program to detect and deter identity theft.

Enforcement of the FCRA is available through dispute resolution, private litigation, and government actions.[9] The dispute resolution infrastructure permits the consumer to fill a request with the CRA to dispute the accuracy of information, and then requires the CRA to investigate the consumer's complaint.[10] If consumers are not satisfied with the dispute resolution process, the individuals have a private right of action, with recent trends including consumers becoming involved in class actions lawsuits.[11] Noncompliance with the FCRA can lead to civil and criminal penalties. In addition to actual damages, as of the writing of this book, violators are subject to statutory damages of at least $1,000 per violation, and at least $3,756 for willful violations.[12]

Government enforcement actions for violations of the FCRA can be brought by the FTC, the CFPB, and state attorneys general.[13] At the federal level, both the FTC and the CFPB share responsibility to enforce the FCRA.[14] Since 1996, state attorneys general have had concurrent enforcement authority with regard to FCRA.[15] The state attorneys general are required to give notice to the FTC prior to filing suit, and the FTC retains the authority to intervene in the cases brought by the state attorneys general.[16]

An example of FTC enforcement is the case against TeleCheck Services, Inc., one of the nation's largest check authorization service companies, and TRS Recovery Services, an associated debt-collection company. In 2014, these companies agreed to pay $3.5 million to settle FTC charges that they violated FCRA. The FTC alleged that TeleCheck, as a CRA, did not comply with dispute procedures for consumers whose checks were denied based on information provided by the business. TRS, a company that handles consumer debt taken on by TeleCheck, was alleged to have violated requirements of the FTC's Furnisher Rule, which requires entities furnishing information to CRAs to ensure the accuracy and integrity of the information provided.[17] The settlement was part of a broader initiative by the FTC to target the practices of data brokers that sell information to companies making decisions about consumers.[18]

An example of CFPB enforcement is the case of Clarity Services, Inc. The CFPB alleged that the company failed to properly investigate consumers who attempted to dispute information on their credit reports and obtained credit reports without a permissible purpose. As a result, Clarity Services agreed to pay an $8 million civil penalty.[19]

Actions by state attorneys general can brought by individual states or collectively by multiple states.[20] An example from 2015 involved more than 30 state attorneys general offices that entered into a settlement with three main reporting agencies, Equifax, Experian and TransUnion. The settlement related to claims concerning credit report errors, monitoring of data furnishers, and marketing of credit monitoring products to consumers. These companies agreed to pay the participating states $6 million and to adjust their business practices.[21]

8.1.1 Notice Requirements Under FCRA

The FTC has published a notice to all users of consumer reports of their obligations under the FCRA.[22] Users include employers who use consumer reports in employment decisions as well as lenders, insurers and others. CRAs are required to provide this notice of their obligations to users of consumer reports.

1. **Users must have a "permissible purpose."** Congress has limited the use of consumer reports to protect consumers' privacy. All users must have a permissible purpose under the FCRA to obtain a consumer report. Such purposes include obtaining reports:
   - As ordered by a court or a federal grand jury subpoena
   - As instructed by the consumer in writing
   - For the extension of credit as a result of an application from a consumer, or the review or collection of a consumer's account
   - For employment purposes, including hiring and promotion decisions, where the consumer has given written permission
   - For the underwriting of insurance as a result of an application from a consumer
   - When there is a legitimate business need, in connection with a business transaction that is initiated by the consumer
   - To review a consumer's account to determine whether the consumer continues to meet the terms of the account
   - To determine a consumer's eligibility for a license or other benefit granted by a governmental instrumentality required by law to consider an applicant's financial responsibility or status
   - For use by a potential investor or servicer, or current insurer, in a valuation or assessment of the credit or prepayment risks associated with an existing credit obligation
   - For use by state and local officials in connection with the determination of child support payments, or modifications and enforcement thereof
   - In addition, creditors and insurers may obtain certain consumer report information for the purpose of making "prescreened" unsolicited offers of credit or insurance (Section 604[c] of the FCRA)
2. **Users must provide certifications.** Section 604(f) of the FCRA prohibits any person from obtaining a consumer report from a CRA unless the person has certified to the CRA the permissible purpose(s) for which the report is being obtained and certifies that the report will not be used for any other purpose.

3. **Users must notify consumers when adverse actions are taken.** The term *adverse action* is defined very broadly to include all business, credit and employment actions affecting consumers that can be considered to have a negative impact, such as denying or canceling credit or insurance, or denying employment or promotion. No adverse action occurs in a credit transaction where the creditor makes a counteroffer that is accepted by the consumer.

The FCRA also details a number of adverse actions that can be taken as result of obtaining or reviewing the information contained within a consumer credit report.

- **Adverse actions based on information obtained from a CRA.** If a user takes any type of adverse action (as defined by the FCRA, action that is based, even in part, on information contained in a consumer report), the FCRA requires the user to notify the consumer. The notification may be done in writing, orally or by electronic means. It must include the following elements:
    - The name, address and telephone number of the CRA (including a toll-free telephone number, if it is a nationwide CRA) that provided the report
    - A statement that the CRA did not make the adverse decision and is not able to explain why the decision was made
    - A statement setting forth the consumer's right to obtain a free disclosure of the consumer's file from the CRA if the consumer makes a request within 60 days
    - A statement setting forth the consumer's right to dispute directly with the CRA the accuracy or completeness of any information provided by the CRA
- **Adverse actions based on information obtained from third parties that are not consumer reporting agencies.** If a person denies (or increases the charge for) credit for personal, family or household purposes based either wholly or partly upon information from a person other than a CRA, and the information is the type covered by the FCRA, Section 615(b)(1) requires that the user clearly and accurately disclose to the consumer his or her right to be informed of the nature of the information that was relied upon, if the consumer makes a written request within 60 days of notification. The user must then provide the disclosure within a reasonable period of time following the consumer's written request.
- **Adverse actions based on information obtained from affiliates.** If a person takes an adverse action involving insurance, employment or a credit transaction initiated by the consumer based on the type of information covered by the

FCRA, and this information was obtained from an entity affiliated with the user of the information by common ownership or control, Section 615(b)(2) requires the user to notify the consumer of the adverse action. The notice must inform the consumer that he or she may obtain a disclosure of the nature of the information relied upon by making a written request within 60 days of receiving the adverse action notice. If the consumer makes such a request, the user must disclose the nature of the information no later than 30 days after receiving the request. If consumer report information is shared among affiliates and then used for an adverse action, the user must make a similar adverse action disclosure.

8.1.2 Disclosures Under FCRA

The FCRA requires disclosure by all persons who use credit scores in making or arranging loans secured by residential real property. These persons must provide credit scores and other information about credit scores to applicants. Further, in some instances the person must provide a risk-based pricing notice to the consumer in accordance with regulations jointly prescribed by the CFPB (formerly the FTC) and the Federal Reserve Board. These notices are required if a consumer report is used by an individual or organization in connection with an application for credit or a grant, extension or provision of credit to a consumer on terms that are less favorable than the most favorable terms available to a substantial proportion of consumers acquiring loans from or through that person.

In 2015, Sprint agreed to pay $2.95 million in civil penalties to settle FTC charges that it violated the FCRA and its Risk-Based Pricing Rule.[23] According to the allegations, Sprint placed consumers with lower credit scores in an Account Spending Limit (ALS) program and charged them a monthly fee of $7.99. According to the FTC, Sprint failed to provide consumers placed in the program with all the required disclosure regarding their credit issues and delayed providing any notice until after the window in which the customer could cancel the service and change to another provider without incurring early termination fees.[24]

8.1.2.1 Consumer Reports and Employment

The FCRA imposes certain additional obligations on organizations that intend to use consumer report information for employment purposes. The user of such information must:

- Make a clear and conspicuous written notification to the consumer before the report is obtained, in a document that consists solely of the disclosure that a consumer report may be obtained by the employer.

- Obtain prior written consumer authorization in order to obtain a consumer report. Authorization to access reports during the term of employment may be obtained at the time of employment.
- Certify to the CRA that the above steps have been followed, that the information being obtained will not be used in violation of any federal or state equal opportunity law or regulation, and that, if any adverse action is to be taken based on the consumer report, a copy of the report and a summary of the consumer's rights will be provided to the consumer.
- Before taking an adverse action, provide a copy of the report to the consumer as well as the summary of the consumer's rights. (The user should receive this summary from the CRA.) An adverse action notice should be sent after the adverse action is taken.

An adverse action notice also is required in employment situations if credit information (other than transactions and experience data) obtained from an affiliate is used to deny employment.

8.1.3 Employee Investigations

The FCRA provides special procedures for investigations of suspected misconduct by an employee or for compliance with federal, state or local laws and regulations or the rules of a self-regulatory organization, and compliance with written policies of the employer. These investigations are not treated as consumer reports as long as (1) the employer or its agent complies with the procedures set forth in the act, (2) no credit information is used and (3) a summary describing the nature and scope of the inquiry is provided to the employee if an adverse action is taken based on the investigation.

8.1.4 Investigative Consumer Reports

Investigative consumer reports contain information about a consumer's character, general reputation, personal characteristics and mode of living. This information is obtained through personal interviews by an entity or person that is a CRA.

Consumers who are the subjects of such reports are given special rights under the FCRA. If a user intends to obtain an investigative consumer report, Section 606 of the FCRA requires that the user of the report disclose its use to the consumer. The disclosure is subject to the following requirements:

- The consumer must be informed that an investigative consumer report may be obtained.

- The disclosure must be in writing and must be mailed or otherwise delivered to the consumer some time before but not later than three days after the date on which the report was first requested.
- The disclosure must include a statement informing the consumer of his or her right to request additional disclosures of the nature and scope of the investigation, and the summary of consumer rights required by the FCRA. The summary of consumer rights will be provided by the CRA that conducts the investigation.
- The user must certify to the CRA that the required disclosures have been made and that the user will make the necessary disclosure to the consumer.
- Upon written request of a consumer made within a reasonable period of time after the required disclosures, the user must make a complete disclosure of the nature and scope of the investigation.
- The nature and scope disclosure must be made in a written statement that is mailed or otherwise delivered to the consumer no later than five days after the date on which the request was received from the consumer or the report was first requested, whichever is later.

8.1.5 Medical Information Under FCRA

FCRA limits the use of medical information obtained from CRAs, other than payment information that appears in a coded form and does not identify the medical provider. If medical information is to be used for an insurance transaction, the consumer must provide consent to the user of the report, or the information must be coded. If the report is to be used for employment purposes—or in connection with a credit transaction, except as provided in regulations issued by the banking and credit union regulators—the consumer must provide specific written consent and the medical information must be relevant. Any user who receives medical information shall not disclose the information to any other person, except where necessary to carry out the purpose for which the information was disclosed, or as permitted by statute, regulation or order.

8.1.6 "Prescreened" Lists

FCRA permits creditors and insurers to obtain limited consumer report information for use in connection with firm unsolicited offers of credit or insurance, under certain circumstances and conditions. This practice is known as prescreening and typically involves obtaining from a CRA a list of consumers who meet certain preestablished criteria. If any person intends to use prescreened lists, that person must: (1) before the offer is made, establish the criteria that will be relied upon to make the offer and to grant credit or insurance and (2) maintain such criteria on file for a three-year period beginning on the date on which the offer is made to each consumer. In addition, any user must include with each written solicitation a clear and conspicuous statement that:

- Information contained in a consumer's CRA file was used in connection with the transaction.
- The consumer received the offer because he or she satisfied the criteria for creditworthiness or insurability used to screen for the offer.
- Credit or insurance may not be extended if, after the consumer responds, it is determined that the consumer does not meet the criteria used for screening or any applicable criteria bearing on creditworthiness or insurability, or the consumer does not furnish required collateral.
- The consumer may prohibit the use of information in his or her file in connection with future prescreened offers of credit or insurance by contacting the notification system established by the CRA that provided the report. The statement must include the address and toll-free telephone number of the appropriate notification system.

Beginning in 2005, the companies that send prescreened solicitations of credit or insurance were required to supply simple and easy-to-understand notices explaining the consumer's right to opt out of receiving such offers. The FTC issued a rule requiring a layered notice with opt-out rights included on the first page. The FTC also issued a new consumer education brochure concerning prescreening.

8.2 The Fair and Accurate Credit Transactions Act

In 2003 Congress passed FACTA, which made substantial amendments to the FCRA.[25] Under FACTA, stricter state laws are preempted in most areas, although states retain some powers to enact laws addressing identity theft.[26] In addition, FACTA specifically identified certain state laws that would remain in effect. With regard to credit scores, state laws in California and Colorado, as well as state insurance laws regulating the use by insurers of credit-based insurance scores, remain in effect.[27] Pertaining to frequency of free credit reports, the federal law permitted state laws in Colorado, Georgia, Maine, Maryland, Massachusetts, New Jersey and Vermont to remain in effect.[28]

FACTA enacted a number of consumer protections. It required truncation of credit and debit card numbers, so that receipts do not reveal the full credit or debit card number. It gave consumers new rights to an explanation of their credit scores. It also gave individuals the right to request a free annual credit report from each of the three national consumer credit agencies—Equifax, Experian and TransUnion. Along with other identity theft protections, FACTA required regulators to promulgate a Disposal Rule and a Red Flags Rule.

In 2010, the FTC issued new rules updating the manner of disclosure required by the companies advertising free credit reports.[29] The updates "include prominent disclosures designed to prevent consumers from confusing these "free" offers with the federally mandated free annual file disclosures." Such a disclosure must be "easily readable," and the rules give examples of fonts that are, and are not, easily readable. As of 2011, the CFPB took over rulemaking authority in this area.[30]

8.2.1 The Disposal Rule

The Disposal Rule requires any individual or entity that uses a consumer report, or information derived from a consumer report, for a business purpose to dispose of that consumer information in a way that prevents unauthorized access and misuse of the data. Consumer reports can be electronic or written. The rule applies to both small and large organizations, including consumer reporting agencies, lenders, employers, insurers, landlords, car dealers, attorneys, debt collectors and government agencies.

"Disposal" includes any discarding, abandonment, donation, sale or transfer of information. The standard for disposal requires practices that are "reasonable" to protect against unauthorized access to or use of the consumer data. Factors to consider include the sensitivity of information being disposed of, the costs and benefits of various disposal methods, and available technology.[31] Examples of acceptable, reasonable measures include developing and complying with policies to:

- Burn, pulverize or shred papers containing consumer report information so that the information cannot be read or reconstructed
- Destroy or erase electronic files or media containing consumer report information so that the information cannot be read or reconstructed
- Conduct due diligence and hire a document destruction contractor to dispose of material specifically identified as consumer report information consistent with the rule

Enforcement of the Disposal Rule is by the FTC, the federal banking regulators and the CFPB. Violators may face civil liability as well as federal and state enforcement actions. Financial institutions that are subject to both the FACTA Disposal Rule and the Gramm-Leach-Bliley Safeguards Rule (discussed in Section 8.3) should incorporate required disposal practices into the information security program that the Safeguards Rule mandates. They should also be aware of any state disposal rules that may impose broader requirements.

8.2.2 The Red Flags Rule

The Red Flags Rule was originally promulgated under FACTA, which required agencies that regulate financial entities to develop a set of rules to mandate the detection, prevention and mitigation of identity theft. The FTC, together with federal banking agencies, authored the Red Flags Rule.[32] As with the rest of the FCRA and FACTA, the CFPB has now gained rule-making and enforcement authority.

The rule requires certain financial entities to develop and implement written identity theft detection programs that can identify and respond to the "red flags" that signal identity theft. Specifically, the rule applies to financial institutions and creditors. "Financial institution" is defined as all banks, savings and loan associations and credit unions. It also includes all other entities that hold a "transaction account" belonging to a consumer. Due to confusion over which entities qualify as covered "creditors," however, enforcement of the rule was delayed several times until a clarification was published in 2010.[33]

The Red Flag Program Clarification Act of 2010 was passed in response to concern that the definition of creditor extended to implicate unintended entities, such as attorneys and health providers, simply because they allow customers to pay their bills after the time of service.[34] The clarification narrows the previously broad definition of creditor, as well as the circumstances under which they are covered by the rule. It eliminates entities that extend credit only "for expenses incidental to a service." The rule still applies to entities that, regularly and in the course of business:

- Obtain or use consumer reports in connection with a credit transaction
- Furnish information to consumer reporting agencies in connection with a credit transaction
- Advance funds to or on behalf of someone, except for expenses incidental to a service provided by the creditor to that person[35]

The new law also authorizes regulations that apply the rule to businesses whose accounts should be "subject to a reasonably foreseeable risk of identity theft." The rule does not provide a checklist for specific red flags that must be included in the identity theft detection programs. Rather, the program should generally identify relevant patterns, practices and specific forms of activity that are red flags of possible identity theft, incorporate these flags into the program and update the program regularly to reflect changes in risks. Each organization is required to develop its own list of red flags, but examples cited by the FTC include alerts, notifications or warnings from a consumer reporting agency; suspicious identification documents; suspicious personal identifying data; and unusual use of a covered account.

8.3 Gramm-Leach-Bliley Act

Title V of the Financial Services Modernization Act of 1999 led to the promulgation of both a Privacy Rule and a Safeguards Rule.[36] The act, also known as GLBA, was major legislation that reflected and codified the consolidation of the U.S. banking, securities and insurance industries in the late 1990s. As previously separate types of financial institutions began to merge, substantial concerns arose over how consumer data would be collected, used and shared among the newly formed holding companies and their subsidiaries within the financial sector.

These privacy provisions were spurred by enforcement actions against major banks for controversial data practices. Prior to GLBA's passage, a number of leading financial institutions were found to have shared detailed customer information, including account numbers and other highly sensitive data, with telemarketing firms. Subsequently, the firms used the account numbers to charge customers for unsolicited services.

One of the most prominent cases involved U.S. Bancorp and the telemarketing firm MemberWorks.[37] The Minnesota attorney general's office brought suit in 1999, as Congress was considering GLBA. The suit resulted in a $3 million settlement for allegations that the bank had sent detailed customer information to the telemarketing firm, including account numbers and related information that enabled the marketer to directly withdraw funds from the customer account. The allegations also stated that the marketing firm was using a "negative option," where customers were charged automatically for services unless they later sent a specific request not to be billed.

The U.S. Bancorp/MemberWorks case focused popular and regulatory attention on the prevalence of data-sharing relationships between banks and third-party marketers. A group of 25 attorneys general brought additional actions against major financial institutions in an attempt to address these practices. Congress responded to these events by including significant privacy and security protections for consumers in GLBA and mandating further rulemaking on privacy and security by the FTC, federal banking regulators and state insurance regulators. Financial institutions were required to substantially comply with GLBA's requirements in 2001.

The passage of GLBA led to major changes in the structure of the financial services industry, and provided for the creation of new financial service holding companies that offer a full range of financial products. It eliminated legal barriers to affiliations among banks, securities firms, insurance companies and other financial services companies. Under GLBA's privacy provisions, financial institutions are required to

- Store personal financial information in a secure manner
- Provide notice of their policies regarding the sharing of personal financial information
- Provide consumers with the choice to opt out of sharing some personal financial information

8.3.1 Scope and Enforcement of GLBA

GLBA applies to "financial institutions," which are defined broadly as any U.S. companies that are "significantly engaged" in financial activities. Financial institutions include entities such as banks, insurance providers, securities firms, payment settlement services, check-cashing services, credit counselors and mortgage lenders, among others.

GLBA regulates financial institution management of "nonpublic personal information," defined as "personally identifiable financial information (i) provided by a consumer to a financial institution, (ii) resulting from a transaction or service performed for the consumer, or (iii) otherwise obtained by the financial institution." Excluded from the definition are publicly available information and any consumer list that is derived without using personally identifiable financial information.[38]

This encompasses a wide range of information that is not exclusively financial in nature. For example, the name of a financial institution's customer is considered nonpublic personal financial information, covered under the act, because it indicates the existence of a relationship between the institution and the consumer that is financial in nature.

GLBA requires financial institutions to protect consumers' nonpublic personal information under privacy rules that were promulgated originally by the FTC and FI regulators. In 2011, with the passage of the Dodd-Frank Act, the CFPB assumed this rule-making power, with exceptions for the Securities and Exchange Commission (SEC) and the Commodity Futures Trading Commission.

As enacted in 1999, federal financial regulators enforced GLBA for the institutions in their jurisdiction, such as for the Federal Reserve, Office of the Comptroller of the Currency, Federal Deposit Insurance Corporation and SEC. Banking and related financial institutions that fail to comply with GLBA requirements can be subject to substantial penalties under the Financial Institution Reform, Recovery and Enforcement Act (FIRREA). FIRREA penalties range from up to $5,500 for violations of laws and regulations, to a maximum of $27,500 if violations are unsafe, unsound or reckless, to as much as $1.1 million for "knowing" violations. For financial institutions not within the jurisdiction of one of the other agencies, the FTC originally had enforcement authority. Under the Dodd-Frank Act, the CFPB also now has enforcement authority for the GLBA Privacy and Safeguards Rules under its general enforcement powers, discussed further in Section 8.4.

At the state level, state attorneys general can enforce GLBA. Stricter state laws are not preempted under GLBA.[39] The validity of stricter state laws, however, can be subject to challenge because there is limited preemption under FCRA, so courts would need to determine which federal financial privacy statute governs for a particular state law. Although there is no private right of action under GLBA, failure to comply with certain notice requirements may be considered a deceptive trade practice by state and federal authorities. Some states also have private rights of action for this type of violation.

GLBA's privacy protections generally apply to "consumers," or individuals who obtain financial products or services from a financial institution to be used primarily for personal, family or household purposes. Many of the act's requirements relate to the subset of consumers who are also "customers"—consumers with whom the organization has an ongoing relationship. Financial services companies that do not have such "consumer customers" are not subject to some of GLBA's requirements, such as those related to notice.

Major components of the GLBA Privacy Rule provide that financial institutions must:

1. Prepare and provide to customers clear and conspicuous notice of the financial institution's information-sharing policies and practices. These notices must be provided when a customer relationship is established and annually thereafter.

2. Clearly provide customers the right to opt out of having their nonpublic personal information shared with nonaffiliated third parties (subject to significant exceptions, including for joint marketing and processing of consumer transactions).

3. Refrain from disclosing to any nonaffiliated third-party marketer, other than a consumer reporting agency, an account number or similar form of access code to a consumer's credit card, deposit or transaction account.
4. Comply with regulatory standards established by certain government authorities to protect the security and confidentiality of customer records and information, and protect against security threats and unauthorized access to or certain uses of such records or information.

8.3.2 GLBA and Privacy Notices

The GLBA Privacy Rule establishes a standard for privacy notices under which a financial institution must provide initial and annual privacy notices to consumers on nine categories of information, and must process opt-outs within 30 days. The privacy notice itself must be a clear, conspicuous and accurate statement of the company's privacy practices and must include the following:

- What information the financial institution collects about its consumers and customers
- With whom it shares the information
- How it protects or safeguards the information
- An explanation of how a consumer may opt out of having his or her information shared through a reasonable opt-out process[40]

Provided this notice standard is met, a financial institution may share any information it has with its affiliated companies and joint marketing partners, which are other financial institutions with whom the entity jointly markets a financial product or service.[41] In addition, other than for defined exceptions, a financial institution may also share consumer information with nonaffiliated companies and other third parties, but only after disclosing information-sharing practices to customers and providing them with the opportunity to opt out.

It should be noted that the GLBA prohibits financial institutions from disclosing consumer account numbers to nonaffiliated companies for purposes of telemarketing and direct mail marketing (including through email), even if the consumer has not opted out of sharing the information for marketing purposes. Also, a financial institution must ensure that service providers will not use provided consumer data for anything other than the intended purpose.

There are certain situations in which the consumer has no right to opt out. For example, a consumer cannot opt out if:

- A financial institution shares information with outside companies that provide essential services like data processing or servicing accounts
- The disclosure is legally required
- A financial institution shares customer data with outside service providers that market the financial company's products or services

In 2009, eight federal regulatory agencies issued a model short privacy notice.[42] The model notice implemented the Financial Services Regulatory Relief Act of 2006, which requires the agencies to propose a succinct and comprehensible model form that allows consumers to easily compare the privacy practices of different financial institutions.[43] Financial institutions that use the model notice satisfy the disclosure requirements for notices, but they are not required to use it.

8.3.3 The GLBA Safeguards Rule

Along with privacy standards and rules, GLBA requires financial institutions to maintain security controls to protect the confidentiality and integrity of personal consumer information, including both electronic and paper records. The regulatory agencies established such standards in the form of a final rule, the Safeguards Rule, that became effective in 2003.[44]

The GLBA Safeguards Rule requires financial institutions to develop and implement a comprehensive "information security program," which is defined as a program that contains "administrative, technical and physical safeguards" to protect the security, confidentiality and integrity of customer information.[45] The program must be appropriate for the size, complexity, nature and scope of the activities of the institution. Thus, like the GLBA Privacy Rule, the Safeguards Rule distinguishes the concepts of security, confidentiality and integrity, but suggests that all three concepts are integral to a complete understanding of security.

The information security program required under the rule must contain certain elements, including a designated employee to coordinate the program, audit systems to determine risk, and certain procedures to take with service providers to ensure that the security of the information is maintained.

Under the GLBA Safeguards Rule, a financial institution must provide the following three levels of security for consumer information:

1. **Administrative security**, which includes program definition, management of workforce risks, employee training and vendor oversight
2. **Technical security**, which covers computer systems, networks and applications in addition to access controls and encryption
3. **Physical security**, which includes facilities, environmental safeguards, business continuity and disaster recovery

Pursuant to the Safeguards Rule, the administrative, technical and physical safeguards to be implemented must be reasonably designed to: (1) ensure the security and confidentiality of customer information, (2) protect against any anticipated threats or hazards to the security or integrity of the information and (3) protect against unauthorized access to or use of the information that could result in substantial harm or inconvenience to any customer.[46] Maintaining the security of this information essentially means protecting the confidentiality and integrity of information, and restricting access to it.

The Safeguards Rule does allow for flexibility in implementing a security program, stating that the program must contain safeguards that are "appropriate" to the entity's size and complexity, the nature and scope of the entity's activities, and the sensitivity of any customer information at issue.[47] The Safeguards Rule requires that certain basic elements be included in a security program. Each institution must:

1. Designate an employee to coordinate the safeguards
2. Identify and assess the risks to customer information in each relevant area of the company's operation and evaluate the effectiveness of the current safeguards for controlling those risks
3. Design and implement a safeguard program and regularly monitor and test it
4. Select appropriate service providers and enter into agreements with them to implement safeguards
5. Evaluate and adjust the program in light of relevant circumstances, including changes in business arrangements or operations, or the results of testing and monitoring of safeguards[48]

8.3.4 California SB-1

California SB-1, also known as the California Financial Information Privacy Act, expands the financial privacy protections afforded under GLBA.[49] SB-1 increases the disclosure requirements of financial institutions and grants consumers increased rights with regard to the sharing of information. Violation of SB-1 in cases of negligent noncompliance can be punished with statutory damages of $2,500 per consumer, up to a cap of $500,000 per occurrence. In cases of willful noncompliance, there is no $500,000 damage cap.

Under the legislation, opt-in and opt-out requirements exist for financial institutions as follows: Written opt-in consent is required for a financial institution to share personal information with nonaffiliated third parties. Opt-in provisions must be presented on a form titled "Important Privacy Choices for Consumers" and be written in simple English. Additionally, SB-1 grants consumers the ability to opt out of information sharing between their financial institutions and affiliates not in the same line of business. A financial institution does not, however, need to obtain consumer consent in order to share nonmedical information with its wholly owned subsidiaries engaged in the same line of business—insurance, banking or securities—if they are regulated by the same functional regulator.

8.4 Dodd-Frank Wall Street Reform and Consumer Protection Act

In response to the financial crisis that became acute in 2008, Congress enacted the Dodd-Frank Wall Street Reform and Consumer Protection Act, which was signed into law in June 2010. Along with numerous other reforms, Title X of the act created the CFPB as an independent bureau within the Federal Reserve.

The CFPB oversees the relationship between consumers and providers of financial products and services. It holds broad authority to examine, write regulations and bring enforcement actions concerning businesses that provide financial products or services, including service providers.[50] The CFPB has assumed rule-making authority for specific existing laws related to financial privacy and other consumer issues, such as the FCRA, GLBA and Fair Debt Collection Practices Act.[51] It has enforcement authority over all nondepository financial institutions,[52] and over all depository institutions with more than $10 billion in assets.[53] For depository institutions with assets of $10 billion or less, CFPB promulgates rules but enforcement power remains with banking regulators.[54]

One potentially important innovation in the act is a change in the usual language about "unfair and deceptive" acts or practices. As discussed in multiple places in this book, the FTC and state attorneys general have long had the power to enforce against unfair and deceptive acts and practices. The CFPB also can now bring enforcement actions for unfairness and deception. In addition, the CFPB has a new power to enforce against "abusive acts and practices." An abusive act or practice:

- *Materially interferes with the ability of a consumer to understand a term or condition of a consumer financial product or service or*
- *Takes unreasonable advantage of—*
    - *A lack of understanding on the part of the consumer of the material risks, costs, or conditions of the product or service;*
    - *The inability of the consumer to protect its interests in selecting or using a consumer financial product or service; or*
    - *The reasonable reliance by the consumer on a covered person to act in the interests of the consumer.*[55]

Because this is new statutory language, the precise meaning of "abusive act or practice" will only become known over time. By its terms, however, enforcement actions for abusive acts or practices may well apply to privacy notices and other aspects of privacy and security protections by financial institutions.

CFPB enforcement authority includes the ability to conduct investigations and issue subpoenas, hold hearings and commence civil actions against offenders.[56] As of the writing of this book, civil penalties vary from $5,526 per day for federal consumer privacy law violations to $27,631 per day for reckless violations and $1,105,241 for knowing violations.[57] Further, state attorneys general are also authorized to bring civil actions in enforcement of the law or regulations.[58]

8.5 Required Disclosure Under Anti-Money-Laundering Laws

The privacy and security rules discussed above typically restrict uses and disclosures of personal information. Financial institutions are also subject to a variety of requirements to retain records and, in some instances, disclose personal financial information to the government. Financial institutions in general have intricate accounting and control systems to document transactions and reduce the risk of fraud. Banks have also long been closely supervised by the government, both to ensure the safety and soundness of the banks and for other reasons. Financial institutions thus have more detailed record retention rules than most other kinds of companies.

In recent decades, anti-money-laundering laws have become a major additional basis for record retention and mandatory disclosure to the government. U.S. anti-money-laundering laws stem from the Bank Secrecy Act of 1970, which targeted organized crime groups and others who used large cash transactions. The laws became stricter as part of the USA PATRIOT Act of 2001, with its focus on antiterrorism efforts. The fundamental goal of anti-money-laundering laws is to "follow the money."[59] The idea of thorough record keeping is that it will help detect and deter illegal activity, and provide evidence for proving illegality.[60]

8.5.1 The Bank Secrecy Act of 1970

The Bank Secrecy Act of 1970 (BSA), also known as the Currency and Foreign Transaction Reporting Act of 1970, authorizes the U.S. treasury secretary to issue regulations that impose extensive record-keeping and reporting requirements on financial institutions.[61] Specifically, financial institutions must keep records and file reports on certain financial transactions, including currency transactions in excess of $10,000, which may be relevant to criminal, tax or regulatory proceedings.

The BSA applies broadly to its own definition of financial institutions, which uses different language than GLBA and so may differ in some cases. The BSA applies to banks, securities brokers and dealers, money services businesses, telegraph companies, casinos, card clubs, and other entities subject to supervision by any state or federal bank supervisory authority. The scope of covered institutions has expanded over time to address the problem that criminals have an incentive to exploit whatever institutions are not already covered by the anti-money-laundering laws.

The BSA contains regulations relating to currency transactions, transportation of monetary instruments and the purchase of currency-like instruments. For example, the BSA generally requires currency transactions of $10,000 or more to be reported to the IRS per the regulations, using a Currency Transaction Report, Form 4789. Similarly, the BSA regulations cover purchases of bank checks, drafts, cashier's checks, money orders or traveler's checks for $3,000 or more in currency. The rules require that the entity collect and report information, including the name and address and Social Security number of the purchaser, the date of purchase, type of instrument, and serial numbers and dollar amounts of the instruments.

The BSA regulates certain wire transfers, including funds transfers and transmittals of funds by financial institutions. Certain funds transfers are exempted from the regulation, however, including funds transfers governed by the Electronic Funds Transfer Act and those made through an automated clearinghouse, ATM or point-of-sale system.

8.5.1.1 Record Retention Requirements

As part of the overall anti-money-laundering strategy, financial institutions are required to retain categories of records for use in investigations or enforcement actions. Financial institutions are required to maintain records of all extensions of credit in excess of $10,000, but this does not include credit secured by real property. Not all records must be maintained—only those with a "high degree of usefulness."[62] Records that are maintained must include the borrower's name and address, credit amount, purpose of credit and date of credit. Such records must be maintained for five years. As to deposit account records, a financial institution must keep the depositor's taxpayer identification number, signature cards, and checks exceeding $100 that are drawn or issued and payable by the bank. With regard to certificates of deposit, the financial institution must obtain the customer name and address, a description of the CD and the date of the transaction. For wire transfers or direct deposits, a financial institution must maintain all deposit slips or credit tickets for transactions exceeding $100.[63] Additionally, the BSA includes detailed rules regarding information that banks must retain in connection with payment orders.

8.5.1.2 Suspicious Activity Reports

Financial institutions must file a Suspicious Activity Report (SAR) in defined situations. The rationale is that SARs can alert government agencies to potentially suspicious transactions. A SAR must be filed with the U.S. Department of the Treasury's Financial Crimes Enforcement Network (FinCEN) in the following circumstances: (1) when a financial institution suspects that an insider is committing (or aiding the commission of) a crime, regardless of dollar amount; (2) when the entity detects a possible crime involving $5,000 or more and has a substantial basis for identifying a suspect; (3) when the entity detects a possible crime involving $25,000 or more (even if it has no substantial basis for identifying a suspect) and (4) when the entity suspects currency transactions aggregating $5,000 or more that involve potential money laundering or a violation of the act.[64]

8.5.1.3 BSA Enforcement

As of the writing of this book, penalties for violations of the BSA and its regulations include the following: civil penalties, including fines up to the greater of $25,000 or the amount of the transaction (up to a $100,000 maximum) as well as penalties for negligence ($500 per violation); additional penalties up to $5,000 per day for failure to comply with regulations; penalties of up to $25,000 per day for failure to comply with the information-sharing requirements of the USA PATRIOT Act; and penalties up to $1 million against financial institutions that fail to comply with due diligence requirements. Criminal penalties include up to a $100,000 fine and/or one-year imprisonment and up to a $10,000 fine and/or five-year imprisonment.[65]

8.5.2 The International Money-Laundering Abatement and Anti-Terrorist Financing Act of 2001

As part of the USA PATRIOT Act, the International Money Laundering Abatement and Anti-Terrorist Financing Act of 2001 expanded the reach of the BSA and made other significant changes to U.S. anti-money-laundering laws.[66] The act gave the U.S. treasury secretary the ability to promulgate broad rules to implement modified Know Your Customer requirements and to otherwise deter money laundering.

For covered financial services companies, the major USA PATRIOT Act compliance issues can be grouped into the following categories:

- Information-sharing regulations and participation in the cooperative efforts to deter money laundering, as required by Section 314
- Know Your Customer rules, including the identification of beneficial owners of accounts—procedures required by Section 326
- Development and implementation of formal money-laundering programs as required by Section 352
- Bank Secrecy Act expansions, including new reporting and record-keeping requirements for different industries (such as broker-dealers) and currency transactions[67]

Going forward, privacy professionals in the financial services sector should be alert to the continuing development of documentation requirements, where the organization may be required to gather and retain personally identifiable information for regulatory purposes.

For example, the Foreign Account Tax Compliance Act of 2010 (FATCA) seeks to target non-compliance with U.S. tax laws for U.S. taxpayers with foreign accounts. To deter tax evasion and require greater withholding of income to these taxpayers, FATCA requires more detailed "know your customer" documentation for both domestic and foreign financial institutions.[68]

8.6 Online Banking and Mobile Banking

Technology has changed the interaction between customers and banks. Customers no longer need to travel to brick-and-mortar buildings, or even to interact with the personnel employed by these banks, to withdraw money, deposit checks or apply for loans. Online banking allows customers to access bank accounts through the Internet, and mobile banking permits customers to engage in financial activities with their banks through the use of their cell phones.[69] By 2014, 74 percent of consumers who had a bank account reported they had engaged in online banking in the last 12 months, and 35 percent reported they used mobile banking in that time frame.[70] These approaches to banking leave customers' financial data susceptible to the vulnerabilities of the technologies at issue: Internet-connected computers and cell phones.[71]

Methods to address concerns regarding online banking require a combination of measures by the financial institution (such as careful design and updating of the relevant software) and education of the individual consumer, with steps including carefully choosing an operating system; selecting an appropriate Internet browser; using firewalls, antivirus programs, and anti-malware programs; and employing strong passwords and encryption.[72]

A similar combination of enterprise-side and user-side practices are important to addressing security and privacy concerns for mobile banking. Enterprises should assure security and privacy throughout the development of an application, and update the application as needed once it has been released. For consumers, privacy and security concerns can be addressed by measures including:[73]

- Letting customers know the type of authentication methods the financial institution has in place
- Informing customers of the dangers of using public Wi-Fi connections
- Empowering customers with information on mobile antivirus and malware detection software
- Creating a mobile privacy policy and having it certified by a reputable third party
- Fostering trust with customers by enabling them to decide which data to share and allowing them to opt out of mobile ad targeting[74]

8.7 Conclusion

Financial institutions are subject to a wide range of government regulations. The FCRA in 1970 was the first major national data privacy law in the United States, applying notably to credit reporting agencies, extensions of credit and purchases of insurance. The overhaul of the financial system in GBLA in 1999 included the GLBA privacy and safeguards requirements. FACTA accessed the credit reporting rules in 2003. These laws, taken together, mean that financial institutions today must carefully examine their practices with personal information, and ensure compliance. As shown by the anti-money-laundering laws, financial institutions at the same time are subject to requirements to retain personal information and disclose it under certain circumstances. The potential complexity of complying with these multiple requirements suggests the usefulness of an overall information management plan for financial institutions, updated over time to meet changing market and regulatory requirements.

Endnotes

1 Fair Credit Reporting (Regulation V), CFPB, www.consumerfinance.gov/policy-compliance/rulemaking/final-rules/fair-credit-reporting-regulation-v/ (accessed November 2017); CFPB Compliance Bulletin 2016-01, CFPB, http://files.consumerfinance.gov/f/201602_cfpb_supervisory-bulletin-furnisher-accuracy-obligations.pdf (accessed November 2017); 12 C.F.R. 1022, www.ecfr.gov/cgi-bin/text-idx?SID=c7ddd10206b3baf14dc7b04e46df3399&mc=true&node=ap12.8.1022_1140.e&rgn=div9 (accessed November 2017).

2 Mark Furletti, "An Overview and History of Credit Reporting," Discussion Paper for the Payment Cards Center of the Federal Reserve Bank of Philadelphia (June 2002), https://www.philadelphiafed.org/-/media/consumer-finance-institute/payment-cards-center/publications/discussion-papers/2002/CreditReportingHistory_062002.pdf (accessed November 2017).

3 Chris Jay Hoofnagle, *Federal Trade Commission: Privacy Law and Policy*, 268-288 (New York: Cambridge 2016); *see generally* EPIC, "The Fair Credit Reporting Act (FCRA) and the Privacy of Your Credit Report," https://epic.org/privacy/fcra/ (accessed November 2017). For a slightly different drafting of the principles, view "Fair Information Principles," FTC, https://www.ftc.gov/reports/privacy-online-fair-information-practices-electronic-marketplace-federal-trade-commission (accessed November 2017).

4 Chris Jay Hoofnagle, *Federal Trade Commission: Privacy Law and Policy*, 270 (New York: Cambridge 2016); *see generally* EPIC, "The Fair Credit Reporting Act."

5 "White House Fact Sheet: President Bush Signs the Fair and Accurate Credit Transactions Act of 2003," December 4, 2003, http://georgewbush-whitehouse.archives.gov/news/releases/2003/12/20031204-3.html (accessed November 2017); also *see* National Consumer Law Center, Analysis of the Fair and Accurate Credit Transactions Act of 2003, Pub. L. No. 108-159 (2003): Summary of FACTA Changes to the FCRA, https://www.nclc.org/images/pdf/credit_reports/archive/analysis-facta.pdf (accessed November 2017).

6 15 U.S.C. § 1681a, https://www.law.cornell.edu/uscode/text/15/1681a (accessed November 2017). For additional discussion, view "Credit Reporting Questions," *Consumer Affairs,* https://www.consumeraffairs.com/credit_cards/credit_reporting.html (accessed November 2017).

7 15 U.S.C. § 1681a, https://www.law.cornell.edu/uscode/text/15/1681a (accessed November 2017).

8 15 U.S.C. § 1681a, https://www.law.cornell.edu/uscode/text/15/1681a (accessed November 2017); 15 U.S.C. § 1681b, https://www.law.cornell.edu/uscode/text/15/1681b (accessed November 2017).

9 Austin Krist, "Large-Scale Enforcement of the Fair Credit Reporting Act and the Role of State Attorney Generals," *Columbia Law Review* (2015), http://columbialawreview.org/content/large-scale-enforcement-of-the-fair-credit-reporting-act-and-the-role-of-state-attorneys-general/ (accessed November 2017).

10 15 U.S.C. § 1681i, https://www.consumer.ftc.gov/articles/pdf-0091-fair-credit-reporting-act-611.pdf (accessed November 2017).

11 15 U.S.C. § 1681p, https://www.law.cornell.edu/uscode/text/15/1681p (accessed November 2017); *see* Hanley Chew and Eric Ball, "Ninth Circuit in Spokeo: Inaccurate Consumer Reports Support Standing in FCRA Cases," Fenwick & West, LLP (August 17, 2017), https://www.fenwick.com/publications/pages/ninth-circuit-in-spokeo-inaccurate-consumer-reports-support-standing-in-fcra-cases.aspx (accessed November 2017).

12 2016 Adjustments of Civil Monetary Penalty Amounts for FCRA violations, https://www.ftc.gov/system/files/documents/federal_register_notices/2016/06/160630civilpenaltyfrn.pdf (accessed November 2017).

13 Austin Krist, "Large-Scale Enforcement of the Fair Credit Reporting Act and the Role of State Attorneys General," *Columbia Law Review* (2015), http://columbialawreview.org/content/large-scale-enforcement-of-the-fair-credit-reporting-act-and-the-role-of-state-attorneys-general/ (accessed November 2017).

14 CFPB Monitor, "How the CFPB and the FTC interact (part 1)," Ballard Spahr (July 7, 2011), https://www.consumerfinancemonitor.com/2011/07/07/how-the-cfpb-and-the-ftc-interact-part-i/ (accessed November 2017). Under the Dodd-Frank Act, rule-making authority shifted from the FTC to the CFPB, Fair Credit Reporting (Regulation V), CFPB, www.consumerfinance.gov/policy-compliance/rulemaking/final-rules/fair-credit-reporting-regulation-v/ (accessed November 2017). *See* Section 8.4 of this chapter for a discussion of the Dodd-Frank Act.

15 "The Consumer Credit Reporting Reform Act of 1996, amending the Fair Credit Reporting Act," https://www.consumer.ftc.gov/articles/pdf-0111-fair-credit-reporting-act.pdf (accessed November 2017); see Peter P. Swire, "The Consumer Credit Reporting Reform Act and the Future of Electronic Commerce Law," *Electronic Banking Law and Commerce Report* (November/December 1996), http://peterswire.net/archive/psccrra.htm (accessed November 2017). Between 1990 and 2010, Congress added explicit grants of state enforcement authority into numerous federal consumer protection laws. Amy Widman and Prentiss Cox, "State Attorney General's Use of Concurrent Public Enforcement Authority in Federal Consumer Protection Laws," University of Minnesota Law School (2011), http://scholarship.law.umn.edu/cgi/viewcontent.cgi?article=1376&context=faculty_articles (accessed November 2017).

16 Austin Krist, "Large-Scale Enforcement of the Fair Credit Reporting Act and the Role of State Attorneys General."

17 Complaint in TeleCheck case, https://www.ftc.gov/sites/default/files/documents/cases/140116telecheckcmpt.pdf (accessed November 2017).

18 "TeleCheck to pay $3.5 million for Fair Credit Reporting Act violations," FTC, https://www.ftc.gov/news-events/press-releases/2014/01/telecheck-pay-35-million-fair-credit-reporting-act-violations (accessed November 2017).

19 In the Matter of Clarity Services, Inc., and Timothy Ranney, United States of America Consumer Financial Protection Bureau Administrative Proceeding File No. 2015-CFPB-0030 (December 1, 2015), http://files.consumerfinance.gov/f/201512_cfpb_consent-order_clarity-services-inc-timothy-ranney.pdf (accessed November 2017); *see* Andrew Smith and Lucille Bartholomew, "Fair Credit Reporting Act and Financial Privacy Update," Covington & Burlington, LLP, https://www.cov.com/-/media/files/corporate/publications/2017/04/fair_credit_reporting_act-and_financial_privacy_update_2016.pdf (accessed November 2017).

20 *See* Amy Widman and Prentiss Cox, "State Attorney General's Use of Concurrent Public Enforcement Authority in Federal Consumer Protection Laws," University of Minnesota Law School (2011), http://scholarship.law.umn.edu/cgi/viewcontent.cgi?article=1376&context=faculty_articles (accessed November 2017).

21 In the Matter of Equifax, Experian, and TransUnion, www.ohioattorneygeneral.gov/Files/Briefing-Room/News-Releases/Consumer-Protection/2015-05-20-CRAs-AVC.aspx (accessed November 2017).

22 "Consumer reports: What information furnishers need to know," FTC, https://www.ftc.gov/tips-advice/business-center/guidance/consumer-reports-what-information-furnishers-need-know (accessed November 2017). For general information, view "Learn more," CFPB, www.consumerfinance.gov/learnmore/ (accessed November 2017).

23 "Sprint will pay $2.95 million penalty to settle FTC charges it violated Fair Credit Reporting Act," FTC, https://www.ftc.gov/news-events/press-releases/2015/10/sprint-will-pay-295-million-penalty-settle-ftc-charges-it (accessed November 2017).

24 Complaint in Sprint case, https://www.ftc.gov/system/files/documents/cases/151021sprintcmpt.pdf (accessed November 2017).

25 16 C.F.R. Part 682, https://www.law.cornell.edu/cfr/text/16/part-682 (accessed November 2017); *see* The Fair Credit Reporting Act (FCRA) and the Privacy of Your Credit Report, https://epic.org/privacy/fcra/ (accessed November 2017).

26 For a detailed analysis of areas of state law preemption under FACTA, *see* the National Consumer Law Center's Analysis of the Fair and Accurate Credit Transactions Act of 2003, Pub. L. No. 108-159 (2003), https://www.nclc.org/images/pdf/credit_reports/archive/analysis-facta.pdf (accessed November 2017).

27 2003 Changes to the Fair Credit Reporting Act, Consumers Union, http://consumersunion.org/pdf/credit_reporting_summary_of_final_law.pdf (accessed November 2017); *see* National Consumer Law Center's Analysis of the Fair and Accurate Credit Transactions Act of 2003.

28 Gail Hillebrand, "After the FACT Act: What States Can Still Do to Prevent Identity Theft," Consumers Union, https://www.nclc.org/images/pdf/credit_reports/archive/cu-analysis-facta.pdf (accessed November 2017); *see* National Consumer Law Center's Analysis of the Fair and Accurate Credit Transactions Act of 2003.

29 16 C.F.R. Part 610.1, https://www.law.cornell.edu/cfr/text/16/610.1 (accessed November 2017).

30 12 C.F.R. Part 1022.130, https://www.law.cornell.edu/cfr/text/12/1022.130 (accessed November 2017).

31 "Disposing of consumer report information? Rules tell how," FTC, https://www.ftc.gov/tips-advice/business-center/guidance/disposing-consumer-report-information-rule-tells-how (accessed November 2017).

32 16 C.F.R. 681, https://www.law.cornell.edu/cfr/text/16/part-681 (accessed November 2017).

33 "FTC extends enforcement deadline for identity theft Red Flags Rule," FTC, https://www.ftc.gov/news-events/press-releases/2010/05/ftc-extends-enforcement-deadline-identity-theft-red-flags-rule (accessed November 2017).

34 S. 3987 (111th), https://www.congress.gov/bill/111th-congress/senate-bill/3987 (accessed November 2017).

35 "Unfurling a new definition of 'creditor' under the Red Flags Rule, FTC, https://www.ftc.gov/news-events/blogs/business-blog/2012/12/unfurling-new-definition-creditor-under-red-flags-rule (accessed November 2017).

36 Gramm-Leach-Bliley Act, 15 U.S.C, Subchapter I, Sec. 6801-6809 (1999), https://www.law.cornell.edu/uscode/text/15/chapter-94/subchapter-I (accessed November 2017). Also *see*, " How To Comply with the Privacy of Consumer Financial Information Rule of the Gramm-Leach-Bliley Act," FTC, https://www.ftc.gov/tips-advice/business-center/guidance/how-comply-privacy-consumer-financial-information-rule-gramm (accessed November 2017).

37 "Consumer Watch: U.S. Bancorp Pays $3 Million in Privacy Case Settlement," Market Watch, July 1, 1999, www.marketwatch.com/story/consumerwatch-us-bancorp-pays-3-million-in-privacy-case-settlement (accessed November 2017).

38 Gramm-Leach-Bliley Act, 15 U.S.C., Subchapter I, Sec. 6809.

39 In Vermont, the state's Department of Banking, Insurance, Securities, and Health Care Administration adopted opt-in provisions for information sharing. To comply with the regulation, some companies have treated all Vermont residents as having opted out under GLBA. www.dfr.vermont.gov/sites/default/files/REG-IH-01-01.pdf (accessed November 2017).

40 Providing a toll-free telephone number or a detachable form with a preprinted address is "reasonable"; requiring someone to write a letter as the only way to opt out is not.

41 The GLBA does not give consumers the right to opt out when the financial institution shares other information with its affiliates. Consumers have this right under the FCRA.

42 "Federal regulators issue final model privacy notice form," FTC, https://www.ftc.gov/news-events/press-releases/2009/11/federal-regulators-issue-final-model-privacy-notice-form (accessed November 2017).

43 Financial Services Regulatory Relief Act of 2006, https://www.gpo.gov/fdsys/pkg/BILLS-109s2856enr/pdf/BILLS-109s2856enr.pdf (accessed November 2017).

44 16 C.F.R. Part 314, https://www.law.cornell.edu/cfr/text/16/part-314 (accessed November 2017).

45 16 C.F.R. Part 314.1(a), https://www.law.cornell.edu/cfr/text/16/part-314 (accessed November 2017).

46 *Id.*

47 16 C.F.R. Part 314.3(a), https://www.law.cornell.edu/cfr/text/16/part-314 (accessed November 2017).

48 16 C.F.R. Part 314.4, https://www.law.cornell.edu/cfr/text/16/part-314 (accessed November 2017).

49 Cal. Fin. Code § 4050 *et seq.*, http://codes.findlaw.com/ca/financial-code/fin-sect-4050.html (accessed November 2017). For additional analysis, view "Analysis of the California Financial Privacy Act (SB1)," www.aba.com/aba/documents/legal/sb1aba.pdf (accessed November 2017).

50 Dodd-Frank Act § 1022, https://www.law.cornell.edu/wex/dodd-frank_title_X (accessed November 2017).

51 *Id.* at 1002(12).

52 *Id.* at 1002(5); (15).

53 *Id.* at 1025.

54 *Id.* at 1026.

55 *Id.* at 5531.

56 *Id.* at 1052(b)-(c).

57 "Civil Penalty Inflation Adjustments," Federal Register, https://www.federalregister.gov/documents/2017/01/12/2017-00521/civil-penalty-inflation-adjustments (accessed January 2018).

58 Dodd-Frank Act § 1041-1042, https://www.law.cornell.edu/wex/dodd-frank_title_X (accessed November 2017).

59 "What We Do," FinCen, https://www.fincen.gov/what-we-do (accessed November 2017).

60 Peter P. Swire, "Financial Privacy and the Theory of High-Tech Government Surveillance," *Washington University Law Quarterly*, 77: 461 (1999), http://papers.ssrn.com/sol3/papers.cfm?abstract_id=133340 (accessed November 2017).

61 Financial Recordkeeping and Reporting of Currency and Foreign Transactions Act of 1970, 31 U.S.C. 1051. In addition to the federal Bank Secrecy Act and other regulations that require reporting to the U.S. government, many states also provide for the disclosure of banking records and financial transaction data to state and local law enforcement agencies.

62 12 U.S.C. § 1829(b), https://www.law.cornell.edu/uscode/text/12/1829b (accessed November 2017).

63 *See* 31 C.F.R. 1010.410, https://www.law.cornell.edu/cfr/text/31/1010.410 (accessed December 2017); 31 C.F.R. 1010.430, https://www.law.cornell.edu/cfr/text/31/1010.430 (accessed December 2017); 31 C.F.R. 1020.410, https://www.law.cornell.edu/cfr/text/31/1020.410 (accessed December 2017).

64 *See* 12 C.F.R. 21.11, https://www.law.cornell.edu/cfr/text/12/21.11 (accessed November 2017); 12 C.F.R. 208.62, https://www.law.cornell.edu/cfr/text/12/208.62 (accessed November 2017); 12 C.F.R. 353.3, https://www.law.cornell.edu/cfr/text/12/part-353 (accessed May 2016).

65 31 U.S.C. § 5321, https://www.law.cornell.edu/uscode/text/31/5321 (accessed November 2017).

66 International Money Laundering Abatement and Anti-Terrorism Financing Act of 2001, https://www.epic.org/privacy/financial/RL31208.pdf (accessed November 2017). For additional information, *see* "Guide to U.S. Anti-Money Laundering Requirements: Frequently Asked Questions," Protiviti, https://www.protiviti.com/en-US/Documents/Resource-Guides/Guide-to-US-AML-Requirements-5thEdition-Protiviti.pdf (accessed November 2017).

67 For an in-depth discussion, view "USA Patriot Act," FinCEN, https://www.fincen.gov/resources/statutes-regulations/usa-patriot-act (accessed November 2017).

68 Foreign Account Tax Compliance Act, IRS, https://www.irs.gov/businesses/corporations/foreign-account-tax-compliance-act-fatca (accessed November 2017).

69 Eleanor Lumsden, "Securing Mobile Technology & Financial Transactions in the United States," *Berkley Business Law Journal* (2013), http://scholarship.law.berkeley.edu/cgi/viewcontent.cgi?article=1095&context=bblj (accessed November 2017).

70 Board of Governors for the Federal Reserve System, *Consumers and Mobile Financial Services* 2015 p.9, (March 2015), www.federalreserve.gov/econresdata/consumers-and-mobile-financial-services-report-201503.pdf (accessed November 2017). The report by the Federal Reserve notes the significant increase in these numbers over a three-year period. In 2011, only 65 percent of consumers who had a bank account reported they had engaged in online banking in the last 12 months, and only 20 percent reported using mobile banking in that same time frame.

71 "Safe Internet Banking—Protect Your Privacy," FDIC, https://www.fdic.gov/bank/individual/online/protect.html (accessed November 2017).

72 "Fact Sheet 36: Securing Your Computer to Maintain Your Privacy," Privacy Rights Clearinghouse, https://www.privacyrights.org/securing-your-computer-maintain-your-privacy (accessed November 2017).

73 Mobile banking concerns include: the small and portable nature of cell phones make them easy to steal, cell phones can become infected with viruses and infect computers that are connected, and users have a limited ability to delete cookies related to mobile applications. http://scholarship.law.berkeley.edu/cgi/viewcontent.cgi?article=1095&context=bblj. For discussion of mobile banking issues, *see* https://www.comscore.com/Insights/Blog/Security-Concerns-Inhibit-Mobile-Banking-Adoption-Among-Older-Consumers (accessed November 2017); www.bankinfosecurity.com/6-top-mobile-banking-risks-a-4735 (accessed November 2017).

74 "FFIEC Releases Supplemental Guidance on Internet Banking Authentication," Federal Financial Institutions Examination Council Press Release, https://www.ffiec.gov/press/pr062811.htm (accessed November 2017).

CHAPTER 9

Education Records and Technology

Education records, for institutions that receive federal funding, have privacy protections under U.S. law. The logic is that grades, disciplinary actions and other school information about a particular student deserve privacy protection. This chapter discusses the Family Educational Rights and Privacy Act of 1974 (FERPA) and the Protection of Pupil Rights Amendment of 1978 (PPRA), as amended. Education in the United States has been governed largely at the state and local level. Practitioners in this area should be careful to follow any state and local laws that apply.[1] This chapter also discusses the emerging issue of education technology, where many new details of students' activity can be collected when they use educational software.

9.1 An Overview of the Family Educational Rights and Privacy Act

FERPA is a federal statute that provides students with control over disclosure and access to their education records.[2] FERPA is also referred to as the Buckley Amendment, in reference to Senator James Buckley, who supported its enactment. The statute generally prevents schools from divulging education record information, such as grades and behavior, to parties other than the student, without that student's consent.[3] FERPA includes major aspects of Fair Information Practice Principles, including notice, consent, access and correction, security and accountability.

FERPA applies to all educational institutions that receive federal funding.[4] Such funding exists for virtually all public and most private schools, especially at the postsecondary level. Specifically, the statute protects the rights of students by providing them with the right to:

- Control the disclosure of their education records to others
- Review and seek amendment of their own education records
- Receive annual notice of their rights under FERPA
- File complaints with the U.S. Department of Education[5]

"Education record" has a broad meaning. FERPA defines it to include all records that are directly related to the student and maintained by the school or by a party on behalf of the school.[6] This extends beyond grades and other academic records to include financial aid records, disciplinary records and others related to the student.

FERPA defines "record" as "any information recorded in a way, not including, but not limited to, handwriting, print, computer media, video or audio tape, film, microfilm, and microfiche."[7] All electronic records and emails are covered by the term "computer media." There are several exceptions to the definition of educational record; these, however, may be protected under other privacy laws. The following records are *not* considered education records under FERPA:

- **Campus police records** created and maintained by school campus police for law enforcement purposes[8]
- **Employment records**, when the employee is not a student at the university[9]
- **Treatment records** or health records, subject to several requirements[10]
- **Applicant records** of those who are not enrolled in the university
- **Alumni records** created by a school after the individual is no longer a student
- **Grades on peer-graded papers**, before they are collected and recorded by a faculty member or other university representative[11]

Disclosure of education records is permitted only if one of the following conditions is met:

- The information is not "personally identifiable"
- The information is "directory information" whose release the student has not blocked
- Consent has been provided by: (1) the parent, or (2) the student once the rights transfer to the student when he or she reaches the age of 18 or attends only a postsecondary institution
- The disclosure is made to (1) the parent or (2) the student himself or herself once the rights transfer to the student when he or she reaches the age of 18 or attends only a postsecondary institution
- A statutory exception applies, such as for health or safety purposes[12]

The Department of Education's definition of "personally identifiable information" is similar to other statutory definitions. It includes, but is not limited to:

- The student's name
- The name of the student's parent or other family members
- The student or student's family's address
- Personal identifiers such as the Social Security number or student number
- Other identifiers, such as date of birth
- Other information that, alone or in combination, can be linked to a student and would allow the student to be identified with reasonable certainty
- Information requested by a person whom the school reasonably believes knows the identity of the student to which the education record is linked[13]

Personally identifiable information may still be disclosed if it is determined to be "directory information."[14] "Directory information" is broadly defined by FERPA to include information that would not generally be considered an invasion of privacy or harmful if disclosed.[15] FERPA does not designate specific information types as directory information for every educational institution but rather allows individual educational institutions to create their own definitions based on lists of examples provided in the statute and rules laid down by the Department of Education.[16] The examples include name, date of birth, address, email address, telephone number, field of study, and honors received.[17]

Before an educational institution can declare information directory information and begin using it as such, the institution must provide students with an opportunity to opt out, or block the release of their directory information. Students cannot use this opt-out to prevent the release of information that falls under a FERPA exception.[18]

The regulations promulgated under FERPA specifically exclude the use of Social Security numbers or student identification numbers as directory information. An educational institution, however, may use student identification numbers as directory information if that number cannot be used to access education records without another factor known only by the authorized user.[19] Therefore, a school cannot use a student identification number as directory information if other information included in directory information combined with the student identification number would enable an unauthorized user to access the student's records.[20] Other than the exceptions noted above, nondirectory information, such as grade point average (GPA), grades or transcripts are not released without student consent.[21]

Valid student consent to disclosure must be signed (by hand or electronically), dated and written. It must also identify:

- The record(s) to be disclosed
- The purpose of disclosure
- To whom the disclosure is being made

Under several statutory exceptions, a school is authorized to disclose personally identifiable information from an education record without student consent. Educational institutions need meet only one exception for the disclosure to be valid. Schools, however, must use "reasonable methods" to verify the identity of the party to whom they disclose the information. Reasonable methods include PINs, passwords, personal security questions, smart cards and tokens, biometric indicators, and other factors known or possessed only by the user.[22]

Exceptions to the FERPA consent requirements include the following:

- Disclosure to school officials who have determined a "legitimate educational interest" in the records. A legitimate educational interest exists if the record is relevant and necessary to the school official's responsibilities. This group includes school employees and board members as well as third-party vendors (1) to whom the school outsources duties and (2) who are under the direct control of the school regarding use and maintenance of the record.[23] These third parties are not permitted to disclose record information to any other party without consent, and cannot use the record for any other purpose than for which the disclosure was made.[24]
- Disclosure to educational institutions in which a student seeks or intends to enroll, or is currently enrolled, when the disclosure is for a purpose related to the student's enrollment or transfer.
- Disclosure in connection with financial aid that the student has received or for which the student will apply, when the purpose of the disclosure is to determine the student's eligibility for aid or conditions to or amount of financial aid.
- Disclosure to organizations doing research studies for, or on behalf of, educational institutions for the purpose of developing predictive tests, administering student aid programs or improving school instruction.
- Disclosure to accrediting organizations to fulfill accrediting duties.
- Disclosure to the alleged victim of a forcible or nonforcible sex offense.

- Disclosure of information related to sex offenders and others when the information is provided to the school under federal registration and disclosure requirements.
- Disclosure to a person or entity that is verified as the party that provided or created that record. For example, if a student transfers high schools, the second school can disclose a student's transcript to the original school to verify its authenticity.
- Disclosure to law enforcement or otherwise to comply with a judicial order or subpoena. The school must make reasonable efforts to notify the student prior to the disclosure unless it is a legal matter that orders nondisclosure.
- Disclosure to appropriate parties in connection with a "health or safety emergency," if knowledge of this information is necessary to protect the health or safety of the student or others. The threat of harm must be "articulable and significant," and the school can take the totality of the circumstances into account in making this determination. Information can be disclosed to any individual with the ability to assist in the situation—this includes parents, law enforcement, school officials, spouse or partner and other educational institutions, among others.[25]

A school is safe from federal scrutiny of its health and safety emergency determination as long as, based on the information available at the time, there is rational basis for the determination. In that case, the Department of Education will not question the determination.

FERPA also provides students with the right to access and review their education records. Once a student has issued a request, the educational institution must provide access to the records within 45 days of that request.[26] It also must respond to reasonable requests from students for explanations of the records. As with other disclosures to third parties, the educational institution must use reasonable measures to verify the identity of the student making the record request.

There are several exceptions to the right of inspection. Students do not have the right to inspect the financial records of their parents, confidential letters of recommendation (if the student has waived the right to inspect those documents), treatment records, attorney-client privileged information or records excluded from the definition of education records (such as law enforcement records). Also, when the request pertains to a record containing information about more than one student, the requesting students may access only the parts pertaining to themselves.[27]

Students can request corrections to their education records if they believe the records to be inaccurate, misleading or in violation of their privacy.[28] This access is intended to allow students to address incorrect records and is not for other purposes. If the request is granted, the records must be corrected within a reasonable time. If the request is denied, the student has a right to request a hearing, which must meet several requirements:

- The student must receive prior and reasonable notice of the time, place and date.
- It must be held within a reasonable time after the request is made.
- It must be conducted by a party without a direct interest in the outcome.
- The student must be afforded a "full and fair" opportunity to present his or her case, with or without assistance or representation.
- The decision must be based on the evidence presented at the hearing, delivered, in writing, within a reasonable amount of time after the hearing, and must contain a summary and explanation for the decision. If the hearing affirms the student's request, the education record must be amended and the student must be notified in writing; if the request is denied, however, the institution must notify the student of his or her right to place a written statement in the file about the contested record. The statement must then be maintained and disclosed with any release of the contested record.

9.2 FERPA and the Protection of Pupil Rights Amendment

FERPA applies only to information stored in education records, defined above as information that (1) directly relates to a student and (2) is maintained by the educational institution or on behalf of the institution. All other general student information that falls outside of this definition is not covered by FERPA's consent and disclosure requirements.[29] This has traditionally allowed schools to sell student directory information to commercial entities such as banks or credit card companies, unless a parent or student opts out.[30]

Congress responded to concerns about the collection and disclosure of student information for commercial purposes by amending FERPA in 1978 with the Protection of Pupil Rights Amendment (PPRA). PPRA provides certain rights to parents of minors with regard to the collection of sensitive information from students through surveys. These areas include:

- Political affiliations
- Mental and psychological problems potentially embarrassing to the student and his/her family
- Sex behavior and attitudes
- Illegal, antisocial, self-incriminating and demeaning behavior
- Critical appraisals of other individuals with whom respondents have close family relationships
- Legally recognized privileged or analogous relationships, such as those of lawyers, physicians and ministers
- Religious practices, affiliations or beliefs of the student or student's parent
- Income (other than that required by law to determine eligibility for participation in a program or for receiving financial assistance under such program)[31]

The No Child Left Behind Act of 2001 broadened the PPRA to limit the collection and disclosure of student survey information.[32] The amended PPRA now requires schools to:

- Enact policies regarding the collection, disclosure or use of personal information about students for commercial purposes[33]
- Allow parents to access and inspect surveys and other commercial instruments before they are administered to students[34]
- Provide advance notice to parents about the approximate date when these activities are scheduled[35]
- Provide parents the right to opt out of surveys or other sharing of student information for commercial purposes[36]

PPRA requirements apply to all elementary and secondary schools that receive federal funding; the statute, however, does not apply to postsecondary schools.

9.3 Interaction Between FERPA and the HIPAA Privacy Rule

FERPA became law in the United States in 1974. When HIPAA was enacted in 1996,[37] one important question for the U.S. Department of Health and Human Services (HHS) to address in the Privacy Rule for HIPAA was whether schools would be covered. Although initial drafts of the HIPAA Privacy Rule included schools, the final version of the Rule exempted schools where educational records were already subject to the privacy regime of FERPA.[38]

This means that the general rule is that health records are subject to FERPA—and not HIPAA—where a public elementary or secondary school provides a nurse for student health issues.[39] By contrast, FERPA does not apply to private elementary or secondary schools that do not receive federal funding. Health records maintained by one of these private schools are thus subject to the HIPAA Privacy Rule if the school qualifies as a "covered entity" under the federal law.[40]

At the postsecondary level, a college or university with a healthcare clinic that treats only students is generally subject to the confidentiality requirements of FERPA relating to the student's health-care records. Both FERPA and the HIPAA Privacy Rule typically apply to the college or university healthcare center that treats both students and nonstudents—such as faculty and staff. In this instance, FERPA applies to the student health records, and the HIPAA Privacy Rule applies to the nonstudent health records.[41]

Practitioners in this area should be aware that there may be instances where it is challenging to determine whether FERPA, HIPAA, or both apply. For example, there has been controversy over school-based healthcare centers that disclose health information to school officials when related to a lawsuit by the student that pertains to those health records, like a rape on campus.[42] Another example is the legal requirements for postsecondary institutions sharing records within the institution and beyond its borders in an effort to prevent tragedies involving students with mental health issues. These fact settings may be difficult to navigate, particularly if the records include those from the high-school and postsecondary levels as well as records from school healthcare providers and nonschool healthcare providers.[43] In these complex legal situations, it may be important to consult an attorney.

9.4 Education Technology

As the use of computers and the Internet is exploding in the educational arena, technology companies are focusing on ways to assist educators in providing content online.[44] These companies enable online hosting of teaching material for students, online posting of homework assignments, online communication between teachers and students, and online delivery of grades to students and parents. Many of these technologies are provided free to those in education settings. These technology company activities are subject to the laws discussed in this chapter.

Google, for example, developed free Apps for Education—a suite of tools that included Gmail, Google Calendar, Google Docs and Google Classroom.[45] In 2014, students in California who used Apps for Education sued Google, accusing the company of scanning millions of emails sent to and received by the students.[46] The Electronic Privacy Information Center, a nongovernmental organization focused on civil liberties and privacy, asserted that Google's practice violated FERPA, and advocated for the Department of Education to investigate the company.[47] Soon after the lawsuit was filed, Google agreed to change its business practices to ensure that the information in the emails could not be used for commercial purposes.[48] During the time period when the lawsuit was pending against Google,[49] the Department of Education issued guidelines to provide assistance in explaining how FERPA applied in the online arena.[50]

Self-regulation has become a prominent source of privacy rules applied in the educational technology space. The Future of Privacy Forum and the Software and Information Industry Association created a student privacy pledge in 2014, with over 250 signatories by 2016, including many leading educational technology providers.[51] The "K-12 School Service Provider Pledge to Safeguard Student Privacy" includes a dozen specific provisions, including a prohibition on selling student personal information and a ban on using information collected in schools for behavioral targeting of advertisements to students.[52] Violation of the pledge would make a company subject to enforcement as a deceptive trade practice under Section 5 of the Federal Trade Commission Act.

9.5 Conclusion

U.S. law provides the major Fair Information Practice Principles related to education records that schools receiving federal funding must abide by. Such educational institutions therefore must examine their practices to ensure compliance with these relatively detailed rules.

High schools as well as colleges and universities should remain alert to the complex interplay that exists regarding student and parent rights related to FERPA. High schools should be aware of the change in legal status that occurs when a student becomes an adult at the age of 18. At that point, the student is the person in control of rights connected to education records, including grades, rather than the parents. If a student has left high school and is attending only a postsecondary institution, the rights under

FERPA are held by the student—regardless of the student's age.[53] Even after the rights under FERPA have transferred to the student, however, a school may disclose to the parents the educational records of the student, without the student's consent, in the circumstance where the student is a dependent for tax purposes.[54]

Privacy professionals should be alert to continuing developments in the educational technology area, because student online activities will continue to generate many new and detailed forms of student personal information.

Endnotes

1 *See* Student Data Privacy, National Conference of State Legislatures (Februay 10, 2017), www.ncsl.org/research/education/student-data-privacy.aspx (accessed November 2017). Numerous states have adopted student data privacy laws. *See*, e.g., Georgia's Student Data Privacy, Accessibility, and Transparency Act, O.C.G.A. §§ 20-2-660 to -668, https://law.justia.com/codes/georgia/2015/title-20/chapter-2/article-15 (accessed November 2017); New York's Education Law, ED-N § 2-d - Unauthorized Release of Personally Identifying Information, requiring Parent's Bill of Rights for Data Protection and Security, http://codes.findlaw.com/ny/education-law/edn-sect-2-d.html (accessed November 2017); Rhode Island's Student Social Media Privacy, Section 16-103-1 to -6, https://law.justia.com/codes/rhode-island/2015/title-16/chapter-16-103/ (accessed November 2017). For an overview of state trends, *see* Sunny Deye, "Schools' Student Data Dilemma," *State Legislatures Magazine*, April 1, 2016, www.ncsl.org/bookstore/state-legislatures-magazine/schools-data-dilemma.aspx (accessed November 2017).

2 20 U.S.C. § 1232g, https://www.law.cornell.edu/uscode/text/20/1232g (accessed November 2017).

3 *Id.*; 34 CFR 99, https://www.law.cornell.edu/cfr/text/34/part-99 (accessed November 2017).

4 20 U.S.C. § 1221, https://www.law.cornell.edu/uscode/text/20/1221 (accessed November 2017).

5 20 U.S.C. § 1232g, https://www.law.cornell.edu/uscode/text/20/1232g (accessed November 2017). There is no private right of action permitted under FERPA.

6 20 U.S.C. § 1232g(a)(4)(A), https://www.law.cornell.edu/uscode/text/20/1232g (accessed November 2017).

7 34 C.F.R. § 99.3, https://www.law.cornell.edu/cfr/text/34/99.3 (accessed November 2017).

8 20 U.S.C. § 1232g(a)(4)(B)(ii); https://www.law.cornell.edu/uscode/text/20/1232g (accessed November 2017). It should be noted, however, that if the records are shared between campus police and other campus administrators, these are considered education records.

9 20 U.S.C. § 1232g(a)(4)(B)(iii); https://www.law.cornell.edu/uscode/text/20/1232g (accessed November 2017).

10 20 U.S.C. § 1232g(a)(4)(B)(iv); https://www.law.cornell.edu/uscode/text/20/1232g (accessed November 2017). Generally, records that are created or maintained by a professional health practitioner for the purpose of treating a student, and not disclosed to anyone except those providing the treatment, are considered treatment records.

11 Owasso Independent School District v. Falvo, 534 U.S. 426 (2002), https://www.law.cornell.edu/supct/html/00-1073.ZO.html (accessed November 2017).

12 Frequently Asked Questions About FERPA, U.S. Department of Education, https://www2.ed.gov/policy/gen/guid/fpco/pdf/ferpafaq.pdf (accessed November 2017); FERPA General Guidance for Students, U.S. Department of Education, https://www2.ed.gov/policy/gen/guid/fpco/ferpa/students.html (accessed November 2017). Even after the rights under FERPA have transferred to the student, one of the statutory exceptions allows many parents to obtain the records without the student's consent. In the situation where the student is claimed as a dependent by either parent for tax purposes, both parents are allowed access to the educational records. 34 CFR § 99.31(a)(8), https://www.law.cornell.edu/cfr/text/34/99.31 (accessed November 2017).

13 34 C.F.R. § 99.3, https://www.law.cornell.edu/cfr/text/34/99.3 (accessed November 2017). *See* generally 20 U.S.C. § 1232g, https://www.law.cornell.edu/uscode/text/20/1232g (accessed November 2017).

14 20 U.S.C. § 1232g(a)(5)(A)-(B), https://www.law.cornell.edu/uscode/text/20/1232g (accessed November 2017).

15 34 C.F.R. § 99.3(b), https://www.law.cornell.edu/cfr/text/34/99.3 (accessed November 2017).

16 20 U.S.C. § 1232g(a)(5)(A)-(B), https://www.law.cornell.edu/uscode/text/20/1232g (accessed November 2017); 34 C.F.R. § 99.3(b)(a), https://www.law.cornell.edu/cfr/text/34/99.3 (accessed November 2017).

17 The statute provides the following list: "the student's name, address, telephone listing, date and place of birth, major field of study, participation in officially recognized activities and sports, weight and height of members of athletic teams, dates of attendance, degrees and awards received, and the most recent previous educational agency or institution attended by the student." https://www.law.cornell.edu/uscode/text/20/1232g (accessed November 2017). The rule provides that "directory information includes: the student's name; address; telephone listing; electronic mail address; photograph; date and place of birth; major field of study; grade level; enrollment status (e.g., undergraduate or graduate, full-time or part-time); dates of attendance; participation in officially recognized activities and sports; weight and height of members of athletic teams; degrees, honors, and awards received; and the most recent educational agency or institution attended." 34 C.F.R. § 99.3, https://www.law.cornell.edu/cfr/text/34/99.3 (accessed November 2017).

18 34 C.F.R. § 99.7, https://www.law.cornell.edu/cfr/text/34/99.7 (accessed November 2017).

19 34 C.F.R. § 99.3(b)(c), https://www.law.cornell.edu/cfr/text/34/99.3 (accessed November 2017). For a discussion of Social Security numbers and student ID numbers as electronic personal identifiers, view "Family Educational Rights and Privacy Act (FERPA): Final Rule 34 CFR Part 99," www2.ed.gov/policy/gen/guid/fpco/pdf/ht12-17-08-att.pdf (accessed November 2017).

20 For a summary of this issue, view "Privacy Concerns: The Effects of the Latest FERPA Changes," https://eric.ed.gov/?id=EJ904659 (accessed November 2017).

21 The U.S. Department of Education provides guidance to schools on information that can be released: "a play bill, showing [the] student's role in a drama production; the annual yearbook; honor roll or other recognition lists; graduation programs; and sports activity sheets, such as for wrestling, showing weight and height of team members." www2.ed.gov/policy/gen/guid/fpco/ferpa/mndirectoryinfo.html (accessed November 2017).

22 34 C.F.R. § 99.31(a)(1)(ii), https://www.law.cornell.edu/cfr/text/34/99.31 (accessed November 2017). For a discussion of identification and authentication of identify, view "Family Educational Rights and Privacy Act (FERPA): Final Rule 34 CFR Part 99."

23 34 C.F.R. § 99.31(a)(1)(i), https://www.law.cornell.edu/cfr/text/34/99.31 (accessed November 2017).

24 The "legitimate educational interest" does not have to be academic, just related to any appropriate school function. Also, reasonable security controls must be in place to ensure that parties with a legitimate educational interest are the only ones to access the records. See 34 C.F.R. § 99.31(a)(1)(ii), https://www.law.cornell.edu/cfr/text/34/99.31 (accessed November 2017).

25 For an overview from the U.S. Department of Education, view www2.ed.gov/policy/gen/guid/fpco/ferpa/parents.html (accessed November 2017).

26 34 C.F.R. § 99.10(b), https://www.law.cornell.edu/cfr/text/34/99.10 (accessed November 2017).

27 20 U.S.C. § 1232g(a)(1)(A), https://www.law.cornell.edu/uscode/text/20/1232g (accessed November 2017). See also 34 C.F.R. § 99.12(a), https://www.law.cornell.edu/cfr/text/34/99.12 (accessed November 2017).

28 20 U.S.C. § 1232g(a)(2), https://www.law.cornell.edu/uscode/text/20/1232g (accessed November 2017).

29 The U.S. Department of Education provides general privacy guidance on FERPA at its Privacy Technical Assistance Center. "Protecting Student Privacy While Using Online Educational Services: Requirements and Best Practices," http://blogs.edweek.org/edweek/DigitalEducation/Student%20Privacy%20and%20Online%20Educational%20Services%20%28February%202014%29.pdf (accessed November 2017). The Department of Education includes model terms of service for protecting student privacy while using online educational services. http://ptac.ed.gov/sites/default/files/TOS_Guidance_Mar2016.pdf (accessed November 2017).

30 Lynn M. Daggett, "FERPA in the Twenty-First Century: Failure to Effectively Regulate Privacy for All Students," *Catholic University Law Review*, 58 (2008): 59, 100, n. 238, http://scholarship.law.edu/lawreview/vol58/iss1/4/ (accessed November 2017).

31 Protection of Public Rights Amendment, https://www.law.cornell.edu/uscode/text/20/1232h (accessed November 2017). For additional information, *see* the website of the Family Policy Compliance Office. http://familypolicy.ed.gov/ppra (accessed November 2017).

32 No Child Left Behind Act, Pub. L. No. 107-110 § 1061, 115 Stat. 1425, 2083 (2002), https://www.law.cornell.edu/uscode/text/20/6301 (accessed November 2017). For additional resources on No Child Left Behind, *see* the U.S. Department of Education's website on the subject, www2.ed.gov/nclb/landing.jhtml (accessed November 2017).

33 20 U.S.C. § 1232h(c), https://www.law.cornell.edu/uscode/text/20/1232h (accessed November 2017).

34 20 U.S.C. § 1232h(c)(1)(F), https://www.law.cornell.edu/uscode/text/20/1232h (accessed November 2017).

35 20 U.S.C. § 1232h(c)(2)(B), https://www.law.cornell.edu/uscode/text/20/1232h (accessed November 2017).

36 20 U.S.C. § 1232h(c)(2)(B), https://www.law.cornell.edu/uscode/text/20/1232h (accessed November 2017).

37 HIPAA is discussed in detail in Chapter 7 of this book.

38 Robert Gellman and Pam Dixon, "Student Privacy 101: Health Privacy in Schools—What law applies?" World Privacy Forum (Originally published February 2015, accessed November 2017), https://www.worldprivacyforum.org/2015/02/student-privacy-101-health-privacy-in-schools-what-law-applies/ (accessed November 2017); S. Barboza, S. Epps, R. Byington and S. Keene, "HIPAA Goes to School: Clarifying Privacy Laws in the Education Environment," *The Internet Journal of*

Law, Healthcare and Ethics (2008) Vol. 6 No. 2), ISPUB.com, http://ispub.com/IJLHE/6/2/3751 (accessed November 2017).

39 "Does the HIPAA Privacy Rule apply to an elementary or secondary school?" Health Information Privacy, U.S. Department of Health and Human Services (created November 25, 2008, last reviewed July 26, 2013), https://www.hhs.gov/hipaa/for-professionals/faq/513/does-hipaa-apply-to-an-elementary-school/index.html (accessed November 2017); *see* Dinsmore and Shohl, LLP, "Understanding the Privacy Rights of HIPAA and FERPA in Schools," *The National Law Review*, January 7, 2011, https://www.natlawreview.com/article/understanding-privacy-rights-hipaa-ferpa-schools (accessed November 2017). In circumstances where a fee is billed to insurance for medical services provided by the school or by a contractor of the school, the transaction may be deemed a HIPAA transaction. In this situation, the HIPAA Administration Simplification Rules for Transactions and Code Sets may apply to those providing the services. Importantly, the records related to the student's personally identifying information are education records protected by FERPA. If, on the other hand, the school or contractor does not bill the student's insurance for the medical services, HIPAA does not apply. *Id.*; *see* S. Barboza, S. Epps, R. Byington and S. Keene, "HIPAA Goes to School," http://ispub.com/IJLHE/6/2/3751 (accessed November 2017).

40 "Are there circumstances in which the HIPAA Privacy Rule might apply to an elementary or secondary school?" Health Information Privacy, U.S. Department of Health and Human Services (created November 25, 2008, last reviewed July 26, 2013), https://www.hhs.gov/hipaa/for-professionals/faq/515/are-there-circumstances-in-which-hipaa-might-apply-to-a-school/index.html (accessed November 2017); *see* Gerald Woods, "The HIPAA Privacy Rule: Information for Private Independent Schools," p. 7, National Association of Independent Schools (January 2003), www.nais.org/Articles/Documents/HIPAAfinal1_03.pdf (accessed November 2017); *see* Robert Gellman and Pam Dixon, "Student Privacy 101," https://www.worldprivacyforum.org/2015/02/student-privacy-101-health-privacy-in-schools-what-law-applies/ (accessed November 2017); The concept of a "covered entity" under HIPAA is discussed in this book in Chapter 7.

41 Milada Goturi and Aaron Lacey, "Is your institution of higher education covered by HIPAA?" Thompson Coburn, LLP, February 3, 2016, https://www.thompsoncoburn.com/insights/blogs/regucation/post/2016-02-03/is-your-institution-of-higher-education-covered-by-hipaa- (accessed November 2017); *see* "Does FERPA or HIPAA apply to records of students at health clinics run by postsecondary institutions?" Health Information Privacy, U.S. Department of Health and Human Services (created November 25, 2008, last reviewed July 26, 2013), https://www.hhs.gov/hipaa/for-professionals/faq/518/does-ferpa-or-hipaa-apply-to-records-on-students-at-health-clinics/index.html (accessed November 2017); *Joint Guidance on the Application of the Family Education Rights and Privacy Act (FERPA) and the Health Insurance Portability and Accountability Act of 1996 (HIPAA) to Student Health Records*, U.S Department of Health and Human Services and U.S. Department of Education (November 2008), https://www2.ed.gov/policy/gen/guid/fpco/doc/ferpa-hipaa-guidance.pdf (accessed November 2017).

42 *See* "DOE Considers HIPAA Privacy Standard for FERPA to Close Rape Disclosure Loophole," *HIPAA Journal*, June 18, 2015, https://www.hipaajournal.com/doe-considers-hipaa-privacy-standards-for-ferpa-to-close-rape-disclosure-loophole-7085/ (accessed November 2017).

43 *See* Gordon Davies, "Connecting the Dots: Lessons from the Virginia Tech Shooting," pp. 11, 14-15, *Change: The Magazine of Higher Learning*, August 7, 2010, http://naspa.tandfonline.com/doi/pdf/10.3200/CHNG.40.1.8-15 (accessed November 2017).

44 *See* Caroline Knorr, "Ask Your Kid's School These Essential Student Privacy and Safety Questions," Common Sense Media (September 18, 2017), https://www.commonsensemedia.org/blog/ask-your-kids-school-these-essential-student-privacy-and-safety-questions (accessed November 2017).

45 "Google hit with a student privacy complaint," nprEd (December 8, 2015), www.npr.org/sections/ed/2015/12/08/458460509/google-hit-with-a-student-privacy-complaint (accessed November 2017).

46 http://digitalcommons.law.scu.edu/cgi/viewcontent.cgi?article=1667&context=historical (accessed May 2016).

47 "Google sued for data mining: California students claim violation of educational privacy." *International Business Times*, March 18, 2014, www.ibtimes.com/google-sued-data-mining-california-students-claim-violation-educational-privacy-1562198 (accessed November 2017).

48 "Google Abandons Scanning of Student Email Accounts," *EdWeek Market Brief*, April 30, 2014, https://marketbrief.edweek.org/marketplace-k-12/google_abandons_scanning_of_student_email_accounts/ (accessed November 2017).

49 "U.S. Department of Education issues guidance on Student Data Privacy," *Education Week*, February 25, 2014, http://blogs.edweek.org/edweek/DigitalEducation/2014/02/us_ed_dept_issues_guidance_on_.html (accessed November 2017).

50 The U.S. Department of Education provides general privacy guidance on FERPA at its Privacy Technical Assistance Center, http://blogs.edweek.org/edweek/DigitalEducation/Student%20Privacy%20and%20Online%20Educational%20Services%20%28February%202014%29.pdf (accessed November 2017).

51 "Student Privacy Pledge – Hits 250 with Launch of New Site," Future Privacy Forum, https://fpf.org/2016/03/30/student-privacy-pledge-hits-250-with-re-launch-of-site/ (accessed November 2017).

52 "K-12 School Service Provider Pledge to Safeguard Student Privacy," Student Privacy Pledge, https://studentprivacypledge.org/privacy-pledge/ (accessed November 2017).

53 Frequently Asked Questions About FERPA, U.S. Department of Education, https://www2.ed.gov/policy/gen/guid/fpco/pdf/ferpafaq.pdf (accessed November 2017); FERPA General Guidance for Students, U.S. Department of Education, https://www2.ed.gov/policy/gen/guid/fpco/ferpa/students.html (accessed November 2017).

54 34 CFR § 99.31(a)(8), https://www.law.cornell.edu/cfr/text/34/99.31 (accessed November 2017).

CHAPTER 10

Telecommunications and Marketing

Telecommunications and marketing involve very important privacy issues. One set of privacy telecommunications issues concerns specific communications channels and methods such as telemarketing, texts and electronic mail. For these channels, U.S. law has specific rules that regulate how organizations can communicate with individuals for direct marketing and related purposes. Another set of marketing issues concerns the rules that apply to personal information (PI) collected by the companies themselves in the course of providing their services. Along with websites themselves, companies in sectors such as telephone, cable, Internet service and social media can potentially learn a great deal about individuals by the phone calls people make, the television shows they watch, and the Internet sites they visit. This chapter examines the statutes that govern the commercial use of that type of telephone, cable and Internet activity.[1]

10.1 Regulations Governing Telemarketing

U.S. federal and state laws place legal limits on the manner in which organizations can call individuals for marketing and fund-raising purposes. Legislators and regulators have issued restrictions in response to complaints by families about deceptive marketing practices as well as unwanted marketing calls.

In examining the legal and theoretical underpinnings of these government actions, it is insightful to compare one traditional privacy tort action known as "intrusion on seclusion" to telemarking regulations. The tort of "intrusion on seclusion" imposes liability on "one who intentionally intrudes, physically or otherwise, upon the solitude or seclusion of another or his private affairs or concerns."[2] To succeed in an intrusion tort claim, the plaintiff must show that "the intrusion would be highly offensive to a reasonable person."[3] In contrast with intrusion tort requirements, telemarketing regulations in the United States address milder intrusions, which do not require a showing of "highly offensive" intrusion.

Telemarketing laws in the United States provide considerable detail about what types of "intrusions" are permitted under federal law. The Federal Communications Commission (FCC) and the Federal Trade Commission (FTC) have coordinated closely in their requirements. The FCC issued regulations under the Telephone

Consumer Protection Act of 1991 (TCPA) that place restrictions on unsolicited advertising by telephone and facsimile, and updated them in 2012 to address robocalls.[4] The FCC has determined that these prohibitions encompass text messages.[5]

The FTC first issued its Telemarketing Sales Rule (TSR) in 1995, implementing the Telemarketing and Consumer Fraud and Abuse Prevention Act. It has since amended the TSR in 2003, 2008, 2010 and 2015.[6] The Telemarketing Sales Rule defines telemarketing as "a plan, program, or campaign which is conducted to induce the purchase of goods or services or a charitable contribution, by use of one or more telephones and which involves more than one interstate telephone call."[7]

The focus of this discussion will be on the FTC rule. This chapter first examines who can receive such calls consistent with the Do Not Call (DNC) list, and then turns to the rules governing how telemarketing calls can be made.

10.1.1 Who Can Be Called: The U.S. National Do Not Call Registry

The U.S. National DNC Registry is perhaps the best known of the FTC's TSR requirements and remains the most popular consumer program ever implemented by the FTC.[8] The program provides a means for U.S. residents to register residential and wireless phone numbers that they do not wish to be called for telemarketing purposes (with specific exceptions, below).

The FTC, the FCC and state attorneys general enforce the DNC Registry, which now contains over 220 million participating phone numbers—and is still growing.[9] As of the writing of this book, violations of the rule can lead to civil penalties of up to $40,654 per violation.[10] In addition, violators may be subject to nationwide injunctions that prohibit certain conduct and may be required to pay redress to injured consumers.[11]

The DNC Registry provisions took effect in 2003 and require sellers and telemarketers to access the registry prior to making any phone-based solicitations. They are also required to update their call lists every 31 days with new registry information.

The registry is accessed via an automated website at www.telemarketing.donotcall.gov. Only sellers, telemarketers and their service providers may access the registry. Each seller must establish a profile by providing identifying information about the organization. The seller then receives a unique Subscription Account Number (SAN) upon payment of the appropriate fee.

Telemarketers accessing the registry on behalf of seller-clients are required to identify the seller-clients and provide the seller-client's unique SAN. (Telemarketers access the registry, at no cost, through the use of their seller-client's unique SANs. Their access is limited to the area codes requested and paid for by the seller-client.)

The FTC's guidance specifically states that:[12]

> *A telemarketer or other service provider working on behalf of a seller may access the registry directly or through the use of its seller-client's SAN. If access is gained through its seller-client's SAN, the telemarketer or service provider will not have to pay a separate fee for that access. The extent of its access will be limited to the area codes requested and paid for by its seller-client.*
>
> *If a telemarketer or service provider is accessing the registry directly—that is, if a telemarketer or service provider decides to obtain the information on its own behalf—it will have to pay a separate fee and comply with all requirements placed on sellers accessing the registry. Such a telemarketer or service provider will be provided a SAN that can be used only by that company. In other words, that SAN is not transferable.*

In other words, each SAN belongs to a specific seller, and SANs are not transferable.

Note that it is a violation of the TSR to place any call to a consumer (absent an exception) unless the registry is checked. In other words, even a call to a consumer whose phone number is not on the registry is a violation of the TSR if the registry was not checked prior to the call.[13]

10.1.1.1 Exceptions to the DNC Rules

DNC rules apply to for-profit organizations and cover charitable solicitations placed by for-profit telefunders. DNC rules do *not* apply to:

- Nonprofits calling on their own behalf
- Calls to customers with an existing relationship within the last 18 months
- Inbound calls, provided that there is no "upsell" of additional products or services[14]
- Most business-to-business calls

10.1.1.1.1 Existing Business Relationship Exception

Sellers (and telemarketers calling on their behalf) may call a consumer with whom a seller has an established business relationship (EBR), provided the consumer has not asked to be on the seller's entity-specific DNC list. The TSR recognizes two distinct types of relationships: "customers" and "prospects."

An EBR exists with a customer if the consumer has purchased, rented or leased the seller's goods or services (or completed a financial transaction with the seller) within 18 months preceding a telemarketing call. The 18-month period runs from the date of the last payment, transaction or shipment between the consumer and the seller.

An EBR exists with a prospect if the consumer has made an application or inquiry regarding the seller's goods and services. This EBR runs for three months from the date of the person's inquiry or application.

10.1.1.1.2 Exception Based on Consent

The TSR allows sellers and telemarketers to call consumers who consent to receive such calls. This consent must be in writing, must state the number to which calls may be made and must include the consumer's signature. (A valid electronic signature is acceptable.)

Note that the seller's request for consent must be "clear and conspicuous." If in writing, the request "cannot be hidden; printed in small, pale, or noncontrasting type; hidden on the back or bottom of the document; or buried in unrelated information where a person would not expect to find such a request."[15] If online, the "please call me" button may not be prechecked. The FTC's guidance also states: "In the FTC's enforcement experience, sweepstakes entry forms often have been used in a deceptive manner to obtain 'authorization' from a consumer to incur a charge or some other detriment. Authorization or permission obtained through subterfuge is ineffective. The FTC scrutinizes any use of such sweepstakes entry forms as a way to get a consumer's permission to place telemarketing calls to her number."[16]

10.1.1.1.3 The Do Not Call Safe Harbor

The TSR has a "DNC Safe Harbor" that sellers and telemarketers can use to reduce the risk of liability. Per the guidance:[17]

> *[I]f a seller or telemarketer can establish that as part of its routine business practice, it meets the following requirements, it will not be subject to civil penalties or sanctions for erroneously calling a consumer who has asked not to be called, or for calling a number on the National Registry:*
>
> - *The seller or telemarketer has established and implemented written procedures to honor consumers' requests that they not be called, [and]*
> - *The seller or telemarketer has trained its personnel, and any entity assisting in its compliance, in these procedures, [and]*
> - *The seller, telemarketer, or someone else acting on behalf of the seller . . . has maintained and recorded an entity-specific Do Not Call list, [and]*

- *The seller or telemarketer uses, and maintains records documenting, a process to prevent calls to any telephone number on an entity-specific Do Not Call list or the National Do Not Call Registry. This, provided that the latter process involves using a version of the National Registry from the FTC no more than 31 days before the date any call is made, [and]*
- *The seller, telemarketer, or someone else acting on behalf of the seller... monitors and enforces compliance with the entity's written Do Not Call procedures, [then]*
- *The call is a result of error.*

This DNC Safe Harbor provides an important protection for sellers and telemarketers because violations of the TSR can result in civil penalties, as of the writing of this book, of up to $40,654 per call.[18]

10.1.2 Rules Governing How Calls Can Be Made Under Telemarketing Laws

The TSR provides detailed rules about many aspects of how telemarketing calls can be made. The vast majority of telemarketing calls are from legitimate businesses trying to achieve their business goals while satisfying consumers. The telemarketing field, however, has also been plagued with a history of intrusive and fraudulent callers. Such callers sometimes intrude repeatedly on consumers, making frequent calls at inappropriate hours and in other ways that bother consumers. Such callers also sometimes take advantage of their anonymity and physical distance from consumers to try to defraud consumers. This combination of intrusiveness and fraud has led to periodic TSR updates to address new forms of problems for consumers.

The TSR requires covered organizations to:

- Call only between 8 a.m. and 9 p.m.
- Screen and scrub names against the national DNC list
- Display caller ID information
- Identify themselves and what they are selling
- Disclose all material information and terms[19]
- Comply with special rules for prizes and promotions
- Respect requests to call back
- Retain records for at least 24 hours
- Comply with special rules for automated dialers

Under the rules, telemarketing is defined as "a plan, program, or campaign . . . to induce the purchase of goods or services or a charitable contribution" involving more than one interstate telephone call.[20] With some exceptions, all businesses or individuals that engage in telemarketing must comply with the TSR (or the FCC counterpart) as well as applicable state laws.[21] Neither the TSR nor the FCC rules preempt state law. As the FTC notes, compliance is required both of "telemarketers," entities that initiate or receive telephone calls to or from consumers, and "sellers," the entities that provide or arrange to provide the goods and services being offered.

10.1.2.1 Entity-Specific Suppression Lists

The TSR prohibits any seller (or telemarketer calling on the seller's behalf) from calling any consumer who has asked not to be called again. Sellers and telemarketers are required to maintain internal suppression lists to respect these DNC requests.

The TSR does provide some latitude for companies that have distinct corporate divisions. In general, such divisions are considered separate sellers under the rule.

The FTC specifies two factors that should be used to determine whether DNC requests should be shared among divisions: (1) whether there is substantial diversity between the operational structure of the divisions and (2) whether the goods or services sold by the divisions are substantially different from each other.

If a consumer tells one division of a company not to call again, a distinct corporate division of the same company may still make calls to that consumer. If the divisions are not distinct, however, the seller may not call the consumer even to offer different goods or services.

10.1.2.2 Required Disclosures

The TSR requires that, at the beginning of the call, before delivering any sales content, telemarketers disclose:

- The identity of the seller
- That the purpose of the call is to sell goods or services
- The nature of those goods or services
- In the case of a prize promotion, that no purchase or payment is necessary to participate or win, and that a purchase or payment does not increase the chances of winning

The FTC has issued guidance on how and when these four basic disclosures must be made. For example, disclosures must be truthful. A company cannot say it is making a "courtesy call" to the consumer if the purpose of the call is telemarketing.

If a call has multiple purposes (such as the sale of different types of products or different overall purposes), disclosures have to be made for all sales purposes. The following examples are from the FTC's "Complying with the Telemarketing Sales Rule" guide:[22]

> *A seller calls a consumer to determine whether he or she is satisfied with a previous purchase and then plans to move into a sales presentation if the consumer is satisfied. Since the seller plans to make a sales presentation in at least some of the calls (the seller plans to end the call if the consumer is not satisfied), the four sales disclosures...must be made promptly during the initial portion of the call and before inquiring about customer satisfaction.*
>
> *However, a seller may make calls to welcome new customers and ask whether they are satisfied with goods or services they recently purchased. If the seller doesn't plan to sell anything to these customers during any of these calls, the four oral sales disclosures are not required. That's the case even if customers ask about the sellers' other goods or services, and the seller responds by describing the goods or services. Because the seller has no plans to sell goods or services during these calls, the disclosures are not required.*

10.1.2.3 Misrepresentations and Material Omissions

The TSR prohibits misrepresentations during the sales call. Telemarketers must provide accurate and complete information about the products and services being offered. They may not omit any material facts about the products or services. There are ten broad categories of information that must always be disclosed:

1. Cost and quantity
2. Material restrictions, limitations, or conditions
3. Performance, efficacy, or central characteristics
4. Refund, repurchase or cancellation policies
5. Material aspects of prize promotions
6. Material aspect of investment opportunities
7. Affiliations, endorsements, or sponsorships
8. Credit card loss protection
9. Negative option features
10. Debt relief services

The rule also was amended to require specific disclosures when a telemarketer accepts payment by means other than a credit card or debit card, such as phone or utility billing. In this case, the seller must obtain "express verifiable authorization." In amending the rule, the commission noted that many new payment methods lacked basic consumer protection provisions that exist in credit card transactions. Because the consumers may not have protections against, for example, unauthorized charges, or recourse in the event they are dissatisfied with the goods or services, the TSR now requires telemarketers to meet a higher standard for proving authorization when consumers use new payment methods.

10.1.2.4 Transmission of Caller ID Information

The TSR requires entities that make telemarketing calls to transmit accurate call identification information so that it can be presented to consumers with caller ID services. In particular, each telemarketer may transmit its own name and phone number, or it may substitute the name of the seller on whose behalf the telemarketer is making the call. The telemarketer may also substitute the seller's customer-service telephone number for its number, provided that the seller's number is answered during normal business hours.

Telemarketers are not liable if, for some reason, caller ID information does not reach a consumer, provided that the telemarketer has arranged with its carrier to transmit this information in every call. The FTC guidance states that "telemarketers who can show that they took all available steps to ensure transmission of Caller ID information in every call will not be liable for isolated inadvertent instances when the Caller ID information fails to make it to the consumer's receiver. Nevertheless, a telemarketer's use of calling equipment that is not capable of transmitting Caller ID information is no excuse for failure to transmit the required information."[23]

10.1.2.5 Prohibition on Call Abandonment

The TSR expressly prohibits telemarketers from abandoning an outbound telephone call with either "hang-ups" or "dead air." Under the TSR, an outbound telephone call is "abandoned" if a person answers it and the telemarketer does not connect the call to a live sales representative within two seconds of the person's completed greeting.

Abandoned calls often result from a telemarketer's use of predictive dialers to call consumers. Predictive dialers promote telemarketers' efficiency by simultaneously calling multiple consumers for every available sales representative. This maximizes the amount of time telemarketing sales representatives spend talking to consumers and minimizes representatives' downtime. But it also means that some calls are abandoned:

Consumers are either hung up on or kept waiting for long periods until a representative is available.

The use of prerecorded-message telemarketing, where a sales pitch begins with or is made entirely by a prerecorded message, also violates the TSR because the telemarketer is not connecting the call to a live sales representative within two seconds of the called person's completed greeting.[24] For a company to use prerecorded sales messages, it must have the prior express consent (opt-in) of the consumer.

10.1.2.6 Abandonment Safe Harbor

According to the FTC guidance, the abandoned call Safe Harbor provides that a telemarketer will not face enforcement action for violating the call abandonment prohibition if the telemarketer:

- Uses technology that ensures abandonment of no more than three percent of all calls answered by a live person, measured per day per calling campaign
- Allows the telephone to ring for 15 seconds or four rings before disconnecting an unanswered call
- Plays a recorded message stating the name and telephone number of the seller on whose behalf the call was placed whenever a live sales representative is unavailable within two seconds of a live person answering the call
- Maintains records documenting adherence to the preceding three requirements

To take advantage of the Safe Harbor, a telemarketer must first ensure that a live representative takes at least 97 percent of the calls answered by consumers. Any calls answered by machine, calls that are not answered at all, and calls to nonworking numbers do not count in this calculation.

This three-percent rule applies to each day and each calling campaign. The FTC does not allow a telemarketer to average abandonment rates, even if it is running simultaneous calling campaigns on behalf of different sellers. The Safe Harbor also requires the telemarketer to let the phone ring at least four times (or for 15 seconds). This requirement is designed to ensure that consumers have sufficient time to answer a call.

For the small number of calls that are abandoned, the TSR's Safe Harbor requires the telemarketer to play a recorded greeting, consisting of the company's name and phone number and a statement that the call was for telemarketing purposes. This recorded message may not contain a sales pitch.[25] The phone number provided in the message must also be one to which the consumer can call to be placed on the company's own DNC list.

Finally, to be within the Safe Harbor, the telemarketer must keep records that demonstrate its compliance with the other Safe Harbor provisions. The records must demonstrate both that the per-day, per-campaign abandonment rate has not exceeded three percent and that the ring time and recorded message requirements have been met.

10.1.2.7 Prohibition on Unauthorized Billing

The detailed rules in the TSR have been amended over time to address specific problems that consumers have experienced. For instance, the TSR strictly prohibits telemarketers from billing consumers for any goods or services without the consumer's "express, informed consent." If the consumer provides the billing account information to the telemarketer during the call, then express, informed consent can be obtained in any nondeceptive manner.

If, on the other hand, the telemarketer has obtained the consumer's account information from some other source ("preacquired account information"), the TSR imposes an array of specific requirements on how express, informed consent must be obtained. In particular, the TSR has special requirements for "free-to-pay conversion" offers (offers that begin with a free trial, but then convert to paid service at the end of the trial period). These rules are designed to combat the high incidence of unauthorized charges made to consumer accounts where consumers did not understand that the service provider would charge the consumer at the end of the trial period. If preacquired account information is used in connection with a free-to-pay conversion offer, the telemarketer must:

- Obtain from the customer at least the last four digits of the account number to be charged
- Obtain the customer's express agreement to be charged for the goods or services using the account number for which the customer has provided at least the last four digits
- Make and maintain an audio recording of the entire telemarketing transaction

If preacquired account information is used in connection with any other type of transaction, the telemarketer must still (at minimum) identify the account with enough specificity for the consumer to understand which account will be charged and obtain the consumer's express agreement to be charged using that account number.

10.1.2.8 Updates to the TCPA Rules Concerning Robocalls and Autodialers

In 2012, the FCC revised its Telephone Consumer Protection Act (TCPA) rules governing prerecorded calls (robocalls) and the use of automatic telephone dialing systems (autodialers) to reconcile its rules with the TSR.[26] First, the FCC revised its established business relationship exemption for robocalls. Now, even if a company has an established business relationship with a consumer, it is required to receive "prior express written consent" for all robocalls to residential lines.[27] Second, the rules include a provision that allows consumers to "opt out of future robocalls during a robocall." In addition, the revisions increase harmonization with the FTC's rules to require "assessment of the call abandonment rate to occur during a single calling campaign over a 30-day period, and if the single calling campaign exceeds a 30-day period, we require that the abandonment rate be calculated each successive 30-day period or portion thereof during which the calling campaign continues." Finally, also consistent with the FTC, robocalls to residential lines made by healthcare-related entities governed by HIPAA are exempt from the above requirements.[28]

10.1.2.9 Updates on the FCC Approach to Robotexts

In 2015, the FCC issued an order explicitly stating that text messages sent to wireless devices are subject to the same consumer protections as voice calls under the TCPA. This means that the TCPA prohibits companies from sending text messages via equipment that sends the messages without human intervention, known as "robotexts"—absent express consent.[29] The order then altered the definition of "prior written consent" to require that the consent obtained must include a "clear and conspicuous disclosure" that telemarking calls or texts can be made with an autodialer or artificial voice. Further, it required that the consent could not be obtained as a requirement of purchase.[30]

In 2017, the FCC provided further guidance on robotexts including: (1) consent can be revoked by the consumer at any time by any reasonable means, (2) the mere fact that a consumer's wireless number appears in the contact list of another wireless customer is not sufficient to establish consent and (3) when a caller has consent for a wireless number and the number has been reassigned, the caller is not liable for the first call but will be liable for subsequent calls if the new consumer makes the caller aware of the change.[31]

10.1.2.10 Record-Keeping Requirements

To make enforcement more effective, the TSR requires sellers and telemarketers to keep substantial records that relate to their telemarketing activities. In general, the following records must be maintained for two years from the date that the record is produced:

- Advertising and promotional materials
- Information about prize recipients
- Sales records
- Employee records
- All verifiable authorizations or records of express informed consent or express agreement

These records may be maintained in whatever manner, format or medium the company uses in the normal course of business. For example, the records may be maintained in electronic or paper formats. Additionally, the TSR requires only one copy of the records to be maintained. In particular, sellers and telemarketers can decide which party should maintain which records as part of the services contract. As the FTC's guidance states:[32]

> *Sellers and telemarketers do not have to keep duplicative records if they have a written agreement allocating responsibility for complying with the recordkeeping requirements. Without a written agreement between the parties, or if the written agreement is unclear as to who must maintain the required records, telemarketers must keep employee records, while sellers must keep the advertising and promotional materials, information on prize recipients, sales records, and verifiable authorizations.*

In the event of dissolution or termination of the business of a seller or telemarketer, the principal of the business must maintain all records of the business. In the event of a sale, assignment or other change in ownership of the seller or telemarketer's business, the successor business must maintain the records.

For each type of record listed above, the TSR includes lists of the information that must be retained. For example, sales records must include: (1) the name and last known address of each customer, (2) the goods or services purchased, (3) the date the goods or services were shipped or provided and (4) the amount the customer paid for the goods or services.

Similarly, for all current and former employees directly involved in telephone sales, records must include: (1) the name (and any fictitious name used), (2) the last known home address and telephone number and (3) the job title(s) of each employee. Additionally, if fictitious names are used by employees, the TSR also requires that each fictitious name be traceable to a specific employee.

10.1.2.11 Other Provisions

The TSR also includes specific regulations designed to address:

- Credit card laundering
- Telemarketing sales of credit repair programs, loss recovery services and advance loans
- "Telefunding" activities (for-profit companies that call on behalf of charitable organizations)

The TSR includes significant enforcement provisions. As noted earlier, the TSR can be enforced by the FTC, the state attorneys general or private individuals.[33] The FTC has aggressively enforced the TSR. As noted, violations of the TSR are currently punishable by civil penalties of up to $40,654 per call. The FCC and state attorneys general also actively enforce their counterpart regulations. Additionally, some states have their own versions of telemarketing sales rules that carry additional penalties and may have different requirements. For example, Louisiana's Public Service Commission's DNC General Order has different allowed time frames for making calls, limits established business relationships to six months, and has established its own penalties for violators.

10.1.3 State Telemarketing Legislation

States have enacted telemarketing laws as well, creating additional legal requirements for telemarketers. For example, more than half the states require that telemarketers obtain a license or register with the state.[34] States can also create their own DNC lists, with differing exceptions, fines or methods of consumer enrollment from their federal counterpart.[35] Some states require that telemarketers identify themselves at the beginning of the call, or that the telemarketer terminate the call without rebuttal if the recipient of the call so desires.[36] Finally, states may require that a written contract be created for certain transactions.[37]

10.2 Fax Marketing

In addition to regulating telemarketing and Internet-to-phone short message service (SMS) marketing, TCPA, enforced by the FCC, prohibits unsolicited commercial fax transmissions. Penalties include a private right of action and statutory damages of up to $500 per fax.[38] In 2001, Hooters of Augusta (Georgia) was found to have violated the act and ordered to pay out $12 million in a class-action suit.[39] In 2003, the FCC approved a $5.4 million fine against Fax.com for violations of the act.[40]

In 2005, Congress passed the Junk Fax Prevention Act (JFPA) in part to clarify whether consent was required for commercial faxing. The JFPA specifically provides that consent can be inferred from an EBR, and it permits sending of commercial faxes to recipients based on an EBR, as long as the sender offers an opt-out in accordance with the act. For purposes of the JFPA, "existing business relationship" has the same definition as it does in the FTC's DNC rule.

Some states have enacted their own laws regulating unsolicited commercial fax transmissions. Notably, California attempted to eliminate the TCPA's EBR exception with legislation applicable to unsolicited faxes sent to or from a fax machine located within the state.[41] The law, however, was declared unconstitutional when applied to interstate fax transmissions due to the TCPA's preemption of interstate regulation.[42]

10.3 Controlling the Assault of Non-Solicited Pornography and Marketing Act of 2003

Along with the rules governing commercial telemarketing and faxes, Congress has created rules for unsolicited commercial electronic mail in the Controlling the Assault of Non-Solicited Pornography and Marketing (CAN-SPAM) Act of 2003.[43] The act applies to anyone who advertises products or services by electronic mail directed to or originating from the United States. The law covers the transmission of commercial email messages whose primary purpose is advertising or promoting a product or service.

CAN-SPAM was never intended to eliminate all unsolicited commercial email, but rather to provide a mechanism for legitimate companies to send emails to prospects and respect individual rights to opt out of unwanted communications. Spam-filtering software is still widely used to screen out as much of the continuing spam as possible. The act nonetheless has fulfilled an important purpose. It has created the rules of the road for how legitimate organizations send emails, including clear identification of the sender and a simple unsubscribe or opt-out. The CAN-SPAM Act:

- Prohibits false or misleading headers
- Prohibits deceptive subject lines
- Requires commercial emails to contain a functioning, clearly and conspicuously displayed return email address that allows the recipient to contact the sender
- Requires all commercial emails to include clear and conspicuous notice of the opportunity to opt out along with a cost-free mechanism for exercising the opt-out, such as by return email or by clicking on an opt-out link

- Prohibits sending commercial email (following a grace period of 10 business days) to an individual who has asked not to receive future email
- Requires all commercial email to include (1) clear and conspicuous identification that the message is a commercial message (unless the recipient has provided prior affirmative consent to receive the email) and (2) a valid physical postal address of the sender (which can be a post office box)
- Prohibits "aggravated violations" relating to commercial emails such as (1) address-harvesting and dictionary attacks, (2) the automated creation of multiple email accounts and (3) the retransmission of commercial email through unauthorized accounts
- Requires all commercial email containing sexually oriented material to include a warning label (unless the recipient has provided prior affirmative consent to receive the email)

CAN-SPAM is enforced primarily by the FTC and carries penalties of fines of up to $40,654 per violation.[44] In addition, deceptive commercial email is subject to laws banning false or misleading advertising. The FTC has the authority to issue regulations implementing the CAN-SPAM Act and did so in 2008 to clarify a number of statutory definitions.[45]

CAN-SPAM distinguishes commercial email messages from "transactional or relationship messages," which are messages whose primary purpose is to:

- Facilitate or confirm an agreed-upon commercial transaction
- Provide warranty or safety information about a product purchased or used by the recipient
- Provide certain information regarding an ongoing commercial relationship
- Provide information related to employment or a related benefit plan
- Deliver goods or services to which the recipient is entitled under the terms of an agreed-upon transaction

CAN-SPAM contains a number of requirements generally applicable to the sender of a commercial email message. A sender is anyone who initiates an email message and whose product or service is advertised or promoted by the message. More than one person may be deemed to have initiated a message. The FTC issued a regulation in 2008 clarifying that the entity identified in the "from" line can generally be considered the single sender as long as there is compliance with the other provisions of CAN-SPAM.[46]

The 2008 regulation also provides additional detail on (1) a prohibition on having the email recipient pay a fee to opt out, (2) the definition of "valid physical postal address" and (3) the application of the term *person* to apply beyond natural persons.

CAN-SPAM grants enforcement authority to the FTC and other federal regulators, along with state attorneys general and other state officials. Internet service providers that have been adversely affected by a violation may sue violators for injunctive relief and monetary damages. Unlike some state spam laws that are now preempted, the act does not provide for a right of action for other parties. For those authorized to sue, the act provides for injunctive relief and damages up to $250 per violation, with a maximum award of $2 million. The act further provides that a court may increase a damage award up to three times the amount otherwise available in cases of willful or aggravated violations. Certain egregious conduct is punishable by up to five years imprisonment.

In an example from 2009, a federal judge shut down a company called 3FN based on the FTC's allegations that it had knowingly distributed spam and malware as well as hosted illegal content, such as child pornography.[47]

CAN-SPAM preempts most state laws that restrict email communications, although state spam laws are not superseded by CAN-SPAM to the extent such laws prohibit false or deceptive activity.

10.3.1 Wireless Message Rules Under CAN-SPAM

In addition to the email rules discussed above, the FCC has issued rules implementing the CAN-SPAM Act with regard to mobile service commercial messages (MSCMs), including many commercial text messages.

The CAN-SPAM Act defines an MSCM as "a commercial electronic mail message that is transmitted directly to a wireless device that is utilized by a subscriber of a commercial mobile service." The message must have (or utilize) a unique electronic address that includes "a reference to an Internet domain." The FCC also notes in its commentary that the rule is designed to apply only to mail addresses designed by carriers for mobile services messaging. Importantly, the FCC's rules cover messages sent using SMS technology, but do not cover phone-to-phone messages.[48]

The FCC rule defers to the FTC rules and interpretation regarding the definitions of "commercial" and "transactional" (with respect to the mail messages) as well as the mechanisms for determining the "primary purpose" of messages. Accordingly, the FCC rule must be analyzed in the context of the FTC regulatory framework for the CAN-SPAM Act.

10.3.2 Express Prior Authorization

The CAN-SPAM Act prohibits senders from sending any MSCMs without the subscriber's "express prior authorization." Express prior authorization must be obtained for each MSCM, regardless of sender or industry. The FCC requirements are quite detailed, and can be summarized as follows:

- "Express prior authorization" must be "express," meaning that the consumer has taken an affirmative action to give the authorization. Authorization may not be obtained in the form of a negative option. If the authorization is obtained via a website, the consumer must take an affirmative action, such as checking a box or hitting a button.
- The authorization must also be given prior to the sending of any MSCMs. There is no provision to grandfather existing authorizations that senders may have obtained. Because of the disclosure requirements in these authorizations, the FCC notes that senders who claim they have obtained authorization prior to the effective date of these rules will not be in compliance unless they can demonstrate that these existing authorizations have met each of the requirements in the rule.
- Consumers must not bear any cost with respect to the authorization or revocation processes.
- Each authorization must include certain required disclosures stating that:

    1. The subscriber is agreeing to receive MSCMs sent to his or her wireless device from a particular (identified) sender.
    2. The subscriber may be charged by his or her wireless provider in connection with the receipt of such messages.
    3. The subscriber may revoke the authorization at any time.

- These disclosures must be clearly legible and in sufficiently large type (or volume, if given via audio). They must be presented in a manner that is readily apparent to the consumer. These disclosures must be separate from any other authorizations contained in another document. Additionally, if any portion of the authorization/disclosure is translated into another language, then all portions must be translated into that language.
- As noted above, the authorization must be specific to the sender and must clearly identify the entity that is being authorized to send the MSCMs. The

FCC rule prohibits any sender from sending MSCMs on behalf of other third parties, including affiliates and marketing partners. Each entity must obtain separate express prior authorizations for the messages it sends.

- Authorization may be obtained in any format, oral or written, including electronic. Although writing is not required, the FCC requires that each sender of MSCMs must document the authorization and be able to demonstrate that a valid authorization (meeting all the other requirements) existed prior to sending the commercial message. The commentary notes that the burden of proof rests with the sender.
- With regard to revocations, senders must enable consumers to revoke authorizations using the same means the consumers used to grant authorizations. (For example, if a consumer authorizes MSCMs electronically, the company must permit the consumer to revoke the authorization electronically.)
- Additionally, the MSCMs themselves must include functioning return email addresses or another Internet-based mechanism that is clearly and conspicuously displayed for the purpose of receiving opt-out requests.

  Note: Consumers must not be required to view or hear any further commercial content during the opt-out process (other than institutional identification).
- The FCC rule maintains the CAN-SPAM–mandated 10-business-day grace period following a revoked authorization, after which messages cannot be sent.

10.3.3 The Wireless Domain Registry

To help senders of commercial messages determine whether those messages might be MSCMs (rather than regular commercial email), the FCC has created a registry of wireless domain names (available on the FCC website).[49] It is updated on a periodic basis, as new domains are added.

Senders are responsible for obtaining this list and ensuring that the appropriate authorizations exist before sending commercial messages to addresses within the domains. In other words, the requirements listed above will apply to messages sent to any address whose domain name is included on the wireless domain name list.

According to the FCC guidance, messages that are not sent to an address for a wireless device, but are only forwarded to a wireless device, are not subject to FCC rules on MSCMs.[50]

With regard to the domain name list, all commercial mobile radio service providers are required under the rule to identify all electronic mail domain names that are dedicated for use by subscribers for wireless devices. The providers are also responsible for updating information on the domain name list to the FCC within 30 days before issuing any new or modified domain names.

10.4 The Telecommunications Act of 1996

The chapter thus far has examined marketing rules for telecommunications channels such as telephones, faxes, emails and texts. The discussion now turns to rules affecting the telecommunications companies themselves in connection with personal information. The Telecommunications Act of 1996 was a major piece of legislation that reshaped numerous aspects of telecommunications markets.[51] Section 222 of the act governs the privacy of customer information provided to and obtained by telecommunications carriers. Prior to the act, carriers were permitted to sell customer data to third-party marketers without consumer consent. The statute imposed new restrictions on the access, use and disclosure of customer proprietary network information (CPNI).

CPNI is information collected by telecommunications carriers related to their subscribers. This includes subscription information, services used, and network and billing information as well as phone features and capabilities. It also includes call log data such as time, date, destination and duration of calls. Certain PI such as name, telephone number and address is not considered CPNI. The CPNI requirements apply to telecommunications carriers and voice-over-Internet protocol (VoIP) providers that are interconnected with telephone service.[52] As discussed in more detail below, they historically did not apply to broadband Internet service providers (ISPs). In 2016 the FCC issued a detailed regulation that was designed to regulate privacy for customers of broadband ISPs. This regulation was repealed under the Trump administration and new FCC leadership, and ISPs today are subject to the general CPNI requirements of Section 222.

The act imposes requirements on carriers to limit access, use and disclosure of CPNI. Specifically, carriers can use and disclose CPNI only with customer approval or "as required by law."[53] However, carriers do not need approval to use, disclose or provide marketing offerings among service categories that customers already subscribe to. Carriers can also use CPNI for billing and collections, fraud prevention, customer service and emergency services.

The rules concerning opt-in and opt-out for use of CPNI have shifted over time. In 1998, the FCC issued a rule requiring carriers to obtain express consent from customers before using CPNI, even for the carriers' own marketing purposes. This rule was struck down in 1999 in U.S. West, Inc. v. Federal Communications Commission.[54] In that case, the Tenth Circuit found that the opt-in requirement violated the First Amendment speech rights of the carriers. Thus, the standard shifted to an opt-out system for carriers' own use of CPNI. In 2002, the FCC issued final rules requiring carriers to obtain express consent before CPNI could be shared with third parties, but allowed sharing of CPNI with joint venture or independent contractors unless customers opted out within 30 days of being notified. In 2007, the FCC issued new CPNI regulations governing carriers' use and sharing of CPNI.[55] The 2007 CPNI order requires customers to expressly consent, or opt in, before carriers can share their CPNI with joint venture partners and independent contractors for marketing purposes.

The 2007 CPNI order imposes requirements aimed at curbing pretexting, or gaining access to CPNI through fraudulent means. First, carriers must notify law enforcement when CPNI is disclosed in a security breach within seven business days of that breach. Second, customers must provide a password before they can access their CPNI via telephone or online account services. The order also establishes carrier CPNI compliance requirements. Carriers must certify their compliance with these laws annually, explain how their systems ensure compliance and provide an annual summary of consumer complaints related to unauthorized disclosure of CPNI.

10.5 The Cable Communications Policy Act of 1984

The Cable Communications Policy of 1984 regulates the notice a cable television provider must furnish to customers, the ability of cable providers to collect PI, the ability of cable providers to disseminate PI and the retention and destruction of PI by cable television providers.[56] It also provides a private right of action for violations of the aforementioned provisions, and allows for actual or statutory damages, punitive damages and reasonable attorney's fees and court costs.[57] The act does not regulate the provision of broadband Internet services via cable because the act defines a "cable service" as "*one-way* transmission to subscribers of . . . video programming or . . . other programming service, and . . . subscriber interaction, if any, which is required for the selection or use of such video programming or other programming service."[58]

At the time of entering into an agreement to provide cable services, and on an annual basis thereafter, cable service providers are required to give subscribers a privacy notice that "clearly and conspicuously" informs subscribers of: (1) the nature of the PI collected, (2) how such information will be used, (3) the retention period of such information and (4) the manner by which a subscriber can access and correct such information.[59] The act further states that a cable TV service provider may only collect

PI that is necessary to render cable services or to detect the unauthorized reception of cable services.[60]

The act limits cable service providers' right to disseminate PI without the "written or electronic consent" of the subscriber, unless the disclosure is subject to a specified exception.[61] A number of exceptions to this provision do exist. Specifically, disclosures may be made (1) to the extent necessary to render services or conduct other legitimate business activities, (2) subject to a court order with notice to the subscriber or (3) if the disclosure is limited to names and addresses and the subscriber is given an option to opt out.[62]

Although the act does not specify a schedule for data retention or destruction, it does mandate that PI be destroyed when it is no longer needed for the purpose for which it was collected and there are no pending requests for access.[63]

The provision allowing for disclosures of PI subject to a court order with notice to the subscriber has been read as creating tension with the Electronic Communications Privacy Act of 1986 (ECPA), which allows such disclosures without notice to the consumer, as notice may negatively impact an ongoing investigation.[64] Courts have resolved this tension in favor of ECPA, due to its later enactment.[65]

10.6 The Video Privacy Protection Act of 1988

The Video Privacy Protection Act of 1988 (VPPA)[66] was passed in response to the disclosure and publication of then-Supreme Court nominee Robert Bork's video rental records.[67] Although the records revealed that Judge Bork watched innocuous films, the disclosure was considered a gross invasion of his privacy.[68]

The act applies to "video tape service providers," who are defined as anyone "engaged in the business, in or affecting interstate or foreign commerce, of rental, sale, or delivery of prerecorded video cassette tapes or similar audio visual materials" as well as individuals who receive PI in the ordinary course of a videotape service provider's business or for marketing purposes.[69] Videotape service providers are prohibited from disclosing customer PI unless an enumerated exception applies.[70] Exceptions are provided for instances in which the disclosure: (1) is made to the consumer themselves; (2) is made subject to the contemporaneous written consent of the consumer; (3) is made to law enforcement pursuant to a warrant, subpoena or other court order; (4) includes only the names and addresses of consumers; (5) includes only names, addresses and subject matter descriptions and the disclosure is used only for the marketing of goods or services to the consumers; (6) is for order fulfillment, request processing, transfer of ownership or debt collection; or (7) is pursuant to a court order in a civil proceeding and the consumer is granted a right to object.[71]

The act requires that PI be destroyed "as soon as practicable, but no later than one year from the date the information is no longer necessary for the purpose for which it was collected and there are no pending requests or orders for access to such information."[72]

The act affords a private right of action for violations and allows for actual or statutory damages, punitive damages, and reasonable attorney's fees and court costs.[73] Statutory damages are set at $2,500.[74] There has been active class-action litigation under the VPPA, and several cases, including those against Blockbuster, Netflix, and Redbox, suggest that the private right of action extends only to disclosure-related violations and not violations based merely on improper retention.[75] Additionally, the VPPA does not preempt more protective state laws, which may give rise to stricter penalties.[76]

Significant changes to the landscape of video delivery have occurred since the law was enacted in 1988. Netflix, which was founded nearly a decade after the enactment of the VPPA, sought to amend the law in 2011 to address the concept of social media integration for users— a prime example of which was a Facebook feature that would allow Netflix users to share their movie-viewing information with social media friends.[77] To address this concern, Congress adopted the Video Privacy Protection Act Amendments Act of 2012 that allowed for one-time consumer consent that was valid for up to two years, replacing the contemporaneity requirement.[78] Despite this amendment, others have suggested that a more comprehensive overhaul of the law is necessary to address changes in technology—such as social media and streaming video.[79] Privacy professionals should be alert to possible legislative change in this area. It is also worth noting that a number of states, such as California, have enacted laws covering the same privacy issues as the VPPA.[80]

10.7 Digital Advertising

As discussed in Chapter 5, digital advertising, which is composed of desktop/laptop and mobile advertising, is an integral part of marketing. As of 2016, digital advertising comprised 36.7 percent of all U.S. advertising dollars. That figure is expected to increase to 51.3 percent by 2021.[81] In addition, the spending on mobile advertising vs. desktop/laptop advertising is anticipated to increase from 10.9 percent of digital advertising in 2014 to 32.9 percent in 2020.[82]

The discussion here focuses on three areas: (1) self-regulatory codes for online advertising, (2) the California Do Not Track law and (3) the 2016 FCC privacy rule for broadband Internet providers. Chapter 5 describes the online advertising ecosystem in more detail.

10.7.1 Self-Regulation for Online Advertising

Realizing the privacy concerns raised by the tracking associated with digital advertising, many companies involved in desktop/laptop advertising and mobile advertising have voluntarily agreed to be bound by self-regulatory principles. Two prominent examples are the Digital Advertising Alliance (DAA) Self-Regulatory Principles for Online Behavioral Advertising and the Network Advertising Initiative (NAI) Code of Conduct.

The DAA is a nonprofit organization that collaborates with businesses, public policy groups and public officials to establish and enforce "responsible privacy practices across industry for relevant digital advertising, providing consumers with enhanced transparency and control." The Self-Regulatory Principles include guidelines for interest-based advertising in the desktop/laptop environment and the mobile environment as well as for cross-device use of data. An important feature of these principles, and related self-regulatory initiatives from the DAA, is the consumer management of opt-outs.

The NAI is a nonprofit self-regulatory association comprised exclusively of third-party digital advertising companies. The NAI Code of Conduct is a list of self-regulatory principles that all NAI members agree to uphold. The Code requires notice and choice with respect to interest-based advertising, limits on the types of data that member companies can use for advertising purposes, and a number of substantive restrictions on member companies' collection, use, and transfer of data used for online behavioral advertising.[83]

Both sets of principles have enforcement mechanisms. For DAA's Self-Regulatory Principles, the Council of Better Business Bureaus and the Direct Marketing Association provide independent oversight and enforcement.[84] The NAI's Code of Conduct is enforced by its board, and sanctions may include revocation of membership and referral of matters to the FTC.[85] For the wide range of industries engaging in digital advertising, the DAA and NAI requirements can be an important area for careful compliance attention—for companies that have agreed to such codes, a violation is considered an "unfair and deceptive" practice that can lead to FTC and state attorney general enforcement actions.

10.7.2 Federal Regulation: FCC Broadband Privacy Rule

Until recently, companies in the United States involved in advertising on the Internet, for both laptop/desktop and mobile advertising, faced federal regulation and enforcement mainly from the FTC (as discussed in Chapter 3). In 2015, the FCC reclassified broadband Internet service as a public utility as part of its "Open Internet" or net neutrality rule.[86] In 2016, the U.S. Court of Appeals upheld the FCC's authority to regulate broadband Internet providers, which include traditional telephone providers such as Verizon and cable companies such as Comcast.[87]

An important effect of the reclassification is that broadband Internet providers also became subject to other requirements of the Telecommunications Act of 1996, notably including the CPNI privacy requirements in Section 222.

Shortly after the court decision upholding reclassification, the FCC proposed new privacy rules for broadband Internet providers and received 50,000 comments concerning these proposed rules.[88] In November 2016, the FCC adopted rules that, among other requirements, would have: (1) required customer opt-in for uses of sensitive personal information, (2) allowed the use of customer opt-out for uses not involving sensitive personal information and (3) permitted inferred customer consent for providing the underlying services and related uses. The rules also provided guidelines for data security and breach notification.[89]

In 2017, Congress voted under the Congressional Review Act to rescind the FCC privacy rule.[90] President Trump agreed with that decision, and signed the law to cancel the rule.[91] This decision did not, however, cancel the reclassification of broadband Internet providers as public utilities. After the congressional vote, the FCC issued an order stating that Section 222 and the CPNI rules continue to apply to broadband Internet providers, under the general provisions of Section 222 and not with the specific and stricter provisions in the FCC rule of 2016.[92]

The events of 2016 and 2017 show a new political prominence for the topic of what privacy rules should apply to broadband Internet providers. In this period, the Republican Party has generally objected to stricter privacy rules for such providers and supported a shift of regulatory jurisdiction from the FCC back to the FTC for such companies. The Democratic Party has generally supported stricter privacy rules for such providers, under FCC enforcement. In light of these political controversies, this area of law may undergo further changes in the coming years.

10.7.3 State Regulation: California Do Not Track Requirements

In 2003, California passed the first law in the nation to require operators of commercial websites, including mobile apps, to "conspicuously post" a privacy policy if they collect personally identifiable information (PII) from those living in California. In 2013, the law, known as the California Online Privacy Protection Act (CalOPPA), was amended by Assembly Bill 370; these amendments, which required privacy policies to include information on how the operator responds to Do Not Track signals or similar mechanisms. The law also requires privacy policies to state whether third parties can collect PII about the site's users.[93]

Specifically, the CalOPPA, including its Do Not Track amendments, requires the operator of a website to display a privacy notice that meets certain content requirements. These include disclosing:

- The categories of PII collected through the site
- The categories of third-party entities with whom the operator may share PII or other content
- How the operator responds to web browsers' Do Not Track signals or other mechanisms that provide consumers the ability to choose regarding collection of PII about an individual consumer's online activities overs time and across third-party websites
- Whether other parties may collect PII about an individual consumer's online activities over time and across different websites when a consumer uses the operator's website[94]

To assist companies in complying with the requirements of the act, the attorney general for the State of California has issued guidance.[95] Privacy professionals seeking to comply with California's Do Not Track requirements should be aware that the Internet ecosystem is complex and rapidly changing, which could result in well-crafted privacy notices becoming inaccurate or outdated over time. One example of how this could occur revolves around the browsers used in this ecosystem. The implementation of Do Not Track by browsers varies. Some set a default that tracking is acceptable unless the user configures the browser to send Do Not Track signals to the requesting site. Others have established Do Not Track as a default. A few browsers have established selective Do Not Track as their default. Another issue is that companies embedding dynamic code from third parties (such as advertisers) on their website may not be fully aware of the tracking activities taking place on their own site over time by those third parties. This evolving landscape poses challenges for site operators to maintain accurate, legally sufficient privacy notices over time.[96]

10.8 Conclusion

This chapter examined the legal rules that apply to important channels for marketing by telephone, fax, text and commercial email. It then considered the rules governing how telecommunications companies can use PI generated in the course of communications activities. Along with the VPPA, special statutes or proposals have long applied to telephone and cable companies, and more recently to broadband Internet providers, based on their potential access to individuals' detailed communication and viewing information. Current law places significant limits on how these infrastructure companies can use and disclose PI that flows through their systems. An important area of ongoing uncertainty is how the political debates in 2016 and 2017 for broadband Internet privacy will turn out—the ongoing debates in this sector may affect privacy rules for other players in the Internet ecosystem.

Endnotes

1 Chapter 12 examines rules for government access to the communications, under wiretap and other statutes, which provide lawful access for the government to that data, subject to search warrants and other restrictions.

2 Restatement of the Law (Second), Torts, § 652B, https://cyber.law.harvard.edu/privacy/Privacy_R2d_Torts_Sections.htm (accessed November 2017).

3 *Id.*

4 47 U.S.C. § 227(b)(1)(A)-(B), https://www.law.cornell.edu/uscode/text/47/227 (accessed June 2016); 47 C.F.R. § 64.1200(a)(2)-(3), https://www.law.cornell.edu/cfr/text/47/64.1200 (accessed November 2017). For an analysis of significant amendments that took effect in 2013, view "New TCPA Rules take effect on October 16, 2013," *Drinker Biddle TCPA Blog*, http://tcpablog.com/new-tcpa-regulations-take-effect-on-october-16th/#_edn1(accessed November 2017).

5 In the Matter of Rules and Regulations Implementing the Telephone Consumer Protection Act of 1991, Report and Order, CG Docket No. 02-278 (February 15, 2012) http://transition.fcc.gov/Daily_Releases/Daily_Business/2012/db0215/FCC-12-21A1.pdf (accessed November 2017).

6 15 U.S.C. § 6101-6108, https://www.gpo.gov/fdsys/granule/USCODE-2011-title15/USCODE-2011-title15-chap87-sec6101 (accessed November 2017); "Complying with Telemarketing Sales Rule," FTC, https://www.ftc.gov/tips-advice/business-center/guidance/complying-telemarketing-sales-rule (accessed November 2017).

7 *Federal Register* 68, no, 19 (January 29, 2003): 4669, https://www.ftc.gov/sites/default/files/documents/reports/federal-trade-commission-report-congress/dnciareportappenda.pdf (accessed November 2017).

8 *See* generally, "Complying with the Telemarketing Sales Rule," FTC, http://business.ftc.gov/documents/bus27-complying-telemarketing-sales-rule#Glance (accessed November 2017).

9 For example, in fiscal year 2015 nearly five million more numbers were added to the registry. *See* "Biennial Report to Congress Reporting on Fiscal Years 2014–2015," FTC, https://www.ftc.gov/reports/biennial-report-congress-under-do-not-call-registry-fee-extension-act-2007-fy-2014-2015 (accessed November 2017).

10 "Complying with the Telemarketing Sales Rule" under "Unauthorized Billing," FTC, https://www.ftc.gov/tips-advice/business-center/guidance/complying-telemarketing-sales-rule#billing (accessed January 2018).

11 For example, the FTC and the Florida attorney general's office assessed a $23 million fine to settle allegations that a Florida-based company defrauded seniors by using robocalls to sell medical alert systems. https://www.ftc.gov/news-events/press-releases/2014/11/settlement-ftc-florida-attorney-general-stops-operations-used (accessed November 2017).

12 "Q&A for Telemarketers & Sellers About DNC Provisions in TSR," under "If I'm a telemarketer or service provider working for a seller, can I use the seller's account number to access the registry?" FTC, https://www.ftc.gov/tips-advice/business-center/guidance/qa-telemarketers-sellers-about-dnc-provisions-tsr#payingforaccess (accessed January 2018).

13 For additional analysis on DNC regulations, view "Telemarketing Regulation: National and State Do Not Call Registries," Congressional Research Services, https://www.fas.org/sgp/crs/misc/R43684.pdf (accessed November 2017).

14 Upselling is the sale of a product or service in addition to the product or service the customer has purchased. https://www.ftc.gov/tips-advice/business-center/guidance/complying-telemarketing-sales-rule (accessed November 2017).

15 "Complying with the Telemarketing Sales Rule," under "Protecting Consumers' Privacy: The Written Permission to Call Exemption," FTC, https://www.ftc.gov/tips-advice/business-center/guidance/complying-telemarketing-sales-rule (accessed November 2017).

16 *Id.*

17 "Complying with the Telemarketing Sales Rule," under "Protecting Consumers' Privacy: Do Not Call Safe Harbor," FTC, https://www.ftc.gov/tips-advice/business-center/guidance/complying-telemarketing-sales-rule#safeharbor (accessed November 2017).

18 "Complying with the Telemarketing Sales Rule" under "Unauthorized Billing," FTC, https://www.ftc.gov/tips-advice/business-center/guidance/complying-telemarketing-sales-rule#billing (accessed January 2018).

19 Material terms may include cost, quantity, restrictions, limitations, conditions, no-refund policies, etc.

20 Intrastate calls are covered by the FCC's regulations under the TCPA (47 U.S.C. § 227), https://www.law.cornell.edu/uscode/text/47/227 (accessed November 2017). These rules are similar to the TSR rules described herein.

21 Not all telemarketing activities are covered by the TSR. For example, most business-to-business calls are excluded from the rule. Additionally, the TSR applies only to entities subject to FTC jurisdiction, with other entities (such as banks) covered solely by the TCPA referenced in note 1. Finally, some types of calls are partially exempt from the rule. As discussed later in this chapter, calls to existing customers are exempt from the DNC Registry provisions. Inbound calls from customers are also excluded, although upselling during the call will bring it back within the scope of the rule with regard to disclosures, payment provisions, etc.

22 "Complying with the Telemarketing Sales Rule," under "Requirements for Sellers and Telemarketers: Multiple Purpose Calls," FTC, https://www.ftc.gov/tips-advice/business-center/guidance/complying-telemarketing-sales-rule (accessed November 2017).

23 "Complying with the Telemarketing Sales Rule," under "Protecting Consumers' Privacy: Transmitting Caller ID Information," FTC, https://www.ftc.gov/tips-advice/business-center/guidance/complying-telemarketing-sales-rule (accessed November 2017).

24 47 C.F.R. § 64.1200(a)(7), https://www.law.cornell.edu/cfr/text/47/64.1200 (accessed November 2017).

25 Including a sales message would violate the FCCs rules under the TCPA (47 U.S.C. § 227), https://www.law.cornell.edu/uscode/text/47/227 (accessed November 2017), and FCC regulations at 47 C.F.R. § 64.1200, https://www.law.cornell.edu/cfr/text/47/64.1200 (accessed November 2017).

26 In the Matter of Rules and Regulations Implementing the Telephone Consumer Protection Act of 1991, Report and Order, CG Docket No. 02-278 (February 15, 2012), https://apps.fcc.gov/edocs_public/attachmatch/FCC-12-21A1.pdf (accessed November 2017).

27 47 C.F.R. § 64.1200(a)(3), https://www.law.cornell.edu/cfr/text/47/64.1200 (accessed November 2017).

28 For an overview, *see* Telephone Consumer Protection Act (TCPA), Robocalls, and Text Messaging, Data & Marketing Association, https://thedma.org/resources/compliance-resources/tcpa/ (accessed November 2017).

29 There are certain narrow exceptions (such as emergency notifications). Laura Phillips and Laura Layton, "What's the purpose of emergency purpose statutory exemption?" DrinkerBiddle (April 10, 2015), http://tcpablog.com/whats-purpose-emergency-purpose-statutory-exemption/ (accessed November 2017).

30 Tanya Forsheit, Alan Friel and Melinda McLellan, "FCC's new TCPA order may require companies to obtain updated consents for marketing calls and texts," Baker Hostetler (July 22, 2015), https://www.dataprivacymonitor.com/enforcement/fccs-new-tcpa-order-may-require-companies-to-obtain-updated-consents-for-marketing-calls-and-texts/ (accessed November 2017).

31 Alan Friel, "FCC closes year with enforcement advisory on text messages," Baker Hostetler (January 3, 2017), www.jdsupra.com/legalnews/fcc-closes-year-with-enforcement-23350/ (accessed November 2017).

32 "Complying with the Telemarketing Sales Rule," FTC, https://www.ftc.gov/tips-advice/business-center/guidance/complying-telemarketing-sales-rule#whomustkeep (accessed November 2017).

33 Private individuals have to meet certain damage requirements to bring suit.

34 "State Regulations," Telemarketing Regulations, http://telemarketingregulations.com/State_Regulations.html (accessed December 2017).

35 For example, *see* Mississippi's Online DNC List registration, https://www.psc.state.ms.us/nocall/nocall.html (accessed June 2016), and Pennsylvania's Online DNC List registration, www.oca.state.pa.us/Industry/TeleCom/other/DoNotCallLists.htm (accessed November 2017).

36 Kan. Stat. Ann. §§ 50-670 and 50-670a, www.kslegislature.org/li_2014/b2013_14/measures/documents/sb308_enrolled.pdf (accessed November 2017). For a summary of the 2014 changes to the Kansas No-Call Act, *see* the webpage on the Kansas State Library, https://kslib.info/Blog.aspx?IID=17 (accessed November 2017).

37 Fla. Stat. § 501.059,www.leg.state.fl.us/Statutes/index.cfm?App_mode=Display_Statute&Search_String=&URL=0500-0599/0501/Sections/0501.059.html (accessed November 2017). For a summary of Florida's law, *see* the website for the Florida Department of Agriculture and Consumer Services, www.freshfromflorida.com/Business-Services/Florida-Do-Not-Call (accessed November 2017).

38 TCPA, 47 U.S.C. 227 (1991), https://transition.fcc.gov/cgb/policy/TCPA-Rules.pdf (accessed November 2017). Also *see* FCC, Telemarketing Policy, https://www.fcc.gov/general/telemarketing-and-robocalls (accessed November 2017).

39 William Glaberson, "Dispute over Faxed Ads Draws Wide Scrutiny After $12 Million Award," *The New York Times*, July 22, 2001, www.nytimes.com/2001/07/22/us/dispute-over-faxed-ads-draws-wide-scrutiny-after-12-million-award.html?pagewanted=all (a accessed November 2017).

40 Tony Pugh, "FCC Fines Fax.com $5 million over ads," *The Seattle Times*, January 6, 2004, http://old.seattletimes.com/html/businesstechnology/2001830436_junkfax06.html (accessed November 2017).

41 California Business & Professions Code § 17538.43, http://leginfo.legislature.ca.gov/faces/codes_displaySection.xhtml?lawCode=BPC§ionNum=17538.43 (accessed November 2017).

42 Chamber of Commerce of the U.S. v. Lockyer, 2006 WL 462482 (E. D. Cal. 2006). For a summary of the case from the U.S. Chamber Litigation Center, view www.chamberlitigation.com/chamber-commerce-et-al-v-lockyer-et-al (accessed November 2017).

43 The CAN-SPAM Act of 2003, 15 U.S.C. 7701, et seq., https://www.gpo.gov/fdsys/pkg/PLAW-108publ187/pdf/PLAW-108publ187.pdf (accessed November 2017).

44 "Complying with the Telemarketing Sales Rule" under "Unauthorized Billing," FTC, https://www.ftc.gov/tips-advice/business-center/guidance/complying-telemarketing-sales-rule#billing (accessed January 2018).

45 "FTC Approves New Rule Provision Under the CAN-SPAM Act," FTC, https://www.ftc.gov/news-events/press-releases/2008/05/ftc-approves-new-rule-provision-under-can-spam-act (accessed November 2017).

46 16 CFR Part 316, https://www.law.cornell.edu/cfr/text/16/part-316 (accessed November 2017).

47 FTC v. Pricewert LLC d/b/a 3FN.net, Triple Fiber Network, APS Communications, and APS Communication, 09 CV-2407 (N.D. Cal. 2009), https://www.ftc.gov/enforcement/cases-proceedings/092-3148/pricewert-llc-dba-3fnnet-ftc (accessed November 2017).

48 In the Matter of Rules and Regulations Implementing the Controlling the Assault of Non-Solicited Pornography and Marketing Act of 2003; Rules and Regulations Implementing the Telephone Consumer Protection Act of 1991, FCC 04-194, (August 12, 2004), https://apps.fcc.gov/edocs_public/attachmatch/FCC-04-194A1.pdf (accessed November 2017).

49 "Domain Name Downloads," FCC, https://transition.fcc.gov/cgb/policy/DomainNameDownload.html (accessed November 2017).

50 "Protecting Your Privacy," under "Protecting You From Unwanted Text Messages on Your Wireless Devices," FCC, https://www.fcc.gov/consumers/guides/protecting-your-privacy (accessed November 2017).

51 Telecommunications Act, 47 U.S.C. §222 (1996), https://www.law.cornell.edu/uscode/text/47/222 (accessed November 2017).

52 Public Notice, Annual CPNI Certifications Due March 1, 2012, (February 16, 2012), http://transition.fcc.gov/Daily_Releases/Daily_Business/2012/db0216/DA-12-170A1.pdf (accessed November 2017).

53 *See* ECPA discussion in Chapter 12.

54 U.S. West, Inc. v. Federal Communications Commission, 182 F.3d 1224 (10th Cir. 1999), http://openjurist.org/182/f3d/1224/us-west-inc-v-federal-communications-commission (accessed November 2017).

55 FCC Report and Order and Further Notice of Proposed Rulemaking, 07-22 (April 2, 2007), https://apps.fcc.gov/edocs_public/attachmatch/FCC-07-22A1.pdf (accessed November 2017).

56 47 U.S.C. § 551 (2006), https://www.law.cornell.edu/uscode/text/47/551 (accessed November 2017).

57 *Id.* at § 551(a).

58 *Id.* at § 522(6)(A) (emphasis added).

59 *Id.* at § 551(a).

60 *Id.* at § 551(b).

61 *Id.* at § 551(c)(1).

62 *Id.* at § 551(c)(2).

63 *Id.* at § 551€.

64 18 U.S.C. §§ 2703 & 2705, https://www.law.cornell.edu/uscode/text/18/2703; https://www.law.cornell.edu/uscode/text/18/2705 (accessed November 2017).

65 *See*, e.g., In re Application of the United States of America for an Order Pursuant to 18 U.S.C. § 2703(D) Directed to Cablevision Systems Corp., 158 F.Supp.2d 644 (2001), http://law.justia.com/cases/federal/district-courts/FSupp2/158/644/2415158/ (accessed November 2017).

66 18 U.S.C. § 2710 (2006), https://www.law.cornell.edu/uscode/text/18/2710 (accessed November 2017).

67 The Video Privacy Protection Act: Protecting Viewer Privacy in the 21st Century, 112th Congress (2012) (statement of Rep. Watt), https://www.judiciary.senate.gov/imo/media/doc/CHRG-112shrg87342.pdf (accessed November 2017).

68 *See* "Video Privacy Protection Act," Electronic Privacy Information Center, https://epic.org/privacy/vppa/ (accessed November 2017).

69 18 U.S.C. § 2710(a)(4) (2006), https://www.law.cornell.edu/uscode/text/18/2710 (accessed November 2017).

70 *Id.* at § 2710(b)(1).

71 *Id.* at § 2710(b)(2).

72 *Id.* at § 2710(e).

73 *Id.* at § 2710(c).

74 *Id.*

75 "Netflix and Blockbuster to amend policies to settle video privacy suits," *Lexology*, www.lexology.com/library/detail.aspx?g=9490362b-5d03-4f20-ae74-3ab4842e0f66 (accessed November 2017); Sterk v. Redbox Automated Retail, LLC, 642 F.3d 535 (7th Cir. 2012), http://media.ca7.uscourts.gov/cgi-bin/rssExec.pl?Submit=Display&Path=Y2014/D10-23/C:13-3037:J:Flaum:aut:T:fnOp:N:1440102:S:0 (accessed November 2017).

76 *See*, e.g., Conn. Gen. Stat. § 53-450, http://law.justia.com/codes/connecticut/2012/title-53/chapter-949f/section-53-450 (accessed November 2017); Mich. L. § 445.1712, www.legislature.mi.gov/(S(1ldubxv5mkknq0qmykkz0g0r))/mileg.aspx?page=getobject&objectname=mcl-445-1712 (accessed November 2017).

77 "Netflix backs amendment to Video Privacy Protection Act," *Hunton & Williams*, July 27, 2011, www.lexology.com/library/detail.aspx?g=2217f175-7a28-4bb0-aac7-40edeed4a6cd (accessed November 2017).

78 Julianne Pepitone, "New video law lets you share your Netflix viewing on Facebook," *CNNtech*, January 10, 2013, http://money.cnn.com/2013/01/10/technology/social/netflix-vppa-facebook/ (accessed November 2017). For the text of the amendment, *see* H.R. 6671 – Video Privacy Protection Act Amendments Act of 2012, https://www.congress.gov/bill/112th-congress/house-bill/6671/text (accessed November 2017).

79 *See* Joshua Jessen and Priyanka Rajagopalan, "Teaching an old law new tricks: The 1988 Video Privacy Protection Act in the modern era," *BloombergBNA*, July 5, 2016, https://www.bna.com/teaching-old-law-n57982076512/?amp=true (accessed November 2017).

80 The VPPA does not preempt state laws. "Video Privacy Protection Act," IAPP, https://www.epic.org/privacy/vppa/ (accessed November 2017); *see* California Civil Code section 1799.3, https://leginfo.legislature.ca.gov/faces/codes_displayText.xhtml?lawCode=CIV&division=3.&title=1.82.&part=4.&chapter=3.&article= (accessed November 2017); *see also* Jeff Kosseff, " 'Video Rental Privacy Act' Covers Magazines, Court Holds," *Inside Privacy*, Covington & Burlington, LLP (August 27, 2014), https://www.insideprivacy.com/advertising-marketing/video-rental-privacy-act-covers-magazines-court-holds/ (accessed November 2017).

81 "US Ad Spending: eMarketer's Updated Estimates and Forecast for 2017", *eMarketer*, September 19, 2017, https://www.emarketer.com/Report/US-Ad-Spending-eMarketers-Updated-Estimates-Forecast-2017/2002134 (accessed November 2017).

82 "Digital Ad Spending to Surpass TV Next Year: By 2020, TV's share of ad spending will drop one-third," *eMarketer*, www.emarketer.com/Article/Digital-Ad-Spending-Surpass-TV-Next-Year/1013671 (accessed November 2017).

83 For the specific language of the NAI Code of Conduct, view www.networkadvertising.org/sites/default/files/NAI_BeyondCookies_NL.pdf (accessed November 2017).

84 For detailed information on DAA's enforcement mechanism, view DAA Enforcement of the Principles, www.aboutads.info/enforcement (accessed November 2017).

85 For detailed information on NAI's enforcement mechanism, view NAI Enforcement, www.networkadvertising.org/code-enforcement/enforcement (accessed November 2017).

86 This discussion of the topic includes the term *net neutrality*, as the regulations are intended to prohibit the companies from engaging in certain business practices such as selectively speeding up websites that pay the providers a fee to do so. "FCC approves net neutrality rule, classifying broadband internet service as a utility," *New York Times*, www.nytimes.com/2015/02/27/technology/net-neutrality-fcc-vote-internet-utility.html?_r=0 (accessed November 2017).

87 Brian Fung, "Cable and telecom companies just lost a huge court battle on net neutrality," *Washington Post*, June 14, 2016, https://www.washingtonpost.com/news/the-switch/wp/2016/06/14/the-fcc-just-won-a-sweeping-victory-on-net-neutrality-in-federal-court/ (accessed November 2017).

88 "FCC Releases Proposed Rules to Protect Broadband Consumer Privacy," FCC, https://www.fcc.gov/document/fcc-releases-proposed-rules-protect-broadband-consumer-privacy (accessed November 2017); "FCC Releases Notice of Proposed Rulemaking for New Broadband ISP Privacy Rules," Paul Hastings, www.paulhastings.com/publications-items/details/?id=1c1ce969-2334-6428-811c-ff00004cbded (accessed November 2017).

89 Sherrese M. Smith and Andrew J. Erber, "FCC releases Order Imposing New Privacy Rules on ISPs and Telecos," Paul Hastings (November 7, 2016), https://www.paulhastings.com/publications-items/details?id=9cc5ea69-2334-6428-811c-ff00004cbded (accessed November 2017).

90 Public Law 115-22, https://www.congress.gov/bill/115th-congress/senate-joint-resolution/34?q=%7B%22search%22%3A%5B%22public+law+115-22%22%5D%7D&r=1 (accessed November 2017).

91 Brian Fung, "Trump Has Signed Repeal of the FCC Privacy Rule; Here Is What Happens Next," *Washington Post*, April, 4, 2017, https://www.washingtonpost.com/news/the-switch/wp/2017/04/04/trump-has-signed-repeal-of-the-fcc-privacy-rules-heres-what-happens-next/?utm_term=.5921ff7e7613 (accessed November 2017).

92 In the Matter of Protecting the Privacy of Customers of Broadband and Other Telecommunications Services, https://apps.fcc.gov/edocs_public/attachmatch/FCC-17-82A1.pdf (accessed November 2017).

93 California Online Privacy Protection Act, www.leginfo.ca.gov/cgi-https://leginfo.legislature.ca.gov/faces/codes_displayText.xhtml?division=8.&chapter=22.&lawCode=BPC; Assembly Bill 370, https://leginfo.legislature.ca.gov/faces/billNavClient.xhtml?bill_id=201320140AB370 (accessed November 2017).

94 Brian Hengesbaugh and Amy de La Lama, "How should I respond to California's Do-Not-Track requirements?" November 26, 2013, IAPP, https://iapp.org/news/a/how-should-i-respond-to-californias-do-not-track-requirements/ (accessed November 2017).

95 "Making Your Privacy Practices Public: Recommendations on Developing a Meaningful Privacy Policy," https://oag.ca.gov/news/press-releases/attorney-general-kamala-d-harris-issues-guide-privacy-policies-and-do-not-track (accessed November 2017).

96 For a discussion of the California Attorney General's Guide to CalOPPA, view "Unpacking the California AG's Guide on CalOPPA," IAPP, https://iapp.org/news/a/unpacking-the-california-ags-guide-on-caloppa/ (accessed November 2017).

CHAPTER 11

Workplace Privacy

This chapter provides an introduction to workplace privacy, with a focus on the sources of law that apply to private-sector employment in the United States. It examines privacy issues before, during and after employment.

11.1 Legal Overview

There is no overarching or organized law for employment privacy in the United States. Federal laws apply in specific areas, such as to prohibit discrimination and regulate certain workplace practices, including employment screening and the use of polygraphs and credit reports. State contract and tort law in some instances provides protections for employees, but usually the employee must show fairly egregious practices to succeed. State legislatures have enacted numerous employment privacy laws, providing protections to employees in a bewildering range of specific situations, which often vary state by state. Taken together, there is considerable local variation and complexity on employment privacy issues.

Along with laws protecting privacy, many labor laws in the United States mandate employee data collection and management practices, for instance, to conduct background checks and to ensure and document a safe workplace environment. Companies also have incentives to gather information about employees and monitor the workplace to reduce the risk of being sued for negligent hiring or supervision of employees.

The regulation of employment privacy in the United States stands in contrast to nations with comprehensive data protection laws. The European Union (EU), for example, includes employee privacy within its general rules applying to the protection of individuals. Monitoring is permitted only with specific legal justification, and background checks are limited in scope. Generally, employees have broad workplace privacy expectations and rights. Companies with employees in the United States and other countries thus must be alert to the possibility that different workplace rules apply in connection with employment privacy.[1] This can be particularly challenging when a multinational corporation's human resources (HR) data systems in one country contain personal information about employees residing in other countries, or even when employees share personal information across borders, such as through email or other communications channels.

11.1.1 Constitutional Law

The U.S. Constitution has significant workplace privacy provisions that apply to the federal and state governments, but it does not affect private-sector employment. Notably, the Fourth Amendment prohibits unreasonable searches and seizures by state actors. Courts have interpreted this amendment to place limits on the ability of government employers to search employees' private spaces, such as lockers and desks.[2]

Some states, including California, have extended their constitutional rights to privacy to private-sector employees.[3] In general for private-sector actors, however, there is no state action and no constitutional law governs employment privacy.

11.1.2 State Contract, Tort and Statutory Law

U.S. law looks at the relationship between the employer and employee as fundamentally a matter of contract law. The general rule in the United States is employment at will, which means that the employer has broad discretion to fire an employee. That discretion, in turn, has been understood to grant the employer broad latitude in defining other aspects of the employment relationship, such as issues about the employer's knowledge about an employee.

A contract, however, can alter the rules between employer and employee. An individual employee, for instance, might negotiate a contract that says that certain private activities are outside the scope of the employment relationship. More generally, negotiation of a contract can create binding obligations on the employer. If the employer makes promises in a contract to honor employee privacy, then violations of those promises can constitute an enforceable breach of contract.

The most important contracts concerning employee privacy are collective bargaining agreements. Unions have often negotiated provisions that protect employee privacy, including, for instance, limits on drug testing and monitoring of the workplace by the employer.

Turning to tort law, at least three common-law torts can be relevant to employee privacy, although U.S. law generally requires a fairly egregious fact pattern before imposing liability on the employer. First is the tort of "intrusion upon seclusion," which states: "One who intentionally intrudes, physically or otherwise, upon the solitude or seclusion of another or his private affairs or concerns, is subject to liability to the other for invasion of his privacy, if the intrusion would be highly offensive to a reasonable person."[4] A classic example of such intrusion is if the employer puts a camera or peephole in a bathroom or employee changing room—a jury may well find that such surveillance is highly offensive to a reasonable person. Another example could be secret wiretaps or other intrusive surveillance of an employee. Although such an employee tort claim may succeed, this chapter will later discuss some of the ways that employers can actually defeat that sort of wiretap claim, such as by an announced policy that the company's computers are owned by the employer and subject to monitoring.

A second tort claim can be "publicity given to private life," which states: "One who gives publicity to a matter concerning the private life of another is subject to liability to the other for invasion of his privacy, if the matter publicized is of a kind that (a) would be highly offensive to a reasonable person and (b) is not of legitimate concern to the public."[5] A plaintiff would need to show a relatively broad dissemination of the facts involved and also that the facts disseminated would be highly offensive to a reasonable person. Courts have been cautious in finding such offensiveness, even for dissemination of a person's salary or other information the employee considers private. Free speech principles under the First Amendment also often provide a defense against such a tort claim.

A third tort claim is for defamation, which focuses on a false or defamatory statement, defined as a communication tending "so to harm the reputation of another as to lower him in the estimation of the community or to deter third persons from associating or dealing with him."[6] For employment law, defamation torts can arise if, for instance, a false drug testing report is issued or if a former employer provides a factually incorrect reference to a possible future employer.

Although the common law thus supplies some possible protections for employees, according to Matthew W. Finkin in *Privacy in Employment Law,* they have a narrow scope: "If privacy is to be protected by law, the task falls largely to the legislatures" rather than to the common-law courts.[7] State legislatures have indeed passed a large number of statutes that affect employee privacy. Finkin cites some striking examples, such as a California law guaranteeing a woman's right to wear pants at work or the Florida right for employees to shop where they will, free of an employer's dictate. Other state statutes prohibit marital status discrimination,[8] and categories of inquiries regarding prospective employees, such as asking whether a worker has ever filed a claim for worker's compensation benefits.[9] In recent years, a number of states have prohibited employers from requiring employees to disclose the passwords of their social network accounts.[10] Statutes vary enormously state by state, leading to "a patchwork of near bewildering complexity and large lacunae," or gaps.[11]

To summarize on state law and employment privacy, employees tend to have narrow protections under contract, tort and statutory law. The free market approach of U.S. law applies broadly, except where a discrete problem has arisen and prompted a response by the legal and political system. Against this general backdrop of employer discretion, however, there may be significant state and local laws that apply in a particular setting.

11.1.3 Federal Laws on Employment Privacy

Given this context of relatively limited constitutional or state law protections, a number of federal statutes have been enacted that bear on employment privacy.

11.1.3.1 U.S. Laws Protecting Employee Privacy

The United States has a number of federal laws that prohibit discrimination. Antidiscrimination laws provide employees with some privacy protection—for example, by limiting questioning with respect to what is being protected, such as age, national origin or disability.

The United States also has federal laws that regulate employee benefits management. These laws offer certain privacy and security protections for benefits-related information. They also often mandate collection of employee medical information. These laws include the following protections:

- The Health Insurance Portability and Accountability Act of 1996 (HIPAA) contains privacy and security rules that regulate "protected health information" for health insurers, including self-funded health plans.[12]
- The Consolidated Omnibus Budget Reconciliation Act (COBRA) requires qualified health plans to provide continuous coverage after termination to certain beneficiaries.[13]
- The Employee Retirement Income Security Act (ERISA) ensures that employee benefits programs are created fairly and administered properly.[14]
- The Family and Medical Leave Act (FMLA) entitles certain employees to unpaid leave in the event of birth or illness of self or a family member.[15]

Other federal laws with employment privacy implications regulate data collection and record keeping:

- The Fair Credit Reporting Act (FCRA) regulates the use of "consumer reports" obtained from consumer reporting agencies (CRAs) in reference checking and background checks of employees[16]
- The Fair Labor Standards Act (FLSA) establishes the minimum wage and sets standards for fair pay[17]

- The Occupational Safety and Health Act (OSHA) regulates workplace safety[18]
- The Whistleblower Protection Act protects federal employees and applicants for employment who claim to have been subjected to personnel actions because of whistleblowing activities[19]
- The National Labor Relations Act (NLRA) sets standards for collective bargaining, which also applies in social media communications[20]
- The Immigration Reform and Control Act (IRCA) requires employment eligibility verification[21]
- The Securities Exchange Act of 1934 requires disclosures about payment and other information about senior executives of publicly traded companies, as well as registration requirements for market participants such as broker-dealers and transfer agents[22]

Later in this chapter we will also discuss two statutory regimes that govern specific monitoring practices by employers:

- The Employee Polygraph Protection Act of 1988, which limits employer use of lie detectors[23]
- Electronic surveillance laws, including the Wiretap Act,[24] the Electronic Communications Privacy Act[25] and the Stored Communications Act (SCA)[26]

11.1.3.2 U.S. Regulatory Bodies that Protect Employee Privacy

Employee privacy is protected by several federal agencies, including the U.S. Department of Labor, the Equal Employment Opportunity Commission (EEOC), the Federal Trade Commission (FTC), the Consumer Financial Protection Bureau (CFPB) and the National Labor Relations Board (NLRB).

The Department of Labor (DOL) oversees "the welfare of the job seekers, wage earners, and retirees of the United States by improving their working conditions, advancing their opportunities for profitable employment, protecting their retirement and health care benefits, helping employers find workers, strengthening free collective bargaining, and tracking changes in employment, prices, and other national economic measurements."[27]

To achieve this mission, the department administers a variety of federal laws, FLSA, OSHA and ERISA.

The EEOC works to prevent discrimination in the workplace. The EEOC oversees many laws, including Title VII of the Civil Rights Act, the Age Discrimination in

Employment Act of 1967 (ADEA) and Titles I and V of the Americans with Disabilities Act of 1990 (ADA).[28]

Both the FTC and the CFPB regulate unfair and deceptive practices and enforce a variety of laws, including the FCRA, which limits employers' ability to receive an employee's or applicant's credit report, driving records, criminal records and other consumer reports obtained from a CRA.[29]

The NLRB administers the National Labor Relations Act. The board conducts elections to determine if employees want union representation and investigates and remedies unfair labor practices by employers and unions.[30]

In addition, each state has an agency, often called the Department of Labor, that oversees the state labor laws. These laws include state minimum wage laws and laws limiting work by minors. The same department in most states may administer state unemployment insurance programs and employee rehabilitation programs. Some departments also conduct safety inspections of worker conditions.

11.2 Privacy Issues Before, During and After Employment

Workplace privacy issues exist in all stages of the employment lifecycle—before, during and after employment. Before employment, employers should consider rules and best practices about background screening, including rules for accessing employee information under the FCRA. During employment, major topics include polygraphs and psychological testing; substance testing; employee monitoring, including of phone calls and emails; and emerging issues such as social network monitoring and "bring your own device (BYOD)." After employment, the main issues are terminating access to physical and informational assets, and proper human resources practices postemployment. It is important to keep in mind that while consumer privacy practices pose a bigger risk for many organizations, HR-related privacy presents a risk for virtually *all* organizations, including organizations in traditional industries that are not focused on data or data privacy.

For privacy professionals whose role encompasses human resources, multiple legal issues can arise in the employment lifecycle. In addition to consulting with the legal and information technology (IT) departments, a privacy professional should keep in close contact with the HR experts in the organization. Even before the IT revolution put personnel records on computers, HR professionals had developed good practices for handling confidential information. It is worth noting that one consequence of the long-standing policies in HR is that these departments may be reluctant to adjust policies at the advice of a recently formed privacy team that is seeking to implement more recent developments in privacy.

HR records are often physically segregated from other organization records or handled within IT systems with strict access controls. Because HR records apply to every person in an organization, including the most senior management, HR professionals have a special responsibility to respect the confidentiality of employee information.

Employment laws in the United States often provide employers with more discretion than laws in the EU and other countries in the handling of personal information. U.S. laws also often vary by state. Organizations thus have to consider which jurisdiction's rules apply to personal information about particular employees.

11.2.1 Privacy Issues Before Employment

Employers today can have access to a wealth of information about applicants, gathered both directly from the candidate and through searches of public records and private databases. In the United States, the FCRA and antidiscrimination laws create national rules that structure how information is gathered and used preemployment. As in other areas of workplace privacy, states often have additional laws, and egregious practices can create tort suits under the common law. Collective bargaining agreements may also apply. As discussed in other chapters of this book, the privacy professional thus must be aware of both the many beneficial uses of personal information and the legal and other risks that can arise from improper handling of personal information.

11.2.1.1 Common Reasons for Employee Background Screening

Before employees are hired—or even brought in for an interview—they are often subject to background screening.[31] The type and extent of screening varies depending on the work environment. There are many reasons and motivations for employers to conduct background screening. Some important trends have stimulated an increase in applicant screening.[32] For example:

- The terrorist attacks of September 11, 2001, resulted in heightened attention to security issues and support for more stringent identity-verification requirements
- Greater attention to child abuse and abductions has led to laws in almost every state requiring criminal background checks for people who work with children
- Business governance scandals, such as those at Enron and WorldCom, spurred passage of the Sarbanes-Oxley Act in 2002, which has increased the incentives for corporate leaders to scrutinize practices in the areas they manage

- The rapid increase of information about candidates from online search and social media sites has made background checks easier[33]

Certain professions are subject to background screening by law. Typically, anyone who works with the elderly, children or the disabled must now undergo background screening. The federal National Child Protection Act authorizes state officials to access the Federal Bureau of Investigation's National Crime Information Center database for some positions that involve contact with children. Many state and federal government jobs require rigorous background checks to obtain a security clearance.[34] Other groups that are targeted in background checks, depending on the state, include emergency medical service personnel, county coroners, humane society investigators, euthanasia technicians in animal shelters, bus and truck drivers, athletic trainers, in-home repair services, firefighters, gaming industry employees, real estate brokers and information technology workers. The EEOC has cautioned businesses that they should carefully review background screening processes, such as denying employment based on criminal convictions, to ensure that their requirements are job related and consistent with business necessity.[35]

Employers use background screening to ensure they are hiring the "best" candidate for the job. Screenings can help determine whether the applicant will fit in the organization's culture and make positive contributions to its growth. Screening can counter false or inflated information provided by job applicants, and helps identify candidates who may damage the organization's brand and reputation. In addition, employers seek to mitigate the risk of liability. Careful background screening can help defeat a later claim for negligent hiring, such as if a person later causes harm when there was prior evidence the employee was dangerous.[36]

Changing information technology has led to changes in screening. An unprecedented amount of candidate data is now available to employers. The sophistication of today's Internet search, coupled with the ever-greater amount of information publicly accessible about many people, has enormously expanded the ability of employers to use "do it yourself" screening on the Internet. Searches of publicly available information have generally been considered a reasonable practice in the United States. Significant privacy issues can accompany such practices, however, as discussed later in this chapter. For instance, Internet searches should not be a basis for making impermissible, discriminatory hiring decisions, and there are emerging laws to prohibit more invasive practices, such as requiring candidates to provide their Facebook or other social network passwords so prospective employers can see information that the candidate has taken steps to keep private.[37]

11.2.1.2 Antidiscrimination Laws as Limits on Background Screening

The United States has a number of federal laws that prohibit discrimination in employment and have sometimes been used to limit background checks, notably:

- Title VII of the Civil Rights Act of 1964 bars discrimination in employment due to race, color, religion, sex and national origin.[38]
- The Equal Pay Act of 1963 bars wage disparity based on sex.[39]
- The Age Discrimination Act bars discrimination against individuals over 40.[40]
- The Pregnancy Discrimination Act bars discrimination due to pregnancy, childbirth and related medical conditions.[41]
- The Americans with Disabilities Act of 1990 bars discrimination against qualified individuals with disabilities.[42]
- The Genetic Information Nondiscrimination Act of 2008 bars discrimination based on individuals' genetic information.[43]
- The Bankruptcy Act provision 11 U.S.C. § 525(b) prohibits employment discrimination against persons who have filed for bankruptcy. There is some ambiguity, however, as to whether the statute applies to discrimination prior to the extension of an offer of employment, and courts have read the statute both ways.[44]

The primary purpose of these laws is to prohibit discrimination in hiring and other employment decisions. A secondary effect, however, is that they often affect how interviews and other background screen activities are conducted. For instance, an employer risks possible discrimination claims for interview questions about national origin or race under Title VII, about current or intended pregnancy under the Pregnancy Discrimination Act, about age under the Age Discrimination Act, or about disability under the Americans with Disabilities Act (ADA). The EEOC has held that Title VII sex discrimination extends to claims based on an individual's sexual orientation or gender identity.[45] Along with these federal laws, many states have their own antidiscrimination laws. Some of these have the same protected classes as the federal laws, and some include additional protected classes. Almost half the states currently prohibit sexual preference discrimination in both public- and private-sector jobs, while other states prohibit such discrimination in public workplaces only.[46] Roughly half the states prohibit discrimination based on marital status.[47]

The complexities of antidiscrimination law are beyond the scope of this book. Extensive case law has grown up under each of these statutes, so that legal research beyond the text of each statute may be needed to assess current good practice. The risk for employers is that their interview questions and other background screening activities may provide evidence of discrimination. On the other hand, information that a candidate is a member of a protected class may be required by statute (such as when age is revealed in the course of verifying eligibility for employment), may be a bona fide occupational qualification or may become known to the employer for some other nondiscriminatory reason.

In practice, HR professionals often receive detailed training about how to collect information relevant to employment decisions while avoiding practices that increase the risk of an antidiscrimination claim. Many companies have established policies that prohibit discrimination and provide more detailed guidance about what interview and background screening practices are permitted. One strategy to reduce risk is to avoid asking questions that elicit information about membership in a protected class. For instance, avoid asking about membership in organizations that reflect religion or national origin. Another strategy is to be consistent and ask the same questions of all candidates. For instance, the company faces a greater risk of pregnancy or sex discrimination claims if women—but not men—are asked about how long they expect to stay on the job.

11.2.1.3 The Americans with Disabilities Act and Medical Screenings

The Americans with Disabilities Act of 1990 (ADA) created important restrictions on medical screening of candidates before employment. The law forbids employers with 15 or more employees from discriminating against a "qualified individual with a disability because of the disability of such individual," and specifically covers "medical examinations and inquiries" as grounds for discrimination.[48] Before an offer of employment is made, the ADA permits such examinations and inquiries only where "job related and consistent with business necessity."[49]

A company may require a medical examination after the offer of employment has been made, and may condition the offer of employment on the results of such an examination. Such an examination is permitted only if: (1) all entering employees are subjected to such an examination regardless of disability, (2) confidentiality rules are followed for the results of the examination and (3) the results are used only in accordance with the statutory prohibitions against discrimination on the basis of disability.[50]

The ADA requires an employer to provide reasonable accommodation to qualified individuals who are employees or applicants for employment, unless to do so would cause undue hardship.[51] During the hiring process and before a conditional offer is made, an employer generally may not ask applicants whether they need a reasonable accommodation for the job, except when the employer knows that an applicant has a disability. After a conditional offer of employment is extended, an employer may inquire whether applicants will need reasonable accommodations so long as all entering employees in the same job category are asked this question.

The ADA restrictions on medical examinations and inquiries significantly affect a range of prehiring practices that previously were widespread.[52] Employers can no longer routinely ask questions about prior injuries and illnesses, including prior worker compensation claims. Psychological tests, previously used to predict conditions such as depression or paranoia, may well qualify as medical examinations. The ADA does not cover the use of drugs or alcohol, although it does cover questions about recovered drug addicts and alcoholics. In general, before hiring employers should use caution about inquiring into the likelihood that a candidate has a covered disability or will seek a reasonable accommodation.

Policies regarding preemployment inquiries should reflect changes to the ADA by the ADA Amendments Act of 2008 (ADAAA).[53] Most importantly, the ADAAA legislatively overturned two U.S. Supreme Court cases under which ADA claims were frequently rejected: Sutton v. United Air Lines[54] and Toyota v. Williams.[55]

In Sutton, the court held that pilots with severe myopia—but correctable with glasses—did not have a disability under the ADA because a "'disability' exists only where an impairment 'substantially limits' a major life activity, not where it 'might,' 'could,' or 'would' be substantially limiting if mitigating measures were not taken."[56]

Toyota further limited the scope of the ADA, rejecting a claim that carpal tunnel syndrome limited a worker's ability to work with power tools, holding that "an individual must have an impairment that prevents or severely restricts the individual from doing activities that are of central importance to most people's daily lives. The impairment's impact must also be permanent or long-term." The ADAAA significantly expanded the scope of ADA protections by broadly defining disabilities to include conditions that are mitigated, in remission or episodic if they would substantially limit a major life activity of an employee when active or absent mitigation.[57] Pursuant to the ADAAA, the EEOC released new regulations addressing the scope of the ADA in 2011.[58]

11.2.1.4 FCRA Restrictions on Background Checks

FCRA, discussed in more detail in Chapter 8 on financial privacy, regulates how employers perform background checks on job applicants. This law is not limited to background credit checks; it also covers any other type of background check, such as criminal records or driving records, obtained from a CRA. A CRA includes any organization that regularly engages in the assembling or evaluating of consumer information for the purpose of furnishing consumer reports to third parties for a fee.[59]

Under the FCRA, the term *consumer report* includes all written, oral or other communications bearing on the consumer's creditworthiness, credit standing, credit capacity, character, general reputation, personal characteristics or mode of living. Examples of inquiries covered by FCRA include a credit report obtained from a credit bureau and a driving history report obtained from an information aggregator. In recent years, the FTC has aggressively enforced FCRA violations against nontraditional CRAs who collect data online and report it to employers.[60] Alleged FCRA violations are frequently litigated by affected individuals as well.

FCRA prohibits obtaining a consumer report unless a "permissible purpose" exists. Permissible purposes, however, include "employment purposes" which in turn include (1) preemployment screening for the purpose of evaluating the candidate for employment and (2) determining if an existing employee qualifies for promotion, reassignment or retention.

The FCRA also permits employers to obtain an "investigative consumer report" on the applicant if a permissible purpose exists. An investigative consumer report is one in which some of the information is acquired through interviews with neighbors, friends, associates or acquaintances of the employee, such as reference checks.

To obtain any consumer report under FCRA, an employer must meet the following standards:

- Provide written notice to the applicant that it is obtaining a consumer report for employment purposes and indicate if an investigative consumer report will be obtained
- Obtain written consent from the applicant
- Obtain data only from a qualified consumer reporting agency, an entity that has taken steps to assure the accuracy and currency of the data
- Certify to the CRA agency that the employer has a permissible purpose and has obtained consent from the employee
- Before taking an adverse action, such as denial of employment, provide a pre-adverse-action notice to the applicant with a copy of the consumer report, in order to give the applicant an opportunity to dispute the report
- After taking adverse action, provide an adverse action notice

If employers do not comply with these requirements, they may face civil and criminal penalties, including a private right of action.

In 2003 the Fair and Accurate Credit Transactions Act (FACTA) amended FCRA. The amendments preempted a wide range of state laws on credit reporting, identity theft and other areas within the FCRA.[61] FACTA, however, specifically left some existing state laws in effect, notably the California Investigative Consumer Reporting Agencies Act (ICRAA).[62] Under the ICRAA, employers must notify applicants and employees of their intention to obtain and use a consumer report. Once disclosure is made, the employer must obtain the applicant or employee's written authorization prior to requesting the report. On the notice and authorization form, employers must enable applicants and employees to check a box to receive a copy of their consumer report any time a background check is conducted. If employers wish to take adverse employment action, they must provide the employee with a copy of the report, regardless of whether the employee waived the right to receive a copy. This exception does not apply to employees suspected of wrongdoing or misconduct.

Disclosure requirements under the ICRAA are more stringent than under the FCRA. Under the ICRAA, any person who acquires an investigative consumer report for employment purposes must provide separate written disclosure to the applicant or employee before the report is obtained. The written disclosure must state:

- The fact that a report may be obtained
- The permissible purpose of the report
- The fact that the disclosure may include information on the consumer's character, general reputation, personal characteristics and mode of living
- The name, address and telephone number of the investigative consumer reporting agency

As of 2012, the disclosure must also include the web address where the applicant or employee "may find information about the investigative consumer reporting agency's privacy practices, including whether the consumer's personal information will be sent outside the United States or its territories."[63] If the CRA does not have a website, then the employer must provide the consumer with a telephone number where the applicant or employee can obtain the same information.

The FCRA and ICRAA also differ with regard to consent requirements. The FCRA allows employers to use the original written consent to get updates to the employee's credit report as needed. The employer, however, must obtain written consent every time a background check is requested under the ICRAA. Also, the FCRA requires that an employer get written consent only if the employer obtains data from a consumer reporting agency. If the employer does the background check itself (for instance, by directly accessing public records from the government records keeper and calling references), it does not need to obtain written consent under the FCRA. The ICRAA, on the other hand, requires employers to give the employee or applicant any public records resulting from an in-house background check unless the employee waives that right. If the investigation results in an adverse action, then the employer must give the employee or applicant a copy of the public records whether he or she waived that right or not. If the employer conducts an in-house reference check, it does not have to give that information to the applicant or employee.[64] Note that if the employer obtains records from any third-party data aggregators, such as online criminal records suppliers, those entities will be deemed to be CRAs under the FCRA.[65]

The FCRA does not preempt states from creating stronger legislation in the area of employment credit history checks, such as the California ICRAA just discussed. Nine other states—Connecticut, Delaware, Hawaii, Illinois, Maryland, Nevada, Oregon, Vermont and Washington—currently limit the use of credit information in employment.[66] These states require that credit history information be used only as related to the position applied for. The requisite degree of relation differs among states. While most states require a substantial relationship,[67] Hawaii requires the applicant's credit history to directly relate to an occupational qualification.[68] Additionally, some states allow credit history checks to be performed if the position applied for fits within predefined occupational categories, generally involving financial or managerial responsibility or exposure to confidential information.[69]

11.2.2 Privacy Issues During Employment

A range of workplace privacy issues can arise once an applicant is hired. The discussion here addresses polygraphs and psychological testing; substance testing; employee monitoring, including of phone calls and emails; and emerging issues such as social network monitoring and BYOD.

11.2.2.1 Polygraphs and Psychological Testing

The **Employee Polygraph Protection Act of 1988** (EPPA) is a prominent example of federal protection of privacy in the workplace.[70] Under the act and its regulations, issued by the Department of Labor, employers are prohibited from using "lie detectors" on incumbent workers or to screen applicants. A lie detector is defined to include polygraphs, voice stress analyzers, psychological stress evaluators, or any similar device used for the purpose of rendering a diagnostic opinion regarding an individual's honesty.[71] The act prohibits employers from requiring or requesting that a prospective or current employee take a lie detector test. Employers cannot use, accept, refer to or inquire about lie detector test results. The act also prohibits employers from taking adverse action against an employee who refuses to take a test.[72]

EPPA has exceptions for certain occupations, including for government employees, employees in certain security services, those engaged in the manufacture of controlled substances, certain defense contractors and those in certain national security functions. Tests are also allowed in connection with "an ongoing investigation involving economic loss or injury to the employer's business," such as theft, embezzlement or industrial espionage. Even for such investigations, there must be reasonable suspicion to test an employee, and other protections for the employee apply. An employee cannot be discharged because of the results of a polygraph or for refusing to submit to a polygraph, unless additional supporting evidence also exists.

EPPA requires employers to post the act's essential provisions in a conspicuous location so that employees are aware of its existence. If the act is violated, employers may be subject to a fine from the Department of Labor, as well as to private lawsuits. Also, state laws are not preempted, and a large number of states have enacted laws further restricting the use of lie detectors in private employment.[73]

EPPA and the ADA together place significant national limits on psychological testing in the workplace. Employers must comply with the rules limiting lie detectors as well as the ADA prohibitions on the use of medical tests, including those designed to test an impairment of mental health. Employers continue to use psychological tests measuring personality traits such as honesty, preferences and habits in hiring and employment, although one expert reports that such tests may be concentrated in specific positions such as management and sales.[74]

11.2.2.2 Substance Use Testing

Employers test for substance use for varied reasons: (1) to reduce costs resulting from lowered productivity, accidents and absenteeism caused by drug use, (2) to reduce medical care costs related to drug use, (3) to reduce theft or other illegal activity in the workplace associated with drug trafficking, (4) to bolster corporate image, and (5) to comply with external legal rules that impose or support a drug testing policy.[75]

There is no federal privacy statute that directly governs employer testing of employees for substances such as illegal drugs, alcohol or tobacco. For public-sector employees, there is considerable case law under the Fourth Amendment about when such testing is reasonable. As previously mentioned, the ADA prohibits discrimination based on disability, although the application of the ADA varies for illegal drugs and alcohol, for current and past use. The ADA specifically excludes current illegal drug use from its protections, and a test for drug use is not considered a medical examination.[76] By contrast, the responsible federal agencies have stated that "an alcoholic is a person with a disability and is protected by the ADA if she or he is qualified to perform the essential functions of the job."[77] Concerning a history of illegal drug use, the U.S. Department of Justice states that "policies that screen out applicants because of a history of addiction or treatment for addiction must be carefully scrutinized to ensure that the policies are job-related and consistent with business necessity."[78]

Federal law mandates drug testing for certain positions within the federal sector, including employees of the U.S. Customs and Border Protection. Federal law also creates regulation for drug testing for employees in the aviation, railroading and trucking industries.[79] The rules preempt state laws that would otherwise limit drug testing.

Drug testing can be used in a variety of settings:

- Preemployment—generally allowed if not designed to identify legal use of drugs or addiction to illegal drugs
- Reasonable suspicion—generally allowed as a condition of continued employment if there is "reasonable suspicion" of drug or alcohol use based on specific facts as well as rational inferences from those facts (e.g., appearance, behavior, speech, odors)
- Routine testing—generally allowed if the employees are notified at the time of hire, unless state or local law prohibits it
- Post-accident testing—generally allowed to test as a condition of continued employment if there is "reasonable suspicion" that the employee involved in the accident was under the influence of drugs or alcohol
- Random testing—sometimes required by law, prohibited in certain jurisdictions, but acceptable where used on existing employees in specific, narrowly defined jobs, such as those in highly regulated industries where the employee has a severely diminished expectation of privacy or where testing is critical to public safety or national security

A majority of states have passed one or more statutes governing the testing of employees for drugs and/or alcohol.[80] States such as Connecticut, Iowa and Minnesota have laws that generally prohibit employee drug tests unless there is reasonable suspicion to test a particular employee,[81] although state law varies on whether employer violation of the statute prevents discharge of an employee who tests positive. There has also been extensive litigation over time under the common law of the various states, on theories including defamation (if the test was inaccurate), negligent testing, invasion of privacy, and violation of contract and collective bargaining agreements.

Generalizing in the face of this state-by-state variation is risky. Cases upholding random drug testing usually involve occupational roles in highly regulated industries or positions that are critical to the protection of life, property or national security. More invasive tests, such as collecting a blood sample, are more prone to scrutiny than less invasive tests, such as a breathalyzer.

11.2.2.3 Lifestyle Discrimination

An employee's lifestyle outside of work has generally been regarded as private, unless these actions negatively affect other people or are criminal.[82] In recent years, concerns have been raised about issues such as employees' weight and smoking habits. Employers must use caution when taking negative actions against employees for lifestyle choices.[83]

Weight. The classic example of weight discrimination was in the field of flight attendants, who were told they must remain under a certain weight to be employed. After numerous discrimination lawsuits in the airline industry, the mandate was changed to one requiring a person's weight to be proportional to their height and age.[84] This illustration shows how restrictions focused on weight can make a company susceptible to being sued for discrimination.

To address the concerns related to increasing obesity in the United States, the ADA was amended in 2009 to protect a person who is 100 pounds overweight from discrimination based on a disability.[85] In the employment context, the EEOC has obtained settlements on behalf of employees who alleged this type of discrimination, yet at least one court has dismissed this type of claim. This means the details of how the disability will be understood legally are still less than certain at this time.[86]

A current trend concerning weight in the workplace arises in wellness programs that are sponsored by the employer. In 2013, CVS Pharmacy gained national attention when employees were required to provide information on weight as part of a wellness program or face a $600 surcharge.[87] Employers should take care to ensure that these attempts to assist their employees do not become avenues for discrimination.

Smoking. Many employers ban smoking tobacco or vaping during work hours or on work property. No federal law protects smokers from discrimination. When designing a policy regarding smoking, employers should be aware that more than half of states have laws that limit smoking bans to the workplace. Under these laws, individuals are protected from discrimination from their employer if they choose to smoke while not at work.[88]

Business who have restrictions related to lifestyle issues should clearly explain the business reason for such policies. While concerned for health insurance costs of employees who engage in certain habits, companies should be careful in carrying out the implementation of such policies.[89]

For the privacy professional, it is important to understand this is a developing area of the law. Numerous state laws have been passed to address various lifestyle issues, and more are being considered.[90] Employer policies should be reviewed and updated in light of new developments.

11.2.2.4 Monitoring in the Workplace

Strong policies both favor and limit monitoring of employees in the workplace. A few reasons for monitoring are to:

- Follow workplace safety and other laws that require or encourage monitoring
- Protect physical security (such as video cameras near entrances) and cybersecurity (such as activity on computer systems)
- Protect trade secrets
- Limit liability for unlicensed transmission of copyrighted material and other confidential company information
- Improve work quality, such as by monitoring service calls with customers
- Try to keep employees on task rather than spending time on personal business, such as surfing the web

In the United States, private-sector employees in general have limited expectations of privacy at the workplace. The physical facilities belong to the employer, and employers in the private sector thus generally have broad legal authority to do monitoring and searches at work.[91] Computers and other IT equipment are similarly understood to be the property of the employer, with consequent broad employer rights about how the equipment is used. These employer rights are frequently more limited in Europe and other countries, where employees often have a broader set of protections against monitoring under data protection, collective bargaining and other employment laws. Companies with employees both in the United States and abroad thus may need to develop different policies and IT systems that conform to the varying laws.

On the other hand, workplace monitoring can intrude on the privacy of employees. Although monitoring is justified in some settings, there can be serious privacy concerns from excessive video monitoring (such as in changing rooms), monitoring of workplace conversations (such as bugs secretly placed by a supervisor to listen to employees) or email and other computer monitoring (such as when emails that an employee believes are personal are reviewed by the employer). Employers often choose not to monitor even where they may have legal ability to do so, for reasons including ethics, cost and morale. Monitoring costs include the legal obligations to detect and act on misconduct revealed by the monitoring program.

Collective bargaining agreements can be an additional limiting factor on an employer's ability to monitor the workplace. Many such agreements contain provisions designed to limit workplace monitoring, or require that a union representative be informed of an employer's monitoring activities.

Technological trends have increased the range of ways that employers can monitor employees. The cost of video cameras and other sensors has fallen sharply over time. The increasing portion of work conducted with computers and personal phones means that a greater portion of the workday, for many employees, is conducted on systems that are subject to monitoring. For instance, many conversations around the old water cooler, which were hard to monitor, have shifted to texts and emails, which leave a record in the employer's IT system. The increase of telecommuting and working from home also mean that lines have blurred between the workday, traditionally under the supervision of the employer, and time at home, which traditionally was considered more private and not usually the business of the boss.

Organizations should consider establishing formal policies about workplace monitoring and accompanying documents, such as acceptable use policies for IT equipment. These policies may also be required by state law in order for such monitoring to be lawful.[92] Such policies often include when monitoring can or will occur, purposes of data use, to whom data may be disclosed, and the consequences to employees for violations. In special circumstances where additional monitoring is conducted, the employer may be required to describe the approval process and document when it is implemented. Providing employees with notices of these policies helps establish their knowledge and reasonable expectations about workplace activities. Such policies have proven broadly effective in addressing employee claims for improper monitoring.[93]

11.2.2.4.1 Legal Obligations or Incentives to Monitor

Employers sometimes have strong legal reasons to monitor the workplace. For example, OSHA requires employers to provide a safe workplace that complies with occupational health and safety standards. These standards require employees to perform tasks in a safe manner, to avoid injury. Thus, ensuring compliance with OSHA is one legal reason to monitor employees.[94]

Call centers and firms that do financial transactions over the phone often record telephone conversations for reasons including agent training, quality assurance and security/liability. If a dispute arises with a customer after the fact, the recording can often resolve what was said or agreed upon. Such recordings, however, must comply with the rules about phone call recording discussed below. As noted in Chapter 10, certain activities that may result in charges placed using preacquired account numbers, such as telemarketing, must be recorded.[95] Note though, for security reasons, call centers often pause the recording functionality when a customer relays full payment card information.

Employers also monitor the workplace as a way to defend against a possible tort claim for negligent supervision, especially where the employer is on notice of a specific risk from one employee to other employees or third parties. The claim of negligent supervision is similar to the claim, discussed above, of negligent hiring. In both instances, there is uncertainty about what a jury will find to have been negligent, and so employers have an incentive to err on the side of caution, to reduce the risk of a successful claim.

Some business lawyers have counseled companies to monitor email and other employee computer usage to reduce the risk that the employer will be held liable for creating a hostile work environment, for example, if sexually explicit or racially derogatory material is viewed at work.[96] An authority on employment law, Professor Matthew Finkin, has disagreed, saying: "The bald fact is that employers have no more a duty to monitor their employees' email, to assure that untoward messages are not being communicated, than they have a duty to place hidden microphones or cameras at the water coolers to detect sexually offensive remarks or leering glances."[97] Courts that have addressed the issue have stressed that the speech involved must be so pervasive as to alter working conditions, and so the risk of such claims may well be lower than business lawyers believed when Internet usage was first becoming common.[98]

11.2.2.4.2 Laws Applying to Types of Monitoring

Federal laws governing wiretaps and access to stored communications are notoriously complex, and electronic monitoring of employees thus should often be done in consultation with a lawyer knowledgeable about the area. Chapter 12 discusses key aspects of these laws. The discussion here focuses on monitoring in the workplace.

Federal and state laws regulate and restrict workplace surveillance activities, including video surveillance, monitoring of telephone calls, and electronic surveillance, such as accessing emails and monitoring Internet activities.[99]

Video surveillance. Cameras and video recordings that do not have sound recordings are outside the scope of the federal wiretap and stored-record statutes. Many U.S. employers use closed-circuit television (CCTV) or other video surveillance in the workplace. Security cameras are often used at the perimeter of a business to deter and detect burglary or other unauthorized intrusion. They are used within a business establishment to deter crimes such as shoplifting and armed robbery, and outside to detect "driveaways" from gas stations or other businesses. They are used within warehouses and other parts of a business to reduce the incidence of stealing by employees, and insurance companies may give companies a discount for installing CCTV systems.[100]

Although federal law generally does not limit the use of either photography or video cameras, state statutes and common law create limits in some settings. California is like other states in forbidding video recording in areas such as restrooms, locker rooms and places where employees change clothes.[101] Michigan's statute is broader, forbidding installation of a device for observing or photographing a "private place" as defined by the statute.[102] Even in the absence of a statute, employees may be able to bring a common-law tort claim for invasion of privacy, especially where a jury would find the use of the camera to be offensive. In addition, as with other areas of workplace monitoring, collective bargaining agreements may apply.

Intercepting communications. As discussed in Chapter 12, the Wiretap Act and the Electronic Communications Privacy Act (ECPA) are generally strict in prohibiting the interception of wire communications, such as telephone calls or sound recordings from video cameras; oral communications, such as hidden bugs or microphones; and electronic communications, such as emails. The exact rules for wire, oral and electronic communications vary, and unless an exception applies, interception of these communications is a criminal offense and provides a private right of action.[103]

Two exceptions to the prohibition on interception often apply in the workplace. Under federal law, interception is permitted:

1. If a person is a party to a call or where one of the parties has given consent [104]

2. The interception is done in the ordinary course of business[105]

An employer who provides communication services, such as a company telephone, or email service, has the ability to intercept provided the interception occurs in the normal course of the user's business.[106] An important distinction exists when an employer listens to an employee's purely personal call. In this instance, the employer risks violation of the wiretap laws. As courts have split on how broadly to define the "ordinary course of business," many employers rely on the consent exception for interception of telephone calls.[107] Privacy professionals should be alert to the requirements of relevant state laws on recording phone calls, because some of these laws require one-party consent while others mandate that all parties to the call consent.[108]

Stored communications. As previously discussed, the SCA creates a general prohibition against the unauthorized acquisition, alteration or blocking of electronic communications while in electronic storage in a facility through which an electronic communications service is provided. Violations for interceptions can lead to criminal penalties or a civil lawsuit. The law provides for exceptions. Two exceptions that may apply to the employer are for conduct authorized:

1. "by the person or entity providing a wire or electronic communications service," (often the employer)[109]

2. "by a user of that service with respect to a communication of or intended for that user"[110]

Generally, employers are permitted to look at workers' electronic communications if the employer's reason for doing so is reasonable and work-related. In the case of City of Ontario v. Quon, the U.S. Supreme Court allowed an employer to review an employee's text messages when the employer was looking at the messages to determine whether the employer's electronic usage policy had been violated. In the case, the employer provided the pager used to send the messages at issue. [111]

ECPA does not generally preempt stricter state privacy protections, and some state laws may protect e-mail communications.

Postal mail monitoring. U.S. federal law generally prohibits interference with mail delivery. Mail is considered "delivered," however, when it reaches a business. As a result, the opening of business letters and packages by a representative of the business does not violate that statute, even if that representative is not the intended recipient. However, there is always some risk involved with monitoring postal mail under state common law. Employers can mitigate this risk by advising employees not to receive personal mail at work, declining to read mail once it is clear that it is personal in nature, and maintaining confidentiality for any personal information obtained in the course of monitoring.

Location-based services (LBS). Mobile phones, GPS devices and some tablet computers provide geolocation data, which enables tracking of the user's physical location and movements. This creates a category of personal information that typically did not exist before the prevalence of these mobile devices.[112] Employers interested in monitoring the location of company vehicles equipped with GPS may generally do so without legal hindrance, provided that the monitoring occurs for business purposes during work hours and employees have been informed beforehand.[113]

A company wishing to monitor the location of its employees themselves, however, may face greater legal barriers. Some state laws limit monitoring of employee geolocation data to an extent. Connecticut, for example, prohibits any type of electronic employee monitoring without written notice, and provides a civil penalty of $500 for a first offense.[114] California has increased protection for its employees by outlawing the use of "an electronic tracking device to determine the location or movement of a person" as a misdemeanor criminal offense.[115] In addition, the utilization of location-based services to monitor employees runs the risk of incurring invasion of privacy claims in situations where the employee has a reasonable expectation of privacy.

11.2.2.4.3 Emerging Technologies to Monitor Employees

Companies today often already have in place a variety of systems to monitor electronic communications. Companies routinely run antispam and antivirus software on emails. The computer security activities of the IT department include a range of intrusion detection and other measures. Depending on the company and job description, there may also be limits on acceptable use of work computers, including bans on accessing websites that are inappropriate for the workplace.

Three emerging areas are: (1) how companies are using social media to monitor prospective and current employees, (2) how the IT department copes with what is called "the consumerization of information technology" or BYOD and (3) how companies implement data loss prevention (DLP) programs.

Using social media to monitor prospective and current employees. Social media sites such as Facebook, Twitter and LinkedIn facilitate easy and immediate sharing, collaboration and interaction. Employers can use social media to their advantage—for example, a strong social media presence helps increase visibility in the marketplace. Social media can be used by employers to stay in touch with customer needs, and its effective use conveys a level of technological sophistication to its followers. It is also a helpful platform for receiving immediate feedback from consumers, clients and employees, at a very low cost.

In recent years, social media has increasingly been used to screen prospective hires. Companies now exist that are dedicated entirely to tracking an individual's online presence and screening candidates for predesignated elements selected by the employer. These may include potential drug use, criminal activity or unsafe behavior. (In doing so, companies should be alert to the possibility that the FCRA applies to these nontraditional providers of background check information.) Social media monitoring is also used to keep track of current employees to mitigate brand or reputation damage.[116]

Despite the advantages of using social media, employers should be aware of potential risks that come with using these mechanisms to monitor employees. Though employers are generally legally permitted to use social media in informing their decisions, they must not violate existing antidiscrimination and privacy laws.[117] Invasive monitoring practices may provide the basis for discrimination lawsuits if the employer accesses and appears to use information that is legally protected. This includes protected classes such as religion, ethnicity, gender or sexual orientation, political affiliations and other sensitive information, all of which is commonly available on individuals's social media pages. Although reading publicly available information is clearly lawful, acting in a discriminatory way in the workplace is not. Employers should thus consider what policies and training should exist to avoid taking actions that could be considered discriminatory, including monitoring information about an employee on social media sites.[118]

Employers face risks when engaging in social engineering—the use of manipulation to gain access to otherwise private information. This includes connecting with potential hires or employees through a false online profile, or requesting access to private networks that are not available to the general public. If employers engage in these practices, they may be confronted with invasion of privacy actions for violating the applicant's or employee's reasonable expectation of privacy.[119]

Finally, employers should not require prospective or current employees to divulge access information to private networks as a condition of employment. In 2012, Maryland was the first state to ban employers from asking applicants or employees for their social network login information and passwords.[120] As of 2017, 24 other states have passed similar laws, and Congress has proposed similar legislation.[121] Employers should proceed with caution when collecting information from social media accounts. Employers have not traditionally had access to an employee's personal e-mail accounts, and similar reasoning should be applied to gaining access to the private parts of a person's social network activities.[122]

Consumerization of information technology (COIT) and BYOD. Individuals today have more information technology options than ever before. Computing devices range from traditional desktop computers and laptops to powerful smartphones, tablet computers and netbooks. Social networks, webmail and applications can be accessed across devices. Marked improvement in device capability and widespread Internet access allow employees to connect to their online networks from almost any location.

Increasingly, individuals are also using their personal devices for work purposes, blurring the line between personal and professional environments. The COIT trend refers not only to the use of personal computing devices in the workplace, but also to online services, such as webmail, cloud storage and social networking. Traditionally, adoption of high-level information technology started with major public- and private-sector organizations, with consumer adoption later after the price became affordable. In recent years the trend has reversed. Today information technology often emerges in the consumer market and is driven by employees who use their personal devices, accounts and applications both in and outside of the office for work tasks.

BYOD is a manifestation of the COIT trend, in which employees use their personal computing devices for work purposes. BYOD offers significant advantages. It allows employees to use the same technology at work that they use at home, which means more flexibility, efficiency and productivity in employee work schedules. Employers benefit from increased accessibility to their employees as well as reduced overhead and workplace device expenses. BYOD, however, presents significant security challenges that stem from the lack of employer control over employee devices. BYOD may expose organizations to security vulnerabilities and threats that they could otherwise protect against with work-issued devices.[123]

Organizations adopting a BYOD strategy must move beyond traditional device management practices to ensure the security of company data. Before implementation, organizations should carefully evaluate their existing security policies to determine how they align with employees' use of personal devices for work purposes. Where there are discrepancies, employers should modify their policies accordingly. For example, if an organization's current policy requires specific security controls for company-owned devices but not personal devices, the company puts itself at risk by allowing employee devices to be used in the workplace. Security controls required for company-owned devices, however, may not be suitable or necessary for personal devices, depending on how they are used. Less security may be adequate for personal devices that are not permitted to store sensitive employer data. One consideration is what information triggers breach notification laws—stricter policies are called for when loss of the device would require breach notices. Ultimately, policies should reflect organization requirements, and devices should be secured in a way that protects employers from liability and legal risk.

BYOD also presents new workplace privacy implications. The same devices that employees use to access personal email accounts and social networking sites and surf the Internet will also be used for work purposes. Though it is generally acceptable for employers to monitor employees' activities on a work network and work-issued devices, it is less clear how employers should handle monitoring of personal devices. Employee expectations of privacy in a BYOD context are likely to be higher because a personal device is involved. As a result, the same surveillance and monitoring activities used for work-issued devices may not be appropriate for personal devices. Further privacy issues arise in event of an investigation or security breach. If an employee's personal device must be searched or analyzed, that employee's personal (nonwork) information is likely to be exposed. Employers can limit the scope of their searches but must be thorough enough to capture evidence of the breach.

In designing BYOD policies, employers should clearly address these issues and convey to employees the privacy limits and risks when using personal devices in the workplace. If the employer is engaged in device monitoring or surveillance, it should disclose that information and obtain employee consent. When monitoring and searching the device, exposure of private employee data should be minimized.[124]

It is worth noting that similar challenges exist for employees' data held in personal online storage accounts, portable media devices and other technology. For security reasons, organizations may find it necessary to adopt policies prohibiting employees from copying the company's confidential information or its customers' personal information onto personal storage or media devices.

When such policies are either not in place or not enforced, employees may be required to provide access to their devices or accounts in response to electronic discovery demands in legal proceedings against the company. For example, an employee who leaves a company for a competitor could be subject to claims such as trade secret theft if the company's data was not completely deleted.[125]

Data loss prevention (DLP). DLP is a strategy used by businesses to ensure that sensitive data is not accessed, misused or lost by unauthorized users. This goal is accomplished by DLP software and tools by monitoring and controlling endpoint activities as well as protecting data as it moves.[126]

Another way of understanding DLP is that it combines: (1) the use of information security tools (2) the utilization of training for employee behavioral modification; and (3) the implementation of effective standards, policies, and procedures.

Successful DLP programs have the following elements:

- Risk assessment
- Data classification
- Data governance
- Regulatory and privacy compliance
- Policies, standards and procedures
- Data discovery
- Training and awareness
- Remediation processes

DLP is designed to ensure that privacy protection is an integral part of the methodology. Privacy assessments are strongly recommended to protect a company's sensitive data by evaluating regulatory and statutory compliance. Risk assessment is also seen as essential to the identification, classification and categorization of data at rest, in motion and at the endpoint.[127]

Despite the efforts to make privacy protection an important part of the process to protect data, privacy concerns have been raised about DLP's impact on employee privacy. This technology can establish a kind of "mass surveillance" in the workplace. The powerful features of modern DLP suites (e.g., recording every key stroke, activating the webcam of laptops or smartphones, tracking the geolocation of the smartphone user without his or her knowledge) may exceed significantly the intrusiveness of traditional forms of surveillance in the workplace.[128] Organizations considering instituting a DLP program should thus consider the likely privacy risks as well as the likely benefits of the program.

11.2.2.5 Investigation of Employee Misconduct

When alleged employee misconduct occurs, the employer should be aware of issues such as the following:

- Be careful to avoid liability or loss due to failure to take the allegations seriously. Ignoring a problem may allow it to grow or otherwise become more difficult to resolve later.
- Treat the employee with fairness during the investigation to reduce possible employee resentment as well as the risk that later litigation will result in harsher penalties if the employer is seen to have been unfair.
- Follow laws and other corporate policies during the investigation. Particular attention should be given to collective bargaining agreements, which often contain provisions concerning investigations of employee misconduct.
- Document the alleged misconduct and investigation to minimize risks from subsequent claims by the employee.
- Consider the rights of people other than those being investigated, such as fellow employees who could be subject to retaliation or other problems.

Investigations are often conducted in cooperation with an organization's HR office. HR policies often apply to investigations. Progressive and documented discipline for initial or minor infractions can provide a reasoned basis for more serious discipline or termination if necessary. The privacy professional should work with the compliance department to determine the appropriate level of documentation.

Frequently, employers use third parties to investigate employee misconduct. Formerly, this exposed corporations to liability under the FCRA. The FCRA generally requires notice and employee consent when the employer obtains a consumer report. According to an opinion letter issued for the FTC known as the "Vail Letter," if an employer hired an outside organization such as a private investigator or background research firm to conduct these investigations, the outside organization constituted a CRA under the FCRA, and any report furnished to the employer by the outside organization was an "investigative consumer report."[129] Under this opinion, an employer that received these reports was required to comply with the FCRA by providing notice to the suspected employee and obtain consent. This destroyed the undercover aspect of investigations.[130]

FACTA amended the FCRA to address the problems created by the Vail Letter.[131] Along with other FCRA and FACTA provisions discussed in Chapter 8 on financial privacy, FACTA provided that (if certain conditions were met) an employer is no longer required to notify an employee that it is obtaining an investigative consumer report on the employee from an outside organization in the context of an internal investigation. Specifically, FACTA changed the definition of "consumer report" under FCRA to exclude communications relating to employee investigations from the definition if three requirements are met:

- The communication is made to an employer in connection with the investigation of: (1) suspected misconduct related to employment, or (2) compliance with federal, state, or local laws and/or regulations, the rules of a self-regulatory organization, or any preexisting written employment policies
- The communication is not made for the purpose of investigating a consumer's creditworthiness, credit standing or credit capacity and does not include information pertaining to those factors
- The communication is not provided to any person except: (1) the employer or agent of the employer; (2) a federal or state officer, agency, or department, or an officer, agency, or department of a unit of general local government; (3) a self-regulating organization with authority over the activities of the employer or employee; (4) as otherwise required by law; or (5) pursuant to 15 U.S.C. § 1681f, which addresses disclosures to government agencies.[132]

If the employer takes adverse action on the basis of these reports, FACTA requires that the employer disclose a summary of the nature and substance of the communication or report to the employee. This report can be issued after the investigation has been conducted and allows employers to maintain the secrecy of the investigation.[133]

11.2.3 Privacy Issues After Employment

At the end of the employment relationship, an employer should restrict or terminate the former employee's access to physical and informational assets, follow the correct termination procedures, minimize risks of post-termination claims, help management to transition after the termination and address any privacy claims that arise.

11.2.3.1 Access to Physical and Informational Assets

When a person leaves a company or is no longer supposed to have access to specific facilities or information, there should be clear procedures for terminating such access. Basic steps include:

- Secure the return of badges, keys, smartcards and other methods of physical access
- Disable access for computer accounts
- Ensure the return of laptops, smartphones, storage drives and other devices that may store company information
- Seek, where possible, to have the employee return or delete any company data that is held by the employee outside of the company's systems
- Remind employees of their obligations not to use company data for other purposes
- Clearly marked personal mail, if any, should be forwarded to the former employee, but work-related mail should be reviewed to ensure that proprietary company information is not leaked

Because the departure of employees is a predictable event, IT systems should be designed to minimize the disruption to the company and other employees when a person no longer has authorized access. Access may end not only for a firm employee, but also for contractors, interns and others who have temporary access to company facilities. To take a simple example, the same password should not be used by multiple people, because of the need to change the password when one employee leaves.

Privacy professionals may also need to consider appropriate practices for maintaining the HR records of former employees. There can be many reasons for retaining such information, such as to provide references, respond to inquiries about benefits and pensions, address health and safety issues that arise, respond to legal proceedings, and meet legal or regulatory retention requirements for particular types of records. There are also countervailing concerns about the privacy and security of sensitive employment records, and in some jurisdictions (such as in the EU), there may need to be a demonstrable business or legal reason to justify retaining certain personal information.

11.2.3.2 Human Resources Issues

The HR office is often significantly involved in the period before an employee leaves, especially when employees are not leaving entirely of their own initiative. The HR office often will have detailed and sensitive information about an employee's performance in the period before termination. This sort of information is gathered, for instance, to document the basis for the company's decisions in case the former employee brings a wrongful termination or other claim against the employer.

A similar level of care is appropriate for post-termination contacts with the employee. External communications to the former employee should be crafted with care, especially if the termination resulted from misconduct. Communications with remaining employees, customers and others should meet company goals while refraining from disparaging the former employee.

When an employer is asked to provide references for the former employee, HR, working with legal counsel, should have basic guidelines but collaborate on an appropriate response in more complex circumstances. Companies balance reasons to provide references with the risk of a suit for defamation. The law can vary significantly state by state.[134] The common law imposes no duty on a former employer to supply a reference for a former employee, but some modern state statutes do require references for specific occupations, such as airplane pilot and public school teacher. The common law provides what is known as a "qualified privilege" for employers to report their experience with and impressions of the employee, to help in defense against defamation suits. In recent years, publicity about winning defamation suits has made some employers reluctant to provide references. On the other hand, state legislatures have responded by passing laws that are designed to encourage accurate reports about former employees. A company also often has good reasons to provide references, including to retain goodwill with former employees, whose statements will affect the company's reputation and with whom the company may do business in the future.

11.3 Conclusion

This chapter introduced major themes relating to privacy in the workplace. In the United States, constitutional protections apply specifically to government employees. Contract and tort remedies can provide protections to employees, but they apply in a relatively narrow set of circumstances. States have enacted a considerable number of statutory protections, but the protections exist against a general backdrop of a free market approach to employment and workplace privacy.

Personal information is involved in virtually every phase of the employment relationship—from evaluation and hiring, to employee management and monitoring, to termination or departure. As organizations grow in size, expand to new geographies and involve larger numbers of outside partners and vendors, the employment privacy challenges become more acute. Global employers must navigate through a complex patchwork of applicable U.S., EU and international workplace privacy laws.

Effective legal compliance and thoughtful management of employee personal information can help reduce the risk of any potential legal claims as well as offer many benefits to both employer and employee. These benefits include minimizing the risk of information mishandling, disclosure or theft; increasing employee morale; and improving the working relationship between employer and employee.

Endnotes

1 *See* Lothar Determann and Lars Brauer, Employee Monitoring Technologies and Data Privacy—No One-Size-Fits-All Globally, 9 The IAPP Privacy Advisor, 1 (2009); Lothar Determann and Robert Sprague, Intrusive Monitoring: Employee Privacy Expectations are Reasonable in Europe, Destroyed in the United States, 26 *Berkeley Technology Law Journal* 979 (2011).

2 O'Connor v. Ortega, 480 U.S. 709 (1987), https://supreme.justia.com/cases/federal/us/480/709/case.html (accessed November 2017).

3 California Constitution, Art. 1, § 1, https://leginfo.legislature.ca.gov/faces/codes_displayText.xhtml?lawCode=CONS&division=&title=&part=&chapter=&article=I (accessed November 2017).

4 Restatement (Second) of Torts, § 652B, https://cyber.law.harvard.edu/privacy/Privacy_R2d_Torts_Sections.htm (accessed November 2017).

5 Restatement (Second) of Torts, § 652D, https://cyber.law.harvard.edu/privacy/Privacy_R2d_Torts_Sections.htm (accessed November 2017).

6 Restatement (Second) of Torts, §§ 558–559, https://yalelawtechdotorg.files.wordpress.com/2013/10/info-privacy-handout.pdf (accessed November 20176).

7 Matthew W. Finkin, *Privacy in Employment Law*, 3d edition (Arlington, VA: BNA Books, 2009), xlv.

8 State Statutes Prohibiting Marital Status Discrimination in Employment, www.unmarriedamerica.org/ms-employment-laws.htm (accessed November 2017). *See*, e.g., Cal. Gov't Code 12940, http://leginfo.legislature.ca.gov/faces/codes_displaySection.xhtml?lawCode=GOV§ionNum=12940. (accessed June 2016); N.Y. Exec. Law § 296, http://www.nyc.gov/html/dcas/downloads/pdf/misc/psb_100_13_296.pdf (accessed November 2017); Del. Code Ann. Tit. 19, § 711, http://delcode.delaware.gov/title19/c007/sc02/ (accessed November 2017).

9 *See*, e.g., Illinois Right to Privacy in the Workplace Act, 820 I.L.C.S. § 55, www.ilga.gov/legislation/ilcs/ilcs3.asp?ActID=2398& (accessed November 2017).

10 "State Laws Ban Access to Worker's Social Media Accounts," Society for Human Resource Management, https://www.shrm.org/ResourcesAndTools/legal-and-compliance/state-and-local-updates/Pages/states-social-media.aspx (accessed November 2017).

11 Matthew W. Finkin, *Privacy in Employment Law.*

12 Health Insurance Portability and Accountability Act, 42 U.S.C. §§ 300gg-300gg-2, http://counsel.cua.edu/fedlaw/hipaa.cfm (accessed November 2017).

13 Consolidated Omnibus Budget Reconciliation Act of 1986, 42 U.S.C. §§ 300bb-1-300bb-8, www.versuslaw.com/usc/42usc/42usc=012-000300-300gg-92@49768.asp (accessed November 2017).

14 Employee Retirement Income Security Act of 1974, 29 U.S.C. §§ 1001-1461, https://www.law.cornell.edu/uscode/text/29/1001 (accessed November 2017).

15 Family Medical Leave Act of 1993, 29 U.S.C. §§ 2601-2654, https://www.law.cornell.edu/uscode/text/29/chapter-28 (accessed November 2017).

16 Fair Credit Reporting Act, 15 U.S.C. §§1681-1681v, https://www.law.cornell.edu/uscode/text/15/1681 (accessed November 2017).

17 Fair Labor Standards Act of 1938, 29 U.S.C. §§ 201-219, https://www.law.cornell.edu/uscode/text/29/chapter-8 (accessed November 2017).

18 Occupational Safety and Health Act of 1970, 29 U.S.C. §§ 651-678, https://www.law.cornell.edu/uscode/text/29/chapter-15 (accessed November 2017).

19 Whistleblower Protection Act of 1989, Public Law No. 101-112, 5 U.S.C. §§ 1201 et seq., https://www.usda.gov/oig/webdocs/whistle1989.pdf; Whistleblower Protection Enhancement Act of 2012, https://www.congress.gov/112/bills/s743/BILLS-112s743enr.pdf (accessed November 2017).

20 National Labor Relations Act, 29 U.S.C. §§ 151-159, https://www.law.cornell.edu/uscode/text/29/151 (accessed November 2017).

21 Immigration Reform and Control Act of 1986, 8 U.S.C. §§ 1324a-b, https://www.law.cornell.edu/uscode/text/8/1324a (accessed November 2017).

22 Securities and Exchange Act of 1934, 15 U.S.C. § 78A, https://www.law.cornell.edu/uscode/text/15/78a (accessed November 2017).

23 Employee Polygraph Protection Act of 1988, 29 U.S.C. §§ 2001-2009, https://www.law.cornell.edu/uscode/text/29/2001 (accessed November 2017).

24 Wiretap Act, 18 U.S.C. §§ 2510-2522, https://it.ojp.gov/PrivacyLiberty/authorities/statutes/1284 (accessed November 2017).

25 Electronic Communications Privacy Act, 18 U.S.C. §§ 2510-2511, https://it.ojp.gov/privacyliberty/authorities/statutes/1285 (accessed November 2017).

26 Stored Communications Act, 18 U.S.C. §§ 2701-2712 https://it.ojp.gov/PrivacyLiberty/authorities/statutes/1285 (accessed November 2017).

27 U.S. Department of Labor, "Our Mission." www.dol.gov/opa/aboutdol/mission.htm (accessed November 2017).

28 Equal Employment Opportunity Commission, "Overview," https://www.eeoc.gov/eeoc/ (accessed November 2017).

29 *See* Fair Credit Reporting Act, 15 U.S.C. §§ 1681 *et seq.*, https://www.law.cornell.edu/uscode/text/15/1681 (accessed November 2017) and "Using Consumer Reports: What Employers Need to Know," FTC, https://www.ftc.gov/tips-advice/business-center/guidance/using-consumer-reports-what-employers-need-know (accessed November 2017).

30 National Labor Relations Board, "What We Do," https://www.nlrb.gov/what-we-do (accessed November 2017).

31 State laws vary on the permissible timing of when a background check can be undertaken. *See* Andy Yoder, "State Laws and Background Checks: What You Need to Know," *Justifacts*, April 4, 2016, https://www.justifacts.com/state-laws-and-background-checks-what-you-need-to-know/ (accessed October 2017).

32 For a detailed discussion of the topic, *see* Julie Totten, "Balancing Workplace Technology and Privacy in the 21st Century," p. 24-35, Orrick (March 22, 2017), https://www.americanbar.org/content/dam/aba/events/labor_law/2017/03/err/papers/balancing_workplace_technology.authcheckdam.pdf (accessed October 2017).

33 *Employment Background Checks: A Jobseeker's Guide*, Privacy Rights Clearinghouse, https://www.privacyrights.org/employment-background-checks-jobseekers-guide (accessed November 2017).

34 *Id.*

35 "Consideration of Arrest and Conviction Records in Employment Decisions Under Title VII of the Civil Rights Act of 1964," EEOC Enforcement Guidelines (2012), https://www.eeoc.gov/laws/guidance/arrest_conviction.cfm (accessed November 2017); "EEOC Updates Guidelines on Criminal Records to Prevent Employment Discrimination During Background Checks," Employment Screening Resources, www.esrcheck.com/wordpress/2013/01/02/eeoc-updates-guidance-on-criminal-records-to-prevent-employment-discrimination-during-background-checks/ (accessed November 2017).

36 "Background Checks: What Employers Need to Know," Joint publication of EEOC and FTC, https://www.eeoc.gov/eeoc/publications/background_checks_employers.cfm (accessed November 2017).

37 "Nebraska's New Workplace Privacy Act Restricts Employer Access to Employee Internet Accounts," Baird Holm LLP, www.bairdholm.com/publications/entry/nebraska-s-new-workplace-privacy-act-restricts-employer-access-to-employee-internet-accounts.html (accessed November 2017).

38 Civil Rights Act of 1964, Title VII, 42 U.S.C. §§ 2000e-2000e-17, https://www.law.cornell.edu/uscode/text/42/2000e (accessed November 2017).

39 Equal Pay Act of 1963, https://www.eeoc.gov/laws/statutes/epa.cfm (accessed November 2017).

40 Age Discrimination in Employment Act of 1967, 29 U.S.C. § 621, https://www.law.cornell.edu/uscode/text/29/chapter-14 (accessed November 2017).

41 Pregnancy Discrimination Act, Title VII, 42 U.S.C. §§ 2000e-2000e-17, https://www.law.cornell.edu/uscode/text/42/2000e (accessed November 2017).

42 Americans with Disabilities Act, 42 U.S.C. §§ 12101-12213, https://www.law.cornell.edu/uscode/text/42/12101 (accessed November 2017).

43 Genetic Information Nondiscrimination Act of 2008, 42 U.S.C. § 2000ff, https://www.law.cornell.edu/uscode/text/42/chapter-21F (accessed November 2017).

44 "Can I Lose My Job if I File for Bankruptcy?" *Georgia Bankruptcy Law Journal*, www.gabankruptcylawyersnetwork.com/2013/11/can-i-lose-my-job-if-i-file-for-bankruptcy/ (accessed November 2017). For an in-depth discussion, view Samantha Orovitz, "The Bankruptcy Shadow: Section 525(b) and the Job Applicant's Sisyphean Struggle for a Fresh Start," *Emory Bankruptcy Developments Journal*, http://law.emory.edu/ebdj/content/volume-29/issue-2/comments/bankruptcy-shadow.html (accessed November 2017).

45 "What you should know about EEOC and the enforcement protections for LGBT workers," EEOC, https://www.eeoc.gov/eeoc/newsroom/wysk/enforcement_protections_lgbt_workers.cfm (accessed November 2017).

46 Map of state nondiscrimination laws covering sexual orientation and gender identity, American Civil Liberties Union, https://www.aclu.org/map/non-discrimination-laws-state-state-information-map (accessed November 2017).

47 State Statutes Prohibiting Marital Status Discrimination in Employment, www.unmarriedamerica.org/ms-employment-laws.htm (accessed November 2017).

48 Americans with Disabilities Act of 1990, 42 U.S.C. § 12112(a), https://www.law.cornell.edu/uscode/text/42/12112 (accessed November 2017).

49 42 U.S.C. § 12112(b)(4).

50 42 U.S.C. § 12112(b)(3).

51 *Enforcement Guide: Reasonable Accommodation and Undue Hardship Under the Americans with Disabilities Act*, https://www.eeoc.gov/policy/docs/accommodation.html (accessed November 2017).

52 Paul F. Gerhart, "Employee Privacy Rights in the United States," *Comparative Labor Law Journal* 17 (1995): 195.

53 *Pub. L.* 110-325 (2008).

54 Sutton v. United Air Lines, 527 U.S. 471 (1999), https://supreme.justia.com/cases/federal/us/527/471/case.html (accessed November 2017).

55 Toyota v. Williams, 534 U.S. 184 (2002), https://supreme.justia.com/cases/federal/us/534/184/case.html (accessed November 2017).

56 527 U.S. at 482-483.

57 *Pub. L.* 110-325, § 4.

58 *See generally* https://www.eeoc.gov/laws/regulations/adaaa_fact_sheet.cfm (accessed November 2017).

59 Fair Credit Reporting Act, 15 U.S.C. § 1581a, https://www.ftc.gov/enforcement/rules/rulemaking-regulatory-reform-proceedings/fair-credit-reporting-act (accessed November 2017).

60 "Where HireRight Solutions went wrong," FTC, https://www.ftc.gov/news-events/blogs/business-blog/2012/08/where-hireright-solutions-went-wrong (accessed November 2017). For an in-depth discussion, view "FTC continues aggressive FCRA enforcement against data brokers," Ballard Spahr, www.ballardspahr.com/alertspublications/legalalerts/2014-01-23-ftc-continues-aggressive-fcra-enforcement-against-data-brokers.aspx (accessed November 2017).

61 Fair Credit Reporting Act, 15 U.S.C. § 1681t, https://www.ftc.gov/enforcement/rules/rulemaking-regulatory-reform-proceedings/fair-credit-reporting-act (accessed November 2017).

62 Investigative Consumer Reporting Agencies Act, 1.6A Cal. Civ. Code §§ 1786-1786.60, https://leginfo.legislature.ca.gov/faces/codes_displayText.xhtml?lawCode=CIV&division=3.&title=1.6A.&part=4.&chapter=&article=1 (accessed November 2017).

63 Cal. Civ. Code §§ 1786.16, 1786.20, http://leginfo.legislature.ca.gov/faces/codes_displaySection.xhtml?lawCode=CIV§ionNum=1786.16 (accessed November 2017).

64 Cal. Civ. Code § 1786.53, https://leginfo.legislature.ca.gov/faces/codes_displayText.xhtml?lawCode=CIV&division=3.&title=1.6A.&part=4.&chapter=&article=4 (accessed November 2017).

65 "FTC Warns Marketers That Mobile Apps May Violate Fair Credit Reporting Act," FTC, February 7, 2012, https://www.ftc.gov/news-events/press-releases/2012/02/ftc-warns-marketers-mobile-apps-may-violate-fair-credit-reporting (accessed November 2017).

66 "Use of Credit Information in Employment 2015 Legislation," National Conference of State Legislatures, www.ncsl.org/research/financial-services-and-commerce/use-of-credit-information-in-employment-2015-legislation.aspx (accessed November 2017).

67 *See*, e.g., Conn. Gen. Stat. § 31-51tt, https://www.cga.ct.gov/current/pub/titles.htm (accessed November 2017); Md. Code, Lab. & Empl. § 3-711, http://mgaleg.maryland.gov/webmga/frmStatutesText.aspx?article=gle§ion=3-711&ext=html&session=2015RS&tab=subject5 (accessed November 2017); Wash. Rev. Code § 19.182.020, http://apps.leg.wa.gov/rcw/default.aspx?cite=19.182.020 (accessed November 2017).

68 Haw. Rev. Stat. § 378-2.7, http://law.justia.com/codes/hawaii/2010/division1/title21/chapter378/378-2-7 (accessed November 2017).

69 *See*, e.g., Cal. Lab. Code § 1024.5, http://leginfo.legislature.ca.gov/faces/codes_displaySection.xhtml?lawCode=LAB§ionNum=1024 (accessed November 2017); 820 Ill. Comp. Stat. § 70/10, www.ilga.gov/legislation/ilcs/ilcs3.asp?ActID=3277&ChapterID=68 (accessed November 2017).

70 Employee Polygraph Protection Act, 29 U.S.C. §§ 2001-2009.

71 29 U.S.C. § 2001(3), https://www.law.cornell.edu/uscode/text/29/chapter-22 (accessed November 2017).

72 Finkin, *Privacy in Employment Law*, 159–173.

73 *Id*. at 175.

74 *Id*. at 184.

75 *Id*. at 67.

76 Americans with Disabilities Act: Questions and Answers, https://www.ada.gov/employmt.htm (accessed November 2017).

77 *Id*.

78 "Questions and Answers: The Americans with Disabilities Act and Hiring Police Officers," U.S. Department of Justice, https://www.ada.gov/copsq7a.htm (accessed November 2017). For additional discussion on the concept of business necessity, view "Consideration of Arrest and Conviction Records in Employment Decisions Under Title VII of the Civil Rights Act of 1964, EEOC Enforcement Guidelines (2012), https://www.eeoc.gov/laws/guidance/arrest_conviction.cfm (accessed November 2017).

79 49 U.S.C. § 1834 (App.) (aviation), https://www.law.cornell.edu/uscode/text/49/subtitle-VII (accessed November 2017); 45 U.S.C. § 431 (App.) (railroading), https://www.law.cornell.edu/uscode/text/45/431 (accessed November 2017); and 49 U.S.C. § 277 (App.) (trucking), https://www.law.cornell.edu/uscode/text/49 (accessed November 2017).

80 "State Drug Testing Laws," OHS Health and Safety Services, www.ohsinc.com/info/state-drug-testing-laws/ (accessed November 2017).

81 Finkin, *Privacy in Employment Law*, 138–140.

82 *See Lifestyle Discrimination in the Workplace: Your Right to Privacy Under Attack*, ACLU, https://www.aclu.org/other/lifestyle-discrimination-workplace-your-right-privacy-under-attack (accessed October 2017).

83 In certain instances, applicants may be able to raise legal claims against potential employers for discrimination based on lifestyle choices of the applicant. *See* Thom Cope, "Lifestyle Discrimination: Is It Legal?" Mesh Clark Rothschild (2017), https://www.mcrazlaw.com/lifestyle-discrimination-is-it-legal/ (accessed October 2017).

84 *See* Carol Kleiman, "Flight Attendants Win Fight Over Weight Rules," *Chicago Tribune*, March 13, 1991, http://articles.chicagotribune.com/1991-03-13/news/9101230213_1_professional-flight-attendants-weight-rules-american-airlines (accessed October 2017).

85 *See* Thom Cope, "Lifestyle Discrimination: Is It Legal?"

86 Jim Griffin, "Is Obesity a Disability Under the ADA?" Management Association (April 19, 2016), https://www.hrsource.org/maimis/Members/Articles/2016/04/April_19/Is_Obesity_a_Disability_Under_the_ADA_.aspx (accessed October 2017).

87 Amy Langfield, "CVS to Workers: Tell Us How Much You Weigh or It'll Cost You $600 a Year," CNBC (March 20, 2013), https://www.cnbc.com/id/100573805 (accessed October 2017).

88 *See* Thom Cope, "Lifestyle Discrimination" ; Ellie Williams, "Can Employers Discriminate Against Smokers?," Chron, http://work.chron.com/can-employers-discriminate-against-smokers-18507.html (accessed October 2017).

89 It is worth noting that the Affordable Care Act prohibits premium increases because someone is obese. *See* Chelan David, "Understanding the legal ramifications of lifestyle discrimination," *Smart Business*, December 2, 2015, www.sbnonline.com/article/understanding-the-legal-ramifications-of-lifestyle-discrimination/ (accessed October 2017).

90 *See* Donna Ballman, "States with Pro-Employee Laws: No Firing for Legal Off-Duty Activity," *LexisNexis Legal Newsroom Labor and Employment Law*, December 18, 2014, https://www.lexisnexis.com/legalnewsroom/labor-employment/b/labor-employment-top-blogs/archive/2014/12/18/states-with-pro-employee-laws-no-firing-for-legal-off-duty-activity.aspx (accessed October 2017).

91 Frank J. Cavico, "Invasion of Privacy in the Private Employment Sector: Tortious and Ethical Aspects," *Houston Law Review* 30 (1993): 1304–1306.

92 For example, *see* Conn. Gen. Stat. § 31-48d, https://www.cga.ct.gov/current/pub/titles.htm (accessed November 2017); 19 Del. C. § 705, http://delcode.delaware.gov/title19/c007/sc01/index.shtml (accessed November 2017).

93 David Bender, *Bender on Privacy and Data Protection* § 10.02 (Dayton, OH: LexisNexis, 2011).

94 Occupational Injury and Illness Recording and Reporting Requirements, OSHA, 29 C.F.R Parts 1904 and 1952 (January 19, 2001), https://www.osha.gov/pls/oshaweb/owadisp.show_document?p_table=FEDERAL_REGISTER&p_id=16312 (accessed November 2017).

95 *See generally* 16 C.F.R. § 310.5(a), https://www.law.cornell.edu/cfr/text/16/310.5 (accessed November 2017).

96 "You & the Law: Quick, Easy-to-Use Advice on Employment Law 2" National Institute of Business Management (2002).

97 Matthew Finkin,"Information Technology and Workers' Privacy: The United States Law," *Comparative Labor Law and Policy Journal* 23 (2002): 471.

98 E.g., Custis v. DiMaio, 46 F. Supp. 2d 206 (E.D.N.Y. 1999), http://law.justia.com/cases/federal/district-courts/FSupp2/46/206/2488236/ (accessed November 2017).

99 For additional information, view "Fact Sheet 7: Workplace Privacy and Employee Monitoring," Privacy Rights Clearinghouse, https://www.privacyrights.org/workplace-privacy-and-employee-monitoring (accessed November 2017). An overview of the issues involved can be found in Julie Totten's "Balancing Workplace Technology and Privacy in the 21st Century," p. 14-24.

100 "5 ways your business can benefit from security cameras," business.com, www.business.com/business-security-systems/5-ways-your-company-can-benefit-from-security-cameras/ (accessed November 2017).

101 Cal. Lab. Code § 435, www.leginfo.ca.gov/cgi-bin/displaycode?section=lab&group=00001-01000&file=430-435 (accessed November 2017).

102 Mich. Comp. Laws § 750.539d, www.legislature.mi.gov/(S(ivmaxvahnreeqqlysth2seun))/mileg.aspx?page=getObject&objectName=mcl-750-539d (accessed November 2017).

103 *See* Julie Totten, "Balancing Workplace Technology and Privacy in the 21st Century," pp. 9-11.

104 18 U.S.C. § 2511(2)(D), https://www.law.cornell.edu/uscode/text/18/2511 (accessed November 2017).

105 18 U.S.C. § 2511(2)(a)(i), https://www.law.cornell.edu/uscode/text/18/2511 (accessed November 2017).

106 Martha W. Barnett and Scott D. Makar, "In the Ordinary Court of Business: The Legal Limits of Workplace Wiretapping," *Communications and Entertainment Law Journal* 10 (1988): 715.

107 Finkin, *Privacy in Employment Law*, 365-369.

108 Summary of Consent Requirements for Taping Telephone Conversations, aapsonline.org, https://www.aapsonline.org/judicial/telephone.htm (accessed October 2017).

109 18 U.S.C. § 2701(c)(1), https://www.law.cornell.edu/uscode/text/18/2701 (accessed November 2017).

110 18 U.S.C. § 2701(c)(2), https://www.law.cornell.edu/uscode/text/18/2701 (accessed November 2017).

111 Although City of Ontario v. Quon illustrates the point, the case itself is more complex because the employer was a government entity. In such an instance, the Fourth Amendment is implicated when monitoring occurs—which means the government would typically need to seek a warrant to conduct the search. In the case, Quon raised claims pursuant to both the Fourth Amendment and the SCA. *See* W. Scott Blackmer, "Quon: US Supreme Court Rules Against Privacy on Employer-Issued Devices," Info Law Group (June 17, 2010), https://www.infolawgroup.com/2010/06/articles/privacy-law/quon-us-supreme-court-rules-against-privacy-on-employer-issued-devices/ (accessed October 2017); "Are my text messages on an employer-provided phone privacy?" Workplace Privacy and Employee Monitoring, Privacy Rights Clearinghouse, https://www.privacyrights.org/consumer-guides/workplace-privacy-and-employee-monitoring (accessed October 2017).

112 "Monitoring your employees through GPS: What is legal and what are best practices?" *Greensfelder*, www.greensfelder.com/business-risk-management-blog/monitoring-your-employees-through-gps-what-is-legal-and-what-are-best-practices (accessed November 2017).

113 "GPS in the Workplace," *Proskauer Privacy Law Blog*, http://privacylaw.proskauer.com/2012/04/articles/workplace-privacy/gps-in-the-workplace/ (accessed November 2017).

114 Conn. Gen. Stat. § 31-48d, http://law.justia.com/codes/connecticut/2014/title-31/chapter-560/section-31-94 (accessed November 2017).

115 Cal. Pen. Code § 637.7, http://codes.findlaw.com/ca/penal-code/pen-sect-637-7.html (accessed November 2017).

116 "Blurred Boundaries: Social Media Privacy and the Twenty-First-Century Employee," *American Business Law Journal*, https://www.researchgate.net/profile/Patricia_Abril/publication/228311105_Blurred_Boundaries_Social_Media_Privacy_and_the_Twenty-First-Century_Employee/links/53d7ad290cf2e38c632dde93.pdf (accessed November 2017).

117 Several recent decisions by the NLRB have found that employees' speech is protected when they use social media to complain about managers, coworkers, or the companies that employ them.

"Even if it enrages your boss, social net speech is protected," *New York Times* (2013),www.nytimes.com/2013/01/22/technology/employers-social-media-policies-come-under-regulatory-scrutiny.html?_r=1&pagewanted=all&pagewanted=print (accessed November 2017).

118 *See* Julie Totten, "Balancing Workplace Technology and Privacy in the 21st Century," pp. 42-43.

119 In 2006, Hewlett Packard's chairman Patricia Dunn authorized the use of false pretenses to investigate press leaks originating from the board of directors, a practice termed "pretexting." The investigative tactics were widely condemned, triggering congressional hearings and both federal and state felony charges against Dunn and others. For a detailed overview of the case, *see* Miriam Hechler Baer, "Corporate Policing and Corporate Governance: What Can We Learn from Hewlett-Packard's Pretexting Scandal?" *University of Cincinnati Law Review* 77: 523 (2008).

120 "Maryland passes nation's first social media privacy protection bill," ACLU, https://www.aclu.org/blog/maryland-passes-nations-first-social-media-privacy-protection-bill (accessed November 2017).

121 "State Social Media Privacy Laws," National Conference of State Legislatures, www.ncsl.org/research/telecommunications-and-information-technology/state-laws-prohibiting-access-to-social-media-usernames-and-passwords.aspx (accessed October 2017).

122 "Questions Remain About Social Media Privacy Rights During Workplace Investigation," *Employment Law Outlook*, www.laborandemploymentlawcounsel.com/2015/10/social-media-privacy-rights-during-workplace-investigations/ (accessed November 2017).

123 "Fact Sheet 40: Bring Your Own Device … at Your Own Risk," Privacy Rights Clearinghouse, https://www.privacyrights.org/bring-your-own-device-risks (accessed November 2017).

124 *See* Julie Totten, "Balancing Workplace Technology and Privacy in the 21st Century," pp. 46-50, https://www.americanbar.org/content/dam/aba/events/labor_law/2017/03/err/papers/balancing_workplace_technology.authcheckdam.pdf (accessed October 2017).

125 The topics related to civil litigation and governments investigations are further discussed in Chapter 12.

126 Nate Lord, "What is Data Loss Prevention (DLP)? A Definition of Data Loss Prevention," *Data Insider*, Digital Guardian, July 27, 2017, https://digitalguardian.com/blog/what-data-loss-prevention-dlp-definition-data-loss-prevention (accessed October 2017).

127 Stephen Holland and Christopher Stevens, "Data Loss Prevention: A Holistic Approach Worth Adopting," *The Privacy Advisor*, IAPP (November 25, 2014), https://iapp.org/news/a/data-loss-prevention-a-holistic-approach-worth-adopting/ (accessed October 2017).

128 Vadim Zdor, "DLP vs. Privacy Laws," *InfoWatch*, September 14, 2011, https://infowatch.com/blog/2328.

129 Advisory Opinion to Vail (04-05-99), https://www.ftc.gov/policy/advisory-opinions/advisory-opinion-vail-04-05-99 (accessed November 2017).

130 Patricia A. Kotze and Eric H. Joss, *Breathing Easier Over Workplace Misconduct*, May 18, 2015, https://www.diversifiedriskmanagement.com/articles/workplace-misconduct./ (accessed November 2017).

131 *Id.*

132 *Id.*

133 *Id.*

134 Finkin, *Privacy in Employment Law*, 267–295.

CHAPTER 12

Privacy Issues in Civil Litigation and Government Investigations

This chapter examines privacy issues that arise when a company is responding to civil litigation and government investigations. Before trial, a company may receive civil "discovery" requests (requests for information by each party in a lawsuit). In the course of a law enforcement or national security investigation, an organization may face requests or orders to produce information. At a civil or criminal trial, the tradition of public records and open courtrooms in the United States means that additional personal information may be revealed.

Historically, outside counsel and in-house lawyers often played the predominant role in determining what personal information would be disclosed in the course of investigations or litigation. Disclosures in litigation were often undertaken manually, after lawyers, paralegals, or other individuals read through document files to determine what had to be produced.

Today, disclosures in investigations and litigation are more likely to be made through cooperative efforts of lawyers with a company's privacy and information technology professionals. Companies that hold large amounts of personal information often have information management plans that set policies for how and when disclosures will occur. Those plans are created through collaborative efforts that include experts on relevant privacy requirements and implementation through automated IT systems. To avoid data breaches, authorization may be required by specific, responsible people in the organization. To ensure implementation of company policies, audit trails are often in place concerning disclosures of sensitive information to third parties, including for investigation and litigation purposes. With this convergence of professionals for privacy, law and IT, organizations thus often need a more systematic approach to responding to investigations and litigation.

This chapter begins with an outline of how disclosures may be required, permitted or forbidden by law. Organizations sometimes are required by law either to disclose or not to disclose personal information. In other situations, the organization faces a choice about whether and how to make such disclosures. The chapter next turns to civil litigation. The U.S. tradition of public records in litigation is paired today with 2007 revisions to the Federal Rules of Civil Procedure, under which lawyers are required to redact certain sensitive personal information before it goes into court files. Since 2006, federal civil litigation has operated under the "e-discovery" rules, which require automated and large-scale production of emails and other corporate documents during the discovery process prior to trial. These large volumes of disclosure raise important privacy issues, illustrating the need for privacy professionals to work closely with lawyers and IT professionals.

The chapter then turns to privacy issues in law enforcement investigations. Protecting privacy is a major theme of the Fourth Amendment to the U.S. Constitution, which prohibits the government from making unreasonable searches and seizures. The Fourth Amendment sets limits on both physical searches and searches for personal information through wiretaps and access to company records. Fourth Amendment principles have also informed a number of statutes, including wiretap laws, the Electronic Communications Privacy Act, the Right to Financial Privacy Act (applying to financial institutions), and the Privacy Protection Act (applying to reporters and media companies). Privacy professionals need to be aware of these statutes, as a company can face legal consequences, depending on the context, for turning over either too much or too little information.

The chapter concludes with an examination of privacy issues and national security investigations in the post-Snowden era. Under the Foreign Intelligence Surveillance Act of 1978 (FISA), telephone companies and other communications providers can face especially complex rules about when and in what way they are permitted or required to provide information to the government. For both the law enforcement and national security discussions in this chapter, the goal is not to provide enough detail to answer the questions of these specialized practitioners. The goal instead is to set forth the basic principles and specific provisions that apply to a wide range of organizations, as well as provide insight into the reforms that were put in place after the Snowden leaks.

12.1 Disclosures Required, Permitted or Forbidden by Law

For investigations and litigation, the law can be complex about when information must be disclosed, when the organization has a choice about whether to disclose, and when the organization is prohibited from disclosing. Sometimes the same statute requires production of information in some circumstances, such as when a judge issues a court order, but prohibits production of the same information in other circumstances, such as when no court order exists.

12.1.1 Disclosures Required by Law

Certain U.S. laws require disclosure of personal information held by an organization. Chapter 8, "Financial Privacy," discussed the Bank Secrecy Act and related reporting requirements designed to reduce money laundering. Other examples of required disclosure:

- The U.S. Food and Drug Administration (FDA) requires health professionals and drug manufacturers to report serious adverse events, product problems or medication errors suspected to be associated with the use of an FDA-regulated drug, biologic, device or dietary supplement under the Food, Drug and Cosmetic Act.[1]
- The U.S. Department of Labor's Occupational Health and Safety Administration (OSHA) requires compilation and reporting of information about certain workplace injuries and illnesses.[2]
- Many states require reporting of certain types of injuries and medical conditions, such as abuse, gunshot wounds, immunization records or specific contagious diseases. The Health Insurance Portability and Accountability Act (HIPAA) permits disclosure of protected health information where disclosure is required by law.[3]

Outside of these regulatory systems, records sometimes must be disclosed during an investigation or in the course of litigation. The discussion in this chapter of e-discovery will describe how parties to civil litigation in the United States are routinely required to produce emails, documents and other company records containing substantial personal information. In litigation, discovery, which essentially means information disclosed to another party in a lawsuit before trial, is governed by the rules of civil and criminal procedure, as overseen by state and federal judges.

Companies with information relevant to a government investigation or in civil litigation may receive a subpoena, which is an instruction to produce a witness or records. For instance, Federal Rule of Civil Procedure 45 says that a subpoena must:

1. State the court from which it is issued
2. State the title of the action and its civil-action number
3. Command each person to whom it is directed to do the following at a specific time and place: attend and testify; produce designated documents, electronically stored information or tangible things in that person's possession, custody or control; or permit the inspection of premises

4. Set out the text of the rules describing a person's right to challenge or modify the subpoena

The party seeking information must "serve" the subpoena (deliver it to the subject in a legally sufficient way), to put that person on notice of the obligation to respond and of the recipient's right to seek to quash or modify the subpoena. The rule states: The issuing court "may hold in contempt a person who, having been served, fails without adequate excuse to obey the subpoena."[4] Contempt of court can result in fines or imprisonment.

Differing legal standards may, of course, apply to civil (private) litigation and to government investigations, and standards also vary depending on the types of records sought. For instance, as discussed further below, law enforcement can get phone numbers called and similar information under a pen register order. A judge issues that type of order under the relatively easy-to-meet standard that the information "is relevant to an ongoing investigation."[5] The stored content of records may be accessed under court orders defined by 18 U.S.C. § 2703(d), which require the government to provide a judge with "specific and articulable facts showing that there are reasonable grounds" to believe communications are relevant to a criminal investigation.[6] One step stricter is the traditional search warrant issued by a judge or magistrate under the Fourth Amendment to the U.S. Constitution, which requires showing that there is probable cause that a crime has been, is, or will be committed. Even stricter is the standard for a telephone wiretap, which has the requirements of a probable cause warrant as well as other requirements, such as that alternative means of getting the evidence have been exhausted.[7] This range of standards is intended to provide more protection for more sensitive information—a list of phone numbers called is easier to get than permission to listen to an entire telephone conversation.

12.1.2 Disclosures Permitted by Law

For some categories of information, an organization is permitted, but not required, to disclose personal information. HIPAA itself, for instance, requires very few disclosures. The Privacy Rule requires covered entities to disclose protected health information (PHI) only to the individual to whom it pertains[8] and to the U.S. Department of Health and Human Services (HHS) in the course of an enforcement action.[9] It permits (but does not require) companies to disclose PHI when required to do so by another applicable law, such as the state laws that require reporting of medical information. HIPAA also permits covered entities to disclose PHI for reasons including public health, law enforcement and national security.

Another example is the "computer trespasser" exception (sometimes called the "hacker trespasser" exception) created by Section 217 of the USA PATRIOT Act.[10] In general, a law enforcement officer needs to have a court order or some other lawful basis to intercept wire or electronic communications. As discussed later in the chapter, the owner or operator of a computer system can face penalties under the Electronic Communication Privacy Act for providing access to law enforcement without following legally mandated procedures. Section 217 of the USA PATRIOT Act permits, but does not require, the owner or operator of a computer system to provide such access in defined circumstances. For computer trespassers,[11] law enforcement can now perform interceptions if:

1. The owner or operator of the protected computer authorizes the interception of the computer trespasser's communications on the protected computer
2. The person acting under color of law (in an official capacity) is lawfully engaged in an investigation
3. The person acting under color of law has reasonable grounds to believe that the contents of the computer trespasser's communications will be relevant to the investigation
4. Such interception does not acquire communications other than those transmitted[12]

12.1.3 Disclosures Forbidden by Law

Many of the privacy laws discussed in this book forbid disclosures of categories of personal information to categories of recipients. These laws often use either an opt-in or an opt-out requirement to help accomplish their restrictions.[13] For instance, HIPAA and the Children's Online Privacy Protection Rule (COPPA) forbid disclosures of covered information to third parties, unless there is opt-in consent or a different exception applies. The Gramm-Leach-Bliley Act (GLBA) forbids disclosures to third parties if the individual has opted out. Many websites of companies not covered by GLBA similarly provide an opt-out, and disclosures in violation of such promises can trigger Section 5 enforcement under the FTC Act.

In the context of investigations and litigation, evidentiary "privileges" can also prohibit disclosure. These privileges are generally defined under state law.[14] One example is the attorney-client privilege, which means that an attorney cannot be compelled to testify or produce records about a client concerning matters within the scope of the representation. As with other privacy rules, there can be exceptions to the attorney-client privilege, such as client consent or to prevent imminent physical harm to another person. Other common evidentiary privileges include doctor-patient, priest-penitent and spousal privilege. Where these apply, a doctor, member of the clergy or spouse cannot be compelled to testify about the other party, absent consent or some other exception. Nationally, a person accused of a crime in state or federal court can assert the privilege against self-incrimination under the Fifth Amendment to the U.S. Constitution.

12.2 Privacy and Civil Litigation

A large amount of personal information may be disclosed to parties in the course of civil litigation. Although the United States has a strong tradition of public access to court records, privacy concerns are also recognized. Courts can issue protective orders to prohibit disclosure of personal information revealed in litigation, and attorneys increasingly are required to redact Social Security numbers and other sensitive information when filing documents with the courts. The systematic management of personal information has also become more prominent since the 2006 adoption of the e-discovery rules, which often require civil litigants to turn over large volumes of a company's electronic records in litigation.

12.2.1 Public Access to Court Records, Protective Orders and Required Redaction

The U.S. has a strong tradition of public access to government records, including under the federal Freedom of Information Act (FOIA) and state open records laws. States and localities often provide access to a wide range of public records, including birth and death records, professional and business licenses, real estate ownership and appraisal records, voter registration records and many more. The activities of courts historically have also been public records. Criminal and civil trials in the United States are almost always open for the public to attend. Historically, people could also go to the local courthouse and read the materials submitted to the court, including documents and other exhibits introduced at trial. With the growth of the Internet, court systems began to consider putting their records online for beneficial reasons such as providing transparency in government and reducing the cost of storing and accessing records.

Placing court records on the Internet, however, also raised privacy issues. Paper records stored in local courthouses provided practical obscurity for most of the information, because of the expense and difficulty of searching the records. Online, searchable public records greatly reduced this obscurity. In 2000, the federal bankruptcy courts proposed placing their records online, including Social Security numbers and the details of the person's financial status, including bank account numbers and the amount in each account. Internet publication of these details raised the risk that these accounts would be the target of identity fraud. The federal government issued a report on the privacy issues,[15] and the bankruptcy court rules were amended to protect Social Security numbers and privacy.[16] In recent years, the Administrative Office of U.S. Courts and the Center for Legal and Court Technology have held an annual conference in Williamsburg, Virginia, with extensive documentation of how state and federal courts address the issues of privacy and public access to court records.[17] Certain categories of records often receive greater protection, including juvenile, financial and medical records.

One response to public access to court records has been for litigants to seek protective orders for personal information. With a protective order, a judge determines what information should not be made public and what conditions apply to those who may access the protected information. Rule 26(c) of the Federal Rules of Civil Procedure states that a party may seek a protective order providing that confidential information may not be revealed or must be revealed in a particular way—such as "attorney's eyes only"—during litigation. The moving party must demonstrate good cause, and a court will apply a three-part test in deciding whether to grant the request. First, the resisting party must show the information to be confidential. Second, the requesting party must show that the information is relevant and necessary to the case. Third, the court must weigh the harm of disclosure against the need for the information.[18]

The HIPAA Privacy Rule, similarly, discusses the standards for a "qualified protective order" (QPO), which applies in state courts that are not covered by the Federal Rules of Civil Procedure. A QPO prohibits the parties from using or disclosing the protected health information for any purpose other than the litigation or proceeding for which such information was requested. It also requires the return to the covered entity or destruction of the protected health information (including copies) at the end of the litigation.[19] If a QPO is in place, a covered entity complies with privacy requirements for disclosure in litigation or administrative proceedings.

More generally, court rules today require redaction of certain personal information by the litigants themselves. **Redaction** is the practice of identifying and removing or blocking information from documents being produced pursuant to a discovery request or as evidence in a court proceeding. One important example is the 2007 adoption of Rule 5.2 of the Federal Rules of Civil Procedure, "Privacy Protection for Filings Made with the Court." The rule applies to both paper and electronic filings and to both parties and nonparties filing documents. Specifically, attorneys are required to redact documents so that no more than the following information is included in court filings:

1. The last four digits of the Social Security number and taxpayer-identification number
2. The year of the individual's birth
3. If the individual is a minor, only the minor's initials
4. The last four digits of the financial account number[20]

Certain exemptions may apply, and parties may request that filings be made under seal without redaction when appropriate. In cases where additional protection may be necessary, parties can seek protective orders. If granted, the protective order may require additional redaction or may restrict electronic access to the court filings.[21] Enforcement and penalties apply as for other violations of court rules.[22]

Rule 49.1 of the Federal Criminal Rules of Procedure and Rule 9037 of the Federal Rules of Bankruptcy Procedure[23] contain similar redaction requirements. In criminal proceedings, city and state of the home address are a fifth category requiring redaction, so that the precise home address is not revealed.[24]

Federal district courts often have supplementary redaction or privacy requirements that apply in their court proceedings. Similarly, state and local courts have increasingly adopted redaction requirements. Attorneys and privacy professionals thus should be mindful of the privacy procedure rules that may apply depending on where the litigation actually takes place.

12.2.2 Electronic Discovery

Prior to trial, the parties usually engage in discovery. In discovery, the information typically is exchanged with the other party or parties and their attorneys. In doing so, as just discussed, there may be confidentiality protections such as protective orders and redaction requirements. Information exchanged in discovery also raises at least the possibility that it will be disclosed more broadly, such as in a trial or public court filing, or because those who receive the information in discovery may disclose it to others.

Since the 2006 revisions to the Federal Rules of Civil Procedure, electronically stored information (ESI) has become an increasingly large focus of pretrial discovery in U.S. litigation.[25] The discovery of ESI, generally known as e-discovery, has become an important subdiscipline in law and technology. E-discovery implicates both domestic privacy concerns and issues arising in transborder data flows.

Managing e-discovery and privacy begins with a well-managed **data retention program**. In designing a retention policy, it should be remembered that ESI takes not only obvious forms such as email or word processing documents, but can also manifest itself as databases, web pages, server logs, instant messaging transcripts, voicemail systems, social networking records, thumb drives or even the microSD cards found in smartphones. An important source of standards and best practices for managing electronic discovery compliance through data retention policies is the Sedona Conference.[26] Regarding email retention, the Sedona Conference offers four key guidelines:

1. Email retention policies should be administered by interdisciplinary teams composed of participants across a diverse array of business units
2. Such teams should continually develop their understanding of the policies and practices in place and identify the gaps between policy and practice
3. Interdisciplinary teams should reach consensus as to policies, while looking to industry standards
4. Technical solutions should meet and parallel the functional requirements of the organization

Database design should also be considered when addressing a company's retention policies. When done in good faith, data that is "transitory in nature, not routinely created or maintained by [d]efendants for their business purposes, and requiring of additional steps to retrieve and store," may be considered outside the duty of preservation.[27] Retention policies should also consider employee hard drives. While it may be an accepted practice to wipe and reimage personal computers after an employee is terminated so that the computer can be provided to a new employee, "in order to take advantage of the good faith exception [to discovery obligations], a party needs to act affirmatively to prevent the system from destroying or altering information, even if such destruction would occur in the regular course of business."[28] One solution to this problem is to collect forensic images of such devices prior to reassignment.

Initial problems with invasion of privacy concerns related to such retention can be countered by clearly articulating a usage policy for employees. For example, by discouraging employees from using their company email accounts for personal communications, a company can reduce the future risk of handing over sensitive or embarrassing information when complying with a discovery request. Similarly, placing limits on the permitted uses of company computers may aid in preventing later forensic discovery of hard drives from revealing private information about employees.

Conversely, employees should be discouraged from conducting company business on personal devices to prevent the subsequent risk of an invasion of privacy if an employer needs to examine such devices.[29]

While these best practices are widely accepted, it should be noted that where discovery obligations are in direct conflict with business practices, the discovery obligations will likely prevail. When a court finds conflict between a corporate retention policy and a discovery request, the court will likely apply a three-factor test: (1) a retention policy should be reasonable considering the facts of the situation, (2) courts may consider similar complaints against the organization and (3) courts may evaluate whether the organization instituted the policy in bad faith.[30] Finally, in regard to retention policies, it must be remembered that even a reasonable policy may need to be suspended in the face of a litigation hold, which exists when the company is on notice of discovery because litigation is already under way.[31]

U.S. sectoral laws such as HIPAA and GLBA create some tension between broad pretrial discovery powers and privacy protections. Generally, however, these laws exist in harmony with discovery obligations. For example, the HIPAA Privacy Regulation specifically addresses when protected health information may be disclosed during discovery. First, a covered entity may disclose PHI if the subject of those records authorizes their release.[32] Second, absent a release, a covered entity may release PHI subject to a court order.[33] Third, a covered entity may disclose PHI subject to a discovery request if satisfactory assurances are provided. An assurance is satisfactory under HIPAA if the parties seeking the request for information have agreed to a qualified protective order and have submitted it to the court, or if the party seeking the information has requested a qualified protective order from the court.[34] A qualified protective order requires both that the parties are prohibited from using or disclosing the PHI for any purpose other than the litigation and that the PHI will be returned or destroyed at the end of the litigation.[35]

Similarly, under GLBA, a financial institution may disclose otherwise protected information "to comply with federal, state, or local laws, rules, and other applicable legal requirements; to comply with a properly authorized civil, criminal, or regulatory investigation or subpoena or summons by federal, state, or local authorities; or to respond to judicial process or government regulatory authorities having jurisdiction over the financial institution for examination, compliance, or other purposes as authorized by law."[36] Federal courts have been willing to read this clause to encompass civil discovery requests, although protective orders should still be obtained by those disclosing the information.[37]

The issue of **transborder data flows** creates a more complicated situation. When engaged in pretrial discovery in U.S. courts, parties can be caught between conflicting demands. On the one hand, they must comply with U.S. discovery rules that expressly recognize the importance of broad preservation, collection and production. The rules therefore generally require the disclosure of all information relevant to the claims or defenses in a case that are in a party's possession, custody or control—and this extends to information globally. On the other hand, parties may also face compliance obligations under foreign laws that place an emphasis of the protection of personal data and recognize privacy as a fundamental right. For instance, the European Union (EU) General Data Protection Regulation (GDPR)[38] makes e-discovery with European nations subject to even more restrictions.[39] Consequently, a conflict can arise between a U.S. requirement to produce documents and another country's laws, which may prohibit transfer of personal information out of that country and/or prohibit disclosure to third parties without the data subject's consent.[40]

Courts have taken different approaches to resolving this conflict. Some courts have sought to resolve this tension by requiring production by those parties that sought to take advantage of U.S. jurisdiction.[41] Other courts, however, have extended data production requirements even to parties that did not seek the benefit of U.S. courts, stating "[i]t is well settled that [foreign] statutes do not deprive an American court of the power to order a party subject to its jurisdiction to produce evidence even though the act of production may violate that statute."[42] Another approach has been to focus on the nature or type of the documents at issue, such as by requiring the foreign parties to prepare a privacy log describing the documents, without disclosing the contents of the documents, so that the court could differentiate among documents.[43] Balancing broad discovery demands with foreign privacy restrictions remains a challenging issue in the United States for many organizations, with no simple resolution thus far of the legal conflicts.

The production of transborder data may also be avoided by invoking the Hague Convention on the Taking of Evidence.[44] Under the treaty, the party seeking to displace the Federal Rules of Civil Procedure bears the burden of demonstrating that it is more appropriate to use the Hague Convention and must establish that the foreign law prohibits the discovery sought. Such prohibitions may be established by expert testimony. Aerospaciale v. S.D. of Iowa outlines the factors that an American court may use to reconcile the conflict.[45] These factors include:[46]

1. The importance of the documents or data to the litigation at hand
2. The specificity of the request

3. Whether the information originated in the United States
4. The availability of alternative means of securing the information
5. The extent to which the important interests of the U.S. and the foreign state would be undermined by an adverse ruling

The fifth factor is often referred to as being the most important. For example, when victims of a terrorist attack sued a British bank for aiding and abetting a terrorist organization, British bank secrecy laws did not preempt the discovery request because the information was central to the case and the disclosure would advance both American and British interests in combatting terrorism.[47] Courts have also been willing to look to additional factors, such as the good faith of the party resisting compliance, in applying such a test. Obtaining evidence through the Hague Convention is far more expensive and time-consuming that typical discovery requests under the Federal Rules; it is often a means of last resort for U.S. litigators with no other recourse for obtaining the necessary evidence.

Prior to the GDPR, an alternative source of guidance was the Article 29 Working Party, which produced a working paper that explored the relationship between the Data Protection Directive and pretrial discovery in transborder lawsuits.[48] Essentially, the processing of data for discovery purposes was done pursuant to a legitimate purpose under Article 7 of the Directive or subject to contractual clauses under Article 26.

Once data has been culled for e-discovery, preservation and transport present final considerations. Data may either be "preserved in place" by maintaining it in its native repository,[49] or it may be preserved in a separate form. For transfer, data should be encrypted, and the key transferred by a secure second method of transport. If shipped as physical media (such as a hard drive or optical media), it should be transported in a manner that preserves an audit trail. Alternatively, data may be transferred by using a secure connection, such as secure file transfer protocol (SFTP). Organizations producing thousands of pages of documents in discovery will often need a plan to address sensitive personal information, including a process for identifying and redacting or withholding such information where possible, maintaining confidentiality under a protective order where it must be disclosed, and seeking to "claw back" or otherwise remediate inadvertent disclosures of such information.

12.3 Law Enforcement and the Role of Privacy Professionals

Along with civil litigation, a company can face requests to provide personal information in connection with criminal investigations and litigation. The discussion here begins with an introduction to Fourth Amendment limits on law enforcement searches. Fourth Amendment cases have articulated some of the most fundamental concepts used by privacy lawyers and other privacy experts in the United States, including the "reasonable expectation of privacy" test developed in the context of government wiretaps.[50] The discussion then moves to other statutes that can apply to criminal investigations, including HIPAA, the Electronic Communications Privacy Act (ECPA), the Stored Communications Act (SCA), the Right to Financial Privacy Act and the Privacy Protection Act.

This chapter does not attempt to provide the many details that prosecutors and criminal defense lawyers need to know about the handling of personal information in criminal litigation. Nor does it go into the complex details of ECPA and the SCA as those laws apply to communications providers such as telephone companies and email services. Instead, the focus is on general principles and issues that can arise in a wide range of companies.

12.3.1 Fourth Amendment Limits on Law Enforcement Searches

The Fourth Amendment to the Constitution provides: "The right of the people to be secure in their persons, houses, papers, and effects, against unreasonable searches and seizures, shall not be violated, and no warrants shall issue, but upon probable cause, supported by oath or affirmation, and particularly describing the place to be searched."

The Fourth Amendment's limits on government power stem in part from objections to "general warrants" used by the British king's customs inspectors before the American Revolution. Officers of the Crown could get one general warrant and search all the houses in a neighborhood or town when looking for contraband goods. At the most basic level, the Fourth Amendment authorizes reasonable government searches while setting limits on their scope and how they are issued. The U.S. Supreme Court has stated: "The overriding function of the Fourth Amendment is to protect personal privacy and dignity against unwarranted intrusion by the State."[51]

The Fourth Amendment provides a ban against "unreasonable searches and seizures" by the government. For search warrants, the government must show "probable cause" that a crime has been, is or is likely to be committed. Search warrants must be supported by specific testimony, often provided by a police officer. A neutral magistrate (judge) approves the search warrant. They cannot be general warrants, but instead must describe the place to be searched with particularity.

Evidence gathered by the government in violation of the Fourth Amendment is generally subject to what is called the "exclusionary rule," meaning that the evidence can be excluded from the criminal trial. The exclusionary rule creates a powerful incentive for criminal defendants to seek to show that the government has violated the Fourth Amendment. Consequently, state and federal courts have issued an enormous number of judicial decisions interpreting the Fourth Amendment, and the case law is notably complex.

Company privacy professionals are not likely to encounter the type of search warrant that provides the police physical entry to a house, automobile or other private space. The legal rules are likely to be more important when the government seeks to conduct surveillance in connection with a company's facilities. For instance, the government might conduct wiretaps using the facilities of a telephone company or email service. In addition, and increasingly over time, the government may seek to gain access to company databases containing personal information about customers, employees, and others.

Telephone wiretap law has been important to the last century of Fourth Amendment jurisprudence. In the 1928 case of Olmstead v. United States, a majority of the Supreme Court held that no warrant was required for wiretaps conducted on telephone company wires outside of the suspect's building.[52] The majority emphasized that the purpose of the Fourth Amendment was to protect the home and other private spaces. In one of the most famous statements about privacy, Justice Louis Brandeis argued in dissent that new technologies meant that the Fourth Amendment must have a "capacity of adaptation to a changing world." He said: "The makers of our Constitution . . . conferred, as against the government, the right to be let alone—the most comprehensive of rights and the right most valued by civilized men. To protect that right, every unjustifiable intrusion by the government upon the privacy of the individual, whatever the means employed, must be deemed a violation of the Fourth Amendment."

The Supreme Court essentially overruled Olmstead in the 1967 case of Katz v. United States.[53] The majority stated: "What a person knowingly exposes to the public, even in his own home or office, is not a subject of Fourth Amendment protection. But what he seeks to preserve as private, even in an area accessible to the public, may be constitutionally protected." The court found that a warrant was needed for a police bug in a restaurant, placed to hear the calls behind the closed doors of a phone booth.

Katz is best remembered today for the widely cited "reasonable expectation of privacy" test. In a concurring opinion, Justice John Marshall Harlan stated: "There is a twofold requirement, first that a person have exhibited an actual (subjective) expectation of privacy and, second, that the expectation be one that society is prepared to recognize as 'reasonable.'"

In practice, important exceptions exist to the requirement of a warrant where a reasonable expectation of privacy exists. The "in public" and "third-party" exceptions are especially important to privacy professionals. Katz itself said that what a person knowingly exposes to the public is not protected by the Fourth Amendment. Police thus have broad discretion to follow a suspect down the street or take advantage of other information that is in plain view. The Supreme Court has also held that information that a person puts into the hand of someone else—a "third party"—is not protected by the Fourth Amendment. For instance, the court has held that the Fourth Amendment does not require a warrant for the police to get a person's checking account records or the list of phone numbers a person has called.[54] The Court has stated that the individual consented to letting the bank or phone company have that information, so the companies can lawfully turn the information over to the government without a search warrant. The third-party doctrine has been especially important in connection with company privacy practices—companies are generally permitted under the Constitution to turn over customer and employee records to the government (although statutory and other legal limits may apply).

In the 2012 case of United States v. Jones, the Supreme Court signaled important changes to the "in public" and third-party exceptions. The court held unanimously that a warrant was needed when the police placed a Global Positioning System (GPS) device on a car and tracked its location for over a month. The majority decision emphasized that the police had trespassed onto the car when they physically attached the GPS device. Four of the nine justices, however, would have held that a search occurred even without the physical attachment, and even for movements that took place entirely in public. A fifth justice seemed to indicate sympathy for this constitutional limit on surveillance of "in public" activities, and also stated that the time had come to reexamine the third-party doctrine.[55]

The 2014 case of Riley v. California was an important decision where the Supreme Court unanimously held that the contents of a cell phone cannot be searched unless law enforcement officers first obtain a search warrant.[56] The justices ruled that the data on a cell phone was quantitatively (the amount of data) and qualitatively (the kind of data) different than the contents that would normally be found in a physical container, which was the analogy the government had proposed to the court. As to the quantity of data, the Court noted the immense storage capacity of cell phones as well as the ability to link to remote storage. With regard to the quality of data, the Court opined that Internet searches can reveal a person's interests, and location information can pinpoint an individual's movement over time.[57]

These two unanimous cases requiring search warrants suggest that the Supreme Court is seeking to update Fourth Amendment doctrine to adapt to changing technology and may be moving to limit the application of the third-party doctrine as it relates to digital data.[58]

12.3.2 Statutes That Go Beyond Fourth Amendment Protections

A number of federal statutes affect law enforcement access to personal information. Some of the statutes placed additional requirements on law enforcement after the Supreme Court held that the Constitution did not require search warrants in the relevant circumstances. For instance, the Right to Financial Privacy Act of 1978[59] was passed after the Supreme Court held that the Fourth Amendment did not apply to checking accounts, and the Electronic Communications Privacy Act of 1986[60] was passed after the Court held that it did not apply to telephone numbers called. In these instances, Congress has required some legal process for law enforcement to access the records, but the requirements are not as strict as a probable cause warrant approved by a neutral magistrate. These two statutes are examples of disclosure to law enforcement that is prohibited unless the statutory requirements are met.

Some law enforcement provisions permit, but do not require, companies to release personal information to law enforcement. HIPAA illustrates the sometimes-complex trade-offs between protecting confidentiality and providing information for law enforcement purposes. The general rule in HIPAA is that protected health information may be disclosed to third parties, including law enforcement, only with opt-in consent from the patient. Unauthorized disclosures can lead to enforcement by HHS. Section 512(f), however, goes into considerable detail about precisely when disclosure to law enforcement is permitted.[61] Disclosure is permitted pursuant to a court order or grand jury subpoena, or through an administrative request if three criteria are met:

1. The information sought is relevant and material to a legitimate law enforcement inquiry
2. The request is specific and limited in scope to the extent reasonably practicable in light of the purpose for which the information is sought
3. De-identified information could not reasonably be used

Disclosure is also permitted in other specific instances, such as about a crime on the premises, about decedents in connection with a suspected crime, in emergencies, and about victims of a crime even in the absence of patient consent if a multifactor test is met. Limited information may in some instances also be released for identification and location purposes.

As discussed at the beginning of the chapter, other statutes require the release of personal information to law enforcement. Companies thus can face multiple, potentially conflicting laws about when and how to disclose to law enforcement. HIPAA addresses this problem by saying that disclosure is permitted when it is "required by law," even if a disclosure does not otherwise fit within the law enforcement or other exception.[62]

12.3.3 The Wiretap Act, Electronic Communications Privacy Act and Stored Communications Act

From strictest to most permissive, federal law has different rules for (1) telephone monitoring and other tracking of oral communications; (2) privacy of electronic communications and (3) video surveillance, for which there is little applicable law. Federal law is also generally stricter for real-time interception of a communication, as contrasted with retrieval of a stored record. In each area, states may have statutes that apply stricter rules. Furthermore, monitoring that is offensive to a reasonable person can give rise to claims under state invasion of privacy or other common-law claims.

12.3.3.1 Intercepting Communications

Federal law is generally strict in prohibiting wiretaps of telephone calls. The law today derives from Title III of a 1968 anticrime law, and its rules are thus often called Title III requirements.[63] The law applies to "wire communications," which includes a phone call or other aural communication made through a network. The law also applies to "oral communications," such as hidden bugs or microphones, and defined as "any oral communication uttered by a person exhibiting an expectation that such communication is not subject to interception under circumstances justifying such expectation."[64] ECPA extended the ban on interception to "electronic communications," which essentially are communications, including emails, that are not wire or oral communications.[65] The exact rules for wire, oral and electronic communications vary. Unless an exception applies, however, interception of these communications is a criminal offense and provides a private right of action.

The prohibition on interception has a number of exceptions, each of which may have its own nuances requiring an expert to analyze. Under federal law, interception is permitted if a person is the party to the call or if one of the parties has given consent.[66]

A number of states, however, have the stricter rule that all of the parties to the call must consent.[67] This all-party consent requirement is why customers often hear a message giving notice that a call is being recorded for quality assurance or other purposes.

A second exception relevant to many companies concerns interception done in the ordinary course of business.[68] This exception can apply where the device used for the interception is "furnished to the subscriber or user by a provider of wire or electronic communication service in the ordinary course of its business."[69] This language, for instance, supports the ability to intercept for an employer who provides the communication service, such as the company telephone or email service. To qualify for the exception, the interception itself must also be in the normal course of the user's business.[70] Normal course of business here would apply to routine monitoring in a call center or scanning of company emails for viruses or other malware. By contrast, the employer listening to an employee's purely personal call would risk running afoul of the wiretap laws. Courts have split on how broadly to define "ordinary course of business,"[71] which is a reason that many employers rely instead on the consent exception for interception of telephone calls. Note that the federal law is not preemptive, so if an organization is monitoring or recording calls, it runs the risk of violating the stricter law in the "all-party consent" states mentioned above—it should not rely on any of these exceptions outside the specific state.[72]

12.3.3.2 Stored Communications

The SCA was enacted as part of ECPA in 1986.[73] It creates a general prohibition against the unauthorized acquisition, alteration or blocking of electronic communications while in electronic storage in a facility through which an electronic communications service is provided. As for interceptions, violations can lead to criminal penalties or a civil lawsuit, so an expert in the SCA should generally be consulted before turning over such records in a law enforcement investigation. For monitoring within a company, the exceptions are simpler than for interceptions. The SCA has an exception for conduct authorized "by the person or entity providing a wire or electronic communications service," which will often be the company.[74] It also has an exception for conduct authorized "by a user of that service with respect to a communication of or intended for that use."[75] In general, legal limits on interceptions are stricter than for access to stored records.

It should also be noted that ECPA does not preempt stricter state privacy protections, and that state laws may protect email communications. For example, Delaware law prohibits employers from "monitor[ing] or otherwise intercept[ing] any telephone conversation or transmission, electronic mail or transmission, or Internet access or usage" without prior written notice and daily electronic notice.[76] Similarly, Connecticut law requires that "each employer who engages in any type of electronic monitoring shall give prior written notice to all employees who may be affected, informing them of the types of monitoring which may occur. Each employer shall post, in a conspicuous place which is readily available for viewing by its employees, a notice concerning the types of electronic monitoring which the employer may engage in."[77]

12.3.3.3 Preservation Orders

The SCA states that a provider of wire or electronic communication services or a remote computing service, upon the request of a governmental entity, shall take all necessary steps to preserve records and other evidence in its possession pending the issuance of a court order or other process.[78]

12.3.3.4 Pen Register and Trap and Trace Orders

Traditionally, a pen register recorded the telephone numbers of outgoing calls, and a "trap and trace" device recorded the telephone numbers that called into a particular number. ECPA provided for pen register and trap and trace orders from a judge under the relatively lenient legal standard of "relevant to an ongoing investigation."[79] The USA PATRIOT Act expanded the definitions beyond telephone numbers to include "dialing, routing, addressing, or signaling information" transmitted to or from a device or process. The USA FREEDOM Act set new rules for national security investigations, prohibiting the use of pen register and trap and trace orders for bulk collection and restricting their use to circumstances where there were specific selectors such as an email address or telephone number.[80]

12.3.4 The Communications Assistance to Law Enforcement Act

The U.S. Communications Assistance to Law Enforcement Act of 1994 (CALEA)[81] (sometimes referred to as the Digital Telephony Bill) lays out the duties of defined actors in the telecommunications industry to cooperate in the interception of communications for law enforcement and other needs relating to the security and safety of the public. It notably requires telecommunications carriers to design their products and services to ensure that they can carry out a lawful order to provide government access to communications. The Federal Communications Commission (FCC) has implemented CALEA through various rule-making processes.[82]

CALEA applies to "telecommunications carriers," but not to other "information services." As enacted, therefore, the law was interpreted not to apply to Internet services. In 2004, however, the U.S. Department of Justice (DOJ), the Federal Bureau of Investigation (FBI) and the Drug Enforcement Administration (DEA) petitioned to expand the interpretation of the scope of the legislation. In 2005, the FCC issued an order that providers of broadband Internet access and voice-over-Internet protocol

(VoIP) services were "telecommunications services" when they interconnect with traditional telephone services, and so they now operate under CALEA requirements.[83]

12.3.5 Cybersecurity Information Sharing Act

The Cybersecurity Information Sharing Act (CISA) became law in 2015. The statute permits the federal government to share unclassified technical data with companies about how networks have been attacked and how successful defenses against such attacks have been carried out.[84] Correspondingly, CISA encourages companies to voluntarily share information with the federal government, state and local governments, as well as other companies and private entities. Under the law, the company's release of information about "cyber threat indicators"[85] and "defensive measures"[86] receives certain protections. These include limitations on liability, non-waiver of privileges, and exemption from FOIA disclosure. Participation by companies is voluntary. In addition, CISA authorizes companies to monitor and implement certain defensive measures on their information systems in an effort to counter cyber threats.[87]

The specific provisions of CISA include:

Authorization for a company to share or receive "cyber threat indicators" or "defensive measures." Pursuant to CISA, a company is authorized to share with the federal government, state and local governments, and other companies and private entities "cyber threat indicators"[88] and "defensive measures"[89] for a "cybersecurity purpose"[90] or to receive such information from these entities.[91]

Requirement for company to remove personal information before sharing. For sharing to qualify for protections under CISA, the company's actions must be done in accordance with certain requirements.[92] For example, a company intending to share a "cyber threat indicator" must first remove, or implement a "technical capacity" configured to remove, any information that is not directly related to a threat and that the company is aware at the time relates to a specific individual.[93]

Sharing information with federal government does not waive privileges. Sharing information with the federal government does not waive privileges, such as attorney-client privilege. Importantly, there is no similar provision for sharing with state and local governments or other companies.[94]

Shared information exempt from federal and state FOIA laws. Information shared pursuant to CISA is exempt from disclosure under FOIA, as well as under any state or local provisions "requiring disclosure of information or records."[95]

Prohibition on government using shared information to regulate or take enforcement actions against lawful activities. Information shared under CISA "shall not be used by any Federal, State, tribal, or local government to regulate, including an enforcement action, the lawful activities of any non-Federal entity or any activities taken by a non-Federal entity pursuant to mandatory standards, including activities related to monitoring, operating defensive measures, or sharing cyber threat indicators." The information may be used, however, to develop or implement new cybersecurity regulations.[96]

Authorization for company's monitoring and operating defensive measures. According to the act, a company is authorized to "monitor" and "operate defensive measures" on its own information system—or, with written authorization, another party's system—for cybersecurity purposes.[97]

Protection from liability for monitoring activities. Under CISA, the company is protected from liability for its monitoring activities. Note, however, that there is no corresponding liability protection for operating defensive measures.[98]

During the discussions prior to the passage of CISA, numerous privacy concerns were raised.[99] In part to address these concerns, the act requires the federal government to publish guidelines concerning the use and dissemination of shared information.[100]

12.3.6 Right to Financial Privacy Act

The special requirements of the Right to Financial Privacy Act (RFPA) of 1978 apply to disclosures by a variety of financial institutions, including banks, credit card companies and consumer finance companies.[101] RFPA states that "no Government authority may have access to or obtain copies of, or the information contained in the financial records of any customer from a financial institution unless the financial records are reasonably described" and meet at least one of these conditions:

1. The customer authorizes access
2. There is an appropriate administrative subpoena or summons
3. There is a qualified search warrant
4. There is an appropriate judicial subpoena
5. There is an appropriate formal written request from an authorized government authority[102]

By its terms, RFPA applies only to requests from federal agencies, although over a dozen states have similar requirements.[103] It applies to the financial records of individuals and partnerships of fewer than five people. With limited exceptions, customers must receive notice in advance of the government request for the records, and they have the right to challenge disclosure of such records. As with other privacy statutes, a number of important exceptions exist. Financial institutions that produce records under the RFPA are eligible for reimbursements for reasonably necessary costs. Penalties for violation can include actual damages to the customer, punitive damages and attorney's fees.

12.3.7 Media Records and the Privacy Protection Act

The Privacy Protection Act (PPA) of 1980 provides an extra layer of protection for members of the media and media organizations from government searches or seizures in the course of a criminal investigation.[104] PPA was passed in the wake of the 1978 Supreme Court case of Zurcher v. Stanford Daily.[105] In that case, police used a search warrant to look through a newspaper's unpublished photographs of a demonstration. Lower courts found the search unlawful, saying that the government should have used less invasive methods than a full search of the newspaper's premises. The Supreme Court, however, found that valid search warrants "may be used to search any property" where there is probable cause to believe that evidence of a crime will be found.

Under PPA, government officials engaging in criminal investigations are not permitted to search or seize media work products or documentary materials "reasonably believed to have a purpose to disseminate to the public a newspaper, book, broadcast or other similar form of public communication." In practice, rather than physically searching a newsroom, "the PPA effectively forces law enforcement to use subpoenas or voluntary cooperation to obtain evidence from those engaged in First Amendment activities."[106]

PPA applies to government officers or employees at all levels of government. It applies only to criminal investigations, not to civil litigation. Several states provide additional protections.[107] Violation can lead to penalties of a minimum of $1,000, actual damages and attorney's fees.

One important exception is if there is probable cause to believe that a reporter has committed or is in the process of committing a crime. This PPA exception does not apply if the member of the media's only crime is possession, receipt or communication of the work product itself. Other exceptions exist, such as to prevent death or serious injury or where there is reason to believe documents will be destroyed or concealed if the materials were requested through a subpoena.[108]

PPA was drafted to respond to police physical searches of traditional newspaper facilities. Going forward, courts may face claims that PPA is significantly broader, because disseminating "a public communication" may apply to blogs, other web publishing and perhaps even social media.[109]

12.3.8 Evidence Stored in a Different Country

With the growth of cloud storage of records, including by web email and social network providers, evidence for a criminal case is more frequently held in a different country, a phenomenon that has been called "the globalization of criminal evidence."[110] Prosecutors and companies thus face an increasing number of cases that raise the issue of whether the domestic rules for accessing evidence apply to communications and other records held abroad.

In July 2016, the federal appellate court in New York ruled, in the case of Microsoft v. United States, that the SCA did not require the company to provide electronic evidence that was stored outside of the United States, meaning the warrant was not valid for the contents of an email account that Microsoft stored overseas.[111] This interpretation, that a warrant could not compel production of electronic evidence held by a U.S. company outside the U.S., surprised some commentators.[112] Until the Microsoft Ireland case (so called because the evidence at issue was housed by Microsoft in Ireland), leading email and social network services have been based in the United States, so the U.S. government could gain evidence in law enforcement investigations by ordering production through the U.S. corporate headquarters.[113] By contrast, other governments have had to meet the requirements of U.S. law, such as ECPA, to gain access to email, social network, or other electronic evidence held by these companies. Other countries aside from the United States have thus needed to use the mutual legal assistance process (MLA), and so had to meet probable cause or other U.S.-defined standards for gaining the evidence. In the wake of Microsoft Ireland, the U.S. government appears to have a greater reason to support MLA reform—to gain evidence from Ireland and other countries where relevant data is stored. While this book was going to press, the Supreme Court agreed to hear the appeal of the Microsoft Ireland case.[114]

12.4. National Security and the Role of Privacy Professionals

Compared with the law enforcement issues discussed in the previous section, somewhat different rules and issues arise when the government seeks personal information for national security purposes. This section briefly explains the key differences. It then provides an overview of FISA,[115] as amended by the USA PATRIOT Act in 2001 and more recently by the 2015 USA FREEDOM Act.[116] As with the discussion above of ECPA, the discussion here does not delve into as many details of the law as would be needed by attorneys who work for the government or communications providers. Instead, the focus is on issues that can arise in a wide range of companies. Notably, any company can be faced with a request for records under Section 215 of the USA PATRIOT Act, and a significant range of companies can receive a National Security Letter (NSL).

12.4.1 Introduction to Debates About National Security Surveillance

National security wiretaps and other national security searches create a fundamental constitutional question. Under Article II of the Constitution, defining executive powers, the president is commander-in-chief of the armed forces, and the Supreme Court has stated the president has "plenary" powers in foreign affairs.[117] On the other hand, Article III of the Constitution grants judicial power to the Supreme Court and lower courts. In 1967, in Katz v. United States, the Supreme Court underscored the importance of judges under the Fourth Amendment—wiretaps require a warrant signed by a neutral magistrate.[118]

The ongoing and difficult question is where the president's inherent authority leaves off, and where judicial and legal limits on that authority apply. The decision in Katz stated that its warrant rules applied for ordinary wiretaps used for domestic law enforcement rather than national security. A few years later, the court expressed skepticism about a general exception for national security cases, in part out of concerns that the term *national security* was too vague and could extend too far. In the Keith case, the court specifically left undecided the extent of the president's power to conduct wiretaps without warrants "with respect to the activities of foreign powers, within or without this country."[119]

In passing FISA in 1978, both supporters and critics of broad surveillance powers achieved important goals. Supporters of surveillance gained a statutory system that expressly authorized foreign intelligence wiretaps, lending the weight of congressional approval to surveillance that did not meet all the requirements of ordinary Fourth Amendment searches. Critics of surveillance institutionalized a series of checks and balances on the previously unfettered discretion of the president and the attorney general to conduct surveillance in the name of national security.

The attacks of September 11, 2001, led to important changes to FISA, as part of the USA PATRIOT Act passed in the wake of attacks. Supporters of the changes emphasized the new types of national security threat posed by Al Qaeda and international terrorism. The original FISA statute was passed during the Cold War, when a major target of national security efforts was to track the activities of agents of the Soviet Union and its allied foreign nation states. For instance, foreign intelligence wiretaps could be used in connection with communications of the Soviet Embassy or people who worked there. By contrast, the war on terrorism after 2001 involved threats from hard-to-detect individuals who had few or no links to foreign governments. Supporters of broader surveillance argued that foreign intelligence wiretaps should be used more often and with more flexible legal limits. The USA PATRIOT Act provided more of that flexibility.

Over time, however, national security surveillance received a major new round of criticism. *The New York Times* and other newspapers published detailed stories that showed large numbers of national security wiretaps and access to stored communications records without judicial authorization.[120] Among other lawsuits, the largest telephone companies were sued for tens of billions of dollars under the SCA for their role in providing records to the government.[121] Other reports revealed that the number of NSLs for communications and other records was orders of magnitude higher than previously stated by the government.[122]

In the wake of these disclosures, Congress accessed FISA once again, notably in the FISA Amendment Act of 2008.[123] This statute gave legal authorization to some of the new surveillance practices, especially where one party to the communication is reasonably believed to be outside of the United States. It granted immunity to the telephone companies, so they would not be liable for the records they had provided to the government in the wake of 9/11. The new rules also required more reporting from the government to Congress, and put limits on some of the secrecy about NSLs and other government requests for records in the national security realm.

Additional public debate and reform proposals emerged after the revelations made by Edward Snowden, which began in June 2013. Snowden released tens of thousands of classified documents to media outlets, detailing government programs collecting massive amounts of information on both citizens and noncitizens. The revelations were met with mixed emotions, with some commentators calling him a patriot or whistleblower for his actions and others calling him a traitor. Whatever the judgment may be about the actions, it is clear that the Snowden revelations reinvigorated the discussion surrounding national security and information privacy.

Beginning soon after June 2013, President Obama worked with two independent review efforts, staffed by people briefed at the TS/SCI level (Top Secret/Sensitive Compartmented Information), the highest level of security clearance. The President's Review Group on Intelligence and Communications Technology ("Review Group"), including the author of this book, Peter Swire, made 46 recommendations in its late 2013 report.[124] When President Obama made his major speech on surveillance reform in January 2014, the Review Group was told that 70 percent of its recommendations were being adopted in letter or spirit, and others have been adopted since. The Privacy and Civil Liberties Oversight Board (PCLOB), an independent agency in the executive branch, released detailed reports on the Section 215[125] and Section 702[126] surveillance programs, making numerous recommendations. Overall, PCLOB made 22 recommendations in its Sections 215 and 702 reports and virtually all have been accepted and implemented.

The Snowden revelations led to significant reforms in U.S. surveillance law and practices. These reforms included passage of the USA FREEDOM Act in 2015, which among multiple provisions ended bulk collection under the Section 215 program, and the Judicial Redress Act of 2016, which extends U.S. Privacy Act protections to certain non-U.S. persons. There have also been numerous administrative changes.[127]

For privacy professionals, the history since the Snowden revelations illustrates the competing values that come into play when the government makes a national security request for personal information. Company employees, including privacy professionals, generally have a strong desire to help where possible with national security requests. On the other hand, as shown by negative reactions to some surveillance activities post-Snowden, providing information too broadly can lead to legal, public relations and civil liberties objections.

Responding to national security requests is more complicated because U.S. privacy laws have varying scope and differing definitions for national security exceptions. For instance, HIPAA permits disclosure of protected health information "to authorized federal officials for the conduct of lawful intelligence, counter-intelligence, and other national security" under the National Security Act.[128] GLBA has a privacy exception that is more vaguely worded, "for an investigation on a matter related to public safety."[129] By contrast, COPPA and its implementing regulation make no mention of a national security exception.[130] Privacy professionals, IT professionals who provide access to records, and attorneys thus may need to do research in particular settings to determine what sorts of national security disclosures are permitted, for what sorts of records, and to which agencies.

Debates about encryption provide another illustration of the tension between national security and law enforcement on the one hand, and civil liberties concerns and limits on lawful sharing of personal information on the other.[131] In the 2016 case of Apple v. FBI that garnered international attention, the FBI sought the assistance of Apple to gain access to the encrypted phone of one of the assailants in the San Bernardino shooting.[132] The FBI obtained a court order requiring Apple to assist the government by creating a custom operating system that would disable key security features on the iPhone.[133] Apple filed a motion with the court asking it to reconsider its decision, expressing the company's concern that complying with the order would result in building a backdoor into the encryption for all iPhones of that particular model phone.[134] On one side of this case, law enforcement sought information in a mass shooting, and they secured a warrant before proceeding. On the other side, a preeminent technology company warned that its compliance with the order could weaken the technology that protects privacy around the world.[135] The specific court case involving Apple ended when the FBI announced that it had gained access to the encrypted phone without the assistance of the company, but the debate about the government accessing encrypted data led to hearings and proposed legislation in Congress.[136] This debate has been framed by national security and law enforcement agencies as the "going dark" problem—the idea that encryption blinds the ability of officials to see evidence—while civil liberties experts have countered that the current environment is the "Golden Age of Surveillance, due to the explosive growth of personal data that is amassed in databases."[137]

12.4.2 Overview of The Foreign Intelligence Surveillance Act

FISA establishes standards and procedures for electronic surveillance that collects "foreign intelligence" within the United States FISA orders can issue when foreign intelligence gathering is "a significant purpose" of the investigation. [138] For law enforcement cases, court orders issue based on probable cause of a crime; FISA orders instead issue on probable cause that the party to be monitored is a "foreign power" or an "agent of a foreign power." FISA orders issue from a special court of federal district court judges, the Foreign Intelligence Surveillance Court (FISC). Historically, only attorneys for the U.S. government appeared before the FISC. The USA FREEDOM Act created a group of independent experts in the area of privacy and civil liberties, called *amicus curiae*, to brief the FISC on novel or significant matters of law.[139]

In addition to wiretap orders, FISA authorizes pen register and trap and trace orders (for phone numbers, email addresses, and other addressing and routing information) and orders for video surveillance.

Due to the secrecy of government surveillance of agents of foreign powers, entities that receive a FISA order to produce records generally cannot disclose the fact of the order to the targets of investigation. There is generally no disclosure after the fact to the target of a FISA wiretap as there is for law enforcement wiretaps. Nonetheless, there have been significant increases in transparency over time about FISA surveillance. Companies are now allowed to publish statistics about the number of FISA orders and NSLs they receive.[140] Under the USA FREEDOM Act, the government issues yearly transparency reports, with more detail than previously, and the U.S. government has declassified a substantial number of orders from the FISA Court.[141] Over time, FISA orders have grown so that they outnumber traditional law enforcement wiretap orders.[142] The legal details of FISA can be important for communication providers, such as telephone companies and email services, but such issues arise much less often for most other companies.[143]

12.4.3 Section 215 Orders

Section 215 of the USA PATRIOT Act received a great deal of public attention after documents released by Edward Snowden stated that the National Security Agency (NSA) had created a database containing a substantial fraction of call detail information for domestic U.S. telephone calls. Section 215 provides that a federal court order can require the production of "any tangible thing" for defined foreign intelligence and antiterrorism investigations.[144] The definition of tangible thing is broad, including "books, records, papers, documents, and other items." Recipients of such an order receive notice that they were forbidden from disclosing the existence or contents of the order.[145] Disclosure is permitted, however, to the persons necessary to comply with the order (such as employees who gather the records) and to an attorney for purposes of receiving legal advice. Production of the records in good faith provides immunity for such production.

The USA FREEDOM Act ended bulk collection conducted under Section 215.[146] Going forward, requests by government officials must be based upon specific selectors, such as a telephone number. Company officials are now permitted to release statistics about the number of such requests they receive in a given time period, and the government is required to report its numbers once a year.[147] In 2015, government officials filed 142 applications for orders for business records pursuant to Section 215.[148]

12.4.4 Section 702

Section 702 refers to a provision in the Foreign Intelligence Surveillance Act Amendments Act of 2008, which revised FISA.[149] Section 702 applies to collection of electronic communications that take place within the United States and only authorizes access to the communications of targeted individuals for listed foreign intelligence purposes. One legal question answered by Section 702 was how to govern foreign-to-foreign communications for interception of content that has been stored within the United States. This inquiry is important because communications between two non-U.S. persons is now often stored within the United States due to the growing use of U.S.-based providers for webmail, social networks and other services.

The basic structure of Section 702 is that the FISC must annually approve certifications by the director of national intelligence and the attorney general setting the terms for Section 702 surveillance.[150] To target the communications of any person, the government must have a foreign intelligence purpose to conduct the collection and a reasonable belief that the person is a non-U.S. citizen located outside of the United States.[151] Section 702 can provide access to the full contents of communications, and not just metadata such as to/from information. The court annually reviews and must approve targeting criteria documenting how targeting of a particular person will lead to the acquisition of foreign intelligence information.[152]

Two surveillance programs are authorized under Section 702: PRISM and Upstream. The PRISM program became famous when it was publicly named in one of the first stories based on the Snowden documents.[153] The operation of PRISM resembles data requests made in other settings to service providers. In PRISM collection, acting under a Section 702 court order, the government sends a judicially approved and judicially supervised directive requiring collection of certain "selectors," such as an email address. The directive goes to a U.S.-based service provider. The company's lawyers have the opportunity to challenge the government request. If there is no appeal to the court, the provider is compelled to give the communications sent to or from that selector to the government.[154]

In addition to PRISM, Section 702 supports intelligence collection commonly referred to as the "Upstream" program. Upstream targets Internet-based communications as they pass through physical Internet infrastructure located within the Unites States.[155] Upstream is designed to only acquire Internet communications that contain a tasked selector. To do so, Upstream filters Internet transactions that pass through the Internet backbone to eliminate potential domestic transactions; these are then further screened to capture only transactions containing a tasked selector. Emails and other transactions that make it through the filters are stored for access by the NSA, while information that does not make it through the filters is never accessed by the NSA or anyone else.

As the book was going to press, Congress was considering possible amendments to Section 702 in connection with the sunset of the Section 702 authorities at the end of 2017.[156]

12.4.5 National Security Letters

An NSL is a category of subpoena that, prior to the PATRIOT Act in 2001, was used narrowly, only for certain financial and communication records of an agent of a foreign power, and only with approval of FBI headquarters.[157] The PATRIOT Act expanded use of NSLs. The number of NSLs rose to tens of thousands per year, with most involving the records of U.S. citizens. Separate and sometimes differing statutory provisions now govern access, without a court order, to communication providers, financial institutions, consumer credit agencies and travel agencies.[158] As the use of NSLs grew after 2001, a series of reports by the inspector general of the DOJ criticized the lack of effective procedures for implementing rules governing NSLs and related investigatory tools.[159]

As amended in 2006, NSLs can be issued by authorized officials, often the special agent in charge of an FBI field office. The precise language in the statutes varies, but NSLs generally can seek records relevant to protect against international terrorism or clandestine intelligence activities. NSLs can be issued without any judicial involvement. Under the 2006 amendments, however, recipients can petition to a federal court to modify or set aside an NSL if compliance would be unreasonable or oppressive.[160]

The USA PATRIOT Act included strict rules against disclosing that an organization had received an NSL. After court decisions questioned this ban on disclosure on First and Fourth Amendment grounds,[161] the 2006 amendments said that recipients are bound to confidentiality only if there is a finding by the requesting agency of interference with a criminal or counterterrorism investigation or for other listed purposes. Recipients were allowed to disclose the request to those necessary to comply with the request and to an attorney for legal assistance. Recipients could also petition a court to modify or end the secrecy requirement. Breach of the confidentiality requirements, however, was treated as a serious offense, punishable by up to five years' imprisonment and fines of up to $250,000 for an individual.[162]

Reforms in the area of NSLs have focused on the indefinite secrecy previously imposed on companies who received these. In 2014, President Obama announced the indefinite secrecy would change. As of 2015, the FBI now presumptively terminates NSL secrecy for an individual order when an investigation closes, or no more than three years after the opening of a full investigation.[163]

12.5 Conclusion

Many privacy issues can arise in the course of investigations and litigation. Companies can face complex legal rules about when they are required to or forbidden from disclosing personal information, and when they have a choice about whether to do so. As the volume of records involved in investigations and litigation has mounted, the earlier case-by-case approach led by lawyers has evolved into a greater role for organization policies and procedures under more comprehensive information management plans.

Lawyers, privacy professionals and IT experts increasingly must work together to meet the organization's goals while still complying with privacy and disclosure requirements.

Endnotes

1 U.S.C. Title 21, Chapter 9 https://www.law.cornell.edu/uscode/text/21/chapter-9 (accessed November 2017).

2 *See* U. S. Department of Labor, Occupational Health and Safety, https://www.osha.gov/pls/oshaweb/owadisp.show_document?p_table=FEDERAL_REGISTER&p_id=16312 (accessed November 2017).

3 45 C.F.R.§ 164.512(a)(1), https://www.law.cornell.edu/cfr/text/45/164.512 (accessed November 2017).

4 Fed. R. Civ. Pro. 45(g), https://www.law.cornell.edu/rules/frcp/rule_45 (accessed November 2017).

5 18 U.S.C. § 3123(a), https://www.law.cornell.edu/uscode/text/18/3123 (accessed November 2017).

6 18 U.S.C. § 2703(d), https://www.law.cornell.edu/uscode/text/18/2703 (accessed November 2017).

7 18 U.S.C. §§ 2510-2522, https://www.law.cornell.edu/uscode/text/18/2510 (accessed November 2017).

8 45 C.F.R. § 164.524; https://www.law.cornell.edu/cfr/text/45/164.524 (accessed November 2017); 45 C.F.R. § 164.528, https://www.law.cornell.edu/cfr/text/45/164.528 (accessed November 2017).

9 45 C.F.R. § 164.502(a)(2), https://www.law.cornell.edu/cfr/text/45/164.502 (accessed November 2017).

10 18 U.S.C. §§ 2510-2511, https://www.law.cornell.edu/uscode/text/18/2510 (accessed November 2017).

11 The USA PATRIOT Act defines a "computer trespasser" as "a person who accesses a protected computer without authorization." 18 U.S.C. § 2510(21), https://www.law.cornell.edu/uscode/text/18/2510 (accessed November 2017).

12 Section 217 of the USA PATRIOT Act, https://www.law.cornell.edu/uscode/text/18/2511 (accessed November 2017).

13 Opt-in provisions require a potential customer to choose to be involved in the organization's services before the organization can act. Opt-out provisions apply to existing customers who receive services from the organization, and who can individually exercise the ability to end receiving such services. Opt-in Policy and Opt-out Policy, The Motive Web Design Glossary, www.motive.co.nz/glossary/opt-in.php?ref (accessed December 2016).

14 The scope of evidentiary privileges in the federal courts is defined by the courts and generally is similar to state law. For civil cases, the evidentiary privileges are governed by Federal Rules of Evidence 501, https://www.law.cornell.edu/rules/fre/rule_501 (accessed November 2017).

15 "The Clinton-Gore Plan to Enhance Consumers Financial Privacy: Protecting Core Values in the Information Age," The White House, http://clinton3.nara.gov/WH/New/html/20000501_4.html (accessed November 2017). For a more detailed discussion, view "Financial Privacy" at PeterSwire.net, http://peterswire.net/archive/psfinancialpage.htm (accessed November 2017).

16 http://origin-www.justice.gov/ust/eo/public_affairs/articles/docs/walton2_ssn2-04.htm (accessed November 2017).

17 10th Conference on Privacy and Public Access to Court Records, Center for Legal & Court Technology, www.legaltechcenter.net/10th-Privacy-Conference/ (accessed December 2016).

18 *See* Madanes v. Madanes, 186 F.R.D. 279, 288 (S.D.N.Y. 1999), http://law.justia.com/cases/federal/district-courts/FSupp/981/241/2282097/ (accessed November 2017).

19 45 C.F.R. § 164.512(e), https://www.law.cornell.edu/cfr/text/45/164.512 (accessed November 2017).

20 Fed. R. Civ. Pro. 5.2, https://www.law.cornell.edu/rules/frcp/rule_5.2 (accessed November 2017).

21 Fed. R. Crim. Pro. 49.1(e), https://www.law.cornell.edu/rules/frcrmp/rule_49.1 (accessed November 2017).

22 11 U.S.C. § 105(a), https://www.law.cornell.edu/uscode/text/11/105 (accessed November 2017).

23 Rule 9037 of the Federal Rules of Bankruptcy Procedure, https://www.law.cornell.edu/rules/frbp/rule_9037 (accessed November 2017).

24 Fed. R. Crim. Pro. 49.1(a)(5), https://www.law.cornell.edu/rules/frcrmp/rule_49.1 (accessed November 2017).

25 *See generally* Federal Rule Changes Affecting E-Discovery Are Almost Here - Are You Ready This Time?, www.ediscoverylaw.com/wp-content/uploads/2015/10/Rules-Amendment-Alert-100115.pdf (accessed November 2017).

26 The Sedona Principles—Third Edition, The Sedona Conference (October 2017 Final Pre-Pub), https://thesedonaconference.org/publication/The%20Sedona%20Principles (accessed November 2017).

27 Arista Records LLC v. Usenet.com, Inc., 608 F. Supp. 2d 409, 413 (S.D.N.Y. 2009), https://www.courtlistener.com/opinion/1465022/arista-records-llc-v-usenet-com-inc/ (accessed November 2017).

28 Doe v. Norwalk Cmty. College, 248 F.R.D. 372, 378 (D. Conn. 2007), https://ralphlosey.files.wordpress.com/2007/07/doe-v-norwalk.doc (accessed November 2017).

29 Cf. Wal-Mart Stores v. Lee, 348 Ark. 707 (Ark. 2002), https://www.courtlistener.com/opinion/1383972/wal-mart-stores-inc-v-lee/ (accessed November 2017).

30 Lewy v. Remington Arms Co., 836 F.2d 1104, 1111 (8th Cir. Mo. 1988), http://cyber.law.harvard.edu/digitaldiscovery/library/spoliation/lewy.html (accessed November 2017)

31 Zubulake v. UBS Warburg LLC, 220 F.R.D. 212, 218 (S.D.N.Y. 2003). ("Once a party reasonably anticipates litigation, it must suspend its routine document retention/destruction policy and put in place a 'litigation hold' to ensure the preservation of relevant documents."), https://cdn2.hubspot.net/hub/179343/file-357162524-pdf/docs/zubulake_v__ubs_warburg_llc.pdf (accessed November 2017).

32 45 C.F.R. § 164.502(a)(1)(iv), https://www.law.cornell.edu/cfr/text/45/164.502 (accessed November 2017).

33 45 C.F.R. § 164.512(e)(1)(I), https://www.law.cornell.edu/cfr/text/45/164.512 (accessed November 2017).

34 45 C.F.R. § 164.512(e)(iv)(A & B), https://www.law.cornell.edu/cfr/text/45/164.512 (accessed November 2017).

35 45 C.F.R.. § 164.512(e)(v), https://www.law.cornell.edu/cfr/text/45/164.512 (accessed November 2017).

36 15 U.S.C. § 6802(e)(8), https://www.law.cornell.edu/uscode/text/15/6802 (accessed November 2017).

37 Marks v. Global Mortg. Group, Inc., 218 F.R.D. 492 (S.D. W. Va. 2003), www.wvsd.uscourts.gov/content/marks-v-global-mortgage-group-inc (accessed November 2017).

38 The GDPR provides extensions of individual rights, including the right to be forgotten, the right to data portability, and implementation of principles of data protection by design and data protection by default. Věra Jourová, "How Does the Data Protection Reform Strengthen Citizens' Rights?" EU (January 2016), http://ec.europa.eu/justice/data-protection/document/factsheets_2016/factsheet_dp_reform_citizens_rights_2016_en.pdf (accessed November 2017).

39 According to the GDPR, orders or judgments from non-EU courts are not a valid basis for transferring data to third countries. Violations of the regulation could result in sanctions of up to four percent of a company's worldwide revenues. Article 48 & 83 of GDPR, www.insidecounsel.com/2016/11/23/the-general-data-protection-regulations-key-implic?page=2&slreturn=1484271077 (accessed November 2017). For an overview of the impacts of GDPR to e-discovery, *see* David Moncure, John Del Piero and Jeffrey McKenna, "The General Data Protection Regulation's Key Implications for E-Discovery," *Inside Counsel*, November 23, 2016, www.insidecounsel.com/2016/11/23/the-general-data-protection-regulations-key-implic?page=2&slreturn=1484271077 (accessed November 2017).

40 *See* Fred H. Cate and Margaret P. Eisenhauer, "Between a Rock and a Hard Place: The Conflict Between European Data Protection Laws and U.S. Civil Litigation Document Production Requirements," BNA Privacy and Security Law Report, www.jstor.org/stable/24052243?seq=1#page_scan_tab_contents (accessed November 2017).

41 Spain v. American Bureau of Shipping, 2006 WL 3208579 (S.D.N.Y. 2006). For an analysis of the case, view *E-discovery and Data Privacy: A Practical Guide*, Catrien Noorda and Stefan Hanloser (Kluwer Law International 2011).

42 Columbia Pictures, Inc. v. Bunnell, 245 F.R.D. 443, 453 (C.D. Cal. 2007), https://www.eff.org/files/filenode/torrentspy/columbia_v_bunnell_magistrate_order.pdf (accessed November 2017).

43 In Re Xarelto (Rivaroxaban) Products Liability Litigation, MDL No. 2592, 2016 WL 2855221 (E.D. La) May 16, 2016. For a discussion of the case, *see* Stephan Cornell, "E-Discovery in Cross-Border Litigation: The 'Blocking Statute Defense,'" Fox Rothschild (May 25, 2016), http://www.foxrothschild.com/publications/e-discovery-in-cross-border-litigation-the-blocking-statute-defense/ (accessed November 2017).

44 20: Convention of 18 March 1970 on the Taking of Evidence Abroad in Civil or Commercial Matters, Hague Conference on Private Internatinoal Law, https://www.hcch.net/en/instruments/conventions/full-text/?cid=82 (accessed November 2017).

45 Societe Nationale Industrielle Aerospatiale v. United States Dist. Court for S. Dist. IA, 482 U.S. 522 (U.S. 1987), https://supreme.justia.com/cases/federal/us/482/522/case.html (accessed November 2017).

46 *Id.* at 568.

47 Weiss v. Nat'l Westminster Bank, PLC, 242 F.R.D. 33 (E.D.N.Y. 2007), http://blogs.reuters.com/alison-frankel/files/2016/04/weissvnatwest-jurisdictionruling.pdf (accessed November 2017).

48 Working Paper 1/2009 (00339/09/EN WP 158), http://ec.europa.eu/justice/policies/privacy/docs/wpdocs/2009/wp158_en.pdf (accessed November 2017). For guidance on e-discovery requests for data held in Europe, view the section entitled "Practical Impact on the Regulation of e-discovery" in

"EU Data Protection Gains a Sword to Go with its Shield," ediscovery.com, www.ediscovery.com/cms/pdf/EU-Data-Protection-Gains-Sword-to-Go-with-Shield.pdf (accessed November 2017).

49 Albert Barsocchini, "Preserve in Place v. Collect to Preserve," *Inside Counsel*, August 24, 2009, www.insidecounsel.com/2009/08/24/preserve-in-place-vs-collect-to-preserve (accessed November 2017).

50 Katz v. United States, 389 U.S. 347 (1967), https://supreme.justia.com/cases/federal/us/389/347/case.html (accessed November 2017).

51 Schmerber v. California, 384 U.S. 757 (1966), https://supreme.justia.com/cases/federal/us/384/757/case.html (accessed November 2017).

52 Olmstead v. United States, 277 U.S. 438 (1928), https://supreme.justia.com/cases/federal/us/277/438/case.html (accessed November 2017).

53 Katz v. United States, 389 U.S. 347 (1967), https://supreme.justia.com/cases/federal/us/389/347/case.html (accessed November 2017).

54 United States v. Miller, 425 U.S. 435 (1976) (checking account records), https://supreme.justia.com/cases/federal/us/425/435/ (accessed November 2017); Smith v. Maryland, 442 U.S. 735 (1979) (phone-calling records), https://supreme.justia.com/cases/federal/us/442/735/case.html (accessed November 2017).

55 United States v. Jones, 132 S. Ct. 945 (2012), https://www.supremecourt.gov/opinions/11pdf/10-1259.pdf (accessed November 2017).

56 Riley v. California, 134 S. Ct. 2473 (2014), https://www.supremecourt.gov/opinions/13pdf/13-132_8l9c.pdf (accessed November 2017).

57 Marc Rotenberg and Alan Butler, Symposium: In Riley v. California, a Unanimous Supreme Court Sets Out Fourth Amendment for Digital Age, (June 26, 2014), www.scotusblog.com/2014/06/symposium-in-riley-v-california-a-unanimous-supreme-court-sets-out-fourth-amendment-for-digital-age/ (accessed November 2017).

58 Marley Degner, "*Riley* and the Third-Party Doctrine," Pillsbury (April 9, 2015), https://www.pillsburylaw.com/siteFiles/Publications/AR_Riley_and_the_thirdparty_doctrine_Degner_4915.pdf (accessed November 2017).

59 12 U.S.C. § 3401 et seq., https://www.law.cornell.edu/uscode/text/12/chapter-35 (accessed November 2017).

60 18 U.S.C. § 2510 et seq., https://www.loc.gov/law/opportunities/PDFs/ElectronicCommunicationsPrivacyAct-PL199-508.pdf (accessed November 2017).

61 45 C.F.R. § 164.512(f), https://www.law.cornell.edu/cfr/text/45/164.512 (accessed November 2017).

62 45 C.F.R. § 164.512(a), https://www.law.cornell.edu/cfr/text/45/164.512 (accessed November 2017).

63 Omnibus Crime Control and Safe Streets Act of 1968, Pub. L. No. 90-351. https://transition.fcc.gov/Bureaus/OSEC/library/legislative_histories/1615.pdf (accessed November 2017)

64 18 U.S.C. § 2510, https://www.law.cornell.edu/uscode/text/18/2510 (accessed November 2017).

65 *Id.*

66 18 U.S.C. § 2511(2)(D), https://www.law.cornell.edu/uscode/text/18/2511 (accessed November 2017).

67 Charles Kennedy and Peter Swire, "State Wiretaps and Electronic Surveillance After September 11," *Hastings Law Journal*, 54: 971 (2003) (Appendix A listing state wiretap laws), http://papers.ssrn.com/sol3/papers.cfm?abstract_id=416586, www.peterswire.net/archive/appendix_A_

state_wiretap_laws.pdf (accessed November 2017). For a current list of state laws, view Reporter's Committee for Freedom of the Press, https://www.rcfp.org/reporters-recording-guide/state-state-guide (accessed November 2017).

68 8 U.S.C. § 2511(2)(a)(i), https://www.law.cornell.edu/uscode/text/18/2511 (accessed November 2017).

69 8 U.S.C. § 2510(5), https://www.law.cornell.edu/uscode/text/18/2510 (accessed November 2017).

70 Martha W. Barnett and Scott D. Makar, " 'In the Ordinary Court of Business': The Legal Limits of Workplace Wiretapping," *Communications and Entertainment Law Journal* 10 (1988): 715.

71 Matthew W. Finkin, *Privacy in Employment Law,* 3d edition (Arlington, VA: BNA Books, 2009), at 365–369.

72 For instance, for a call from a state with one-party telephone recording notification to California, the latter's two-party notification law outweighs the one-party notification law—that is, both or all parties must consent to the telephone call recording. Kearney v. Salomon Smith Barney Inc., 39 Cal. 4th 95 (2006), http://caselaw.findlaw.com/ca-supreme-court/1099204.html (accessed November 2017).

73 18 U.S.C. §§ 2701-2712, https://www.law.cornell.edu/uscode/text/18/part-I/chapter-121 (accessed November 2017).

74 18 U.S.C. § 2701(c)(1), https://www.law.cornell.edu/uscode/text/18/2701 (accessed November 2017).

75 18 U.S.C. § 2701(c)(2), https://www.law.cornell.edu/uscode/text/18/2701 (accessed November 2017).

76 19 Del. C. § 705, http://codes.findlaw.com/de/title-19-labor/de-code-sect-19-705.html (accessed November 2017).

77 Conn. Gen. Laws. Chap. 557, § 31-48d, https://www.cga.ct.gov/current/pub/chap_557.htm (accessed November 2017).

78 18 U.S.C. § 2703(f), https://www.law.cornell.edu/uscode/text/18/2703 (accessed November 2017).

79 18 U.S.C. § 3123, https://www.law.cornell.edu/uscode/text/18/3123 (accessed November 2017).

80 "USA FREEDOM Act, https://judiciary.house.gov/issue/usa-freedom-act/ (accessed November 2017). For additional information, view Peter Swire, "US Surveillance Law, Safe Harbor, and Reforms Since 2013," https://fpf.org/wp-content/uploads/2015/12/White-Paper-Swire-US-EU-Surveillance.pdf (accessed November 2017).

81 Communications Assistance to Law Enforcement Act of 1994, 47 U.S.C. §§ 1001-1021 (1994), https://www.law.cornell.edu/uscode/text/47/chapter-9 (accessed November 2017).

82 *See* "Communications Assistance for Law Enforcement," FCC, https://www.fcc.gov/public-safety-and-homeland-security/policy-and-licensing-division/general/communications-assistance (accessed November 2017).

83 American Council on Education v. FCC, 451 F.3d 226 (D.C. Cir. 2006), http://openjurist.org/451/f3d/226/american-council-on-education-v-federal-communications-commission (accessed November 2017).

84 The act authorizes classified information to be shared with entities that have the appropriate security clearances. Cybersecurity Information Sharing Act, Section 103(a), https://epic.org/privacy/cybersecurity/Cybersecruity-Act-of-2015.pdf (accessed November 2017); *see* Boris Segalis, Andrew Hoffman, and Kathryn Linsky, *Federal Cybersecurity Information Sharing Act signed into law,* Data Protection Report, Norton Rose Fulbright (January 3, 2016), www.dataprotectionreport.

com/2016/01/federal-cybersecurity-information-sharing-act-signed-into-law/ (accessed November 2017).

85 Examples of "cyber threat indicators" include malware found on a company's network and IP addresses associated with botnet command and control servers. Hanley Chew and Tyler Newby, "The Cybersecurity Information Sharing Act of 2015: An Overview," *Fenwick Privacy Bulletin*, Fall 2016, Fenwick & West LLP (October 24, 2016), https://www.fenwick.com/Publications/Pages/Fenwick-Privacy-Bulletin-Fall-2016.aspx (accessed November 2017); *see* Rick Link, "What You Need to Know about the Cybersecurity Information Sharing Act of 2015," *The Nexus: Cyber News Converged*, ISACA (October 10, 2016), www.isaca.org/cyber/cyber-security-articles/Pages/what-you-need-to-know-about-the-cybersecurity-information-sharing-act-of-2015.aspx?utm_referrer= (accessed November 2017).

86 The configuration of a firewall mechanism would be an example of a "defensive measure." Hanley Chew and Tyler Newby, "The Cybersecurity Information Sharing Act of 2015"; *see* Rick Link, "What You Need to Know about the Cybersecurity Information Sharing Act of 2015."

87 Brad S. Karp, Paul, Weiss, Rifkind, Wharton & Garrison LLP, "Federal Guidelines on the Cybersecurity Information Sharing Act of 2015," Harvard Law School Forum on Corporate Governance and Financial Regulation (March 3, 2016), https://corpgov.law.harvard.edu/2016/03/03/federal-guidance-on-the-cybersecurity-information-sharing-act-of-2015/ (accessed November 2017); *see* Boris Segalis, Andrew Hoffman, and Kathryn Linsky, "Federal Cybersecurity Information Sharing Act signed into law.

88 CISA defines "cyber threat indicator" as "[I]nformation that is necessary to describe or identify:
(A) malicious reconnaissance, including anomalous patterns of communications that appear to be transmitted for the purpose of gathering technical information related to a cybersecurity threat or security vulnerability;
(B) a method of defeating a security control or exploitation of a security vulnerability;
(C) a security vulnerability, including anomalous activity that appears to indicate the existence of a security vulnerability
(D) a method of causing a user with legitimate access to an information system or information that is stored on, processed by or transiting an information system to unwittingly enable the defeat of a security control or exploitation of a security vulnerability;
(E) malicious cyber command or control;
(F) the actual or potential harm caused by an incident, including a description of the information exfiltrated as a result of a particular cybersecurity threat;
(G) any other attribute of a cybersecurity threat, if disclosure of such attribute is not otherwise prohibited by law;
(H) any combination thereof,";
Cybersecurity Information Sharing Act, Section 102(6), https://epic.org/privacy/cybersecurity/Cybersecruity-Act-of-2015.pdf (accessed November 2017).

89 CISA defines "defensive measures" as:
"(A) In General.—Except as provided in subparagraph (B), the term 'defensive measure' means an action, device, procedure, signature, technique, or other measure applied to an information system or information that is stored on, processed by, or transiting an information system that detects, prevents, or mitigates a known or suspected cybersecurity threat or security vulnerability;
(B) Exclusion.—The term "defensive measure" does not include a measure that destroys, renders unusable, provides unauthorized access to, or substantially harms an information system or information stored on, processed by, or transiting such information system not owned by:

i. the private entity operating the measure
ii. another entity or Federal entity that is authorized to provide consent and has provided consent to that private entity for operation of such measure."
Id. at Section 102(7).

90 CISA defines a "cybersecurity purpose" as "the purpose of protecting an information system or information that is stored on, processed by or transiting an information system from a cybersecurity threat or security vulnerability." *Id.* at Section 102(4).

91 *Id.* at Section 104(c)(1).

92 *Id.* at Section 106(b)(1).

93 *Id.* at Section 104(d)(2)(A), (B).

94 *Id.* at Section 105(d)(1).

95 *Id.* at Section 105(d)(3).

96 *Id.* at Section 105(d)(5)(D)(i), (ii).

97 *Id.* at Section 104(a)(1)(A)-(C), (b)(1)(A)-(C).

98 *Id.* at Section 106(a); *see* generally Brad Karp, "Federal Guidelines on the Cybersecurity Information Sharing Act of 2015."

99 *See* Boris Segalis, Andrew Hoffman and Kathryn Linsky, "Federal Cybersecurity Information Sharing Act signed into law"; Graeme Caldwell, "Why You Should be Concerned about the Cybersecurity Information Sharing Act," *TechCrunch*, February 7, 2016, https://techcrunch.com/2016/02/07/why-you-should-be-concerned-about-cisa/ (accessed November 2017).

100 Privacy and Civil Liberties Final Guidelines: Cybersecurity Information Sharing Act of 2015, U.S. Department of Homeland Security and U.S. Department of Justice (June 15, 2016), https://www.us-cert.gov/sites/default/files/ais_files/Privacy_and_Civil_Liberties_Guidelines_%28Sec%20105%28b%29%29.pdf (accessed November 2017).

101 12 U.S.C. §§ 3401-3422, https://www.law.cornell.edu/uscode/text/12/chapter-35 (accessed November 2017).

102 12 U.S.C. § 3402, https://www.law.cornell.edu/uscode/text/12/3402 (accessed November 2017).

103 The Right to Financial Privacy Act, Electronic Privacy Information Center, https://epic.org/privacy/rfpa/ (accessed November 2017).

104 42 U.S.C. §§2000aa to 2000aa-7, https://www.law.cornell.edu/uscode/text/42/chapter-21A (accessed November 2017).

105 Zurcher v. Stanford Daily, 436 U.S. 547 (1978), https://supreme.justia.com/cases/federal/us/436/547/case.html (accessed November 2017).

106 Chapter Three: Existing Federal Privacy Laws, Center for Democracy & Technology, https://cdt.org/insight/existing-federal-privacy-laws/ (accessed November 2017).

107 Nine states are listed at https://epic.org/privacy/ppa/ (accessed November 2017).

108 42 U.S.C. § 2000aa(b)(3), https://www.law.cornell.edu/uscode/text/42/2000aa (accessed November 2017).

109 For an in-depth discussion of evolving technology, view Elizabeth Uzelac, "Reviving the Privacy Protection Act of 1980," *Northwestern University Law Review*, http://scholarlycommons.law.northwestern.edu/cgi/viewcontent.cgi?article=1057&context=nulr (accessed November 2017).

110 Peter Swire, "Why Cross-Border Government Requests for Data Will Keep Becoming More Important," *Lawfare*, May 23, 2017, https://www.lawfareblog.com/why-cross-border-government-requests-data-will-keep-becoming-more-important (accessed November 2017).

111 Microsoft v. United States, 829 F.3d 197, 220 (2d Cir. 2016). At the writing of this book, the case is on appeal to the United States Supreme Court. William Fry, "U.S. Department of Justice Appeals Microsoft Decision to U.S. Supreme Court," *Lexology*, November 3, 2016, www.lexology.com/library/detail.aspx?g=9a358e84-ba7a-42ca-aefa-513c8885b80b (accessed November 2017).

112 Jennifer Granick, The Microsoft Ireland Case and the Future of Digital Privacy, *JUSTSECURITY* (July 18, 2016), https://www.justsecurity.org/32076/microsoft-ireland-case-future-digital-privacy/ (accessed November 2017).

113 It is worth noting that not all federal judges in the U.S. have adopted the approach set forth in the Microsoft Ireland case. As of the writing of this book, federal magistrate judges in various states—including California, Florida, Pennsylvania and Wisconsin—have ruled that a warrant issued pursuant to ECPA reaches all data held by U.S. service providers, even if that data is physically located outside of the country. *See* Statement of Jennifer Daskal, associate professor of American University Washington College of Law, Committee on the Judiciary Subcommittee on Crime and Terrorism United States Senate, Hearing on Law Enforcement Access to Data Stored Across Borders: Facilitating Cooperation and Protecting Rights (May 10, 2017), p. 3-4, https://www.judiciary.senate.gov/imo/media/doc/05-10-17%20Daskal%20Testimony.pdf (accessed November 2017).

114 See Greg Stohr, "Microsoft Email-Access Fight With U.S. Gets Top Court Review," *Bloomberg Politics*, October 16, 2017, https://www.bloomberg.com/news/articles/2017-10-16/microsoft-email-access-fight-with-u-s-gets-supreme-court-review (accessed November 2017); Andrew Woods, "A Primer on Microsoft Ireland, the Supreme Court's Extraterritorial Warrant Case," *Lawfare* blog, October 16, 2017, https://www.lawfareblog.com/primer-microsoft-ireland-supreme-courts-extraterritorial-warrant-case (accessed November 2017).

115 The Foreign Intelligence Surveillance Act of 1978, Pub. L. No. 95-511, 92 Stat. 1783 (1978), http://legcounsel.house.gov/Comps/Foreign%20Intelligence%20Surveillance%20Act%20Of%201978.pdf (accessed November 2017).

116 "USA Freedom Act: What's in, what's out," *The Washington Post*, https://www.washingtonpost.com/graphics/politics/usa-freedom-act/ (accessed November 2017).

117 United States v. Curtiss-Wright Export Corp., 299 U.S. 304 (1936), https://supreme.justia.com/cases/federal/us/299/304/case.html (accessed November 2017).

118 Katz v. United States, 389 U.S. 347 (1967), https://supreme.justia.com/cases/federal/us/389/347/case.html (accessed November 2017).

119 United States v. United States District Court, 407 U.S. 297 (1972), https://supreme.justia.com/cases/federal/us/407/297/case.html (accessed November 2017).

120 James Risen and Eric Lichtblau, "Bush Lets U.S. Spy on Callers Without Courts," *New York Times*, December 16, 2005, A1, www.nytimes.com/2005/12/16/politics/bush-lets-us-spy-on-callers-without-courts.html?_r=0 (accessed November 2017).

121 Peter Swire and Judd Legum, "Telcos Could Be Liable for Tens of Billions of Dollars for Illegally Turning Over Phone Records," *ThinkProgress*, May 11, 2006, http://thinkprogress.org/politics/2006/05/11/5300/telcos-liable/ (accessed November 2017).

122 Testimony of Peter Swire before the U.S. Senate Judiciary Committee, "Responding to the Inspector General's Findings of Improper Use of National Security Letters by the FBI" (2007), https://www.americanprogress.org/wp-content/uploads/issues/2007/04/pdf/swire_senate_judiciary_testimony.pdf (accessed November 2017).

123 Foreign Intelligence Surveillance Act Amendments Act of 2008, Pub. L. 110-261, 2008.

124 One of the Review Group's report most widely publicized findings was that the use of Section 215 telephony metadata was not essential to preventing attacks and could readily have been obtained in a timely manner using conventional Section 215 orders. The full report is available at "Liberty and Security in a Changing World: Report and Recommendations of the President's Review Group on Intelligence and Communications Technology," https://obamawhitehouse.archives.gov/sites/default/files/docs/2013-12-12_rg_final_report.pdf (accessed November 2017).

125 "Report on the Telephone Records Program Conducted under Section 215 of the USA PATRIOT Act and on the Operations of the Foreign Intelligence Surveillance Court," Privacy and Civil Liberties Oversight Board (January 23, 2014), https://www.pclob.gov/library/215-Report_on_the_Telephone_Records_Program.pdf (accessed November 2017).

126 "Report on the Surveillance Program Operated Pursuant to Section 702 of the Foreign Intelligence Surveillance Act, Privacy and Civil Liberties Oversight Board (July 2, 2014), https://www.pclob.gov/library/702-Report.pdf (accessed November 2017).

127 A full list of reforms is presented in "US Surveillance Law, Safe Harbor, and Reforms Since 2013," Peter Swire, https://fpf.org/wp-content/uploads/2015/12/White-Paper-Swire-US-EU-Surveillance.pdf (accessed November 2017).

128 45 C.F.R. § 164.512(k)(2), https://www.law.cornell.edu/cfr/text/45/164.512 (accessed November 2017).

129 15 U.S.C. § 6803(e), https://www.law.cornell.edu/uscode/text/15/6803 (accessed November 2017).

130 15 U.S.C. § 6501, https://www.law.cornell.edu/uscode/text/15/6501 (accessed November 2017).

131 Leslie Harris, "House Passage of Cybersecurity Bill CISPA Wasn't a Complete Loss," *Daily Beast*, April 30, 2012, www.thedailybeast.com/articles/2012/04/30/house-passage-of-cybersecurity-bill-cispa-wasn-t-a-complete-loss.html (accessed November 2017).

132 Elizabeth Weise, "Apple v. FBI timeline: 43 days that rocked tech," *USA Today*, March 15, 2016, https://www.usatoday.com/story/tech/news/2016/03/15/apple-v-fbi-timeline/81827400/ (accessed November 2017).

133 For specifics of the request by the FBI and the order issued by the court, *see* Apple v. FBI, EPIC.org, https://epic.org/amicus/crypto/apple/ (accessed November 2017).

134 Arjun Kharpal, "Apple vs FBI: All you need to know," CNBC, March 29, 2016, https://www.cnbc.com/2016/03/29/apple-vs-fbi-all-you-need-to-know.html (accessed November 2017).

135 Jedidah Bracy, "Why the Apple crypto case goes beyond one company's privacy battle," IAPP (February 18, 2016), https://iapp.org/news/a/why-the-apple-crypto-case-goes-beyond-one-companys-privacy-battle/ (accessed November 2017).

136 "Apple, FBI go to Capitol Hill to talk encryption," IAPP (March 2, 2016), https://iapp.org/news/a/apple-fbi-go-to-capitol-hill-to-talk-encryption/ (accessed November 2017).

137 For a discussion of the debate, view Peter Swire and Kenesa Ahmad, " 'Going Dark' versus a 'Golden Age of Surveillance," Stanford, https://stanford.edu/~jmayer/law696/week8/Going%20Dark%20or%20Golden%20Age.pdf (accessed November 2017). For an analysis of encryption encountered

in U.S. wiretaps, view "2015 Wiretap Report: No wiretap denied, encryption rarely encountered," *ComputerWorld*, www.computerworld.com/article/3091824/security/2015-wiretap-report-no-wiretap-denied-encryption-rarely-encountered.html (accessed November 2017).

138 FISA is codified at 50 U.S.C. §§ 1801-1811, https://www.law.cornell.edu/uscode/text/50/chapter-36/subchapter-I (accessed November 2017).

139 This is one of the reforms instituted in the USA FREEDOM Act. USA FREEDOM Act, Sec. 401, https://iapp.org/media/pdf/resource_center/Freedom_Act_Amendments_FINAL.pdf (accessed November 2017).

140 USA Freedom Act, Sec. 604, https://www.congress.gov/114/bills/hr2048/BILLS-114hr2048enr.pdf (accessed November 2017). Examples of these reports are located on the websites of Facebook and Google. Facebook United States Report, https://govtrequests.facebook.com/country/United%20States/2015-H2/ (accessed November 2017); Google Transparency Report, https://www.google.com/transparencyreport/userdatarequests/US/ (accessed November 2017).

141 2015 FISA Report, https://www.justice.gov/nsd/nsd-foia-library/2015fisa/download (accessed November 2017).

142 Wiretap reports, www.uscourts.gov/statistics-reports/analysis-reports/wiretap-reports (accessed November 2017).

143 For detailed analysis of USA FREEDOM Act amendments to FISA, view https://iapp.org/media/pdf/resource_center/Freedom_Act_Amendments_FINAL.pdf (accessed November 2017).

144 50 U.S.C. § 1861(a), https://www.law.cornell.edu/uscode/text/50/1861 (accessed November 2017).

145 50 U.S.C. § 1861(d), https://www.law.cornell.edu/uscode/text/50/1861 (accessed November 2017).

146 "So what does the USA Freedom Act do anyway?" *Lawfare*, https://www.lawfareblog.com/so-what-does-usa-freedom-act-do-anyway (accessed November 2017).

147 Peter Swire, "US Surveillance Law, Safe Harbor, and Reforms Since 2013," https://fpf.org/wp-content/uploads/2015/12/White-Paper-Swire-US-EU-Surveillance.pdf (accessed November 2017).

148 https://epic.org/privacy/surveillance/fisa/stats/#foot22text (accessed November 2017). For additional information, view "IC on the Record," Office of the Director of National Intelligence, https://icontherecord.tumblr.com/ppd-28/2015/privacy-civil-liberties#section-215 (accessed November 2017).

149 FISA Amendments Act of 2008, Pub. L. 110-261 (2008), https://www.govtrack.us/congress/bills/110/hr6304/text (accessed November 2017).

150 *See* NSA Director Of Civil Liberties And Privacy Office Report, "NSA's Implementation Of Foreign Intelligence Surveillance Act Section 702" (April 16, 2014), https://www.nsa.gov/about/civil-liberties/reports/assets/files/nsa_report_on_section_702_program.pdf (accessed November 2017).

151 President's Review Group on Intelligence and Communications Technologies, *Liberty and Security in a Changing World: Report and Recommendations of The President's Review Group on Intelligence and Communications Technologies*, Appendix A at 263 (December 12, 2013), https://obamawhitehouse.archives.gov/sites/default/files/docs/2013-12-12_rg_final_report.pdf (accessed November 2017).

152 Peter Swire, "Chapter 3: Systemic Safeguards in the US System of Foreign Intelligence Surveillance Law," Professor Peter Swire Testimony in Irish High Court Case, Alston & Bird, https://www.

alston.com/-/media/files/insights/publications/peter-swire-testimony-documents/chapter-3--systemic-safeguards-in-the-us-sytem-of.pdf?la=en (accessed November 2017).

153 The initial story about PRISM was incorrect in important respects, but those inaccuracies have been widely repeated. The actual PRISM program is not even a bulk collection program, much less the basis for "mass and indiscriminate surveillance" when data is transferred from the EU to the U.S. See Peter Swire, "US Surveillance Law."

154 Privacy and Civil Liberties Oversight Board, *Report on the Surveillance Program Operated Pursuant to Section 702 of the Foreign Intelligence Surveillance Act*, 7 (July 2, 2014), https://www.pclob.gov/library/702-Report.pdf (accessed November 2017).

155 "Upstream collection is different from PRISM collection because the acquisition occurs not with the compelled assistance of United States [Internet service providers], but instead with the compelled assistance (through a Section 702 directive) of the providers that control the telecommunications backbone over which communications transit." Privacy and Civil Liberties Oversight Board, Report on the Surveillance Program."

156 *See* Peter Swire and Richard Clarke, "Reform Section 702 to Maintain Fourth Amendment Principles," *Lawfare*, October 19, 2017, https://www.lawfareblog.com/reform-section-702-maintain-fourth-amendment-principles (accessed November 2017); Susan Hennessey and Benjamin Wittes, "Don't Reform Section 702 Just for the Sake of Reform," *Lawfare*, October 16, 2017, https://www.lawfareblog.com/dont-reform-section-702-just-sake-reform (accessed November 2017).

157 Peter Swire,"Responding to the Inspector General's Findings of Improper Use of National Security Letters by the FBI," Testimony of Peter Swire before the U.S. Senate Judiciary Committee (2007), https://www.americanprogress.org/wp-content/uploads/issues/2007/04/pdf/swire_senate_judiciary_testimony.pdf (accessed December 2016). For additional detail, view Peter Swire, "The System of Foreign Intelligence Surveillance Law," 72 George Washington Law Review 1306 (2004), http://ssrn.com/abstract=586616 (accessed November 2017).

158 Charles Doyle, "National Security Letters in Foreign Intelligence Investigations: Legal Background," Congressional Research Service (2015), www.fas.org/sgp/crs/intel/RL33320.pdf (accessed November 2017).

159 *A Review of the Federal Bureau of Investigation's Use of Exigent Letters and Other Informal Requests for Telephone Records*, Office of the Inspector General, U.S. Department of Justice, (2010), https://oig.justice.gov/special/s1001r.pdf (accessed November 2017).

160 18 U.S.C. § 3511, https://www.law.cornell.edu/uscode/text/18/3511 (accessed November 2017).

161 Doe v. Ashcroft, 334 F.Supp. 2d 471 (S.D.N.Y. 2004), www.clearinghouse.net/detail.php?id=12966 (accessed November 2017); Doe v. Gonzales, 386 F.Supp.2d 66 (D.Conn. 2005), https://www.courtlistener.com/opinion/2372515/doe-v-gonzales/ (accessed December 2016).

162 18 U.S.C. § 1510, https://www.law.cornell.edu/uscode/text/18/part-I/chapter-73 (accessed November 2017).

163 Exceptions are permitted only if a senior official determines that national security requires otherwise in the particular case and explains the basis in writing. "IC on the Record," Office of the Director of National Intelligence, https://icontherecord.tumblr.com/ppd-28/2015/privacy-civil-liberties#section-215 (accessed November 2017). For additional information, view Peter Swire, *"US Surveillance Law."*

CHAPTER 13

Emerging Issues

Big Data and the Internet of Things

This chapter focuses on the future. Privacy issues proliferate as new technologies develop. This chapter highlights two technology trends that are changing the landscape of privacy concerns: Big Data and the Internet of Things (IoT).

Big Data is a term used to describe the nearly ubiquitous collection of data about individuals from multitudinous sources, coupled with the low costs to store such data and the new data mining techniques used to draw connections and make predictions based on this collected information.[1] On the positive side, Big Data provides the basis for modern analytics, and the significant insights that can be derived from such data. On the cautionary side, Big Data and modern analytics can be a difficult fit for the fair information privacy practices (FIPPs), sometimes called fair information practices (FIPs), because there may not be clear notice of how data is used, and advanced analytics may not be within the purposes the individual expected when the data was collected.

The data analyzed by analytics programs, algorithms, machine learning, and other data mining techniques—the underpinnings of the term Big Data—are often gathered by devices collectively known as IoT.[2] IoT represents a new development in the ways that individuals interact with computing devices. In the early 1980s, individuals dealt with desktop computers. Later, people adapted to laptops and eventually smartphones. The next evolution, which is rapidly unfolding, combines sensors almost anywhere with connection to the Internet. Examples include wearable technology and connected cars as well as so-called smart homes and smart cities. These technologies allow real-time collection of data about everything from heartbeats (when an individual is in a particular room within a house) to driving patterns (tied to a specific route such as from home to work) to information regarding how long a person remains in a parked vehicle on a city street (and perhaps even what their heartbeat is while they are at that location). Organizations and regulators face a myriad of privacy and security questions about how data is collected and shared, and how to safeguard data in transit.[3] The amount and variety of data collected by the IoT helps to explain the privacy impacts of Big Data and illuminates the interconnectedness of these two technological developments.[4] The topics of Big Data and IoT illustrate how privacy professionals face continuous change in information technology, leading to ever-emerging new issues in the effective governance of personal information.

13.1 Historic Context

In the last several decades, the world has seen a revolution in the types of technology that can generate electronic data—in large part from the proliferation of cell phones and sensors. There are now more cell phones in use than people on the earth.[5] The number of sensors connected to the Internet is now counted in the tens of billions.[6] From a privacy perspective, cell phones provide intimate details of a person's life—from location information to lists of friends to personal preferences as diverse as shopping habits and medical conditions. Sensors have been put in places that previously would have been almost unimaginable—on street light poles, within car fuel injectors, on asthma inhalers, and inside human hearts.

Despite the recent surge in the number and type of these data-collecting devices, key issues that underlie the new developments were envisioned more than 50 years ago. Cofounder of Intel Gordon Moore predicted the exponential increase in computing power needed to handle the massive amounts of data, and science fiction writer Isaac Asimov discussed the social and ethical implications of the cognitive computing power that would come from such rich data analysis.

13.1.1 Moore's Law

In 1965, Moore published a now-iconic article in which he observed that the number of transistors that would fit onto a circuit board doubled each year.[7] A decade after this publication, the principle, dubbed "Moore's Law," was tweaked to say that the number of transistors on a circuit board doubled every 18 to 24 months.[8] For most nonengineers, this law is understood to say that computing power doubles every 18 months.[9] Moore's Law is not a mathematical law, but instead is a useful simplification about the exponential growth in computing for the last several decades. Moore's Law is a useful way to explain the development of two of the technological phenomena emerging at the time of the writing of this book—Big Data and IoT.[10]

With Big Data, a new law has emerged—the amount of data doubles each year. In 2016, humans produced as much data as in the entire history of humankind through 2015. By 2025, it is estimated that amount of data will double every 12 hours.[11] Big Data analytics is a direct outcome of Moore's Law. Big Data is characterized by the "three Vs":

velocity (how fast the data is coming in), volume (the amount of data coming in), and variety (what different forms of data are being analyzed). Velocity and volume come directly from greater processing capability. Variety, derived from the combination of network environments, draws from disparate sources as well as disparate capabilities that can be turned into more uniform categories of data.[12]

The computing power available today allows sensors to go everywhere and be networked together. From a practical standpoint, the basic definition of IoT is that there are inexpensive, precise sensors that can send an unprecedented amount of data into a network.[13] Ordinary individuals experience this with the cameras built into their smartphones. Each picture contains millions of pixels—known today as megapixels. This provides an example of the change in the volume of sensed information and storage, which was unimaginable a few years ago. Digital cameras first became popular in 2004, with the 1.3-megapixel (million pixels) camera.[14] Now the standard smartphone has a 12-megapixel camera, and the computing infrastructure (collection, transmission and storage) continues to shift to far higher, and growing, amounts of information.

13.1.2 Asimov's Law of Robotics

Big Data is the fuel that runs algorithms and analytics, which will enable artificial intelligence (AI) systems connected to the cloud. Kant's famous statement that "thoughts without content are empty; intuitions without concepts are blind" can be modernized as "algorithms without data are empty; data without algorithms are blind."[15]

In the 1940s, Asimov spoke in terms of robots. In today's world, these emblematic laws apply not just to robots, but to algorithms, machine learning, and AI, meaning that Asimov's three "laws," to the extent they apply in practice, will apply to the practices in IoT, Big Data and the cloud.[16] The three laws are as follows:

1. "A robot may not injure a human being or, through inaction, allow a human being to come to harm"
2. "A robot must obey orders given it by human beings except where such orders would conflict with the First Law"
3. "A robot must protect its own existence as long as such protection does not conflict with the First or Second Law"[17]

In a synthesis of Asimov's principles with modern concepts of privacy, Mark Rotenberg of the Electronic Privacy Information Center suggested two additions to Asimov's iconic laws to address transparency in algorithms and AI. These are as follows:

1. "Robots should always reveal the basis of their decisions"

2. "Robots must always reveal their identities"[18]

Paying homage to the starting point provided by Asimov, Microsoft's CEO Satya Nadella proposed a list of AI design principles, including several that focus on privacy issues: "AI must be designed to help humanity, AI must be designed for intelligent privacy, AI must be transparent, and AI needs algorithmic accountability so humans can undo unintended harm."[19]

The "laws" and design principles discussed here do not operate today as actual legal rules that apply to an organization's privacy practices. Instead, they vividly suggest how profound the issues are that organizations will face as IoT and Big Data become pervasive.

13.2 Big Data

Big Data's extensive collection of data related to consumers' activities, both online and offline, and the subsequent analysis of that data is fraught with risks—financial risk, business risk, security risk and privacy risk.[20]

13.2.1 A Case Study in Big Data

To understand the concerns that arise with Big Data, consider a case study of a major financial services firm that decides to create an "All Customer Funds" (ACF) database, showing all transactions and balances for customers' checking accounts, savings accounts, securities, real estate and other assets.[21] The ACF software collects a tremendous amount of data, with granular financial information about tens of millions of customers. Data at this scale enables advanced analytics, with potentially great benefits to customers (higher return on investment) and the bank (greater profit per customer).

Along with these potentially great benefits, there are also potential risks. The bank will not be pleased if the Big Data product turns into a Big Data breach—a centralized database can create the possibility of larger breaches than previously. Such a breach can be quite expensive, due to the costs of responding to the breach (such as notice to customers under data breach laws), fraudulent account activity (when a hacker is able to withdraw money from customer accounts), and identity theft (when the information in the accounts is used to impersonate the customers in other settings).

The specter of a Big Data Breach shows the importance of information security in determining how an organization should collect and manage Big Data. The scale of the database creates a more attractive target for hackers. Along with external hackers, the organization should address the risk of insiders accessing information at scale. The example of Edward Snowden taking many tens of thousands of records from the National Security Agency (NSA) illustrates the magnitude of a possible breach by an insider. The organization must thus create and implement a comprehensive security plan for its major databases, including firewalls (to keep intruders away) and intrusion detection (to find intruders that get in). The organization should study the "threat models" of who wants to attack the organization and why they want to do so, and raise the level of security preparedness to match the level of the threats. One tip for senior managers in implementing the comprehensive information plan is the "friends and family test"—would the managers feel comfortable if data on themselves and their family and friends were in the database, subject to possible breach? For instance, would managers at the bank feel comfortable with their own family's data going into the ACF database? If not, that is a reason to take greater precautions.

13.2.2 Fair Information Privacy Practices, Data Minimization and Anonymization

The assembly and use of unprecedented amounts of personal information raises multiple issues about how to apply the FIPPs, also called FIPs, discussed in Chapter 1. In the European Union (EU), the FIPPs have essentially been codified into the Data Protection Directive and the General Data Protection Regulation. In the United States, the FIPPs have often been incorporated into companies' privacy policies, and violation of those policies can lead to enforcement under the Federal Trade Commission (FTC) Act or other statutes. Relevant FIPPs include:

- **Collection Limitation:** obtain data by lawful and fair means and (where possible) with the knowledge and consent of the data subject
- **Purpose Specification:** use the data as initially intended or for other purposes that are not incompatible with that purpose (meaning there are limitations on secondary uses of the data)
- **Use Limitation:** do not use or disclose data beyond those purposes except with consent or by authority of law[22]

In practice, two themes are especially important in applying privacy protections to Big Data: (1) data minimization, to avoid privacy and security risks of Big Data where possible and (2) de-identification, to avoid privacy and security risks that arise when previously de-identified data can be re-identified.

13.2.2.1 Data Minimization

In some organizations, there is an unexamined assumption that more data is better, that the organization will know more and do more effective analytics by pulling more data into a centralized system such as the ACF database. As discussed, this simplistic approach to Big Data can lead to a Big Data Breach—a single failure can compromise a potentially enormous number and variety of records. Logical responses to this risk include access controls (only employees with a need to know can access the personal information) and segregation of databases, to prevent one lapse from harming the entire company.

The FIPPs add privacy-based reasons for caution about the idea that more data is always better. Legal rules and company policy, in many settings, implement the guiding principles of FIPPs such as collection limitation, purpose specification and use limitation.

The principle of data minimization is a useful way to summarize why more data is not always better. As one prominent example, the employees doing data analytics often have no need to see the customers' names and full account numbers—the analytics can proceed just as well without those data fields. Identifiers are not needed for many Big Data applications, so the benefits of analytics can be achieved while reducing the privacy and security risks. Similarly, data should be disposed of when no longer needed by the organization—proper disposal reduces the risk that a security or privacy breach will occur down the road because of paper left in a dumpster or records left on an old hard drive.

This practice of data minimization reduces the risk that data will be used in ways that violate the FIPPs, for instance, in ways not intended by the customer. To reduce privacy and security risks, companies should examine their data practices to best approach the collection, use, and retention of customers' data. They can decide not to collect certain data, to collect only those fields of data necessary to provide the service or product being offered, to collect only data that is less sensitive or to de-identify data once it is collected.[23]

13.2.3 Data De-identification, Pseudonymization and Anonymization

Big Data is often defined as having a great volume, variety, and velocity of data. As such, Big Data poses a risk to the anonymization or de-identification of data. In the United States, quite a few people share the same height (within an inch) and weight (within five pounds), and eye color. Imagine combining those three data fields with dozens of other data fields—zip code, religion, purchasing habits, social media public posts and so forth. These extra data fields are typical of the increasing volume and variety of data. Where that wealth of data exists, a company analyst or someone else with access to the data can quite possibly re-identify the data—determine the name of the person, or at least narrow the list of names down to a small number.

Big Data thus can call into question the traditional line between personally identifiable information, which is subject to stricter privacy rules, and de-identified information, where privacy rules traditionally no longer apply. As an overall goal, organizations are seeking to gain the benefits from analyzing data, while seeking to suppress the portions of records that can reveal individuals' identities.[24] The highest privacy risks apply to what are called "direct identifiers," which are data that identify an individual with little or no additional effort. A phone number is an example of a direct identifier, because there are look-up services that provide the name for most phone numbers. As the volume and variety of data fields increase in a database, organizations also pay increasing attention to "indirect identifiers"—data such as age or gender that can increase the likelihood of identifying an individual.

The Future of Privacy Forum has developed a useful chart that illustrates the multiple ways data can vary from fully identified (a person's name) to fully statistical or aggregate.[25] This chart, for instance, distinguishes among subtly different terms:

- **Pseudonymous data:** Information from which the direct identifiers have been eliminated. Indirect identifiers remain intact.[26]
- **De-identified data:** Direct and known indirect identifiers have been removed.
- **Anonymous data:** Direct and indirect identifiers have been removed or technically manipulated to prevent re-identification.

These categories do not result from a single method or from reducing the identifiability of data. Instead, reduction of the risk of re-identification results from a collection of techniques that can be applied to different kinds of data with differing levels of effectiveness.[27] Data minimization was discussed above, such as ensuring that the people doing the analytics do not see names or other direct identifiers. Some other commonly used approaches include:

- **Blurring.** This technique reduces the precision of disclosed data to reduce the certainty of individual identification. For example, date of birth is highly identifying (because a small portion of people are born on a particular day of a particular year), but year of birth is less identifying. Similarly, a broader set of years (such as 1971-1980, or 1981-1990) is less identifying than year of birth.
- **Masking.** This technique masks the original values in a data set with the goal of data privacy protection. One way this may be accomplished is to use perturbation—make small changes to the data while maintaining overall averages—to make it more difficult to identify individuals.[28]
- **Differential Privacy.** This technique uses a mathematical approach to ensure that the risk to an individual's privacy is not substantially increased as a result of being part of the database.[29]

Because many organizations have stricter rules for personally identifiable information (PII) than for de-identified data, these sorts of statistical techniques are becoming a more prominent feature for organizations that wish to use Big Data analytics. Failure to use effective techniques may result in an enforcement action. Suppose, for instance, that the company privacy policy states that the company does not share PII with third parties, but there is a long-established practice of sharing anonymized data. If the data is not truly anonymized and can instead be re-identified easily by those receiving the data, then the FTC or state attorneys general may have a valid claim for a deceptive trade practice.

Faced with this risk of re-identification, companies in their Big Data practices should develop and implement policies to reduce that risk.[30] Along with technical measures, such as the statistical methods mentioned here, companies should consider effective administrative measures to control the data. For instance, customer names held in one part of the company can be suppressed when transferred to the analytics division (a technical measure); in addition, audits and other administrative policies can be instituted to help prevent the persons doing analytics from seeking to re-identify the data.[31]

Many Big Data efforts face a tension between the utility of analytics and the risk of re-identification or other security or privacy risks. Some technical experts have stressed the great difficulty of effectively de-identifying data,[32] and debates are likely to continue about what mix of technical and administrative controls (if any) are sufficient to treat data as aggregated enough to fall outside of the definition of PII in the United States or "personal data" in Europe.

13.2.4 FTC Reports on Big Data

In recent years, the FTC has issued reports that examine issues that arise as a result of the use of Big Data. Privacy practitioners are encouraged to become familiar with the key points in these reports as they can indicate areas where the federal agency will focus its future efforts.

13.2.4.1. FTC Report, "Data Brokers: A Call for Transparency and Accountability"

In this 2014 report, the FTC expressed concern about the vast amount of personal information collected by data brokers.[33] The FTC characterized the data broker industry as: collecting consumer data from numerous sources, usually without consumers' knowledge or consent; storing billions of data elements on nearly every U.S. consumer; analyzing data about consumers to draw inferences about them; and combining online and offline data to market to consumers online.

The FTC identified three broad categories of products offered by data brokers at that time: (1) marketing (such as appending data to customer information that a marketing company already has), (2) risk mitigation (such as information that may reduce the risk of fraud) and (3) location of individuals (such as identifying an individual from partial information). For each of these segments of the industry, the FTC suggested that data brokers engage in data minimization practices, review collection practices carefully as they relate to children and teens, and take reasonable precautions to ensure that downstream users did not use the data for discriminatory or criminal purposes.[34]

At the time of the report, the FTC requested legislation to require data broker practices be more transparent for consumers whose information was being collected and manipulated as well as to provide greater control to consumers regarding their own information.[35]

After the 2014 report was issued, the FTC successfully brought an enforcement action against LeapLab for its failure to protect data that was sold to a third party. According to the FTC, LeapLab bought sensitive information, including Social Security numbers and bank account numbers, from payday loan websites and, acting as a data broker, sold the information to businesses that LeapLab knew had no legitimate use for the information. LeapLab's actions allowed scammers to steal millions of dollars from individuals' accounts. The court issued an order in 2016 prohibiting LeapLab from continuing these business practices. The court also issued a $5.7 million money judgment against the business and its officers, but suspended the payment of the judgment based on sworn affidavits that the defendants could not pay the amount.[36]

13.2.4.2 FTC Report, "Big Data: A Tool for Inclusion or Exclusion?"

This 2016 report discussed the era of Big Data as being brought about by dramatic reduction in the cost of storage, collection of consumer data from almost innumerable sources (as discussed in the IoT section), and increase in computer capabilities to analyze this data. The FTC noted that the era of Big Data was still in its infancy in 2016, but that the analytics resulting from Big Data already benefited areas such as marketing, human resources and fraud prevention.

The agency expressed its understanding that Big Data brought with it significant benefits coupled with significant risks. Examples of the benefits identified included providing healthcare tailored to individual patients, enhancing educational opportunities by tailoring the experience to the individual student, and increasing equal access to employment. Examples of the risks included: exposing sensitive information; reinforcing existing disparities; and creating new justifications for exclusion.

Issues of particular concern to the FTC revolved around: privacy of sensitive information, security of large sets of data, and disparate impacts on individuals from inappropriate or inaccurate inferences drawn from analytics. The FTC cautioned companies that numerous federal laws already applied to handling Big Data: the Fair Credit Reporting Act, the Equal Credit Opportunity Act, and the Federal Trade Commission Act.[37]

13.3 Internet of Things

In 2016, estimates for the number of IoT devices in use topped 15 billion worldwide, with spending on these devices approaching $1 trillion globally.[38] By 2020, the number of wearable device shipments is estimated to be more than 200 million.[39] Predictions are that 90 percent of new cars will be connected by 2020, with estimates that a quarter of a billion connected vehicles will be on the road by that time.[40]

When reading accounts like these in the media, note that there is not one universally accepted definition of the term IoT. A critical aspect of IoT is that the devices can connect to the Internet (and each other) without the need for human interaction.[41] The FTC has examined privacy and security issues using the following definition of IoT: "Devices or sensors—other than computers, smartphones, or tablets—that connect, communicate, or transmit information with or between each other through the Internet."[42]

When thinking of a privacy framework, the initial screen is to look at the data to determine where it falls on a spectrum that plots personal data at one end and impersonal data on the other. It is worth noting that much of IoT—such as temperature, traffic statistics, and sensors around industrial production—often does not implicate PII.[43] For example, traffic sensors that count cars generally will not create PII, but sensors that take pictures of license plates likely do. Often with networked sensors there are few, if any, privacy concerns because the data is impersonal.[44] In assessing privacy risks, practitioners should be vigilant to understand the definition of IoT being used in a particular context, and the prevalence, if any, of PII.

Most IoT devices share two characteristics that are important for privacy and cybersecurity discussions: (1) the devices interact with software running elsewhere (often in the cloud) and function autonomously and (2) when coupled with data analysis, the devices may take proactive steps and make decisions about or suggest next steps for users.[45]

Concerns regarding privacy and cybersecurity stem from: (1) limited user interfaces in the products; (2) lack of industry experience with privacy and cybersecurity; (3) lack of incentives in the industries to deploy updates after products are purchased; and (4) limitations of the devices themselves, such as lack of effective hardware security measures.[46]

Along with analysis of prominent reports about IoT, the following IoT devices will now be examined in more detail: (1) wearables, such as sensors to monitor health and track patterns of daily activities; (2) connected cars, including devices that allow cars to report the maintenance issues directly to the dealer; (3) smart homes, for example, heating systems that adjust as the occupants move from room to room in the house; and (4) smart cities, such as the use of sensors in cities to help regulate traffic congestion.

13.3.1 Wearables

Electronic devices that are worn on the body and collect data in real time are known as wearables. They range from headwear used by soldiers on the battlefield to wrist devices that check heart beats during exercise. Analysis of the data from these devices presents the possibility of benefits as well as significant challenges. Possible benefits of health-related data include information to help individuals meet their fitness goals, or data that can serve as a basis for a reduction in health insurance rates.[47] Privacy challenges exist, however, when the devices collect health-related information such as heart rate, blood pressure and even more complex information such as blood alcohol content. Most of this information is not protected by HIPAA, because HIPAA applies only to the activities of covered entities such as providers and health insurance plans.[48]

The challenges related to wearables data have been examined in research that focused on users' privacy concerns regarding wearables:

- **"Right to forget."** Users are concerned that tracking data daily will make it difficult for them to get rid of documentation of actions that they would rather forget.
- **Impact of location disclosure.** Users expressed concern that criminals might gain access to this information to track or stalk them.
- **Concern that screens will be read.** Users pointed out that many devices, such as smart watches, have a display that can be read by those who are near the user.
- **Video and audio recording where those involved were unaware.** Users discussed that head-mounted devices, such as Google glasses, raise privacy concerns because video and audio recording can take place without those in the recording being aware that the documentation is occurring.
- **Lack of control of the data.** Users are concerned that government and organizations may use the data without their consent or knowledge.
- **Automatic syncing with social media.** Users are concerned that some devices sync instantaneously with social media, without providing an effective opportunity to restrict such sharing.
- **Facial recognition.** Users noted a concern that systems may identify them individually.[49]

In 2016, the Future of Privacy Forum issued a set of best practices for the privacy of consumer wearables. These include access, deletion, and correction rights; opt-in consent for sharing with third parties; sharing of data for scientific research purposes, with informed consent; compliance with leading app platform standards and global privacy frameworks; strong data security requirements; and strong requirements for de-identification.[50]

13.3.2 Connected Cars

Connected cars collect and transmit data about the vehicle, the driver's driving habits, and the driver's preferences. One example would be a vehicle that wirelessly alerts the dealership when tires need to be rotated. Another would be an app from a car insurance company that records braking habits. Additionally, information may be transmitted from the car to the Internet from multiple sources, such as users' phones, video systems, cameras, GPS systems, and entertainment centers.[51]

As cars move toward being autonomous, more systems and subsystems will have digital information sent to the Internet. The various systems, both those operating the vehicle and those for keeping the user's electronics operating, have different levels of interoperability and security. Privacy experts raise concerns that these configurations place sensitive information at risk to unauthorized access or hacking. The complexity of these issues has led to a situation where numerous federal agencies are considering regulating connected cars: the National Highway Traffic Safety Administration (NHTSA), FTC, and the Federal Communications Commission (FCC).[52]

13.3.3 Smart Homes

Smart homes have multiple devices that are connected to the Internet to enhance the home environment experience. These devices are typically user controlled—a task that is often accomplished via a smartphone or another small electronic device. The types of devices in these houses include refrigerators that can update grocery lists (or contact the grocery store directly), thermostats that change the temperature in a given room based on the occupants' presence, beds that adjust the mattress as per the preferences of the user, video monitors that allow parents to check on a baby from another room, and electricity sensors that ensure efficient use of resources.[53] The smart homes market is expected to surpass $43 billion by 2020.[54]

As the home has long been seen as a bastion of privacy, the collection and storage of intimate information from smart homes has raised significant privacy concerns. These issues are intensified even further by the massive amounts of data collected, the fact that much of the data is reported back to companies over the Internet (often without the awareness of the user), and the reality that these systems can be hacked or hijacked (and often the data streams are not encrypted).[55]

Examples of privacy issues with smart homes include:

- **Smart thermostats.** IoT devices, including thermostats, are vulnerable to attack by hackers and criminals in part because users often do not reset factory set passwords. In 2016, white-hat researchers demonstrated that smart devices are susceptible to ransomware, which involves malicious actors locking down a system, such as a thermostat, and demanding money to return it to working order.[56]

- **Smart TVs.** As with many IoT devices, the Internet connection with a smart TV has often not been effectively secured. Experts currently discourage users from providing bank information over a Smart TV or even from accessing social media sites. Additional advice includes covering the camera on the device and disconnecting the device from the Internet when not in use. One smart TV manufacturer has even warned customers not to have private conversations in the vicinity of the devices, because those conversations will be recorded and reviewed in an effort to comply with any commands that may be in the speech.[57]

- **Communication systems.** Homes with multiple devices often use wireless technology to allow devices to communicate. For example, a laptop may transmit data wirelessly to a printer. With access to the home network, a malicious actor can eavesdrop on these transmissions, monitoring email and phone conversations, and potentially stealing passwords, bank accounts and other sensitive information.[58]
- **Security systems.** Security systems that are connected to the Internet to provide the user with the ability to remotely lock doors or open the garage also provide hackers with the means to access the house.[59]

13.3.4 Smart Cities

Smart cities is a term that primarily refers to municipalities and other government entities using sensors to monitor functions and improve government services.[60] For example, a city could embed wireless sensors into existing lighting fixtures, then analyze this data to allow targeted law enforcement practices, improved parking efficiency and increased environmental monitoring.[61] The demand for smart cities technologies, which can help manage everything from traffic to garbage collection to parking meters, is expected to continue to grow—with estimates that the global market for these technologies will be $27.5 billion by 2023.[62]

The reliance of smart cities on automated sensors and algorithms raises concerns about software vulnerabilities, data security breaches and potential invasions of privacy.[63] In 2015, the U.S. Department of Homeland Security (DHS) issued a report highlighting three themes in cybersecurity risks that arise when integrating cyber-physical systems with city infrastructure in Smart Cities:

- **Changing seams.** From the seams between legacy and new infrastructure to those between urban and rural systems, these boundaries are moving or disappearing as systems are networked and upgraded.
- **Inconsistent adoption.** Factors such as user preferences, resource availability and scale of technological system will lead to inconsistent adoption. These inevitable inconsistencies will introduce security challenges for industry, government and people living with the technology.
- **Increased automation.** Although automation can reduce certain risks, removal of human interaction from many aspects of cyber-physical infrastructure

> has the potential to introduce new security challenges, including increasing the number of access points (and the possible attack vectors), cascading failures (where no humans are present to witness developing problems), and unintentional removal of manual overrides.[64]

Privacy threats from the technologies used by smart cities include real-time surveillance capabilities, invasion of physical private space, identification of habits, and collection of aggregated details about personal life.[65] Privacy discussions with regard to smart cities differ somewhat from the previous discussion of wearables, connected cars and smart homes, because municipalities are government actors. The conceptual framework can best be seen as part of a spectrum. The discussion at the beginning of the IoT section introduced a spectrum to analyze whether data was PII or not. For data held by government, purpose is another criterion that is important to consider. With regard to the purpose aspect of privacy for government's use of data, service is on one end of the spectrum and surveillance on the other. Privacy concerns are fairly low, or even nonexistent, for collected information that falls in the area of impersonal data and is used for a service purpose. An example would be a trash bin with smart technology that allows government officials to know when the receptacle should be emptied. Privacy concerns are heightened if either personal data or surveillance purpose is implicated. Concerns about privacy can become even greater when both personal data and surveillance purpose are at issue. A few changes to the previous example move the scenario into this category. In an amended version where the municipality wants to prevent illegal dumping, an authentication card is required to dump trash—meaning the refuse deposited in any particular trash bin can be linked back to a specific individual.[66]

13.3.5 BITAG Report

In 2016, the Broadband Internet Technical Advisory Group issued a set of recommendation for IoT privacy and security practices. The main recommendations include:

- IoT devices should follow security and encryption best practices
- For devices that can be customized by the users, the company should test the IoT devices in different possible configurations
- IoT devices should be designed to facilitate automated, secure software updates
- IoT devices should be secured by default by the inclusion of a password
- IoT devices should be shipped originally with reasonably up-to-date software

- IoT devices should be shipped with a privacy policy that is understandable and easy to find
- IoT devices should communicate with restrictive rather than permissive protocols
- IoT devices should continue to function if Internet connectivity is disrupted or if cloud back-up fails[67]

The threat from IoT is not so much that an individual device will be compromised, but that IoT will allow an avenue for attack of a network. Organizations should develop a programmatic approach to address these risks.[68]

In 2016, one of the first known malware attacks using IoT devices occurred in the United States. The attack affected an Internet infrastructure company, causing significant delays in Internet traffic in key areas throughout the country. Companies heavily affected by the outages included Amazon, Netflix, Reddit, Spotify, Tumblr and Twitter.[69] The attack was accomplished by exploiting weak security in smart video cameras and DVRs to launch a distributed denial of service (DDoS) attack.[70]

13.3.6 FTC Report on IoT

In 2014, the FTC undertook its first enforcement action involving an Internet-connected device against a company that provided consumers with Internet-connected cameras for use inside the home. In its complaint, the FTC alleged that TRENDnet failed to encrypt customer log-in credentials and failed to test consumers' privacy settings. Hackers utilized these security vulnerabilities to post hundreds of live video feeds featuring babies sleeping in cribs and adults engaging in daily activities. The agency's complaint resulted in an order requiring the company to bring its practices into line with FTC requirements and to establish its compliance by undergoing assessments every 2 years for the next 20 years.[71]

The year after this order, the FTC issued a report, "Internet of Things: Privacy and Security in a Connected World."[72] With regard to privacy of personal information, the FTC pointed out that the sheer volume of information collected as well as the deeply personal nature of the information obtained heightened the need for protection. The FTC explained that traditional models of providing consumer disclosure and choice may need to be modified by companies involved in this industry. The FTC is keenly aware of the practical difficulty of providing choice when there is no consumer interface and suggests that companies look at utilizing one or more of the following: choice at point of sale, video tutorials, codes on the devices, choice during setup, management portals or dashboards, icons, emails or texts, general privacy menus, or a user experience approach.

IoT security risks identified by the FTC include: lax security that could allow intruders access to personal information collected by the devices, security vulnerabilities on a consumer's device that could lead to attacks on networks connected to the device, and security issues with the devices that could place physical safety at issue, such as changes to instructions for an insulin pump or to a lock on a front door to a house. In addressing these concerns, the FTC urged companies to: implement security by design, ensure personnel employ good security, engage in good vendor management practices, utilize a defense-in-depth approach where security measures are considered at several levels, implement reasonable access controls to ensure that access by unauthorized persons to a customer's device is limited, and continue to monitor products throughout the device's lifecycle, patching vulnerabilities when possible.[73] In sum, the FTC has expressed a concern about both the privacy and security aspects of IoT.

13.4 Conclusion

The discussion of Moore's Law highlighted the continuous and exponential increase that has existed for decades in computing capabilities. This constant change in information technology means constant change in the challenges facing privacy professionals. This chapter's discussion of Big Data and the IoT analyzes two areas that have emerged since roughly 2013 yet are already dominating the work of many privacy professionals.

The discussion in this chapter suggests that privacy professionals serve themselves well by a process of lifelong education in information technology, as well as the organizational practices and legal changes that come from the changes in computing. Keeping pace with this change can seem overwhelming. A more optimistic perspective is that privacy professionals are at the forefront of crucial changes in society. The terms *Big Data* and *Internet of Things* were unknown a decade ago. A decade from now, privacy professionals will face new, emerging challenges, applying durable values to changing times.

Privacy issues will continue to emerge as new technologies come onto the market. Concerns around Big Data and IoT will proliferate as these two developments pave the way for analytics to evolve into AI. Privacy professionals should seek out best practices in their industry to address these topics.

Endnotes

1 "Big Data: Seizing Opportunities, Preserving Data," Executive Office of the President (May 2014), pp. 1-7, https://obamawhitehouse.archives.gov/sites/default/files/docs/big_data_privacy_report_may_1_2014.pdf (accessed November 2017).

2 For a discussion of the ethical obligations concerning the collection of data needed for Big Data and IoT, *see* "With Big Data Comes Big Responsibility," *Harvard Law Review* (November 2014), https://hbr.org/2014/11/with-big-data-comes-big-responsibility (accessed December accessed November 2017).

3 The 2014 White House report defines IoT as "a term used to describe the ability of devices to communicate with each other using embedded sensors that are linked through wired and wireless networks; "Big Data: Seizing Opportunities, Preserving Data," p.2.

4 For a detailed look at privacy concerns related to Big Data, *see* Big Data and Privacy: Making Ends Meet, Future of Privacy Forum, https://fpf.org/wp-content/uploads/Big-Data-and-Privacy-Paper-Collection.pdf (accessed November 2017). For an in-depth discussion of privacy issues related to IoT, view Broadband Internet Technical Advisory Group IoT Security and Privacy Recommendations (November 2016), https://www.bitag.org/report-internet-of-things-security-privacy-recommendations.php (accessed November 2017).

5 Roger Cheng, "By 2020, more people will own a phone than have electricity: The proliferation of mobile phones will continue as mobile traffic jumps tenfold over the next four years, according to a study by Cisco," *CNET*, February 3, 2016, https://www.cnet.com/news/by-2020-more-people-will-own-a-phone-than-have-electricity/ (accessed November 2017). See Murithi Mutiga and Zoe Flood, "Africa calling: mobile phone revolution to transform democracies," *The Guardian*, August 8, 2016.

6 John Greenough, "34 billion devices will be connected to the Internet by 2020," *Business Insider*, January 26, 2016, www.businessinsider.com/34-billion-devices-will-be-connected-to-the-internet-by-2020-2016-1 (accessed November 2017).

7 Gordon E. Moore, "Cramming More Components onto Integrated Circuits," *Electronics*, pp. 114-117 (April 19, 1965), https://cis.upenn.edu/~cis501/papers/mooreslaw-reprint.pdf (accessed November 2017).

8 Matthew Bey, "Analysis: Fifty Years Later, Moore's Computing Law Holds," Stratfor (April 19, 2015), https://www.stratfor.com/analysis/fifty-years-later-moores-computing-law-holds (accessed December 2016); "1965: "Moore's Law" Predicts the Future of Integrated Circuits," www.computerhistory.org/siliconengine/moores-law-predicts-the-future-of-integrated-circuits/ (accessed November 2017).

9 Jonathan Strickland, "How Moore's Law Works," HowStuffWorks, http://computer.howstuffworks.com/moores-law.htm (accessed November 2017).

10 When discussing privacy and security concerns, it is important to understand that there are no bright lines that separate Big Data concerns from IoT concerns. "This lack of clarity is partially due to the challenge of defining both Big Data and the Internet of Things." Richard Rutledge, Aaron Massey, Annie Antón and Peter Swire, "Clarifying the Internet of Things by Defining the Internet of Devices," Sensity, p. 39:28, http://peterswire.net/wp-content/uploads/Clarifying-the-Internet-of-Things-by-Defining-the-Internet-of-Devices.pdf (accessed November 2017).

11 Dirk Heilbing, Bruno S. Frey, Gerd Gigerenzer, Ernst Hafen, Michael Hagner, Yvonne Hofstetter, Jeroen van Hoven, Roberto V. Zicari and Andrej Zwitter, "Will Democracy Survive Big Data and

Artificial Intelligence?" *Scientific American*, February 25, 2017, https://www.scientificamerican.com/article/will-democracy-survive-big-data-and-artificial-intelligence/ (accessed November 2017).

12 David Gewirtz, "Volume, velocity, and variety: Understanding the three V's of big data," *ZDNet*, April 20, 2016, www.zdnet.com/article/volume-velocity-and-variety-understanding-the-three-vs-of-big-data/ (accessed November 2017). IBM adds a fourth category: veracity—the uncertainty of data. "The Four Vs of Big Data, Infographics & Animations," IBM Big Data & Analytics Hub, www.ibmbigdatahub.com/infographic/four-vs-big-data (accessed November 2017).

13 The common usage of IoT generally references it as an umbrella term that encompasses Internet of Devices (IoD)—ID devices, remote sensors, smart devices, application-specific computers (such as a mall kiosk), and general-purpose computing devices (such as desktop computers and laptops). For a detailed discussion of the nuances of the definitions of IoT and IoD as well as the resulting impacts on privacy and security, see Richard Rutledge, Aaron Massey, Annie Antón and Peter Swire, "Clarifying the Internet of Things by Defining the Internet of Devices," Sensity, http://peterswire.net/wp-content/uploads/Clarifying-the-Internet-of-Things-by-Defining-the-Internet-of-Devices.pdf (accessed November 2017).

14 Simon Hill, "From J-Phone to Lumina 1020: A Complete History of the Camera Phone," *Digital Trends*, August 11, 2013, www.digitaltrends.com/mobile/camera-phone-history/ (accessed November 2017).

15 Jack Balkin, "The Three Laws of Robotics in the Age of Big Data," SSRN, *Ohio State Law Journal* (August 27, 2017) (citing Immanuel Kant, *Critique of Pure Reason*), https://papers.ssrn.com/sol3/papers.cfm?abstract_id=2890965 (accessed November 2017).

16 Jack Balkin, "The Three Laws of Robotics in the Age of Big Data," SSRN, *Ohio State Law Journal* (August 27, 2017), https://papers.ssrn.com/sol3/papers.cfm?abstract_id=2890965 (accessed November 2017).

17 Isaac Asimov: The Three Laws of Robotics, video on YouTube, https://www.youtube.com/watch?v=AWJJnQybZlk (accessed November 2017).

18 Mark Rotenberg, "Privacy in the Modern Age: The Search for Solutions," PowerPoint Presentation presented at 38th ICDPCC in Marrakech, Morocco (October 19, 2016). For further discussion, *see* Stephen Gardner, "Artificial intelligence Poses Data Privacy Challenges," *Bloomberg BNA*, October 26, 2016, https://www.bna.com/artificial-intelligence-poses-n57982079158/ (accessed November 2017).

19 Satya Nadella, "The Partnership of the Future: Microsoft's CEO explores how humans and A.I. can work together to solve society's greatest challenges," *Slate*, June 28, 2016, www.slate.com/articles/technology/future_tense/2016/06/microsoft_ceo_satya_nadella_humans_and_a_i_can_work_together_to_solve_society.html (accessed November 2017). Amazon, Facebook, Google, IBM, and Microsoft have entered into a partnership to advance best practices in AI. "Industry leaders establish partnership on AI best practices," Partnership on AI (September 28, 2016), https://www.partnershiponai.org/2016/09/industry-leaders-establish-partnership-on-ai-best-practices/ (accessed November 2017).

20 Timothy Morey, Theodore Forbath and Allison Schoop, "Customer Data: Designing for Transparency and Trust," *Harvard Business Review*, May 2015, https://hbr.org/2015/05/customer-data-designing-for-transparency-and-trust (accessed November 2017).

21 This case study was created by Peter Swire for teaching executive education classes about Big Data. Peter Swire, Professor of Law and Expert on Privacy and Cybersecurity, http://peterswire.net/ (accessed November 2017).

22 Appendix D - Fair Information Practices, Guide to Protecting the Confidentiality of Personally Identifiable Information (PII), National Institute of Standards and Technology (NIST), http://nvlpubs.nist.gov/nistpubs/Legacy/SP/nistspecialpublication800-122.pdf (accessed November 2017).

23 *See* "Internet of Things: Privacy and Security in a Connected World," FTC (January 2015), p. iv, https://www.ftc.gov/system/files/documents/reports/federal-trade-commission-staff-report-november-2013-workshop-entitled-internet-things-privacy/150127iotrpt.pdf (accessed November 2017).

24 See Felix Yu, "Defining Privacy and Utility in Data Sets," 84 *University of Colorado Law Review* 1117 (2013), http://lawreview.colorado.edu/wp-content/uploads/2013/11/13.-Wu_710_s.pdf. Cynthia Dwork and Aaron Roth, "The Algorithmic Foundations of Differential Privacy," *Foundations and Trends in Theoretical Computer Science*, Vol. 9, Nos. 3-4 (2014), pp. 6-10, https://www.cis.upenn.edu/~aaroth/Papers/privacybook.pdf (accessed November 2017). For additional information on this topic, view Simson Garfinkel, "De-Identification of Personal Data," National Institute of Standards and Technology (NIST) (October2015), http://nvlpubs.nist.gov/nistpubs/ir/2015/NIST.IR.8053.pdf (accessed November 2017).

25 A Visual Guide to Practical Data De-Identification, Future of Privacy Forum, https://fpf.org/wp-content/uploads/2016/04/FPF_Visual-Guide-to-Practical-Data-DeID.pdf (accessed November 2017). For additional information on this topic, *see* Simson Garfinkel, "De-Identification of Personal Data."

26 In the EU, the GDPR encourages pseudonymization of data. Gabe Maldoff, "Top 10 Operational Impacts of the GDPR: Part 8 - Pseudonymization," Privacy Advisor, February 12, 2016, https://iapp.org/news/a/top-10-operational-impacts-of-the-gdpr-part-8-pseudonymization/ (accessed November 2017).

27 Christopher Achatz, "At a Glance: De-Identification, Anonymization, and Pseudonymization," Bryan Cave (February 28, 2016), https://www.bryancave.com/en/thought-leadership/at-a-glance-de-identification-anonymization-and-pseudonymization.html (accessed November 2017). For an in-depth discussion of data de-identification, view Jules Polonetsky, Omer Tene and Kelsey Finch, "Shades of Gray: Seeing the Full Spectrum of Practical Data De-Identification," SSRN (April 1, 2016), https://papers.ssrn.com/sol3/papers.cfm?abstract_id=2757709 (accessed November 2017).

28 For an in-depth discussion on de-identification techniques, *see Guide to Protecting the Confidentiality of Personally Identifiable Information (PII)*, National Institute of Standards and Technology (NIST), http://nvlpubs.nist.gov/nistpubs/Legacy/SP/nistspecialpublication800-122.pdf (accessed November 2017).

29 For an overview of the concept of differential privacy, view Anthony Tockar, "Differential Privacy: The Basics," Neustar Research (September 8, 2014), https://research.neustar.biz/2014/09/08/differential-privacy-the-basics/ (accessed February, 2017). An in-depth analysis can be found at Cynthia Dwork and Aaron Roth, "The Algorithmic Foundations of Differential Privacy," *Foundations and Trends in Theoretical Computer Science*, Vol. 9, Nos. 3-4 (2014), https://www.cis.upenn.edu/~aaroth/Papers/privacybook.pdf (accessed November 2017).

30 "Data De-Identification: An Overview of Basic Terms," Privacy Technical Assistance Center, U.S. Department of Education, http://ptac.ed.gov/sites/default/files/data_deidentification_terms.pdf (accessed November 2017). *See* Dr. Khaled El Emam, "Perspectives on Health Data De-Identification," Privacy Analytics, https://iapp.org/media/pdf/knowledge_center/Perspectives_on_Health_Data_De-Identification_final.pdf (accessed November 2017); Guidance regarding

methods for de-identification of protected health information in accordance with HIPAA, https://www.hhs.gov/hipaa/for-professionals/privacy/special-topics/de-identification/ (accessed November 2017).

31 Yianni Lagos and Jules Polonetsky, Public vs. Nonpublic Data: The Benefits of Administrative Controls, 66 Stan. L. Rev. Online 103 (2013), https://www.stanfordlawreview.org/online/privacy-and-big-data-public-vs-nonpublic-data/ (accessed November 2017).

32 Cybersecurity specialists warn that truly anonymized data could not be used for further analysis, meaning that data techniques that are intended to anonymize individuals within the set often do not fully achieve that goal. Cynthia Dwork and Aaron Roth, "The Algorithmic Foundations of Differential Privacy." *Privacy—Preserving Data Analysis, Data Cannot be Fully Anonymized and Remain Useful*, https://www.cis.upenn.edu/~aaroth/Papers/privacybook.pdf (accessed November 2017); *see* Paul Ohm, "Broken Promises of Privacy: Responding to the Surprising Failure of Anonymization," *UCLA Law Review*, 2009 (discussing the scientists ability to re-identify or de-anonymize individuals in data sets where those individuals were thought to be anonymous), www.uclalawreview.org/pdf/57-6-3.pdf (accessed November 2017).

33 A data broker is a type of business that collects data on consumers, generally creates profiles of individuals, and then sells the information to other organizations. Data Broker, WhatIs.com, http://whatis.techtarget.com/definition/data-broker-information-broker (accessed November 2017).

34 "Data Brokers: A Call for Transparency and Accountability," FTC (May 2014), https://www.ftc.gov/system/files/documents/reports/data-brokers-call-transparency-accountability-report-federal-trade-commission-may-2014/140527databrokerreport.pdf (accessed November 2017).

35 "FTC Recommends Congress Require the Data Broker Industry to be More Transparent and Give Consumers Greater Control Over Their Personal Information," FTC, https://www.ftc.gov/news-events/press-releases/2014/05/ftc-recommends-congress-require-data-broker-industry-be-more (accessed November 2017).

36 "Data Broker Defendants Settle Charges They Sold Sensitive Personal Information to Scammers," FTC (February 18, 2016), https://www.ftc.gov/news-events/press-releases/2016/02/data-broker-defendants-settle-ftc-charges-they-sold-sensitive (accessed November 2017). For details of the court order, view https://www.ftc.gov/system/files/documents/cases/160218leaplabsitesearch.pdf (accessed November 2017).

37 "Big Data: A Tool for Inclusion or Exclusion—Understanding the Issues," FTC, https://www.ftc.gov/system/files/documents/reports/big-data-tool-inclusion-or-exclusion-understanding-issues/160106big-data-rpt.pdf (accessed November 2017).

38 Leo Sun, "Internet of Things in 2016: 6 Stats Everyone Should Know," *The Motley Fool*, January 18, 2016, www.fool.com/investing/general/2016/01/18/internet-of-things-in-2016-6-stats-everyone-should.aspx (accessed November 2017).

39 "IDC Forecasts Worldwide Shipments to reach 213.6 Million Units Worldwide in 2020 with Watches and Wristbands Driving Volume While Clothing and Eyewear Gain Traction," IDC (June 15, 2016) https://www.idc.com/getdoc.jsp?containerId=prUS41530816 (accessed November 2017).

40 Telefonica IoT Team, "90% of New Cars Will be Connected in 2020," *Telefonica*, June 24, 2013, https://iot.telefonica.com/blog/90-of-new-cars-will-be-connected-by-2020 (accessed November 2017); "Gartner Says by 2020, a Quarter Billion Connected Vehicles Will Enable New In-Vehicle Services and Automated Driving Capabilities," Gartner, January 26, 2015, www.gartner.com/newsroom/id/2970017 (accessed November 2017).

41 The "things" can be anything from an automobile with a built-in sensor to a human with heart monitor implant. Margaret Rouse, "Definition: Internet of Things (IoT)," *TechTarget*, http://internetofthingsagenda.techtarget.com/definition/Internet-of-Things-IoT (accessed November 2017). "Simply put, this is the concept of basically connecting any device with an on and off switch to the Internet (and/or to each other)." Jacob Morgan, "A Simple Explanation of the 'Internet of Things,'" *Forbes*, May 13, 2014, www.forbes.com/sites/jacobmorgan/2014/05/13/simple-explanation-internet-things-that-anyone-can-understand/#760160d46828 (accessed November 2017).

42 The FTC further limits its discussion to those devices or sensors "that are sold to or used by consumers." "Internet of Things: Privacy and Security in a Connected World," FTC Staff Report (January 2015), p. 6, https://www.ftc.gov/system/files/documents/reports/federal-trade-commission-staff-report-november-2013-workshop-entitled-internet-things-privacy/150127iotrpt.pdf (accessed November 2017).

43 For example, the sector known as the Industrial Internet of Things, or IIoT, focuses on the application of IoT to manufacturing and has relatively few privacy issues. *See* "Industrial Internet of Things (IIoT)," *TechTarget*, http://internetofthingsagenda.techtarget.com/definition/Industrial-Internet-of-Things-IIoT (accessed November 2017).

44 *See generally* the discussion in Liesbet van Zoonen, "Privacy Concerns in Smart Cities," www.sciencedirect.com/science/article/pii/S0740624X16300818 (accessed November 2017). For an in-depth discussion of this topic, view Richard Rutledge, Aaron Massey, Annie Antón and Peter Swire, "Clarifying the Internet of Things."

45 Broadband Internet Technical Advisory Group (BITAG) Internet of Things (IoT) Security and Privacy Recommendations (November 2016), p. i, https://www.bitag.org/report-internet-of-things-security-privacy-recommendations.php (accessed November 2017).

46 *Id.*, p. ii.

47 "How Wearables Will Bring Health Insurers Closer to Customers," Telus International (May 19, 2016), https://www.telusinternational.com/articles/wearables-bring-health-insurers-closer-customers/ (accessed November 2017).

48 Kenneth Corbin, "IoT Makes Security and Privacy Top Challenges for Wearables," *CIO*, March 8, 2016, www.cio.com/article/3041637/wearable-technology/iot-makes-security-and-privacy-top-challenges-for-wearables.html (accessed November 2017).

49 Scott Amyx, "Data Privacy Playbook for Wearables and IoT," *Information Week*, June 8, 2015, www.informationweek.com/mobile/mobile-devices/data-privacy-playbook-for-wearables-and-iot/a/d-id/1320690 (accessed November 2017). To view the research paper, see Vivian Gerano Motti and Kelly Caine, "Users' Privacy Concerns about Wearables: Impact in Form Factor, Sensors, and Type of Data Collected," Clemson University, http://fc15.ifca.ai/preproceedings/wearable/paper_2.pdf (accessed November 2017).

50 Melanie Bates, "Future of Privacy Forum Releases Best Practices for Consumer Wearables and Wellness Apps and Devices," Future of Privacy Forum (August 17, 2016), https://fpf.org/2016/08/17/future-privacy-forum-releases-best-practices-consumer-wearables-wellness-apps-devices/ (accessed November 2017).

51 Craig Timberg, "Web-Connected Cars Bring Privacy Concerns," *The Washington Post*, March 5, 2013, https://www.washingtonpost.com/business/technology/web-connected-cars-bring-privacy-concerns/2013/03/05/d935d990-80ea-11e2-a350-49866afab584_story.html?utm_term=.396ea92fd638 (accessed November 2017).

52 Ellen S. Pyle, "The Connected Car and the Race to Keep Consumers in the Driver's Seat on Data Privacy," *Bloomberg BNA*, February 2, 2016, https://www.bna.com/connected-car-race-n57982066853/ (accessed November 2017).

53 Diana Olick, "Just what is a 'smart home' anyway?" CNBC (May 10, 2016), www.cnbc.com/2016/05/09/just-what-is-a-smart-home-anyway.html (accessed November 2017).

54 Deborah Weinswig, "Why Smart Homes Will be a Million Times Better than 'The Jetsons,'" *Forbes*, April 19, 2016, www.forbes.com/sites/deborahweinswig/2016/04/19/why-smart-homes-will-be-a-million-times-better-than-the-jetsons/#5d4bff2a41bb (accessed November 2017).

55 "On Privacy and Security in Smart Homes," IOTAP at Malmo University, https://medium.com/@iotap/on-privacy-and-security-in-smart-homes-543f62aa9917#.n9t5k82ja (accessed November 2017).

56 Lorenzo Franceschi-Biccierai, "Hackers Make the First-Ever Ransomware for Smart Thermostats," *Motherboard*, August 7, 2016, http://motherboard.vice.com/read/internet-of-things-ransomware-smart-thermostat (accessed November 2017).

57 "Samsung warns customers not to discuss personal information in front of Smart TVs," *The Week*, February 9, 2017, http://theweek.com/speedreads/538379/samsung-warns-customers-not-discuss-personal-information-front-smart-tvs (accessed November 2017).

58 Smart Home Networking Technologies, https://www.researchgate.net/figure/232923869_fig3_Figure-3-Smart-home-networking-technologies (accessed November 2017).

59 Rick Delgado, "5 Security Concerns to Consider When Creating Your Smart Home," MUO (May 28, 2015), www.makeuseof.com/tag/5-security-concerns-consider-creating-smart-home/ (accessed November 2017).

60 The term is also referred to as *smart communities*. *See* Shanna Freeman, "How Smart Communities Will Work," *Home & Garden*, http://home.howstuffworks.com/smart-communities.htm (accessed November 2017).

61 "Sensity Systems Join Panasonic's CityNow Initiative to Accelerate the Transformation of Smart Cities," Sensity (April 20, 2016), www.sensity.com/pressrelease/sensity-systems-joins-panasonics-citynow-initiative-to-accelerate-the-transformation-of-smart-cities (accessed November 2017).

62 "Smart City Technology Will Reach $27.5 Billion in Annual Revenue by 2023," Navigant Research (July 7, 2014), https://www.navigantresearch.com/newsroom/smart-city-technology-will-reach-27-5-billion-in-annual-revenue-by-2023 (accessed November 2017).

63 Tod Newcombe, "Security, Privacy, Governance Concerns about Smart Cities technologies grow," *Government Technology*, June 7, 2016, www.govtech.com/Security-Privacy-Governance-Concerns-About-Smart-City-Technologies-Grow.html (accessed November 2017).

64 "The Future of Smart Cities: Cyber-Physical Infrastructure Risk," U.S. Department of Homeland Security (August 2015), pp. 3-4, https://ics-cert.us-cert.gov/Future-Smart-Cities-Cyber-Physical-Infrastructure-Risk (accessed November 2017).

65 A. Bartoli, J. Hernandez-Serrano, M. Soriano, M. Dohler, A. Kountouris and D. Barthel, "On the Ineffectiveness of Today's Privacy Regulations for Secure Smart Cities Networks," www.cttc.es/publication/on-the-ineffectiveness-of-todays-privacy-regulations-for-secure-smart-city-networks/ (accessed November 2017).

66 Liesbet van Zoonen, "Privacy Concerns in Smart Cities," *ScienceDirect*, July 2016, www.sciencedirect.com/science/article/pii/S0740624X16300818 (accessed November 2017).

67 Internet of Things (IoT) Security and Privacy Recommendations, BITAG, p. iv-vii.

68 Taylor Armerding, "The IoT: Gateway for enterprise hackers," *CSO*, December 8, 2016, www.csoonline.com/article/3148806/internet-of-things/the-iot-gateway-for-enterprise-hackers.html (accessed November 2017).

69 Brian Krebs, "Hacked Cameras, DVRs Powered Today's Massive Internet Outage," *KrebsOnSecurity*, October 21, 2016, https://krebsonsecurity.com/2016/10/hacked-cameras-dvrs-powered-todays-massive-internet-outage/ (accessed November 2017).

70 Michael Kan, "An IoT Botnet is Partly Behind Friday's Massive DDoS Attack," *PCWorld*, October 21, 2016, www.pcworld.com/article/3134056/hacking/an-iot-botnet-is-partly-behind-fridays-massive-ddos-attack.html (accessed November 2017).

71 In the Matter of TRENDnet, Inc., FTC, https://www.ftc.gov/enforcement/cases-proceedings/122-3090/trendnet-inc-matter (accessed November 2017).

72 The FTC explained in the report that its consideration of the topic is limited to sensors or devices sold to consumers. "Internet of Things: Privacy and Security in a Connected World," FTC (January 2015), https://www.ftc.gov/system/files/documents/reports/federal-trade-commission-staff-report-november-2013-workshop-entitled-internet-things-privacy/150127iotrpt.pdf (accessed November 2017). *See* "Internet of Things Urges Companies to Adopt Best Practices to Address Consumer Privacy and Security Risks," FTC, https://www.ftc.gov/news-events/press-releases/2015/01/ftc-report-internet-things-urges-companies-adopt-best-practices (accessed November 2017).

73 "ASUS Case Suggests 6 Things to Watch for in the Internet of Things," https://www.ftc.gov/news-events/blogs/business-blog/2016/02/asus-case-suggests-6-things-watch-internet-things (accessed November 2017).

About the Authors

Peter Swire, CIPP/US

Peter Swire is the Holder Chair of Law and Ethics at the Georgia Institute of Technology Scheller College of Business. He has appointments by courtesy with the College of Computing and School of Public Policy and is associate director for policy at the Institute for Information Security and Privacy at Georgia Tech. Swire is senior counsel with the cyber-security and privacy practice of Alston & Bird, LLP.

In 2015, the International Association of Privacy Professionals awarded Swire its Privacy Leadership Award. In 2013, he served as one of five members of President Obama's Review Group on Intelligence and Communications Technology. Prior to that, he was co-chair of the global Do Not Track process for the World Wide Web Consortium. In 2009-2010, he was special assistant to the president for economic policy, in the National Economic Council. He is Senior Fellow with the Future of Privacy Forum, and a member of the National Academy of Sciences Forum on Cyber-Resilience.

Under President Clinton, Swire was the chief counselor for privacy in the U.S. Office of Management and Budget. He was the first person to have U.S. governmentwide responsibility for privacy policy. In that role, his activities included being White House coordinator for the Health Insurance Portability and Accountability Act medical privacy rule, chairing a White House task force on how to update wiretap laws for the Internet age, and helping negotiate the U.S.-EU Safe Harbor agreement for transborder data flows.

Swire is author of six books and numerous scholarly papers. He has testified often before Congress and is quoted regularly in the press.

Swire graduated from Princeton University, summa cum laude, and from the Yale Law School, where he was an editor of the *Yale Law Journal*.

DeBrae Kennedy-Mayo, CIPP/US

DeBrae Kennedy-Mayo is a research faculty member at the Georgia Institute of Technology, where she engages in research on legal and policy issues related to privacy and cybersecurity. Kennedy-Mayo has spent most of her legal career working in government, acting as both an assistant attorney general for the state of Georgia and as an assistant district attorney in several Georgia counties. In 2002, Kennedy-Mayo's first cyber-related paper, "In Search of a Balance Between Police Power and Privacy in the Cybercrime Treaty," was published in the *Richmond Journal of Law and Technology*. In 2009, this paper was republished in a book, *Computer Crime*, which is part of Ashgate Publishing's series entitled "The International Library of Criminology, Criminal Justice, and Penology." Kennedy-Mayo graduated with honors from Emory Law School in Atlanta.

Index

A

Abandoned call Safe Harbor, 239–240
Acceptance, in contract law, 31
Access, defined, 34
Account Spending Limit (ALS) program, 193
Accountability, FTC on, 351
Accountability participation principle, OECD Guidelines, 7
Active data collection, 112
Ad exchanges, 123
AdChoices system, 59
Administrative enforcement actions, 40
Administrative law judge (ALJ), 40, 44
Administrative Office of U.S. Courts, 307
Administrative Procedure Act (APA), 40
Administrative security controls, 136
Adobe Flash, 96, 120
Advertising
  digital, 252–255
  online networks, 115
Adware, 118
Aerospaciale v. S.D. of Iowa, 311–312
Affirmative consumer consent (opt-in), 78. *See also* Opt-in/opt-out
Age Discrimination in Employment Act of 1967 (ADEA), 267–268, 271
AI (artificial intelligence), 345
Alaska
  breach notification laws, 146
  data destruction laws, 152
ALJ. *See* Administrative law judge (ALJ)
ALS (Account Spending Limit) program, 193
Amazon, Inc., 358
American Institute of Certified Public Accountants, 100
American Recovery and Reinvestment Act of 2009, 173
Americans with Disabilities Act of 1990, 268, 271–273, 277–278
Analytics. *See* Big data
Andreessen, Mark, 93
Anonymous data, 347–350
Anti-money-laundering laws, 206–209
Antidiscrimination laws, 271–272
Antivirus software, 99
APA. *See* Administrative Procedure Act (APA)
APEC. *See* Asia-Pacific Economic Cooperation (APEC)
Apple v. FBI (2016), 326–327
Apps for Education (Google), 225
Aristotle International Inc., 22
Arizona, data destruction laws, 152
Arkansas, breach notification law in, 143
ARPA. *See* U.S. Advanced Research Projects Agency (ARPA)
ARPAnet, 91
Article 29 Working Party, of European Union (EU), 312
Artificial intelligence (AI), 345
Asia-Pacific Economic Cooperation (APEC), 60
  Cross-border Privacy Enforcement
    Arrangement (CPEA), 60
  customer access and redress, 81–82
  Privacy Framework, 8–11, 110–111
Asimov, Isaac, 344–346
Asimov's law of robotics, 345–346

Attorney-client privilege, 305–306
Attorneys general, state. *See* State attorneys general
Autodialers, in telemarketing, 241
Availability, information security and, 136

B

Background screening of employees, 269–270, 273–276
Bank Secrecy Act (BSA) of 1970, 207–209
Banking, online and mobile, 210. *See also* Financial privacy
Bankruptcy Act provision 11, 271
Berners-Lee, Tim (Sir), 92
Better Business Bureau, 58
  online verification and certification services, 100
  as Trustmark example, 108
"Big Brother" *(1984)*, 13
Big Data
  Asimov's law of robotics, 345–346
  case study on, 346–347
  data de-identification in, 349–350
  fair information privacy practices in, 347–348
  FTC reports on, 351–352
  Moore's Law, 344–345
  overview, 343–344
Binding Corporate Rules (BCRs), 85–86
BITAG (Broadband Internet Technical Advisory Group), 357–358
BitTorrent, 99
Blockbuster, Inc., 252
Blurring, to reduce precision of data, 350
Bodily privacy, 2
Bork, Robert, 251
Brandeis, Louis, 1, 314
Breach notification laws, 57
  lack of federal, 142
  vendor requirements, 83
Breach notification laws, state, 142–151
  covered entities definition, 144
  harm and definition of security breach, 144–145
  penalties and right of action, 151
  personal information definition in, 143
  what to include, 147–148
  when to notify, 147
  whom to notify, 145–147
Breaches, Big Data, 347
Broadband Internet Technical Advisory Group (BITAG), 357–358
BSA (Bank Secrecy Act) of 1970, 207
Buckley, James, 217
Business associate, 75, 115
BYOD (bring your own device), 268, 286–288

C

Cable Communications Policy Act of 1984, 250–251
Caching, 95
CALEA. *See* Communications Assistance to Law Enforcement Act (CALEA) of 1994, 319–320
California
  breach notification law in, 36, 57, 137, 142–145, 147–148, 150
  California Investigative Consumer Reporting Agencies Act (ICRAA), 275–276
  California Medical Information Privacy Act (CMIA), 164
  California Online Privacy Protection Act (CalOPPA), 254–255
  constitutional privacy provisions, 3
  data destruction laws, 152
  Do Not Track law, 252, 254–255
  Medical Information Privacy Act, 164
  mobile apps privacy and, 58
  Privacy Rights for California Minors in the Digital World, 106
Call abandonment, in telemarketing, 238–240
Caller ID information, telemarketing transmission of, 238

Camden, Lord (Britain), 3
CAN-SPAM Act of 2003, 29–30, 102, 244–246
  FTC and, 43
  preemption of state laws and, 33
  state enforcement and, 57
  user preferences and, 79–81
Cars, connected, in Internet of Things, 354–355
Cascading style sheets (CSS), 96
Case law, 30
Case study on Big Data, 346–347
Cell tower triangulation, 133n104
Center for Internet Security's Critical Security Controls, 137
Center for Legal and Court Technology, 307
CFPB. *See* Consumer Financial Protection Bureau (CFPB)
Checkboxes, 112
Children, online privacy and, 105–107
Children's Advertising Review Unit (CARU), 22, 35
Children's Online Privacy Protection Act (COPPA), 22, 30, 33, 43, 46, 59, 78, 106, 305
Choice
  defined, 33–34
  simplified consumer, 53–54
Choice and consent, fair information practices and, 5
CISA. *See* Cybersecurity Information Sharing Act (CISA) of 2014
Cities, smart, 356–357
City of Ontario v. Quon, 284
Civil litigation, 39–40
Civil litigation and government investigation, 301–341
  Communications Assistance to Law Enforcement Act of 1994, 319–320
  Cybersecurity Information Sharing Act of 2014, 320–321
  disclosure statutes, 316–317
  disclosures in, 303–306
  evidence stored in different countries and, 323
  Fourth Amendment limits on law enforcement searches, 313–316
  national security (*See* National security)
  overview, 301–302
  privacy and civil litigation, 306–312
  Privacy Protection Act of 1980, 322
  Right to Financial Privacy Act of 1978, 321–322
  Wiretap Act, Electronic Communications Privacy Act, and Stored Communications Act, 317–319
Civil Rights Act, 175–176, 267, 271
Clarity Services, Inc., 190
Cloud storage, 323
CMIA. *See* California Medical Information Privacy Act (CMIA)
CNN Money, 135
COBRA. *See* Consolidated Omnibus Budget Reconciliation Act (COBRA)
Co-branded sites, 115
COIT. *See* Consumerization of information technology (COIT)
Collection limitation
  APEC privacy framework, 10
  as FIPP, 347
  OECD Guidelines, 7
Collection of personal information, fair information practices and, 5
Colorado, breach notification law in, 146
Comcast, Inc., 254
Commodity Futures Trading Commission, 201
Common law, 30
Commonly accepted practices, 79
Communications
  intercepting, 283, 317–318
  storing, 283–284
Communications Assistance to Law Enforcement Act (CALEA) of 1994, 319–320
Communications privacy, 2
Communication systems, smart devices connected by, 356
Comprehensive Alcohol Abuse and Alcoholism Prevention, Treatment and Rehabilitation Act of 1970, 164
Comprehensive model of data protection, 19–20

"Computer trespasser" exception, 305
Confidentiality, information security and, 136
Confidentiality of Patient Records for Alcohol and Other Drug Treatment Rule, 166
Confidentiality of Substance Use Disorder Patients Records Rule, 163, 165
Confidentiality provision, in vendor contract, 82
Confirmed opt-in, 79
Congressional Review Act of 2017, 254
Connected cars, in Internet of Things, 354–355
Connecticut, breach notification law in, 143–146, 148–150
Consent decree, 30
  FTC and, 44, 87n7
Consideration, in contract law, 31
Consolidated Omnibus Budget Reconciliation Act (COBRA), 266
Constitutions, as source of law, 29
Consumer choice (opt-out). *See also* Opt-out
"Consumer Data Privacy in a Networked World" ("White House Report"), 52–53, 59
Consumer Financial Protection Bureau (CFPB), 34, 40
  consumer and financial providers
    relationship overseen by, 205–206
  creation of, 187
  employee privacy protected by, 267–268
  FCRA enforced by, 190
  GLBA rule-making assumed by, 200–201
  risk-based pricing notices required by, 193
"Consumer Privacy Bill of Rights," 52–53
Consumer protection, new technologies and, 56
Consumer Protection Project, National Association of Attorneys General, 57
Consumer reporting agencies (CRAs), 188–189
Consumerization of information technology (COIT), 286–288
Contract law, 31
  employer-employee relationship as, 264
Controller, 75
Controlling the Assault of Non-Solicited Pornography and Marketing. *See* CAN-SPAM Act of 2003, 244–246
Convention for the Protection of Individuals with Regard to the Automatic Processing of Personal Data (1981), 8
Cookies
  information contained in, 123, 133n100
  See also HTML cookies
COPPA. *See* Children's Online Privacy Protection Act (COPPA)
Co-regulation, as privacy protection source, 18
Co-regulatory model of data protection, 22
Council of Europe Convention, fair information practices (FIPs), 8
CPNI. *See* Customer proprietary network information (CPNI)
CRAs. *See* Consumer reporting agencies
Credit. *See* Financial privacy
Credit Reporting Agencies (CRAs), breach notification to, 146
Criminal litigation, 40
Cross-border Law Enforcement Access to Company Data—Current Issues Under Data Protection and Privacy Law, 61
Cross-border privacy enforcement issues, 60–61
Cross-device tracking, digital advertising and, 125–126
Cross-site scripting (XSS). *See* XSS code
CSS. *See* Cascading style sheets (CSS)
Currency and Foreign Transaction Reporting Act of 1970, 207–209
Customer access, redress and, 81–82
Customer proprietary network information (CPNI), 249–250, 254
CVS Pharmacy, Inc., 279
Cybersecurity Information Sharing Act (CISA) of 2014, 320–321

D

DAA. *See* Digital Advertising Alliance (DAA)
Data & Marketing Association, 80, 100
Data accountability, determining, 73–75
Data breaches
  managing, 140–142
  notification laws, 140

types of incidents, 139–140
Data breach law, 74
lack of federal, 142
See also Breach notification laws; Breach notification laws, state
Data brokers, 54, 351
Data classification, controls for managing, 73
Data controller, 17
Data destruction laws, state, 151–152
Data flows, documenting, 73
Data inventory, controls for managing, 72–73
Data loss prevention (DLP), 288–289
Data privacy law, 1
Data processor, 17
Data protection
advent of IT and, 13
organization chart for activities, 71
Data protection authority (DPA), 19
Data Protection Directive and the General Data Protection Regulation, of European Union (EU), 20, 347
Data protection, world models of, 19–23
co-regulatory and self-regulatory models, 22–23
comprehensive model, 19–20
sectoral model (U.S.), 21
Data protection law, 1
first, in German state of Hesse, 13
reasons for, 20
Data quality
Council of Europe Convention, 8
Madrid Resolution on, 12
OECD Guidelines, 7
Data retention program, e-discovery and, 309–310
Data security
APEC privacy framework, 10
Council of Europe Convention, 8
FTC investigations, 55
Data sharing, controls for managing, 72–75
Data subject, 17
Data subject access, fair information practices and, 5
Data transfer
controls for managing, 72–75
lawful bases for, 85–86
DDoS (distributed denial of service) attacks, 358
De-identification of data, 349–350
Deceptive trade practices, FTC enforcement actions and, 47–48
Defamation torts, 265–266
Delaware, Online and Personal Privacy Protection Act, 106
Demand-side advertising platforms, 123
Denial of service (DoS) attacks, 358
DesignerWare, LLC, 51–52
Desktop computer, digital advertising ecosystem on, 123
Differential privacy, for data privacy protection, 350
Digital advertising, 116–126, 252–255
cross-device tracking, 125–126
desktop/laptop ecosystem, 123
digital fingerprinting, 121
mobile ecosystem, 123–125
online social networking, 122–123
overview, 116–118
search engines, 122
web beacons, 121
web cookies, 118–120
Digital Advertising Alliance (DAA), 59, 117
opt-out system and, 80
Self-Regulatory Principles for Online Behavioral Advertising, 253
Digital fingerprinting, 121
Digital photographs, data size of, 345
Direct identifiers, in Big Data, 349
Direct Marketing Association, 35, 100
Disclosure(s)
in civil litigation and government investigation, 303–306
Fair Credit Reporting Act (FCRA) of 1970 requirements for, 193–194
Family Educational Rights and Privacy Act (FERPA) of 1974 on, 219–221

of personal information, fair information practices and, 5
privacy policies and, 75–78
statutes on, 316–317
in telemarketing regulations, 236–237
Disclosure laws, cross-border enforcement conflicts, 60–61
Discovery process in civil litigation, 301
Disposal Rule for consumer reports, 197–198
Distributed denial of service (DDoS) attacks, 358
District of Columbia, breach notification law in, 142, 146
DNC Safe Harbor, 234–235
Do Not Call rules, 80 (*See also* U.S. National Do Not Call (DNC) Registry)
Do Not Track approach, 117
Do Not Track mechanism, 54
Doctor-patient privilege, 306
Dodd-Frank Wall Street Reform and Consumer Protection Act of 2010, 200, 205–206
DOJ. *See* U.S. Department of Justice (DOJ)
DOL. *See* U.S. Department of Labor (DOL)
DoS (denial of service) attacks, 358
Double opt-in, 79
"Drive-by downloads," 103
Drones, consumer privacy and, 56
Drug Abuse Prevention, Treatment and Rehabilitation Act of 1972, 164–165

E

EBR. *See* Established business relationship (EBR)
e-discovery, 302, 308–312
Education privacy, enforcement of, 41
Education records, 217–230
Family Educational Rights and Privacy Act (FERPA) of 1974, 217–222
HIPAA and FERPA interaction, 224
Protection of Pupil Rights Amendment (PPRA) of 1978 to Family Educational Rights and Privacy Act (FERPA) of 1974, 222–223
technology for, 224–225
Educational Research Center of America, deceptive trade practices by, 106
EHR. *See* Electronic Health Record (EHR)
Electronic commerce, privacy laws to promote, 20
Electronic Communications Privacy Act (ECPA) of 1986, 251, 267, 283, 302, 305, 316–319
Electronic data, collection and use of
active *v.* passive collection, 112–113
desktop products with web interfaces, 113–114
online data collection, 111–112
onward transfers, 115–116
third-party interactions, 114–115
Electronic discovery, 302, 308–312
Electronic Health Record (EHR), 174–175
Electronic Privacy Information Center, 225, 346
Electronically stored information (ESI), 308
Eli Lilly and Company, FTC enforcement action against, 46–47
Email, spam, 101–102
Email security, 101
Emerging issues. *See* Big Data; Internet of Things
Employee Polygraph Protection Act of 1988, 267, 276–277
Employee Retirement Income Security Act (ERISA), 175, 266
Employment. *See* Workplace privacy
Encryption, 68
breach notification laws and, 149–150
debates on, 326
in transit, 74
Enforcement agencies, cooperation between cross-border, 60
Enforcement, privacy law. *See* Federal Trade Com (FTC), enforcement actions
Enron, Inc., business governance scandal at, 269
Entertainment Software Rating Board (ESRB), 22

Entity-specific suppression lists, for telemarketing, 236
Equal Credit Opportunity Act, 352
Equal Employment Opportunity Commission (EEOC), 267–268, 270
Equal Pay Act of 1963, 271
Equifax consumer reporting agency (CRA), 188, 190, 197
ERISA. *See* Employee Retirement Income Security Act (ERISA)
ESI. *See* Electronically stored information (ESI)
Established business relationship (EBR), telemarketing and, 233–234
EU Cookie Directive, 117
EU Data Protection Directive
    customer access and redress, 81
    customer access to information, 110
    secondary use of information and, 108
EU Electronic Privacy Directive of 2002, on information in cookies, 118–119
EU-U.S. Privacy Shield agreement. *See* Privacy Shield agreement
European Convention for the Protection of Human Rights and Fundamental Freedoms Article 8, 3
European Court of Justice, Safe Harbor program and, 85
European Privacy Seal (EuroPriSe), 100
European Union (EU)
    Article 29 Working Party of, 312
    Data Protection Directive of, 20, 347
    employee privacy in, 263
    General Data Protection Regulation (GDPR) of, 311, 347
    IP address as personal information in, 95
    privacy regime, terms used in, 75
E-Verify program, 42
Evidence
    Hague Convention on the Taking of Evidence, 311–312
    stored in different countries, 323
Exclusionary rule, in Fourth Amendment to U.S. Constitution, 314
Executive branch (U.S.), 27–28
Experian consumer reporting agency (CRA), 188, 190, 197
"Express prior authorization" for MSCMs, 247–248
Extensible markup language (XML), 93

F

Facebook, 122, 252, 285
Facial recognition, wearable IoT devices for, 354
Fair and Accurate Credit Transactions Act (FACTA) of 2003, 43, 196–199, 275, 290
Fair Credit Reporting Act (FCRA) of 1970, 13, 40, 42
    Big Data regulated by, 352
    consent options and, 78
    customer access to information, 81, 110
    data destruction laws and, 151–152
    delinquent debts and, 87n7
    disclosures under, 193–194
    employee background checks and, 266, 268, 273–274
    employee investigation procedures in, 194
    FACTA amendments to, 275–276
    investigative consumer reports in, 194–195
    medical information under, 195
    notice requirement of, 190–193
    overview, 187–190
    "prescreened" lists and, 195–196
    Vail Letter problems and, 290
Fair Debt Collection Practices Act, 205
Fair information practices (FIPs), 4–12, 130n61
    APEC privacy framework, 8–11
    controls on information, 5
    Council of Europe Convention, 8
    information lifecycle, 5
    Madrid Resolution, 11–12
    management and, 5–6
    OECD Guidelines, 6–7
    rights of individuals, 4–5
    U.S. Health, Education and Welfare, 6
Fair Information Privacy Practices (FIPPs), 4

Big Data *versus*, 343
in company privacy policies, 347–348
in FERPA, 217
See also Fair information practices (FIPs)
Fair Labor Standards Act (FLSA), 266
Family and Medical Leave Act (FMLA) of 1993, 176, 266
Family Educational Rights and Privacy Act (FERPA) of 1974
HIPAA interaction with, 170, 224
overview, 217–222
Protection of Pupil Rights Amendment (PPRA) of 1978 to, 222–223
FATCA. *See* Foreign Account Tax Compliance Act (FATCA) of 2010
Fax.com, 243
Fax marketing, 243–244
FCC. *See* Federal Communications Commission (FCC)
FCRA. *See* Fair Credit Reporting Act (FCRA)
Federal Aviation Administration (FAA), 41
Federal Bureau of Investigation (FBI)
on Internet inclusion in CALEA, 319, 326
National Crime Information Center database of, 270
on NSLs, 330
Federal Communications Commission (FCC), 34
CALEA implemented by, 319
on connected cars, 355
on customer proprietary network information (CPNI), 249–250
on fax marketing, 243
net neutrality rule of, 253–254
privacy law enforcement and, 39
privacy rule on broadband Internet providers of, 252
on telemarketing laws, 231–232
Federal Criminal Rules of Procedure, 308
Federal Privacy Reports
2012, 52–54
2016 update, 55–56
Federal Reserve, 34, 40
Federal Reserve Board, 193
Federal Rules of Bankruptcy Procedure, 308
Federal Rules of Civil Procedure, 301, 307, 311
Federal Trade Commission (FTC), 30
authority of, 28
on Big Data, 351–352
CAN-SPAM enforced by, 245
on connected cars, 355
consent decrees of, 30, 44
data security investigations, 55
employee privacy protected by, 267–268
endorsement of OECD Guidelines, 6–7
enforcement process, 43
FCRA enforced by, 190
FIPPs enforced by, 347
FTC Act, Section 5, 42–43, 46, 49, 58
"FTC Report," 52–54, 59
FTC v. Wyndham Worldwide Corp., 48, 63n33
on Internet of Things, 352, 358–359
on IP addresses, 15
jurisdiction of, 42–43
K-12 School Service Provider Pledge to Safeguard Student Privacy violations and, 225
mobile privacy notices best practices, 109–110
privacy law enforcement and, 39–66
"Protecting Consumer Privacy in an Era of Rapid Change," 79
on telemarketing laws, 231–232
Federal Trade Commission (FTC), enforcement actions
deceptive trade practices and, 47–48
future of federal enforcement, 52–56
privacy policies/notices and early, 45–47
unfair trade practices and, 48
Federal Trade Commission Act, 352
Feinstein Institute for Medical Research, 170
Feinstein, Diane (Senator), 142
FERPA. *See* Family Educational Rights and Privacy Act (FERPA) of 1974
Fifth Amendment to U.S. Constitution, 3, 306
File sharing, 99

Financial Crimes Enforcement Network (FinCEN), 42, 208
Financial Institution Reform, Recovery and Enforcement Act (FIRREA), 201
Financial privacy, 187–216
anti-money-laundering laws, 206–209
California SB-1 (California Financial Information Privacy Act), 204–205
Dodd-Frank Wall Street Reform and Consumer Protection Act of 2010, 205–206
enforcement of, 40
Fair and Accurate Credit Transactions Act (FACTA) of 2003, 196–199
Fair Credit Reporting Act (FCRA) of 1970, 187–196
Gramm-Leach-Bliley Act of 1999, 199–204
online and mobile banking, 210
Financial Services Modernization Act of 1999. *See* Gramm-Leach-Bliley Act of 1999
Financial Services Regulatory Relief Act of 2006, 203
Financial software, 114
Finkin, Matthew W., 265, 282
FIPPs. *See* Fair Information Privacy Practices (FIPPs)
Firewall software, 68
online identity protection and, 99
as web client, 93
FIRREA. *See* Financial Institution Reform, Recovery and Enforcement Act (FIRREA)
First-party cookie, 120
FISA. *See* Foreign Intelligence Surveillance Act (FISA)
FISC. *See* Foreign Intelligence Surveillance Court (FISC)
Flash. *See* Adobe Flash
Flash cookie, 120
Florida, breach notification law in, 143, 145, 146, 147
FLSA. *See* Fair Labor Standards Act (FLSA), 266
FOIA. *See* Freedom of Information Act (FOIA)
Forbes, 135
Forbidden disclosures in civil litigation, 305–306
Foreign Account Tax Compliance Act (FATCA) of 2010, 209
Foreign Intelligence Surveillance Act (FISA), 302, 324, 327–329
Foreign Intelligence Surveillance Act Amendments Act of 2008 (FISA Amendment Act), 328
Foreign Intelligence Surveillance Court (FISC), 327
Fortune, 135
Fourth Amendment to U.S. Constitution
limits on law enforcement searches, 302, 313–316
privacy provisions, 3
probable cause requirements of, 304, 313
Freedom of Information Act (FOIA), 306, 320
FTC. *See* Federal Trade Commission (FTC)
Full notice, 109
Future of Privacy Forum
on Big Data, 349
on consumer wearable IoT devices, 354
on educational technology, 225

G

GDPR. *See* General Data Protection Regulation (GDPR)
General Data Protection Regulation (GDPR), 61, 79, 311
data breach notifications and, 140
key new provisions in, 84–85
U.S. compliance with, 84
valid consent under, 89n43
General *v.* specific authority, in U.S. privacy law, 33
Genetic Information Nondiscrimination Act (GINA) of 2008, 175–177, 271
GeoCities, Inc., 46
Geolocation data, 105, 284–285
Georgia, breach notification law in, 144, 146

Germany
first modern data protection law, 13
strict data protection laws in, 20
GLBA. *See* Gramm-Leach-Bliley Act (GLBA)
Global Positioning System (GPS) devices, 124, 284, 315
Global Privacy Enforcement Network (GPEN), 60
"Golden Age of Surveillance," 327
Google, 23, 225
Government investigation. *See* Civil litigation and government investigation
Government, U.S., branches of, 27–28. *See also* U.S. legal framework
GPEN. *See* Global Privacy Enforcement Network (GPEN)
Gramm-Leach-Bliley Act (GLBA) of 1999, 41, 43, 46
data destruction laws and, 151–152
disclosures of covered information to third parties and, 305
information security laws and, 137
opt-out request and, 80
overview, 199–200
pretrial discovery powers and, 310
privacy notices and, 202–203
Safeguards Rule of, 72, 149, 203–204
scope and enforcement of, 200–202
service provider and, 75, 115
user preferences and, 79
Griswold v. Connecticut, 37n1

H

"Hacker trespasser" exception, 305
Hacking, 139
Hague Convention on the Taking of Evidence, 311–312
Harlan, John Marshall, 315
"Harm-based model," 52
Harvard Law Review, 1
Hawaii, breach notification law in, 145, 146, 147
Health Information Technology for Economic and Clinical Health Act (HITECH) of 2009, 21, 173–175
Health Information Trust Alliance (HITRUST), 100
Health Insurance Portability and Accountability Act (HIPAA) of 1996, 29, 40, 42, 46
"business associates" and, 17, 75, 115
consent options and, 78
customer access to information, 81, 110
data breach notification laws and, 149
data destruction laws and, 151–152
disclosures and, 303
e-discovery and, 310
FERPA interaction with, 224
in employment privacy, 266
information security laws and, 137
overview, 166–168
privacy rule of, 168–171
qualified protective order standards in, 307
security rule of, 172–173
staff training for interacting with PI and, 77
HHS. *See* U.S. Department of Health and Human Services (HHS)
Hippocratic Oath, 163
HITECH (Health Information Technology for Economic and Clinical Health Act) of 2009, 43, 173–175
Homes, smart, 355–356
Hooters of Augusta (GA), 243
HTML. *See* Hypertext markup language (HTML)
HTML cookies, 118, 120. *See also* Cookies
HTML5, 93, 96
HTTP. *See* Hypertext Transfer Protocol (HTTP)
HTTPS. *See* Hypertext Transfer Protocol Secure (HTTPS)
Hyperlink, 94
Hypertext markup language (HTML), 92, 98
Hypertext transfer protocol (HTTP), 92
Hypertext Transfer Protocol Secure (HTTPS), 74, 93

I

ICANN. *See* International Corporation for Assigned Names and Numbers (ICANN)
ICRAA. *See* California Investigative Consumer Reporting Agencies Act (ICRAA)
Idaho, breach notification law in, 144, 145
Identity Theft Resource Center, 140
iKeepSafe, 22
Illinois
  breach notification law in, 143–145, 147
  data destruction laws, 152
Immigration and Customs Enforcement, 42
Immigration Reform and Control Act (IRCA), 267
In the Matter of DesignerWare, LLC, 51–52
In the Matter of GeoCities, Inc., 46
In the Matter of LabMD, Inc., 50
In the Matter of LifeLock, Inc., 50–51
In the Matter of Nomi, 47
In the Matter of Snapchat, 47–48
In the Matter of TRUSTe, Inc., 48
In the Matter of Wyndham Worldwise Corp., 49
Indiana, breach notification law in, 146
Indirect identifiers, in Big Data, 349
Individual participation principle, OECD Guidelines, 7
Infinite loop, 127n16
Information
  controls on, 5
  nonpersonal, 14
personal, 13–16 (*See also* Personal information)
Information lifecycle, 5
Information management
  access requests, 81–82
  contact and vendor management, 82–84
  data sharing and transfer, 72–75
  global perspective, 84–86
  privacy policies and disclosure, 75–78
  privacy professional's role, 67–68
  program development, 69–72
  risks of improper use, 68–69
  user preferences, 78–81
Information privacy, 2
  advent of IT and, 13
Information Privacy Case Book, The (IAPP), 46
Information privacy law, 1
Information security (IS), 136
Information security laws
  Social Security Numbers and, 139
  state laws, 137–138
Information security provisions, in vendor contracts, 83
Information technology (IT)
  continued evolution of, 20
  information privacy, data protection and, 13
InMobi, 55
Insider data breach, 139
Integrity, information security and, 136
Intel, Inc., 344
Intentional torts, 32
Intercepting communications, 283
Internal Revenue Service (IRS), 42
International Chamber of Commerce, 61
International Conference of Data Protection and Privacy Commissioners, Madrid Resolution, 11–12
International Corporation for Assigned Names and Numbers (ICANN), 127n11
International Harvester Co., Unfairness Policy Statement, 63n31
International Money-Laundering Abatement and Anti-Terrorist Financing Act of 2001, 209
Internet, commercial activity on, 45–46, 91
Internet of Things (IoT), 352–359
  Broadband Internet Technical Advisory
    Group report on, 357–358
  connected cars, 354–355
  FTC report on, 358–359
  overview, 352–353
  smart cities, 356–357
  smart homes, 355–356
  wearables, 353–354
"Internet of Things: Privacy and Security in a Connected World" (FTC report), 358
Internet protocol (IP), 95
Internet protocol (IP) address, 15, 95, 121

Iowa, breach notification law in, 144, 145, 147
IP. *See* Internet protocol (IP)
IPv6, 95
IRCA. *See* Immigration Reform and Control Act (IRCA)
IRS. *See* Internal Revenue Service (IRS)
IS. *See* Information security (IS)
ISP. *See* Internet Service Provider (ISP)

J

Japan Information Processing Development Center, 100
Javascript, 96
JIPDEC, 100
Judicial branch (U.S.), 27–28
Judicial Redress Act of 2015, 81
Judicial Redress Act of 2016, 326
Junk Fax Prevention Act (JFPA) of 2005, 244
Jurisdiction, use of term in U.S. privacy law, 32
Justices of the Peace Act (England), 2

K

Kansas, breach notification law in, 145, 146
Katz v. United States (1967), 314, 324
Kentucky, breach notification law in, 146
kidSAFE, 22
Know Your Customer rules, 209

L

LabMD, Inc., 50
Laptop computer, digital advertising ecosystem on, 123
Law
  as privacy protection source, 18
U.S., 35–37 (*See also* Sources of U.S. law; U.S. legal framework)
Law enforcement, Fourth Amendment limits on searches and seizures by, 313–316
Lawfulness and fairness, principle of, Madrid Resolution, 12
Lawrence v. Texas, 37n1
Layered notices, 108–109
LeapLab (data broker), 351
Legislation, as source of U.S. law, 29
Legislative branch (U.S.), 27–28
Leibowitz, Jon, 52
Lifecycle, information, 5
Lifestyle discrimination of employees, 279–280
LinkedIn, 122, 285
Location data, mobile devices transmission of, 124
Location-based services (LBS), 105, 284–285
Login, 99
Louisiana, breach notification law in, 144, 145

M

MAC. *See* Media access control (MAC)
MAC address, 124
Madrid Resolution, 11–12
Magnuson-Moss Warranty Federal Trade Commission Improvement Act, 43
Maine, breach notification law in, 146
Majoris, Deborah Platt, 52
Malware, 97, 103
Malware attacks, IoT devices used in, 358
Marketing. *See* Telecommunications and marketing
Marketing privacy, enforcement of, 41
Markets, as privacy protection source, 18
Maryland, breach notification law in, 146, 147
Masking, for data privacy protection, 350
Massachusetts
  breach notification law in, 142, 146, 147, 148
  data destruction laws, 152
  Internet security law in, 138
  Massachusetts Personal Information Security Regulation, 150
Media, Privacy Protection Act for, 322
Media access control (MAC), 62n24
Media player applications, 113
Medical privacy, 163–186
  21st Century Cures Act of 2016, 177–178
  enforcement of, 40

in FCRA, 195
Genetic Information Nondiscrimination Act (GINA) of 2008, 175–177
Health Information Technology for Economic and Clinical Health Act (HITECH) of 2009, 173–175
Health Insurance Portability and Accountability Act of 1996, 163–171
substance use disorder confidentiality, 164–166
Megapixels, in digital photographs, 345
MemberWorks telemarketing firm, 199–200
Michigan, breach notification law in, 144, 146, 147
Microsoft Corporation, 23, 346
Microsoft v. United States (2016), 323
Minimization of data, 347–348
Minnesota
breach notification law in, 146
Internet security law in, 138
Misconduct, employee, 289–290
Missouri, breach notification law in, 143, 145, 146, 147
Mobile apps, California task force on, 58
Mobile banking, 210. *See also* Financial privacy
Mobile devices
advertising ecosystem on, 123–125
malware and, 103
online privacy and, 105
privacy notices, 109–110
Mobile service commercial messages (MSCMs), 246–248
Mobile services, self-regulation of, 54
Mohammed, 2
Money-laundering, laws against, 206–209
Monitoring in workplace
consumerization of information technology (COIT) and BYOD, 286–288
data loss prevention (DLP), 288–289
emerging technologies for, 285
intercepting communications, 283
legal obligations for, 281–282
of location-based services (LBS), 284–285
overview, 280–281
of postal mail, 284
social media for, 285–286
storing communications, 283–284
video surveillance, 282–283
Montana, breach notification law in, 143, 146, 147
Moore, Gordon, 344
Moore's Law, 344–345, 359
MSCMs (mobile service commercial messages), 246–248
Muris, Timothy, 52
Mutual legal assistance (MLA) process, 323

N

Nadella, Satya, 346
National Association of Attorneys General, Consumer Protection Project, 57
National Center for Supercomputing Applications (NCSA), 93
National Child Protection Act, 270
National Crime Information Center database of FBI, 270
National Health Information Network, 174
National Highway Traffic Safety Administration (NHTSA), 41, 355
National Institutes of Health (NIH), 177
National Labor Relations Act (NLRA), 267
National Labor Relations Board (NLRB), 267–268
National Science Foundation, 91
National security
Foreign Intelligence Surveillance Act, 327–328
national security letters, 329–330
overview, 323–324
Section 702 of Foreign Intelligence Surveillance Act, 328–329
Section 215 of USA PATRIOT Act, 328
surveillance, debates on, 324–327
National Security Agency (NSA), 68, 347
National security letters (NSLs), 325, 329–330

National Telecommunications and Information Administration (NTIA), 59
NCSA. *See* National Center for Supercomputing Applications (NCSA)
Nebraska, breach notification law in, 144
Negligent torts, 32
Net neutrality rule, of FCC, 253–254
Netflix, Inc., 252, 358
Network Advertising Initiative, 35, 80, 100, 253
Nevada
  breach notification law in, 143, 146
  Internet security law in, 138
New Hampshire, breach notification law in, 143, 146, 147
New Jersey, breach notification law in, 146
New Mexico
  breach notification law in, 144, 147
  data destruction laws, 152
New York
  breach notification law in, 146, 147, 148
  Internet security law in, 138
New York Times, 325
NHTSA. *See* National Highway Traffic Safety Administration (NHTSA)
NIH. *See* National Institutes of Health (NIH)
1984 (Orwell), 13
NIST Cybersecurity Framework, 87n6
NLRA. *See* National Labor Relations Act (NLRA)
NLRB. *See* National Labor Relations Board (NLRB)
No Child Left Behind Act of 2001, 223
No consumer choice (no option), 79
Nomi, 47
Nonpersonal information, 14–16
Nonpublic information, 16
North Carolina
  breach notification law in, 144, 146, 147–148
  data destruction laws, 151–152
North Dakota, breach notification law in, 143, 144, 145
Norton
  online verification and certification services, 100
  as Trustmark example, 108
Notice(s), 4
  APEC privacy framework, 9
  defined, 33
  fair information practices and, 4
  privacy policy disclosure through, 76
  transparency in, 54
  See also Online privacy notices; Privacy notice
NSA. *See* National Security Agency (NSA)
NSLs. *See* National security letters (NSLs)

O

Obama administration
  Consumer Privacy Bill of Rights, 52
  national security letters reform, 330
  Personal Data Notification Act proposal, 142
  privacy enforcement reports, 52–56
  Review Group on Intelligence and Communications Technology, 325
Occupational Safety and Health Act (OSHA), 267, 281
OECD Guidelines, 4, 6–7
  customer access and redress, 81
  privacy framework, 6–7
  secondary use of information and, 108
Offer, in contract law, 31
Office of Civil Rights, 40
Office of Management and Budget (OMB). *See* U.S. Office of Management and Budget (OMB)
Office of the Comptroller of the Currency, 34, 40
Office of the Director of National Intelligence, Privacy Shield and, 85
Office of the National Coordinator for Health Information Technology, 173
Office productivity applications, 113
Ohio, breach notification law in, 146, 147
Olmstead v. United States (1928), 314

One-line text boxes, 112
Online advertising networks, 115
Online and Personal Privacy Protection Act (Delaware), 106
Online attacks
malware, 103
phishing, 102–103
spam email, 101–102
Online banking, 210. *See also* Financial privacy
Online identity, protecting, 99–100
Online privacy
children's, 105–107
collection and use of electronic data, 111–116
digital advertising, 116–126
mobile devices and, 105
online attacks on users, 101–107 (*See also* Online attacks)
online security and, 97–101
privacy notices, 107–111 (*See also* Online privacy notices)
threats to, 97
web technologies overview, 91–96
Online privacy notices, 107–111
customer access to information, 110–111
layered notices, 108–109
mobile privacy notices, 109–110
web privacy notices, 107–108
Online security, 97–101
email security, 101
online verification and certification, 100
protecting online identity, 99–100
transport layer security (TLS), 99
web access, 98
Online social networking
digital advertising and, 122–123
See also Social media
Onward transfer of information, 115–116
Openness principle
Madrid Resolution, 12
OECD Guidelines, 7
Opt in/opt out, 34, 78–79
Oregon, breach notification law in, 143, 144, 145, 146, 147
Organisation for Economic Co-operation and Development Guidelines Governing the Protection of Privacy and Transborder Flows of Personal Data
privacy issues and, 41
Recommendation on Cross-Border Co-operation in the Enforcement of Laws Protecting Privacy, 60
See also OECD Guidelines
Organization chart, for privacy and data protection activities, 71
Orwell, George, 13

P

Passive data collection, 112
Password, 99
Payment card fraud, 139
Payment Card Industry Data Security Standard (PCI-DSS), 22, 49, 58, 69, 138
Payment Card Industry Security Standards Council (PCI SSC), 128n26
PCI DSS. *See* Payment Card Industry Data Security Standard (PCI DSS)
PCI SSC. *See* Payment Card Industry Security Standards Council (PCI SSC)
PCLOB. *See* Privacy and Civil Liberties Oversight Board
Pennsylvania, breach notification law in, 146
Permitted disclosures in civil litigation, 304–305
Persistent cookie, 119–120
Person, use of term in U.S. privacy law, 32
Personal information (PI), 13–16
APEC privacy framework, 10
benefits and risks of using, 67–69
cookies as, 118
customer access to their, 110–111
definition in breach notification laws, 143
Educational Rights and Privacy Act and, 218–219
information lifecycle and, 5

IP address as, in EU, 95
line between nonpersonal and, 14–16
processing, 17
protecting, on websites, 100
risks of improper use, 68–69
sources of, 16
See also User information
Personally identifiable information (PII), 13, 218–219
breaches of, 141
rules for, 350
See also Personal information
Perturbation, for data privacy protection, 350
PHI. *See* Protected health information (PHI)
Phishing, 97, 102–103
Physical loss, as data breach, 139
Physical security controls, 136
PII. *See* Personally identifiable information (PII)
PINs, 99
Pitofsky, Robert, 52
Pitt, William, 3
Pop-up ads, 118
Portable device, data breaches and, 139
Postal mail, monitoring of, 284
PPRA. *See* Protection of Pupil Rights Amendment (PPRA) of 1978
Preemption, use of term in U.S. privacy law, 33
Pregnancy Discrimination Act, 271
President's Review Group on Intelligence and Communications Technology, 325
Priest-penitent privilege, 306
PRISM surveillance program, 329
Privacy
classes of, 2
defined, 1
historical and social origins of, 2
See also Data privacy; Information privacy
Privacy Act
IP addresses and, 15
secondary use of information and, 108
Privacy Act of 1974, 41
Privacy and Civil Liberties Oversight Board (PCLOB), 325–326
Privacy and Data Security Update (2015), 54–55
Privacy and Data Security Update (2016), 55–56
Privacy by design, 53
Privacy framework, OECD Guidelines, 6–7
"Privacy fundamentalist," 68
Privacy in Employment Law (Finkin), 265
Privacy law, 1
Privacy law enforcement, 39–66
cross-border conflicts, 60–61
federal, outside of FTC and FCC, 40–42
FTC enforcement process and consent decrees, 44–45
FTC jurisdiction, 42–43
future of federal, 52–56
privacy policies and notices, 45–46
self-regulation and, 58–59
state enforcement, 57–58
types of litigation and, 39–40
See also Federal Trade Commission (FTC), enforcement actions; Federal Trade Commission, enforcement actions
Privacy notice, 69, 107–111
Privacy policies
disclosure and, 75–78
version control, 77–78
use of term, 33, 69
Privacy professional
role of, 67–68
understanding of third-party interactions, 114
Privacy protection, sources of, 18–19
Privacy Protection Act of 1980, 302, 322
Privacy Rights for California Minors in the Digital World, 106
Privacy Shield, 59
customer access to information, 110
data transfer and, 85–86
onward transfers and, 116
Privacy Shield certifications, 47
"Privacy unconcerned," 68
Private right of action, in U.S. privacy law, 33

PRIVO, 22
Probable cause requirements, of fourth Amendment to U.S. Constitution, 304, 313
Processing, use of term, 17
Processors, 115
Proportionality principle, Madrid Resolution, 12
Protected health information (PHI), 304
"Protecting Consumer Privacy in an Era of Rapid Change" (FTC report), 52–54, 79
Protection of Pupil Rights Amendment (PPRA) of 1978, 222–223
Proxy server, 94
Pseudonymous data, 349–350
Psychological testing of employees, 276–277
Public charging stations, protecting online identity on, 100
Public computers, protecting online identity on, 100
Public Health Service Act, 176
Public records, as personal information source, 16
Publicly available information, 16
Puerto Rico, breach notification law in, 142, 144, 145, 147
Purpose specification principle
  Madrid Resolution, 12
  OECD Guidelines, 7
Purpose specification, as FIPP, 347

Q

Qualified protective order (QPO) standards, in HIPAA, 307
Quality, data, Council of Europe Convention on, 8
Quality, information, 5
Qur'an, privacy in, 2

R

Radio buttons, 112
Ransomware, 104
  consumer privacy and, 56
  smart devices and, 355
"Reasonable expectation of privacy" test, 315
Recommendation on Cross-Border Co-operation in the Enforcement of Laws Protecting Privacy (OECD), 60
Red Flag Program Clarification Act of 2010, 198
Red Flags Rule for identity theft detection, 198–199
Redaction practice, 307–308
Redbox, Inc., 252
Reddit.com, 358
Regulatory agencies, U.S., 30
Regulatory authorities, U.S., 34
Required disclosures in civil litigation, 303–304
Retention of data e-discovery and, 309–310
Retention of personal information, 5
Rhode Island, breach notification law in, 143, 145, 147
Right to Financial Privacy Act (RFPA) of 1978, 302, 316, 321–322
"Right to Privacy, The" (Warren & Brandeis), 1
Riley v. California (2014), 315–316
Robocalls, 241
Robotexts, 241
Robotics, Asimov's law of, 345–346
Roe v. Wade, 37n1
Rotenberg, Mark, 346

S

Safe Harbor certifications, 47
Safe Harbor program, European Court of Justice and, 85
SAN (Subscription Account Number), for telemarketers, 232–233
SANS Top 20, 137
SAR (Suspicious Activity Report), 208
Sarbanes-Oxley (SOX) Act of 2002, 269
SCA (Stored Communications Act) of 1986, 267, 283–284, 317–319
Schrems v. Data Protection Commission, 85
Scrolling text boxes, 112
Search engines, digital advertising and, 122

Searches and seizures, Fourth Amendment limits on law enforcement, 313–316
Section 702 of Foreign Intelligence Surveillance Act, 326–329
Section 215 of USA PATRIOT Act, 326, 328
Section 217 of USA PATRIOT Act, 305
Sectoral model of data protection (U.S.), 21
Securities Exchange Act of 1934, 267
Securities and Exchange Commission (SEC), 201
Security
  data, Council of Europe Convention on, 8
  information, 5
Security breach notification law (California), 36
Security controls, types of, 136
Security safeguards principle, OECD Guidelines, 7
Security systems, smart, 356
Security warning, false, 104
Sedona Conference, 309
Self-incrimination, privilege against, 306
Self-regulation
  industry guidelines for, 71
  of mobile services, 54
  privacy law enforcement and, 58–59
  as privacy protection source, 18–19
Self-regulatory model of data protection, 22–23
Sensitive personal information, 14
Sensitivity of information, data classification and, 74
Session cookie, 119
Short notice, 109
Simplified consumer choice, 53–54
Smart cities, 356–357
Smart homes, 355–356
Smart TVs, consumer privacy and, 56
Smoking, discrimination against, 279–280
Snapchat
  "Find Friends" feature, 47–48
  FTC enforcement action against, 47–48
Snowden, Edward, 68, 325–326, 328, 347
Social engineering, 97
Social media
  digital advertising and, 122–123
  for monitoring in workplace, 285–286
  Privacy Protection Act and, 322
  wearable IoT devices synced with, 354
Social Security Act, 175
Social Security numbers
  information security laws and, 139
  privacy protection and, 68
Software and Information Industry Association, 225
Sources of U.S. law, 28–32
  case law, 30
  consent decree, 30–31
  constitutions, 29
  contract law, 31
  legislation, 29
  regulations and rules, 30
  tort law, 31–32
South Carolina, breach notification law in, 145, 146
SOX. *See* Sarbanes-Oxley (SOX) Act of 2002
Spam, 101–102
Spam filtering software, 244
Spear phishing, 97, 103
Spousal privilege, 306
Sprint, Inc., 193
Spyware, 103
Standard Contract Clauses (SCCs), 85–86
Stare decisis, 30
State attorneys general
  consumer protection law enforcement by, 57
  as regulatory authority, 34
State constitutions, 29
State legislatures, 29
Static IP address, 95, 125
Stationary device, data breaches and, 139
Stored Communications Act (SCA) of 1986, 267, 283–284, 317–319
Strict liability torts, 32
Structured query language (SQL) injection, 97
Subcontractors, vendor contracts and, 83
Subscription Account Number (SAN), for telemarketers, 232–233

Substance abuse testing, 277–279
Substance use disorder, confidentiality of records on, 164–166
Supply-side advertising platforms, 123
Surveillance
debates on, 324–327
workplace, 282–283
See also National security
Suspicious Activity Report (SAR), 208
Sutton v. United Airlines, 273
Swire, Peter, 325
Syndicated content, 114

T

TCP. *See* Transmission control protocol (TCP)
TCPA. *See* Telephone Consumer Protection Act (TCPA) of 1991
Technical security controls, 136
Technically based attacks, 97
Technology, as privacy protection source, 18
TeleCheck Services, Inc., 190
Telecommunications Act of 1996, 249–250
Telecommunications and marketing, 231–262
Cable Communications Policy Act of 1984, 250–251
Controlling the Assault of Non-Solicited Pornography and Marketing (CAN-SPAM) Act of 2003, 244–246
digital advertising, 252–255
"express prior authorization" for MSCMs, 247–248
fax marketing, 243–244
Telecommunications Act of 1996, 249–250
Video Privacy Protection Act (VPPA) of 1988, 251–252
wireless domain registry, 248–249
See also Telemarketing regulations
Telemarketing and Consumer Fraud and Abuse Prevention Act, 232
Telemarketing privacy, enforcement of, 41
Telemarketing regulations
call abandonment, 238–240
caller ID information, 238
calling rules, 235–236
disclosures, 236–237
entity-specific suppression lists, 236
misrepresentations and material omissions, 237–238
overview, 231–232
record-keeping requirements, 241–242
robocalls and autodialers, 241
state-based, 243
U.S. National Do Not Call Registry, 232–235
unauthorized billing, 240
Telemarketing Sales Rules (TSRs)
user preferences and, 81
See also Telecommunications and marketing
Telephone Consumer Protection Act (TCPA) of 1991, 232, 241
Telephone wiretaps, standards for warrants for, 304, 314, 317
Tennessee, breach notification law in, 146, 147, 150
Territorial privacy, 2
Texas, breach notification law in, 143, 144, 145, 146
Thermostats, smart, 355
Third Amendment to the U.S. Constitution, privacy provisions, 3
Third Circuit Court of Appeals, 49
Third Reich, Hitler's, personal information abuses under, 13
Third-party cookie, 120
Third-party doctrine, 315–316
Third-party interactions, collection and use of electronic data and, 114–115
Third-party privacy seal and certification programs, 58
Third party online verification and certification services, 100
Third-party vendors, user preferences and, 81
TLS. *See* Transport layer security (TLS)
Tort law, employee privacy in, 264–266
Toyota v. Williams, 273
Transborder data flows, 8, 311
Transmission control protocol (TCP), 96

Transparency
FTC on, 53, 351
in privacy notices, 54
"White House Report" on, 53
Transport layer security (TLS), 96, 99
Transportation Security Administration, 42
TransUnion consumer reporting agency (CRA), 188, 190, 197
TRS Recovery Services, 190
Trump, Donald, 249, 254
TrustArc, 22, 58
online verification and certification services, 100
opt-out system and, 80
as Trustmark example, 108
See also TRUSTe, Inc.
TRUSTe, Inc., 22, 48
Trustmarks, 108
TSRs. *See* Telemarketing Sales Rules (TSRs)
TS/SCI level (Top Secret/Sensitive Compartmented Information) of security clearance, 325
Tumblr.com, 358
Turn, Inc., 56
TVs, smart, 355–356
twenty-first 21st Century Cures Act of 2016, 177–178
Twitter, 122, 285, 358

U

U.S. Advanced Research Projects Agency (ARPA), 91
U.S. Bancorp/MemberWorks case (Minnesota, 1999), 199–200
U.S. Congress
legislation in, 29
as legislative branch, 27–28
U.S. Constitution
privacy and, 3, 29
as source of law, 29
U.S. Customs and Border Protection, 278
U.S. Department of Commerce (DOC), 34, 41
U.S. Department of Education, 217–219, 225
U.S. Department of Energy, 42
U.S. Department of Health and Human Services (HHS), 34, 167–168, 224, 304
Office of Civil Rights, 40
U.S. Department of Health, Education and Welfare, 4, 6
U.S. Department of Homeland Security (DHS), 42, 356–357
U.S. Department of Justice (DOJ)
criminal prosecution by, 40
enforcement actions by, 42
HIPAA compliance enforced by, 170–171
on Internet inclusion in CALEA, 319–320
Privacy Shield and, 85
on substance abuse screening, 278
U.S. Department of Labor (DOL), 267, 303
U.S. Department of State, 41
U.S. Department of the Treasury, 42, 208
U.S. Department of Transportation (DOT), 34, 41
U.S. Drug Enforcement Administration (DEA), 165, 319
U.S. Food and Drug Administration (FDA), 303
U.S. Government Accounting Office, 114
U.S. law. *See* Sources of U.S. law; U.S. legal framework
U.S. legal framework
branches of government, 27–28
key definitions, 32–33
regulatory authorities, 34
self-regulation, 35
sources of law, 28–32. *See also* Sources of U.S. law
understanding laws, 35–37
U.S. National Do Not Call (DNC) Registry, 232–235
U.S. Office of Management and Budget (OMB), 41, 141
U.S. Supreme Court
authority of, 28
City of Ontario v. Quon, 284
on Fourth Amendment to U.S. Constitution, 313

Katz v. United States (1967), 314–315, 324
Olmstead v. United States (1928), 314
Riley v. California (2014), 315–316
Sutton v. United Airlines, 273
Toyota v. Williams, 273
United States v. Jones (2012), 315
Zurcher v. Stanford Daily (1978), 322
U.S. Virgin Islands, breach notification law in, 142
U.S. West, Inc. v. Federal Communications Commission (1999), 250
UDAP statutes. *See* Unfair and Deceptive Acts and Practices (UDAP) statutes
Unauthorized access, 97
Unauthorized billing, telemarketing regulations on, 240
Unfair and Deceptive Acts and Practices (UDAP) statutes, 57–58
Unfair trade practices, FTC enforcement actions and, 48–52
Unfairness Policy Statement (International Harvester Co.), 63n31
Uniform resource locator (URL), 94, 121
Unintended disclosure, as data breach, 139
United Nations
privacy issues and, 41
Universal Declaration of Human Rights, 3
United States v. Jones (2012), 315
Universal Declaration of Human Rights (UN), 3
Unreasonable searches and seizures, Fourth Amendment to U.S. Constitution ban on, 313–314
Upstream surveillance program, FISA authorization of, 329
URL. *See* Uniform resource locator (URL)
USA FREEDOM Act
on communications interception, 319, 326, 328
independent privacy expert group created by, 327
USA PATRIOT Act
anti-money-laundering laws and, 207
on communications interception, 319
International Money-Laundering Abatement and Anti-Terrorist Financing Act of 2001 in, 209
national security and, 324
on NSLs, 330
Section 215 of, 328
Section 217 of, 305
USA Today, 135
Use limitation principle, OECD Guidelines, 7
Use limitation, as FIPP, 347–348
Use of personal information, 5
User information
Web form soliciting, 111–112
See also Personal information (PI)
User preferences
managing, 80–81
no option, 79
opt-in/opt-out, 78–79. *See also* Opt-in; Opt-out
Utah, data destruction laws, 152

V

Vail Letter, 290
Variety, of Big Data, 345
Velocity, of Big Data, 344–345
Vendor contracts, 82–83
Vendor due diligence, 83–84
Verizon, Inc., 254
Vermont, breach notification law in, 146, 147
Video Privacy Protection Act (VPPA) of 1988, 79, 251–252
Video Privacy Protection Act Amendments Act of 2012, 252
Video surveillance of employees, 282–283
Virginia, breach notification law in, 143, 145, 146, 147
Virtual private networks (VPNs), 94–95
Volume of Big Data, 345
VPPA. *See* Video Privacy Protection Act (VPPA) of 1988
Vulcan, FTC data security case against, 56

W

Warren, Samuel, 1
Washington
breach notification law in, 146, 147
Internet security law in, 138
Wearables, in Internet of things, 353–354
Web access, 98
Web beacons, 121
Web cookies, 118–120
Web form, 111–112
Web infrastructure, 94–96
Web interfaces, desktop products with, 113–114
Web privacy notices, 107–108
Web server, 94
Web server log, 95
Web services, 114
Web technologies, 91–96
Web widgets, 115
Websites
privacy protection on, 45–46
protecting personal information on, 100
Weight discrimination of employees, 279
West Virginia, breach notification law in, 146, 147
Whaling, 103
WhatsApp, 122
Whistleblower Protection Act, 267
White-hat researchers, on smart devices, 355
"White House Report," 52–53, 59
Wireless domain registry, 248–249
Wiretap Act, 267, 317–319
Wisconsin, breach notification law in, 143, 144, 146, 147
Workplace privacy, 263–300
enforcement of, 41
Fair Credit Reporting Act (FCRA) of 1970 and, 194
legal overview of, 264–268
post-employment, 291–292
Workplace privacy, during employment
Employee Polygraph Protection Act of 1988, 276–277
lifestyle discrimination, 279–280
misconduct of employees, 289–290
monitoring, 280–289
substance abuse testing, 277–279
Workplace privacy, prior to employment
Americans with Disabilities Act of 1990, 272–273
antidiscrimination laws, 271–272
background screening, 269–270, 273–276
World Wide Web
developments in technology of, 93–94
historic development of, 92–93
Web infrastructure, 94–96
WorldCom, Inc., business governance scandal at, 269
Wyndham Worldwide Corp., 48–49
Wyoming, breach notification law in, 143, 144, 147

X

XML. *See* Extensible markup language (XML)
XSS code, 96, 97, 114

Z

Zurcher v. Stanford Daily (1978), 322